T0254749

Lecture Notes in Business Information Processing 251

More information about this series at http://www.springer.com/series/7911

Helen Sharp · Tracy Hall (Eds.)

Agile Processes in Software Engineering and Extreme Programming

17th International Conference, XP 2016 Edinburgh, UK, May 24–27, 2016 Proceedings

Editors
Helen Sharp
Computing and Communications Department
The Open University
Milton Keynes
UK

Tracy Hall
Computer Science Department
Brunel University London
Middlesex
UK

ISSN 1865-1348 ISSN 1865-1356 (electronic)
Lecture Notes in Business Information Processing
ISBN 978-3-319-33514-8 ISBN 978-3-319-33515-5 (eBook)
DOI 10.1007/978-3-319-33515-5

Library of Congress Control Number: 2016937949

Printed on acid-free paper

This Springer imprint is published by Springer Nature
The registered company is Springer International Publishing AG Switzerland

Preface

Agile software development continues to be adopted widely, and the submissions to XP 2016 reflected a diversity of concerns. Alongside challenges that have traditionally been the subject of discussion and research such as scalability, UX design, and agile measurement, this year's submissions included an increased focus on domains that originally shied away from agile working, such as safety-critical systems and other regulated environments. In addition, submissions considered agile sustainability, both across a software system's life, and within the organizational context.

The XP conference attracts a large number of software practitioners and researchers, providing a rare opportunity for interaction between the two communities. In order to leverage this opportunity, a new Empirical Studies track was introduced this year. In this track, researchers who wanted to collect empirical data from practitioners during XP 2016 were invited to submit their research plans. Accepted plans were then associated with accepted industry and practice sessions to collect empirical data live during XP 2016 sessions. Accepted study plans are included here; papers resulting from the studies appear in a later special section of the *Information and Software Technology* journal.

These proceedings contain full research papers, experience reports, empirical study plans, and doctoral symposium papers. All of these submissions went through a rigorous peer-review process commensurate with their track. In all, 42 research papers were submitted; each was reviewed by three members of the Program Committee, and 14 were accepted (an acceptance rate of 33 %). Experience reports were initially submitted as two-page outlines, and after initial screening, they were then shepherded to produce the papers seen in this volume. Empirical studies papers were reviewed and ranked by the track chairs and discussed with the industry and practice chairs in order to ensure suitable sessions were available to run the planned empirical study. Of the 12 study plans submitted, five were accepted (an acceptance rate of 42 %).

Together, the papers presented here represent a set of high-quality contributions to the literature on agile research and experience addressing a wide range of contemporary topics.

The conference program featured a rich set of session topics and session types that extend beyond the papers contained in these proceedings. Sessions focusing on practical hands-on activities, on teaching agile in academic and industry settings, and coping with change were complemented by ad hoc lightning talks and a vibrant Open Space track. Materials from all of the sessions are available on the conference website at www.xp2016.org.

XP 2016 attendees were also treated to a number of high-profile keynote speakers. Elisabeth Hendrickson spoke about "XP at Scale," Mary Poppendieck discussed the role of "Software Engineering in a Digitized World," and Professor Lionel Briand explained that "Documented Requirements Are Not Useless After All." Finally, Steve

Freeman and Nat Pryce battled it out as "The Odd Couple," considering how good code should be, and what to do about poor-quality code.

Over 330 submissions were received across all of XP 2016 tracks, excluding workshop papers, and it was a mammoth effort to review these and bring them together into a coherent program. We would like to thank everyone who contributed to this effort including paper authors, session presenters, track chairs, Program Committee members, shepherds, volunteers, and sponsors. Without their support the event would not have been as successful.

March 2016

Helen Sharp
Tracy Hall

Organization

Organizing Committee

General Chair

Seb Rose | Claysnow Limited, UK

Academic Chair

Helen Sharp | The Open University, UK

Scientific Workshops

Katie Taylor | University of Central Lancashire, UK
Peggy Gregory | University of Central Lancashire, UK

Industry and Practice Track

Giovanni Asproni | Asprotunity, UK
Andrea Provaglio | andreaprovaglio.com, Italy

Experience Reports

Rebecca Wirfs-Brock | Wirfs-Brock Associates, USA
Ken Power | Cisco, Ireland

Teaching Agile Track

Bruce Scharlau | University of Aberdeen, UK
Chris Murray | University of Sheffield, UK

Empirical Studies Track

Tracy Hall | Brunel University London, UK
Nat Pryce | Technemetis Ltd., UK

Posters

Ville T. Heikkilä | Aalto University, Finland

Research Papers

Helen Sharp | The Open University, UK
Tracy Hall | Brunel University London, UK

Doctoral Symposium

Darja Smite	Blekinge Institute of Technology, Sweden
Brian Fitzgerald	Lero – the Irish Software Research Centre, Limerick, Ireland

Open Space

Charlie Poole	Independent, USA
Andy Mell	Independent, UK

Bridging Research and Practice

Morten Elvang	Nordea, Denmark
Nils Brede Moe	SINTEF, Norway

Program Committee (Research Papers)

Barroca, Leonor	The Open University, UK
Bjarnason, Elizabeth	Lund University, Sweden
Counsell, Steve	Brunel University London, UK
Digsøyr, Torgeir	SINTEF, Norway
Erdogmus, Hakan	Carnegie Mellon University, USA
Fitzgerald, Brian	Lero – Irish Software Engineering Research Centre, Ireland
Garbajosa, Juan	Universidad Politecnica de Madrid/Technical University of Madrid (UPM), Spain
Goldman, Alfredo	University of São Paulo, Brazil
Greer, Des	Queens University Belfast, UK
Gregory, Peggy	University of Central Lancashire, UK
Hall, Tracy	Brunel University London, UK
Hoda, Rashina	The University of Auckland, New Zealand
Holmström Olsson, Helena	Malmö University, Sweden
Kelly, Tim	University of York, UK
Lassenius, Casper	MIT, USA
Madeyski, Lech	Wroclaw University of Science and Technology, Poland
Marchesi, Michele	DIEE – University of Cagliari, Italy
Marczak, Sabrina	PUCRS, Canada
Mishra, Alok	Atilim University, Turkey
Moe, Nils Brede	SINTEF, Norway
Noble, James	Victoria University of Wellington, New Zealand
Paasivaara, Maria	Aalto University, Finland
Petersen, Kai	Blekinge Institute of Technology/Ericsson AB, Sweden
Prechelt, Lutz	Freie Universität Berlin, Germany
Pries-Heje, Jan	Roskilde University, Denmark

Rolland, Knut H.	Westerdals Oslo School of Arts, Communication and Technology, Norway
Rumpe, Bernhard	RWTH Aachen University, Germany
Schneider, Kurt	Leibniz Universität Hannover, Germany
Sharp, Helen	The Open University, UK
Smite, Darja	Blekinge Institute of Technology, Sweden
Tonelli, Roberto	University of Cagliari, Italy
Van Solingen, Rini	Delft University of Technology, The Netherlands
Wang, Xiaofeng	Free University of Bozen-Bolzano, Italy
Yague, Agustin	Universidad Politecnica de Madrid, Spain

Reviewers and Shepherds (Experience Reports)

Wirfs-Brock, Rebecca	Wirfs-Brock Associates, USA
Power, Ken	Cisco, Ireland
Eckstein, Jutta	IT communication, Germany
Yoder, Joseph	The Refactory, Inc., USA
Poupko, Avraham	Cisco, Israel
Passivaara, Maria	Aalto University, Finland
Zuill, Woody	Independent, USA
Hvatum, Lise	Schlumberger, USA
Ville, Heikkilä T	Aalto University, Finland
Kelly, Allan	Software Strategy Ltd., UK
Rothman, Johanna	Rothman Consulting, USA

Reviewers (Industry and Practice)

Asproni, Giovanni	Asprotunity, UK
Barbini, Uberto	gamasoft.com, UK
Braithwaite, Keith	Zuhlke Engineering Ltd., UK
Brown, Simon	Coding the Architecture, UK
Chatley, Robert	Develogical Ltd., UK
Clapham, John	Cotelic, UK
Dalgarno, Mark	Software Acumen, UK
Eckstein, Jutta	IT communication, Germany
Freeman, Steve	M3P, UK
Gaillot, Emmanuel	/ut7, France
García, Vicenç	Valtech, UK
Hellesøy, Aslak	Cucumber, UK
Holyer, Steve	Steve Holyer Consulting, Switzerland
Larsen, Diana	FutureWorks Consulting, USA
Lewitz, Olaf	trustartist.com, Germany
Mell, Andrew	Independent
Milne, Ewan	IPL, UK
Murray, Russell	Murray Management Services Ltd., UK
Nagy, Gaspar	Spec Solutions, Hungary

Provaglio, Andrea	andreaprovaglio.com, Italy
Rose, Seb	Claysnow Limited, UK
Skelton, Matthew	Skelton Thatcher Consulting Ltd., UK
Vandenende, Willem	QWAN, The Netherlands
Webber, Emily	Tacit, UK
Wloka, Nils	codecentric AG, Germany

Sponsors

Crown Jewels Sponsor

Sky Plc

Chieftain Sponsors

JP Morgan
Cisco
Head Resourcing

Tartan Sponsors

Amazon
Cucumber
NDC Conferences

Munro Sponsors

Scotland IS
Redgate
Claysnow Limited
Endava
Stattys
Calba
Cultivate
NewRedo
QWAN

Regional Support

Marketing Edinburgh
SICSA*
Visit Scotland

Contents

Full Research Papers

Full Research Papers

Focal Points for a More User-Centred Agile Development

Silvia Bordin(✉) and Antonella De Angeli

Department of Information Engineering and Computer Science, University of Trento, via Sommarive 9, 38123 Trento, Italy
{bordin,antonella.deangeli}@disi.unitn.it

Abstract. The integration of user-centred design and Agile development is becoming increasingly common in companies and appears promising. However, it may also present some critical points, or communication breakdowns, such as a variable interpretation of user involvement, a mismatch in the value of documentation, and a misalignment in iterations. We refine these themes, emerging from both literature and previous fieldwork, by analysing a case study performed in an IT company that adopts both software engineering approaches, and we further extend the framework with a new theme related to task ownership. We argue that communication breakdowns can become focal points to drive action and decision for establishing an organisational context acknowledging the value of user involvement: to this end, we suggest the adoption of design thinking and the active engagement of the customer in embracing its values.

Keywords: Communication breakdowns · Organisational culture · Case study

1 Introduction

In recent years we have witnessed a growing interest in the integration of Agile methodologies with user-centred design (UCD), in order to achieve a more holistic software engineering approach. In fact, UCD and Agile show some complementary aspects: on the one hand, UCD does not address how to implement the software, while Agile provides large flexibility in accommodating changing requirements; on the other hand, Agile does not directly address user experience (UX) aspects, although valuing customer involvement in the development process.

However, even though the integration of UCD and Agile appears promising, it also presents some issues and no fully satisfactory approach to it has been found yet. In particular, three communication breakdowns [4] hampering such integration have been identified [5], namely a variable interpretation of user involvement, a mismatch in the value of documentation, and a misalignment in iteration phases. In this paper, we refine this framework by discussing a new case study looking at the practices of a software and interaction design company. To support our analysis, we define the main actors involved and how they are mutually linked in a communication network, comparing the latter with the one resulting from the case study presented in [5]. Despite the differences in the two working contexts, the three themes manifest anyway and an additional point, related to task ownership, emerges. We conclude by discussing how these

H. Sharp and T. Hall (Eds.): XP 2016, LNBIP 251, pp. 3–15, 2016.
DOI: 10.1007/978-3-319-33515-5_1

communication breakdowns can become focal points to support action and decision in companies adopting UCD and Agile; moreover, we argue that possible solutions to these issues need to be backed by a supportive organisational culture that recognises the value of user contribution and actively endorses it with the customer.

2 Related Work

User-centred design (UCD) is an umbrella term used to denote a set of techniques, methods, procedures that places the user at the centre of an iterative design process [25]. The benefits of involving users in systems design are widely acknowledged [1, 14, 16, 18]: they include improved quality and acceptance of the system [11], and cost saving, since unnecessary features or critical usability issues are spotted early in the development process [23]. In recent years, there have been several attempts at integrating UCD with Agile software development, as witnessed for instance by the literature reviews in [15, 26]. Despite the large common ground that the two approaches share, there are at least three themes on which their perspectives diverge [5]: we frame these themes by drawing on the concept of communication breakdown, that is a "disruption that occurs when previously successful work practices fail, or changes in the work situation (new work-group, new technology, policy, etc.) nullify specific work practices or routines of the organizational actors and there are no ready-at-hand recovery strategies" [4]. Although originally discussed with respect to global software development, we believe that this concept can support a reflection on the synthesis of different software engineering approaches: we argue, in fact, that it refers to issues occurring at "work practice level" that are due to an "underdeveloped shared context of meaning" [4], which could also be interpreted as the incomplete establishment of a common ground [10] between designers and developers of the same company.

The three communication breakdowns in the integration of UCD and Agile were formalised during a field study carried out within the Smart Campus project [5], where UCD and Scrum were integrated in a process of mobile application development for a community of users, namely students of the University of Trento campus. The goal of this R&D project was to create an ecosystem fostering students' active participation in the design and development of mobile services for their own campus [12]; more details about the aims and results of the project can be found in [6, 12, 34]. In the following, we will illustrate the three communication breakdowns identified by drawing on the literature review that supported the findings of the Smart Campus field study.

User Involvement. In UCD, user involvement can range from informative, to consultative, to participative [11]. In Agile instead, the emphasis is rather put on the customer [1], who acts as a representative of users, but may or may not have direct and regular contact with them [27, 28], to the point that some authors question the extent of such representativeness [30] and others recommend that the customer role is supported by members of the project team [9].

Documentation. Both UCD and Agile encourage frequent communication among team members; however, there can be issues in the communication between designers and developers [1] and in the role of documentation in this respect. In fact, UCD suggests the use of several artefacts such as personas and prototypes to record requirements and design rationales [28], while Agile promotes face-to-face conversation as the most effective means of communication in its fundamental principles [3], to the point of incorporating the customer in the development team.

Synchronisation of Iterations. There are different schools of thought about whether UCD and Agile should be merged into a unified software engineering process, leveraging on their common practices [19, 35, 37], or should just proceed in parallel [20, 24, 33].

3 H-umus

We will now discuss a field study performed in H-umus, presented in their website as a "software and interaction design company". Born in 2007 in one of the most well known Italian venture incubators, H-umus designs and develops mobile sales tools for the fashion industry and now belongs to a large Italian software and services business. The personnel include a CEO, a CTO, four project managers (two of whom are also interaction designers), and five developers. The company adopts a customised version of Scrum for the development and follows a loose interaction design approach. At present, H-umus offers two main products to an established customer portfolio: a B2B merchandising platform and a time and expenses accounting tool. The company also follows some ad-hoc projects for more occasional customers: we consider here the development of a mobile tool for a leading fashion brand that we will call FashionX.

3.1 Field Study Methodology

The field study was carried out by one of the authors and is summarised in Table 1: it consisted of 20 h of observation of working practices, semi-structured interviews, attendance to meetings. Furthermore, artefacts used to support work were examined, while interviews were transcribed and thematically analysed [29].

Table 1. Summary of field study activities performed at H-umus.

Day	Activity	Duration
October 26th, 2015	Attendance of sprint planning meeting; interviews with the CEO, a project manager, a designer and a developer	7 h
November 20th, 2015	Interviews with both designers and the CTO	6 h
December 14th, 2015	Attendance of sprint planning meeting; interviews with two developers, a designer, and a project manager	7 h

3.2 Communication Network

This section will illustrate the actors involved in H-umus and how, possibly through some artefacts, they are connected in a network, as shown in Fig. 1. The dialogue with users is completely mediated by the customer, usually represented by the IT department of a large fashion business. The customer in turn communicates with H-umus through a project manager of this company, who is often also an interaction designer; such dialogue is supported by a series of artefacts such as requirements documents, prototypes, and cost or time estimates, which will be described more in detail in later paragraphs. The project manager is then usually the only point of contact between the inside and outside of H-umus: he collaborates with the management (i.e. the CEO) in the early stages of an approach to a new customer, with the CTO in the definition of the technical analysis, and with developers during the implementation. Internal communication is also supported by a range of artefacts. Finally, the owner group refers to the management for products developed on their behalf.

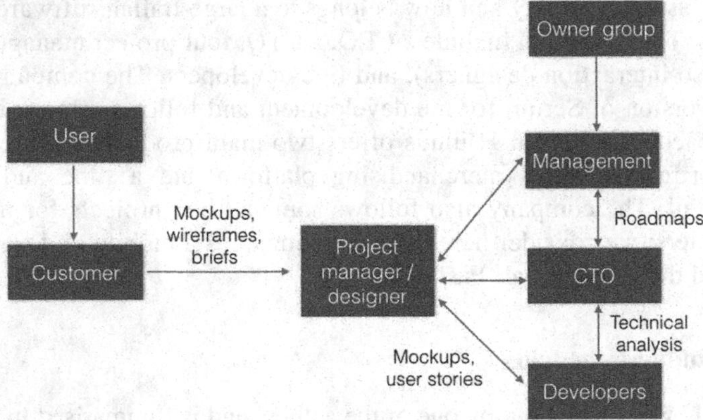

Fig. 1. Communication network in H-umus.

3.3 Artefacts

A variety of artefacts are used in H-umus to support communication, both internally and with the customer. In this paragraph, we will describe the most relevant ones.

Mockups and Wireframes. In the case of enhancements to already consolidated products, designers prepare high-fidelity mockups relying on the existing interface; in the case of software built from scratch instead, they prepare wireframes, representing interaction flows and layouts. Mockups and wireframes are then iteratively discussed with the customer: this allows to check that requirements have been correctly understood, to ensure that the customer is aware of project status and will not change his mind later, and to skip formal validation steps at the end of each sprint.

Briefs. Prototypes and requirements are integrated in documents called briefs, which crystallise the requirements; they are then iteratively revised with the customer to ensure that both parties share the same understanding of requirements and status of advancement.

Roadmaps. For each project, the relevant project manager keeps a chart showing the evolution of the product at a high level, including milestones to be delivered to the customer. This chart is often linked to other documents reporting, for instance, more extensive descriptions of functionalities or specifications of the customer's target platforms. Roadmaps are used internally, at management level: the CEO, the CTO and project managers refer to them to supervise the status of each project. However, if the customer requires so, roadmaps are also used to provide long-term visibility on the articulation of the project.

Technical Analysis. The CTO elaborates this document for each project: it includes finalised interface mockups, a description of the data flow and of the data structure, cost and time estimates, and a finer-grained breakdown of development tasks. The technical analysis serves two purposes: internally, it is a reference for developers to determine what to implement in the next sprints; externally and if needed, it can provide the customer with a detailed understanding of the implementation process.

3.4 Findings

In the following, we discuss the results of the interviews with the H-umus staff, categorising the narratives according to the three communication breakdowns constituting our framework. Citations in the next paragraphs will be attributed to interviewees as follows: *Dev* for developers; *Des* for designers; *PM* for project managers who are not designers; *Mgmt* for the CTO and the CEO.

User Involvement. The distinction between customers and users is very sharp and project managers usually communicate only with the customer, who can be represented by different employees at different stages of the same project. Especially when the customer is a large company, its most appropriate representative to liaise with can be difficult to identify and often changes over time:

Dev2: "The most difficult thing in communicating with the customer is understanding who you should be talking to."

In general, the customer representative is the IT department:

Mgmt2: "You would not believe how conservative IT departments can be. Whatever change may affect their working routine, it's a no-no."

There are, however, exceptions to this situation: for example, a few demos were arranged with business and sales representatives of FashionX, i.e. with a sample of final users, in order to collect feedback that could supplement the requirements provided by the IT department of the company. Yet, this only happens occasionally: usually, and as shown in Fig. 1, the customer completely mediates user needs, requirements, and feedback. This causes some concern in the H-umus management:

Mgmt2: "Then it is difficult to determine how to handle the feedback we receive and how relevant it actually is with respect to the customer or with respect to the needs users may truly have. […] Sometimes I wonder whom we should really satisfy. Is it the business department or the IT department? We usually speak only to the latter. I believe this causes a large drop in the value we deliver with our products."

H-umus designers acknowledge that it would be desirable to apply a proper user-centred design methodology, involving real users in requirement gathering and interface evaluation. However, this is very hard to achieve in practice, because of two main reasons: first, the time for design is constrained; second, it is difficult to gain access to users. In fact, the customer is not always interested in being actively involved in the design of the commissioned product: sometimes H-umus may only be asked to prototype a new graphical interface for an existing software. The customer may even believe that users are not able to provide any sensible contribution:

Dev1: "I do not have any contact with users […] Sometimes they are even described to me as being as dumb as an ox, so it is paramount to design products that are very easy to use, and I guess this is a major challenge for designers."

Documentation. The staff has a small size and is co-located in the same open space: hence, most coordination occurs face to face or at most through instant messaging, both among developers and between developers and designers. This leads to a scarcity of documentation for internal use. However, in order to avoid knowledge gaps in case someone leaves the company, pair programming is adopted when a part of the code needs to be modified: the task is in fact assigned both to the developer who already worked on that code and to a "fresh" developer at the same time. In this way, in the long run everybody will have at least an overview of all the code produced. Working in pairs is also a common practice in the early stages of a new project, where a designer and a developer cooperate in order to shape the design space quickly and based on an understanding of what can be technically feasible.

PM1: "Everybody has an overview, but also a specific responsibility."

Documentation is instead actively and carefully maintained to support the relationship with the customer. Despite the Agile principle [3] of "embracing change", the management highlighted the need of making the customer responsible for his requirements and committed to them. The CTO and the project managers in fact insisted on their strong need to shield H-umus from sudden, important changes in customer requirements; being the company so small, this could cause a lot of work to be wasted and not paid, causing in turn potentially severe financial issues.

PM1: "H-umus is a small company. If the customer first says he wants a mobile app, and then after six months he comes and says that now he wants a standalone application... We cannot afford that. Unless the customer is paying for the extra time, of course."

Des2: "We do not have much development capacity. It can become a big issue if I draw the mockup and then we have to go back and change fundamental parts of it."

This protection is achieved by using several artefacts that are admittedly not typically Agile: documents such as requirements lists and technical analyses are shared with the customer, iteratively discussed and then signed off.

Mgmt1: "We make the customer sign the requirements document, so nobody can come up and say: "This is not what we agreed upon". Whatever extra, we discuss it and it is billed on top."

Des2: "Being able to tell the customer: "Look, this is what we suggested and you approved it" is something that can cover our back when we need to ask for more funding or when we just say that something is not feasible".

The strong perception of documentation as having a purpose mainly in relation to the customer emerges very clearly also in relation to other themes:

Mgmt1: "I'll show you the technical analysis we did for FashionX [...] Please write down in your notes that to me this is complete nonsense. The risk estimates and the planning poker and stuff... It is obvious that these numbers are meaningless. Yet the customer wants to have a long-term perspective on the project, so here it is."

Synchronisation of Iterations. Given the small size of the company, designers and developers work together, so synchronisation is handled through constant, direct communication. Indeed, there is no separate process for design and for development: for instance, design tasks such as prototyping are listed as regular user stories in the Agile management tool in use:

Des1: "UX aspects are regarded as common functionalities."

Despite a general awareness among the staff of the company transitioning towards a more design-oriented culture, the overall attitude appears to be still strongly technical. For instance, sprint meetings only involve developers:

Mgmt1: "We are born as a data-driven company [...] Sprint meetings are too technical; designers would waste time attending them."

Furthermore, a different theme emerges, related to the recognition of designers' expertise in a technically dominant environment. Several times designers referred to their competence in UX as being interpreted as common sense in the company:

Des2: "Why should the CEO's opinion be more relevant than mine, if I designed the interface from the beginning? Sometimes [Des1] and I refer to it as a class conflict with the developers"

Des2: "Everybody feels entitled to comment on the design, just because each of us is a technology user, while nobody would comment on the code unless competent. So [developers] bring in their own use cases, but we are not developing, say, Instagram, which only has a couple of functionalities: it is totally different. Sometimes the comments are just "I don't like it". I can take it from the customer, if he pays for the extra time needed to rework the design, otherwise I'd expect some sounder feedback."

The rest of the team perceives this issue as well, although in variable ways:

Dev1: "Interfaces are subjective [...] usability is subjective too: you need to design stuff that is comfortable for the user, more than functional. [Des1 and Des2] do a great job in my opinion in this respect."

PM1: "The best way to work shouldn't be to tell the designer how to do the things, but just what you need; unfortunately, the customer is often unable to articulate what he wants, and anyway we must give priority to the development to save time."

Dev2: "We all give our opinion, but in the end it is the designer who decides."

4 Discussion

Despite a positive attitude towards UCD, H-umus found objective difficulties in integrating it with Agile in practice. These difficulties were partially overlapping with the communication breakdowns identified in Smart Campus [5], although the working context of the latter was quite different from the H-umus one as illustrated by Fig. 2, which represents the main actors in Smart Campus and their communication network.

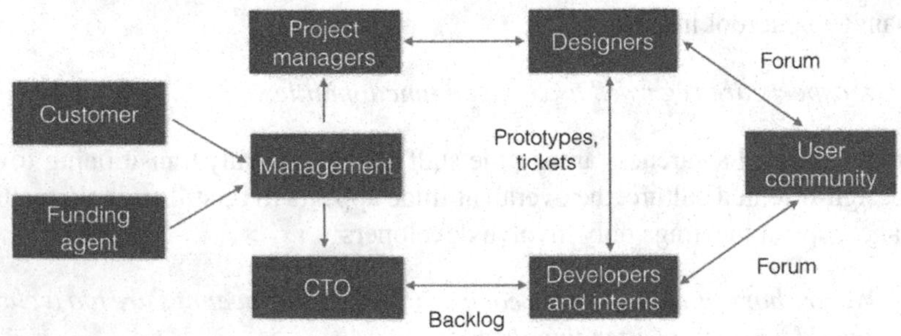

Fig. 2. Communication network in Smart Campus.

The analysis of the H-umus case study allowed us to refine our framework, broadening the scope of identified communication breakdowns as follows.

User Involvement. In Smart Campus, the customer and the user community were two clearly differentiated actors; most of the team had direct contact only with the users through a variety of communication channels such as a forum. However, the perception of user involvement appeared to be variable between designers and developers, denoting an underlying mismatch in the understanding of this concept: while designers struggled to promote a participative role of the user community, developers intended such role as informative or at most consultative instead [11]. In H-umus, the extent of user involvement remains problematic, although with a different flavour: the customer completely mediates the interaction with the user, so the role of the latter is practically less than informative [11]. Therefore, we can argue that the understanding of the extent of user involvement should be shared not only inside the company (among designers, developers, managers), but also outside, by the customer.

Documentation. In Smart Campus, documentation did not appear to have an intrinsic value as a communication tool for developers; however, it became increasingly relevant to keep the development team aligned when the latter became more distributed due to the introduction of interns working at variable times and often remotely. Yet, how to effectively support the need for a shared knowledge base remained an open point, particularly referring to design artefacts, although the team tried to adopt a variety of articulation platforms. In H-umus instead, the team is co-located: in this case, besides being a tool for tracing the history of the software and the rationale of related design and development choices, documentation can also have an instrumental function in balancing the power relationship with the customer, protecting the company against unsustainable changes in requirements.

Synchronisation of Iterations. The Smart Campus project was oriented towards a large and strong user community, whose feedback escalated quickly and was not mediated (for instance by a customer). This caused severe difficulties in synchronising the iterations of UCD and Agile: designers struggled to elaborate requirements and provide suggestions in a timely manner that could fit the development pace, while developers often took the initiative of fixing interfaces regardless of the overall UX vision. In general, designers resorted to several ad-hoc interventions, elaborated together with the developers requesting them. In H-umus instead, the team is co-located and quite small, so synchronisation can easily occur through face-to-face communication. Furthermore, the existence of signed documents prevents the customer from changing requirements with the same frequency witnessed in Smart Campus with the user community.

Task Ownership. An additional communication breakdown strongly emerged from the interviews conducted in H-umus. Several interviewees argued that, in order for an effective communication to occur, it is advisable that the whole team shares a common language. Additionally, our observations suggested that the team should also share a common understanding about who is responsible for each task, especially in the case of UX activities, and in particular for taking final decisions over it. This will help avoid situations in which a technically predominant environment interprets UX as mere "common sense", which are not conducive to endorsing the added value that UX can provide to a product and which seem to reflect a long-lasting contrast between soft and hard sciences. To this end, we point to the concept of boundary objects, i.e. mediating artefacts that allow knowledge sharing and promote collaboration since their interpretive flexibility facilitates "an overlap of meaning while preserving sufficient ambiguity" for different groups to read their own meanings [2]. The briefs used in H-umus can be considered as boundary objects in this sense, as they gather mockups from designers, technical specs from developers, and business requirements from the customer, and they act as a common reference point for monitoring the evolution of the product.

5 Conclusion

In this paper we have discussed four communication breakdowns that may affect the integration of user-centred design and Agile development and that emerged from an analysis of working practices in companies. Possible solutions can derive from discount usability techniques [e.g. 13, 22] or more recent research on automatic usability evaluation tools [e.g. 21, 31]. However, we remark that communication breakdowns are manifested at the work process level [4, 5]: hence, we suggest that their solution could be found in a supportive organisational environment [5, 8, 11, 17], whose fundamental importance is reiterated by the present study. As seen in H-umus, not even having designers play the role of project managers is enough to fully endorse the UCD component of the working process. To leverage the full potential of the integration of UCD and Agile, the management should actively counteract the so-called "developer mindset" [1, 14], i.e. an approach that is overly focused on technical aspects rather than on customer and user satisfaction, and commit to an explicit inclusion of UCD in company goals and financial allocation [36].

We claim that the four communication breakdowns discussed in this paper can become focal points to drive action and decision in companies, facilitating communication between designers and developers and supporting management in the construction of a favourable context. Our current research is addressing the development of specific guidelines concerning how to apply such focal points in practice through additional case studies. Nonetheless, and as already suggested in [5], we believe that design thinking [7] can be an appropriate methodology in this respect: grounded on a "human-centred design ethos", it advocates a "designer's sensibility" pervading the whole organisation, so that also technical personnel (be it part of the development or of the management) can be aware of the importance of meeting users' needs with what is technologically feasible. Inspired by design thinking, the organisational culture is likely to empathise more with the user and to share the ownership of the UX vision among all members of the company: this is in turn also likely to address the task ownership theme introduced above.

However, the benefits of this internal culture may be limited if the customer does not share its same values, preventing access to users or completely mediating the communication with them. A direct contact with users can allow the company to deliver a product that, although requiring a possibly longer design period, will be more suited to the needs of people ultimately using it and will therefore bring more value to the customer for its money. Even after many years from [23], we still need to address the "developer mindset" [1, 14] and persuade the customer and the technical personnel (at least partially) of the positive cost-benefit trade-off of devoting time to user studies and usability [32]. We insist that attainable benefits should be clearly presented to the customer in order to win its buy-in of the principles of design thinking, its acknowledgement of the advantages of involving the users and its active collaboration in this. We point out to the research community that however, to this end, a set of actionable measures that can more objectively assess the positive impact of user involvement on the quality of produced software [18] is still lacking, together with a set of less resource-intensive practices to put such involvement in place.

Acknowledgments. Smart Campus was funded by TrentoRISE. The present work has been possible thanks to the funding granted by the Italian Ministry of Education, University and Research (MIUR) through the project "Città Educante", project code CTN01_00034_393801. We wish to thank the Smart Campus team, the students who contributed to the project, and the H-umus team for their kind support.

References

1. Ardito, C., Buono, P., Caivano, D., Costabile, M.F., Lanzilotti, R.: Investigating and promoting UX practice in industry: an experimental study. Int. J. Hum. Comput. Stud. **72**(6), 542–551 (2014)
2. Barrett, M., Oborn, E.: Boundary object use in cross-cultural software development teams. Hum. Relat. **63**(8), 1199–1221 (2010)
3. Beck, K., et al.: Manifesto for Agile software development. http://www.Agilemanifesto.org
4. Bjørn, P., Ngwenyama, O.: Virtual team collaboration: building shared meaning, resolving breakdowns and creating translucence. Inf. Syst. J. **19**(3), 227–253 (2009)
5. Bordin, S., De Angeli, A.: Communication breakdowns in the integration of user-centred design and Agile development. To appear. In: Cockton, G., Larusdottir, M.K., Gregory, P., Cajander, A. (eds.) Integrating User Centred Design in Agile Development. Springer, London (2016)
6. Bordin, S., Menéndez Blanco, M., De Angeli, A.: ViaggiaTrento: an application for collaborative sustainable mobility. EAI Endorsed Trans. Ambient Syst. **14**(4), (2014)
7. Brown, T.: Design thinking. Harvard Bus. Rev. **86**(6), 84 (2008)

8. Cajander, Å., Larusdottir, M., Gulliksen, J.: Existing but not explicit - the user perspective in scrum projects in practice. In: Kotzé, P., Marsden, G., Lindgaard, G., Wesson, J., Winckler, M. (eds.) INTERACT 2013, Part III. LNCS, vol. 8119, pp. 762–779. Springer, Heidelberg (2013)
9. Chamberlain, S., Sharp, H., Maiden, N.A.M.: Towards a framework for integrating Agile development and user-centred design. In: Abrahamsson, P., Marchesi, M., Succi, G. (eds.) XP 2006. LNCS, vol. 4044, pp. 143–153. Springer, Heidelberg (2006)
10. Clark, H.H., Brennan, S.E.: Grounding in communication. Perspect. Socially Shared Cogn. **13**, 127–149 (1991)
11. Damodaran, L.: User involvement in the systems design process-a practical guide for users. Behav. Inf. technology **15**(6), 363–377 (1996)
12. De Angeli, A., Bordin, S., Menéndez Blanco, M.: Infrastructuring participatory development in information technology. In: Proceedings of the 13th Participatory Design Conference: Research Papers(1), pp. 11–20. ACM (2014)
13. Gothelf, J.: Lean UX: Applying Lean principles to improve user experience. O'Reilly Media Inc, Redwood Shores (2013)
14. Hussain, Z., Milchrahm, H., Shahzad, S., Slany, W., Tscheligi, M., Wolkerstorfer, P.: Integration of extreme programming and user-centered design: Lessons learned. In: Abrahamsson, P., Marchesi, M., Maurer, F. (eds.) Agile Processes in Software Engineering and Extreme Programming, pp. 143–153. Springer, Heidelberg (2006)
15. Jurca, G., Hellmann, T.D., Maurer, F.: Integrating Agile and user-centered design: a systematic mapping and review of evaluation and validation studies of Agile-UX. In: Proceedings of Agile, pp. 24–32. IEEE (2014)
16. Kujala, S.: User involvement: a review of the benefits and challenges. Beh. Inf. Technol. **22**(1), 1–16 (2003)
17. Lárusdóttir, M.K., Cajander, Å., Gulliksen, J.: The big picture of UX is missing in Scrum projects. In: Proceedings of the 2nd International Workshop on The Interplay between User Experience Evaluation And Software Development, in Conjunction with the 7th Nordic Conference on Human-Computer Interaction (2012). http://ceur-ws.org/Vol-922/I-UxSED-2012-Proceedings.pdf#page=49
18. Mao, J.Y., Vredenburg, K., Smith, P.W., Carey, T.: The state of user-centered design practice. Commun. ACM **48**(3), 105–109 (2005)
19. Memmel, T., Gundelsweiler, F., Reiterer, H.: Agile human-centered software engineering. In: Proceedings of the 21st British HCI Group Annual Conference on People and Computers: HCI… but not as We Know It vol. 1, British Computer Society, pp. 167–175 (2007)
20. Miller, L.: Case study of customer input for a successful product. In: Proceedings of Agile, pp. 225–234 (2005)
21. Miniukovich, A., De Angeli, A.: Computation of Interface Aesthetics. In: Proceedings of the CHI, pp. 1163–1172 (2015)
22. Nielsen, J. Guerrilla HCI: Using discount usability engineering to penetrate the intimidation barrier. In: Cost-justifying Usability, pp. 245–272 (1994)
23. Nielsen, J.: Usability Engineering. Elsevier, New York (1994)
24. Nodder, C., Nielsen, J.: Agile Usability: Best Practices for User Experience on Agile Development Projects. Nielsen Norman Group, Freemont (2010)
25. Rogers, Y., Sharp, H., Preece, J.: Interaction Design: Beyond Human-Computer Interaction. John Wiley & Sons, New York (2011)
26. Salah, D., Paige, R.F., Cairns, P.: A systematic literature review for agile development processes and user centred design integration. In: Proceedings of the 18th International Conference on Evaluation and Assessment in Software Engineering, p. 5. ACM (2014)

27. Schwartz, L.: Agile-User Experience Design: does the involvement of usability experts improve the software quality? Int. J. Adv. Softw. **7**(3&4), 456–468 (2014)
28. Sharp, H., Robinson, H.: Integrating user-centred design and software engineering: a role for extreme programming? (2004). http://citeseerx.ist.psu.edu/viewdoc/download?doi=10.1.1.99.4554&rep=rep1&type=pdf
29. Smith, C.P.: Motivation and Personality: Handbook of Thematic Content Analysis. Cambridge University Press, New York (1992)
30. Sohaib, O., Khan, K.: Integrating usability engineering and agile software development: a literature review. In: International Conference on Computer Design and Applications, vol. 2, pp. V2–32. IEEE (2010)
31. Staiano, J., Menéndez, M., Battocchi, A., De Angeli, A., Sebe, N.: UX_Mate: from facial expressions to UX evaluation. In: Proceedings of the DIS, pp. 741–750. ACM (2012)
32. The Standish Group CHAOS report (2014). https://www.projectsmart.co.uk/white-papers/chaos-report.pdf
33. Sy, D.: Adapting usability investigations for Agile user-centered design. J. Usability Stud. **2**(3), 112–132 (2007)
34. Teli, M., Bordin, S., Blanco, M.M., Orabona, G., De Angeli, A.: Public design of digital commons in urban places: a case study. Int. J. Hum Comput Stud. **81**, 17–30 (2015)
35. Ungar, J.M., White, J.A.: Agile user centered design: enter the design studio – a case study. In: Proceedings of the CHI, pp. 2167–2177. ACM Press (2008)
36. Venturi, G., Troost, J., Jokela, T.: People, organizations, and processes: an inquiry into the adoption of user-centered design in industry. Int. J. Hum. Comput. Interact. **21**(2), 219–238 (2006)
37. Wolkerstorfer, P. et al.: Probing an Agile usability process. In: Proceedings of the CHI, pp. 2151–2157. ACM Press (2008)

Agility Measurements Mismatch: A Validation Study on Three Agile Team Assessments in Software Engineering

Konstantinos Chronis[1] and Lucas Gren[1,2(✉)]

[1] Chalmers and University of Gothenburg, 412 96 Gothenburg, Sweden
konstantinos.chronis@gmail.com, lucas.gren@cse.gu.se
[2] University of São Paulo, São Paulo 05508–090, Brazil

Abstract. Many tools have been created for measuring the agility of software teams, thus creating a saturation in the field. Three agile measurement tools were selected in order to validate whether they yield similar results. The surveys of the tools were given to teams in Company A ($N = 30$). The questions were grouped into agile practices which were checked for correlation in order to establish convergent validity. In addition, we checked whether the questions identified to be the same among the tools would be given the same replies by the respondents. We could not establish convergent validity since the correlations of the data gathered were very few and low. In addition, the questions which were identified to have the same meaning among the tools did not have the same answers from the respondents. We conclude that the area of measuring agility is still immature and more work needs to be done. Not all tools are applicable to every team but they should be selected on the basis of how a team has transitioned to agile.

Keywords: Validation · Agile measurement · Empirical study

1 Introduction

Agile and plan-driven methodologies are the two dominant approaches in the software development. Although it has been almost 20 years since the former were introduced, the companies are quite reluctant in following them [1].

Software development teams started adopting the most known agile methodologies, such as eXtreme Programming [2], Feature Driven Development (FDD), [3], Crystal [4], Scrum [5] and others. Most companies use a tailored methodology by following some of the aforementioned processes and practices which better suit their needs. Williams et al. [6] report that all XP practices are exercised rarely in their pure form, something on which Reifer [7] and Aveling [8] also agree based on the results of their surveys, which showed that it is common for organizations to partially adopt XP. The most important issue that tends to be neglected though, is how well these methodologies are adopted.

H. Sharp and T. Hall (Eds.): XP 2016, LNBIP 251, pp. 16–27, 2016.
DOI: 10.1007/978-3-319-33515-5_2

According to Escobar-Sarmiento and Linares-Vasquez [9], the agile methodologies are easier to misunderstand. The previous statement is also supported by Taromirad and Ramsin [10], who argue that the agile software development methodologies are often applied to the wrong context. Sidky [11] defines the level of agility of a company as the amount of agile practices used. Considering this statement, a group that uses pair programming and collective code ownership at a very low level is more agile than a group which uses only pair programming but in a more efficient manner.

Williams et al. [12] pose the question "*How agile is agile enough*"? According to a survey conducted by Ambysoft [13], only 65 % of the agile companies that answered met the five agile criteria posed in the survey. Poonacha and Bhattacharya [14] mentioned that the different perceptions of agile practices when they are adopted are troublesome, since even people in the same team understand them differently, according to the result of a survey [15].

Since agile methodologies become more and more popular, there is a great need for developing a tool that can measure the level of agility in the organizations that have adopted them. For over a decade, researchers have been constantly coming up with models and frameworks in an effort to provide a solution.

This case study comprises three tools which claim to measure the agility of software development teams using surveys. These tools are Perceptive Agile Measurement (PAM) [16], Team Agility Assessment (TAA) [17], Objectives Principles Strategies (OPS) [18]. The first one has been validated with a large sample of subjects, the second one is well-used by companies and the third one covers many agile practices. Since all three tools measure agility, convergent validity should be established among them to corroborate this. The surveys from the three tools were given to Company *A* employees to answer. The analysis of the data was performed by grouping the survey questions in accordance to to agile practices. The correlation of these practices were the indications for establishing the convergent validity. Moreover, questions identified to have the same meaning among the tools should have the same answers from the respondents. The purpose of this study is to check whether these three tools will yield similar results.

Research Questions.

1. Will PAM, TAA and OPS yield similar results?
   (i) Does convergent validity exist between the tools?
   (ii) Will the questions that are exactly the same in the tools yield the same results?

2 Case Study

Any effort to see if the selected agility measurement tools are valid in what they do, would require to apply them to real software developments teams. According to Runeson and Host [19], a case study is "a suitable research methodology for software engineering research since it studies contemporary phenomena in their natural context". As a result, a case study was selected as the most suitable means.

2.1 Subject Selection

Company *A* is a United States company which operates in the Point Of Sales (POS) area. It has four teams with mixed members of developers and testers. The teams do not follow a specific agile methodology, but rather a tailored mix of the most famous ones which suits the needs of each team. Methodology A, as we can name it, embraces the practices from the various agile methodologies, some of them to a larger and some of them to a smaller extent. The analysis process created by Koch [20] was used for identifying these methodologies. The identification of the practices was done by observing and understanding how the teams work.

2.2 Data Collection

In order to collect the data, an online survey was considered to be the best option, since it could be easily answered by each subject.

For each of the tools, four surveys were created (one for each team). The data collection lasted about one month, while the surveys for each tool were conducted every ten days. None of the subjects was familiar with any of the tools.

Two subjects were requested to answer to the surveys first, in order to detect if there were any questions which could cause confusion, but also to see how much time is needed to complete a survey. Once the issues pointed out by the two subjects were fixed, the surveys were sent to the rest of the company's employees.

The links for the surveys were sent to the subjects via email, and they were asked to spend 15–20 min to reply to the survey. The employees who belonged to more than one team were asked a couple of days later to take the other survey in order to verify that their answers matched in both surveys.

OPS agility measurements are based on three aspects: Adequacy, Capability and Effectiveness. Effectiveness measurement focuses on how well a team implements agile methodologies. Since the rest of the tools focus on the same thing, it was decided only to use the survey from Effectiveness and not to take into account the Adequacy and Capability aspects.

The surveys for PAM, TAA and OPS were answered on a Likert scale 1–7 (never having done what is asked in the question to always doing what is asked in the question).

The employees who were asked to answer to the surveys were all members of the software development teams, which consisted of software and QA engineers. All of the participating employees have been in the company for over a year and most of them have more than five years of work experience in an agile environment. Employees who had been working for less than six months in the company were not asked to participate, since it was considered that they were not fully aware of the company's procedures or that they were not familiar enough with them. Each participant replied to 176 questions in total. Initially, 34 surveys were expected to be filled in, but in the end, 30 of them were filled in, since some employees chose not to participate.

2.3 Data Preparation

All three tools have different amount of questions and cover different practices. For this reason, we preferred to do a grouping of the questions based on the practices/areas to which they belong.

Team Agility Assessment – Areas. Team Agility Assessment (TAA) does not claim that it covers specific agile practices, but rather areas important for a team. It focuses on product ownership for Scrum teams but also on the release, iteration planning and tracking. The team factor plays a great role, as well as the development practices and the work environment. Automated testing and release planning are important here as well.

Perceptive Agile Measurement – Practices. The Perceptive Agile Measurement (PAM) tool focuses on the iterations during software development, but also on the stand-up meetings for the team members, their collocation and the retrospectives they have. The access to customers and their acceptance criteria have a high importance as well. Finally, the continuous integration and the automated unit testing are considered crucial in order to be agile.

Objectives, Principles, Strategies (OPS) – Practices. Objectives, Principles, Strategies (OPS) Framework is the successor of the Objectives, Principles, Practices (OPP) Framework [21]. OPP identified 27 practices as implementations of the principles which later on were transformed into 17 strategies.

Practices Covered Among The Tools. We have abstracted some of the OPP practices to OPS strategies in order to avoid repeating the mapping of the questions. The connection between the practices and the strategies is done based on the questions of each tool.

Mapping of questions among tools. PAM has its questions divided on the basis of agile practices, while on the other hand, TAA has divided them based on areas considered important. Although all practices/areas from PAM and TAA are mapped onto OPP and OPS, not all of their questions are under OPP practices or OPS strategies. This can be explained due to the different perception/angle that the creators of the tools have and what is considered important for an organization/team to be agile.

2.4 Data Analysis

The data gathered from the surveys were grouped on the basis of the practices covered by the OPP, and as a consequence, the OPS.

Convergent Validity Analysis. Since all the tools claim to be measuring agility and under the condition that convergent validity exists among them, then, by definition, they should yield similar results.

In similar studies [22,23], the correlation analysis was selected as the best way to check similar tools and this was followed here as well. We decided to use the practices covered by each tool and see if they correlate with the same practices from the other two tools. The idea is based on the *multitrait-multimethod matrix*, presented by Campbell and Fiske [24]. The matrix is the most commonly used way for providing construct validity.

In order to select which correlation analysis method to choose from, the data were checked if they had normal distribution by using the Shapiro-Wilk test which is the most powerful normality test, according to a recent paper published by Razali and Wah [25]. The chosen alpha level was 0.05, as it is the most common one.

Out of the 42 normality checks (three for each of the 14 practices), only 17 concluded that the data are normally distributed. The low level of normally distributed data gave a strong indication that Spearman's rank correlation coefficient, which is more adequate for non-parametric data, was more appropriate to use, rather than the Pearson's product-moment correlation.

In order to use the Spearman's rank correlation coefficient, a monotonic relationship between two variables is required. In order to check for the monotonicity, plots were drawn between the results of each tool for all 14 practices. The plots surprisingly showed that only eight out of 42 were monotonic, which indicates no correlation what-so-ever.

Direct Match Questions Analysis. We want to find which questions are the same among the tools. In order to achieve this, the mapping described in Subsect. 2.3 was used. Afterward, the questions were checked one by one to identify the ones which had the same meaning. When we finalized the groups of questions which were the same, we requested from the same employees who were taking the pilot surveys to verify if they believed the groups were correctly formed. Their answer was affirmative, so we continued by checking if the answers of the subjects were the same. Surprisingly, OPS–TAA have 20 questions with the same meaning, while OPS–PAM and TAA–PAM only four and three respectively.

Out of the 35 normality checks (two for each group and three for one group), only 2 concluded that the data are normally distributed. Since the samples are also independent (they do not affect one another), there is a strong indication that the MannWhitney U test is appropriate. For the group *Smaller And Frequent Product Releases*, we used the Kruskal–Wallis one-way analysis of variance method, which is the respective statistical method for more than two groups.

The hypothesis in both cases was:

H_0: *There is no difference between the groups of the same questions*
H_1: *There is a difference between the groups of the same questions*

3 Results

3.1 Correlations

As it was previously stated, only eight out of 42 plots were monotonic. The more interesting than the correlations result is the non-existence of monotonicity in the other 34 relationships, which leads us to the conclusion that there is little convergence among the tools. This is surprising because tools claiming to measure the same thing should converge.

3.2 Direct Match Questions Results

The groups of direct match questions showed some unexpected results. Questions which are considered to have the same meaning should yield the same results, which was not the case for any of the question groups, apart from one group concerning the *Software Configuration Management.* On the other hand, the *Product Backlog* practice had the lowest score with only six respondents giving the same answer. The maximum difference in answers was up to two Likert-scale points.

As far as the results from the Mann-Whitney U test and Kruskal-Wallis one-way analysis of variance are concerned, the p-values from the majority of the groups are more than the alpha level of 0.05. As a result, we cannot reject the H_0 hypothesis. Such practices are *Iteration Progress Tracking and Reporting - group #2*, *High-Bandwidth Communication* and others. On the other hand, the p-value of group *Software Configuration Management* cannot be computed, since all the answers are the same, while for other groups the p-value is below the alpha level which means that the H_0 hypothesis can be rejected. Such practices are *Continuous Integration - group #2*, *Iteration Progress Tracking and Reporting - group #4* and others.

4 Discussion

4.1 Will PAM, TAA and OPS Yield Similar Results?

The plots drawn by the data gathered showed an unexpected and interesting result. Not only do the tools lack a correlation, but they do not even have a monotonic relationship when compared to each other for the agile practices covered, resulting in absence of convergent validity. This could indicate two things; the absence of monotonicity and the negative or very low correlations show that the questions used by the tools in order to cover an agile practice do it differently as well as that PAM, TAA and OPS measure the agility of software development teams in their own unique way.

Almost all groups had different responses to the same questions. With regards to the research question ***"Does convergent validity exist among the tools?"***, we showed that convergent validity could not be established due to the low (if existing) correlations among the tools. Concerning the research question ***"Will the questions that are exactly the same among the tools yield the same results?"***, we saw that a considerable amount of respondents' answers were different.

The reasons for this somewhat unexpected results are explained in the following paragraphs.

Few or no questions for measuring a practice. A reason for not being able to calculate the correlation of the tools is that they cover slightly or even not at all some of the practices. An example of this is the *Smaller and Frequent Product Releases* practice. OPS includes four questions, while on the other hand, PAM and TAA have a single question each. Furthermore, *Appropriate Distribution of Expertise* is not covered at all by PAM. In case the single question gets a low score, this will affect how effectively the tool will measure an agile practice. On the contrary, multiple questions can better cover the practice by examining more factors that affect it.

The same practice is measured differently. Something interesting that came up during the data analysis was that although the tools cover the same practices, they do it in different ways, leading to different results. An example of this is the practice of *Refactoring*. PAM checks whether there are enough unit tests and automated system tests to allow the safe code refactoring. In case the course unit/system tests are not developed by a team, the respondents will give low scores to the question, as the team members in Company *A* did. Nevertheless, this does not mean that the team never refactors the software or does it with bad results. All teams in Company *A* choose to refactor when it adds value to the system, but the level of unit tests is very low and they exist only for specific teams. On the other hand, TAA and OPS check how often the teams refactor, among other aspects.

The same practice is measured in opposite questions. The *Continuous Integration* practice has a unique paradox among TAA, PAM and OPS. The first two tools include a question about the members of the team having synchronized to the latest code, while OPS checks for the exact opposite. According to Soundararajan [18], it is preferable for the teams not to share the same code in order to measure the practice.

Questions phrasing. Although the tools might cover the same areas for each practice, the results could differ because of how a question is structured. An example of this is the *Test Driven Development* practice. Both TAA and PAM ask about automated code coverage, while OPS just asks about the existence of code coverage. Furthermore, TAA focuses on 100 % automation, while PAM does not. Thus, if a team has code coverage but it is not automated, then the score of the respective question should be low. In case of TAA, if the code coverage is not fully automated, its score should be even lower. It is evident that the abstraction level of a question has a great impact. The more specific it is, the more a reply to it will differ, resulting in possible low scores.

Better understanding of agile concepts. In pre-post studies there is a possibility of the subjects becoming more aware of a problem in the second test due to the first test [26]. Although the *testing* threat, as it is called, does not directly apply here, the similar surveys on consecutive weeks could have enabled the respondents to take a deeper look into the agile concepts, resulting in better understanding of them, and consequently, providing different answers to the surveys' questions.

How people perceive agility. Although the concept of agility is not new, people do not seem to fully understand it, as Conboy and Wang [27] also mention. This is actually the reason behind the existence of so many tools in the field which are trying to measure how agile the teams are or the methodologies used. The teams implement agile methodologies differently and researchers create different measurement tools. There are numerous definitions of what agility is [28–31], and each of the tool creators adopt or adapt the tools to match their needs. Their only common basis is the agile manifesto and its twelve principles [32], which are (and should be considered as) a compass for the agile practitioners. Nevertheless, they are not enough and this resulted in the saturation of the field. Moreover, Conboy and Fitzgerald [33] state that the agile manifesto principles do not provide practical understanding of the concept of agility. Consequently, all the reasons behind the current survey results are driven by the way in which tool creators and tool users perceive agility.

The questions in the surveys were all based on how their creators perceived the agile concept which is quite vague, as Tsourveloudis and Valavanis [34] have pointed out. None of the Soundararajan [18], So and Scholl [16], Leffingwell [17] claimed, of course, to have created the most complete measurement tool, but still, this leads to the oxymoron that the tools created by specialists to measure the agility of software development teams actually do it differently and without providing substantial solution to the problem. On the contrary, this leads to more confusion for the agile practitioners.

Considering that the researchers and specialists in the agile field perceive the concept of agility differently, it would be naive to say that the teams do not do the same. The answers to surveys are subjective and people reply to them depending on how they understand them. Ambler [15] stated the following: "I suspect that developers and management have different criteria for what it means to be agile". This is also corroborated by the fact that, although a team works in the same room and follows the same processes for weeks, it is rather unlikely that its members will have the same understanding of what a retrospection or a releasing planning meeting means to them, a statement which is also supported by Murphy et al. [35].

5 Threats to Validity

5.1 Construct Validity

We consider that the construct validity concerning the surveys given to the subjects was already handled by the creators of the tools which were used. Our own construct validity lies in establishing the convergent validity. The small sample of subjects was the biggest threat in establishing convergent validity, making the results very specific to Company *A* itself. Future work on this topic should be performed at other companies to mitigate this threat. In order to avoid mono-method bias, some employees were asked to fill in the surveys first in order to detect any possible issues. All the subjects were promised to remain anonymous, resulting in mitigating the evaluation apprehension [36].

5.2 Internal Validity

The creators of PAM, TAA and OPS have already tried to mitigate internal validity when creating their tools. Yet, there are still some aspects of internal validity, such as selection bias maturation and testing effect. With regard to maturation, this concerns the fatigue and boredom of the respondents. Although the surveys were small in size and did not require more than 15–20 min each, still the similar and possibly repetitive questions on the topic could cause fatigue and boredom to the subjects. This could result in the participants giving random answers to the survey questions. The mitigation for this threat was to separate the surveys and conduct them during three different periods. In addition, the respondents could stop the survey at any point and continue whenever they wanted. As far as the testing effect is concerned, this threat could not be mitigated. The testing effect threat applies to pre-post design studies only, but due to the same topic of the surveys, the subjects were to some extent more aware of what questions to expect in the second and third survey. Finally, selection could also not be mitigated, since the case study focused on a specific company only.

5.3 Conclusion Validity

Although the questions of the surveys have been carefully phrased by their creators, still there may be uncertainty about them. In order to mitigate this, for each survey a pilot one was conducted to spot any questions which would be difficult to understand. In addition, the participants could ask the first author about any issue they had concerning the survey questions. Finally, the statistical tests were run only for the data that satisfied the prerequisites, with the aim to mitigate the possibility of incorrect results.

5.4 External Validity

This case study was conducted in collaboration with one company and 30 subjects only. Consequently, it is hard to generalize the outcomes. Nevertheless, we believe that any researcher replicating the case study in another organization with teams which follow the same agile practices as those used in Company *A* would get similar results.

5.5 Reliability

To enable other researchers to conduct a similar study, the steps followed have been described and the reasons for the decisions made have been explained. Furthermore, all the data exist in digital format which can be provided to anyone who wants to review them. The presentation of the findings could probably be a threat to validity because of the first author's experience at the company. In order to mitigate this, the findings were discussed with a Company *A* employee who did not participate in the case study.

6 Conclusions and Future Work

6.1 Conclusions

This paper contributes to the area of measuring the agility of software developments teams. This contribution can be useful for the research community, but mostly for practitioners. We provided some evidence that tools claiming to measure agility do not yield similar results. The expertise of the tool creators is unquestionable, but nevertheless, their perception of agility and their personal experience have led them to create a tool in the way they consider appropriate. A measurement tool which satisfies the needs of one team may not be suitable for other teams. This derives not only from the team's needs but also from the way it transitioned to agile. Companies need a tool to measure agility in order to identify their mistakes and correct them with the total purpose to produce good quality software for their customers. There is still work to be done in order to find a universal tool for measuring agility, and such a tool should be scientifically validated before it is used.

6.2 Future Work

It would be interesting to see the results of a study that would be conducted at more companies, in order to compare them to the results of the present study. In addition, another way of forming the data samples could indicate different results, which is worth looking into. Moreover, future work in the field could check for establishing convergent validity among other agility measurement tools, combine them, validate them, and finally, only use them where their output is relevant in context.

References

1. Sureshchandra, K., Shrinivasavadhani, J.: Moving from waterfall to agile. In: Agile Conference (AGILE 2008), pp. 97–101, August 2008
2. Beck, K., Andres, C.: Extreme Programming Explained: Embrace Change. The XP Series. Addison-Wesley, Reading (2004)
3. Palmer, S.R., Felsing, M.: A Practical Guide to Feature-Driven Development. Pearson Education, London (2001)

4. Cockburn, A.: Crystal Clear a Human-powered Methodology for Small Teams. Addison-Wesley Professional, Boston (2004)
5. Schwaber, K., Beedle, M.: Agile Software Development with Scrum. Series in Agile Software Development. Prentice Hall, Englewood Cliffs (2001)
6. Williams, L., Krebs, W., Layman, L., Antón, A., Abrahamsson, P.: Toward a framework for evaluating extreme programming. In: Empirical Assessment in Software Engineering (EASE), pp. 11–20 (2004)
7. Reifer, D.J.: How to get the most out of extreme programming/agile methods. In: Wells, D., Williams, L. (eds.) XP 2002. LNCS, vol. 2418, pp. 185–196. Springer, Heidelberg (2002)
8. Aveling, B.: XP lite considered harmful? In: Eckstein, J., Baumeister, H. (eds.) XP 2004. LNCS, vol. 3092, pp. 94–103. Springer, Heidelberg (2004)
9. Escobar-Sarmiento, V., Linares-Vasquez, M.: A model for measuring agility in small and medium software development enterprises. In: 2012 XXXVIII Conferencia Latinoamericana En Informatica (CLEI), pp. 1–10, October 2012
10. Taromirad, M., Ramsin, R.: Cefam: Comprehensive evaluation framework for agile methodologies. In: 32nd Annual IEEE Software Engineering Workshopp, SEW 2008, pp. 195–204, October 2008
11. Sidky, A.: A structured approach to adopting agile practices: The agile adoption framework. Ph.D. thesis, Virginia Polytechnic Institute and State University (2007)
12. Williams, L., Rubin, K., Cohn, M.: Driving process improvement via comparative agility assessment. In: Agile Conference (AGILE 2010), pp. 3–10 (2010)
13. Ambysoft.: How agile are you? (2013)
14. Poonacha, K., Bhattacharya, S.: Towards a framework for assessing agility. In: 2012 45th Hawaii International Conference System Science (HICSS), pp. 5329–5338, January 2012
15. Ambler, S.W.: Has agile peaked? (2011)
16. So, C., Scholl, W.: Perceptive agile measurement: new instruments for quantitative studies in the pursuit of the social-psychological effect of agile practices. In: Abrahamsson, P., Marchesi, M., Maurer, F. (eds.) Agile Processes in Software Engineering and Extreme Programming. LNBIP, vol. 31, pp. 83–93. Springer, Heidelberg (2009)
17. Leffingwell, D.: Scaling Software Agility: Best Practices for Large Enterprises. The Agile Software Development Series. Addison-Wesley Professional, Boston (2007)
18. Soundararajan, S.: Assessing Agile Methods, Investigating Adequacy, Capability and Effectiveness. Ph.D. thesis, Virginia Polytechnic Institute and State University (2013)
19. Runeson, P., Hst, M.: Guidelines for conducting and reporting case study research in software engineering. Empir. Softw. Eng. **14**(2), 131–164 (2008)
20. Koch, A.: Agile Software Development: Evaluating The Methods For Your Organization. Artech House, Incorporated, Boston (2005)
21. Soundararajan, S., Arthur, J., Balci, O.: A methodology for assessing agile software development methods. In: Agile Conference (AGILE 2012), pp. 51–54 (2012)
22. Jalali, S., Wohlin, C., Angelis, L.: Investigating the applicability of agility assessment surveys: A case study. J. Syst. Softw. **98**, 172–190 (2014)
23. Delestras, S., Roustit, M., Bedouch, P., Minoves, M., Dobremez, V., Mazet, R., Lehmann, A., Baudrant, M., Allenet, B.: Comparison between two generic questionnaires to assess satisfaction with medication in chronic diseases. PLoS ONE **8**(2), 56–67 (2013)
24. Campbell, D.T., Fiske, D.W.: Convergent and discriminant validation by the multitrait-multimethod matrix. Psychol. Bull. **56**(2), 81–105 (1959)

25. Razali, N., Wah, Y.B.: Power comparisons of shapiro-wilk, kolmogorov-smirnov, lilliefors and anderson-darling tests. J. Stat. Model. Anal. **2**(1), 21–33 (2011)
26. Campbell, D.T., Stanley, J.: Experimental and Quasi-Experimental Designs for Research. Cengage Learning, New York (1963)
27. Conboy, K., Wang, X.: Understanding agility in software development from a complex adaptive systems perspective. In: ECIS (2009)
28. Kidd, P.T.: Agile Manufacturing: Forging New Frontiers. Addison-Wesley, Reading (1994)
29. Kara, S., Kayis, B.: Manufacturing flexibility and variability: an overview. J. Manuf. Technol. Manage. **15**(6), 466–478 (2004)
30. Ramesh, G., Devadasan, S.: Literature review on the agile manufacturing criteria. J. Manuf. Technol. Manage. **18**(2), 182–201 (2007)
31. Nagel, R.N., Dove, R.: 21st Century Manufacturing Enterprise Strategy: An Industry-Led View. Diane Pub Co, Collingdale (1991)
32. Beck, K., Beedle, M., van Bennekum, A., Cockburn, A., Cunningham, W., Fowler, M., Grenning, J., Highsmith, J., Hunt, A., Jeffries, R., Kern, J., Marick, B., Martin, R.C., Mellor, S., Schwaber, K., Sutherland, J., Thomas, D.: Manifesto for agile software development (2001)
33. Conboy, K., Fitzgerald, B.: Toward a conceptual framework of agile methods: A study of agility in different disciplines. In: Proceedings of the 2004 ACM Workshop on Interdisciplinary Software Engineering Research, WISER 2004, pp. 37–44 (2004)
34. Tsourveloudis, N., Valavanis, K.: On the measurement of enterprise agility. J. Intell. Robot. Syst. **33**(3), 329–342 (2002)
35. Murphy, B., Bird, C., Zimmermann, T., Williams, L., Nagappan, N., Begel, A.: Have agile techniques been the silver bullet for software development at microsoft? In: 2013 ACM / IEEE International Symposium on Empirical Software Engineering and Measurement, pp. 75–84, October 2013
36. Wohlin, C., Ohlsson, M.C., Wessln, A., Hst, M., Runeson, P., Regnell, B.: Experimentation in Software Engineering. Springer, Berlin Heidelberg (2012)

Scaling up the Planning Game: Collaboration Challenges in Large-Scale Agile Product Development

Felix Evbota[1,2], Eric Knauss[1,2(✉)], and Anna Sandberg[3]

[1] Department of Computer Science and Engineering, Chalmers University of Technology, Gothenburg, Sweden

[2] Department of Computer Science and Engineering, University of Gothenburg, Gothenburg, Sweden

fevbota@gmail.com, eric.knauss@cse.gu.se

[3] Ericsson AB, Gothenburg, Sweden

Abstract. One of the benefits of agile is close collaboration of customer and developer. This ensures good commitment and excellent knowledge flows of information about priorities and efforts. However, it is unclear if this benefit can be leveraged at scale. Clearly, it is infeasible to use practices such as planning game with several agile teams in the room. In this paper, we investigate how a large-scale agile organization manages, what challenges exist, and which opportunities can be leveraged. We found challenges in three areas: (i) the ability to estimate, prioritize, and plan; (ii) the context of planning with respect to working environment, team build-up, and team spirit; and (iii) the ceremonial agreement which promises to allow leveraging abilities in a given context.

Keywords: Large-scale agile · Planning · Collaboration · Communication

1 Introduction

One of the advantages associated with agile software development is the focus on customer collaboration and the ability to deliver customer value quickly and incrementally [8]. Popular agile methods such as Scrum [18] and eXtreme Programming (XP) [17] have powerful planning mechanisms in place, around practices such as backlog grooming, distinction between product and sprint backlog, and defining Sprint goals in Scrum, or user stories, onsite customer, acceptance testing, and planning game in XP. These practices facilitate excellent information flows: Agile development teams learn about priorities of customers, while customer representatives (product owner or onsite customer) gain knowledge about feasibility and costs of implementing their needs.

Consequently, agile methods have been applied to more and more complex development endeavors, including large and embedded software systems [1, 7]. In such contexts, it is necessary to scale up agile principles and even though this is not an easy task to do, successes have been reported, especially on reducing time-to-market of features or average times for solving customer requests [1].

H. Sharp and T. Hall (Eds.): XP 2016, LNBIP 251, pp. 28–38, 2016.
DOI: 10.1007/978-3-319-33515-5_3

Despite these successes, challenges remain, e.g. in coordination and communication of large teams [10]. In this paper we present a qualitative case study based on ten semi-structured interviews that explores how program and project leaders, product owners, line managers, and developers of cross-functional teams coordinate around planning work in a large-scale agile setting.

Contribution. Our contribution in this paper is two-fold. First, we provide insights about the challenges of aligning the views of product owners and product developers during planning in large-scale agile. Secondly, we provide a model on the relationship of different challenge types that shows how technical abilities (e.g. to estimate, to prioritize, or to plan) depend on contextual aspects (such as team build-up, work environment, and team spirit). Our study indicates that ceremony agreement plays a crucial role for enabling technical abilities of estimation, prioritization, and planning in a given context defined by the team structure and its environment.

2 Background and Related Work

Agile software development is incremental, cooperative, and adaptive [6] and facilitates responding to change quickly and frequently [8]. According to Leffingwell [1] it leads to the following business benefits: increase in productivity, increase in team morale and job satisfaction, faster time to market, and increase in quality. In this paper, we refer to the agile methods Scrum and XP [1, 8] and we are inspired by the XP practice Planning Game, wich suggest that developers, managers, and customers meet at the start of each iteration to estimate and prioritize requirements (user stories) for the next release [6, 8].

Agile methods rely heavily on face-to-face communication [3, 5, 9]. However, if the number of the involved developers (and teams) grows, it becomes extremely difficult to practice face-to-face communication between different teams [3, 5, 9]. Such growth is usually triggered by a large number of complex requirements and there is a considerable challenge to manage them [3, 4]. While Larman and Vodde suggest the use of area product owners to scale the product owners role [2], Lassenius and Paavi report that collaboration and communication between teams and product owners in such a setup were challenging and did not work well [4]. These challenges are related to the fact that area product owners work with different teams and that teams could receive different user stories from several area product owners, which thereby become difficult to prioritize [4]. Also, the introduction of Scrum of Scrums meeting (SoS– a meeting where the Scrum masters of all Scrum teams meet on a daily or weekly basis to discuss the state of every team) was found to be ineffective because of the large number of Scrum masters that were involved. As a consequence of this large audience, it was difficult to get everybody interested in the coordination meetings [4].

Products with long lifecycle (e.g. complex systems like ships or planes) tend to have very comprehensive backlogs [20]. According to Larman and Vodde, it is the responsibility of the product owner to prioritize the product backlog to improve return on investment or delivery of value [20]. For this, they suggest using planning poker to assign effort and relative value points (RVP) as a lightweight proxy for 'value' (e.g. on a scale of 1–7). The product owner then prioritizes items based on low effort estimate and high

RVP as well as other factors, such as stakeholders' preferences, strategic alignment, impact on profit, and risk [20]. Daneva et al. describe requirements prioritization in large-scale agile software development as a decision-making process [19]. In this process, priority drives the packaging of requirements into releases: requirements with highest priorities are packaged for development first [13] and usually the main criterion for such prioritization is the business value of clients and vendors [19]. Agile development however implies incremental development prioritization, which is hard to maintain: Priorities of requirements change, so there is always a need to update the priority list [13]. Thus, for being able to carry out a successful decision in prioritization, it is of paramount importance to continuously consider the roles involved, the contextual setting of the prioritization process, the prioritization criteria being used, and the kind of trade-offs being made [19]. Yet, according to Daneva et at. [19], there is a lack of (empirical) knowledge about how requirements prioritization is done in large-scale agile software development [19], a gap that we aim at exploring in this paper.

3 Research Method

The setting for this case study is Ericsson AB in Gothenburg, Sweden. Ericsson was founded in the year 1876 and is a world leading Swedish telecommunication company. Ericsson has its headquarter in Stockholm in Sweden and has more than 110, 000 employees from different parts of the world such as Sweden, China, United States of America, South Africa, United Kingdom, Germany, Nigeria, and other countries. Ericsson is involved in the development of several products, such as, cable TV, network systems, Internet Protocol, networking equipment, video systems, mobile, and fixed broadband. Ericsson also renders extensive services to its customers. Ericsson uses agile methods at a large-scale in development of their products and their methods include for example Scrum, Extreme programming, and Kanban.

This paper presents a case study conducted at Ericsson in which we explore collaboration challenges during planning of large-scale agile development efforts. We choose a qualitative case study approach that allows studying large-scale agile planning in its context [12, 15, 16]. Accordingly, we selected ten participants based on their ability in order to cover the following roles: operative product owner (OPO), line manager, program leader, project leader, release leader, team leader and developer. Through this setup, we were able to investigate collaboration challenges between teams, product owners, and program leaders in large-scale agile software development in depth. Some of our participants have about 30 years of working experience at Ericsson. The interviews were based on an interview guide with open-ended and probing questions [15]. The interview questions focus on the collaboration challenges that teams, operative product owners, and program leaders face while planning, estimating, prioritizing, and delivery of features/tasks both on the teams and program levels at Ericsson.

We carried out a verbatim transcription of the interviews data that we collected and analyzed it qualitatively to form themes and identify patterns using the six steps suggested by Braun and Clarke's thematic analysis approach [11]:

Step 1: Familiarizing with your data. We transcribed the interviews and read it several times to familiarize ourselves with the data.

Step 2: Generating initial codes. We highlighted quotes in the transcriptions that related to our research and assigned initial codes.

Step 3: Searching for themes. We grouped all codes from phase two into a number of themes.

Step 4: Reviewing the themes. We reviewed the candidate themes from phase three several times and created a thematic map containing seven categories of challenges as well as some sub challenges.

Step 5: Defining and naming themes. We further reviewed the themes we generated from phase four by checking them with interview data and the codes generated from previous phases. Codes that we found assigned to wrong themes were moved to their rightful themes. In addition to that, we also reviewed the names we gave to the themes based on the sub challenges we have in each of the themes to ascertain suitable and distinctive naming.

Step 6: Producing the report. For this paper we further analyzed the themes to identify key challenges of large-scale agile planning in order to present and discuss our findings.

In our analysis we coded the interview data by taking our research question into consideration [11]. The analysis of the interview data was not linear, meaning that we did not always follow the suggested steps in their exact order. The analysis phase was instead recursive; meaning that while we were in Step 3 for example, we often had to revisit Step 2 and even Step 1.

4 Findings: Technical Abilities, Context, and Ceremonies

Our research method resulted in a number of observations that can be arranged into seven major themes, as shown in Fig. 1: The technical *ability to estimate, prioritize*, and *plan*, the context of planning in terms of *team build-up, work environment*, and *team spirit*, and finally the *ceremony agreement* that plays a key role in aligning technical abilities and context. In this section, we will describe our findings with respect to each of the themes before we will discuss relationships between the themes as well as their implications to research and practice in Sect. 5.

4.1 Technical Ability Challenges

For adequate planning, agile teams (regardless of their scale) need to bring together the *ability to estimate* required work, *prioritize* it with respect to business value, and to combine this knowledge into a good *plan* for the coming iteration(s). At a large-scale, where a hierarchy of product owners manages backlog items for a large number of teams, we identify (communication) challenges in all three parts.

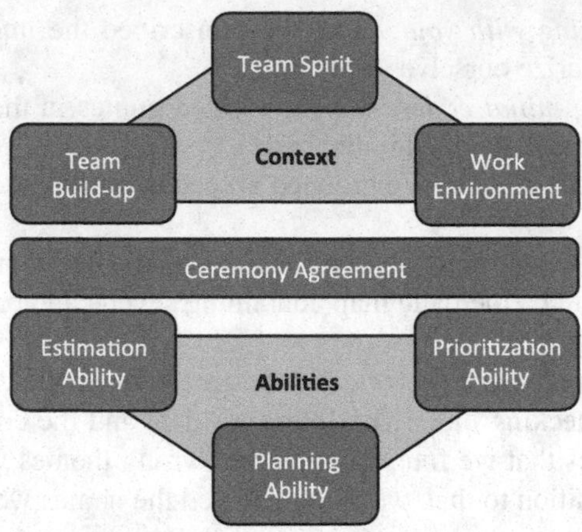

Fig. 1. Relevant themes of large-scale agile planning concern technical abilities as well as context of planning. Ceremony agreement plays a key role to connect both spheres.

Estimation Ability. According to our interviewees, it is extremely challenging to make a long-term estimation (i.e. making estimates for several months) because of the amount of content (i.e. product backlog items) is too big. This experience has lead teams to become *skeptical about estimation* in general. In addition, the fast pace and large-scale leads to a significant amount of troubleshooting, which is hard to anticipate and impacts available resources during a sprint:

> *"[Previously we] estimated on available days in the sprint, that is not a good way because you do not include the unexpected things" [OPO]*

Another challenge with estimation in large-scale agile is the *need to monitor discussions* during story estimation. Our interviewees reported that without systematic monitoring of such discussions, they could go on in circles for hours without making significant progress.

In the context of cross-functional teams, an unstructured estimation session can also lead to a pathological situation, where team members should *estimate tasks that do not fit their role*, as for example shown by the following quote from one of our interviewees:

> *"[Sometimes we have a] tester estimating design tasks and a designer estimating test tasks. It is important to know whose estimation should be looked at". [Line manager]*

Most of our interviewees stated that they are not experts in estimation and the challenges of large-scale agile estimation create a steep learning curve, especially for new team members. Estimation is based learning from past iterations and experience in the team.

Prioritization Ability. Large-scale agile product development implies a more or less *complex structure of product owners and backlogs* on different levels (such as total product, product area, operational level). It is hard to establish a shared vision with so many stakeholders, leading to disagreements and continued discussions about priorities.

> *"The challenge is if you have a lot of small backlog you are not in control at all because if you have one common backlog and you decide on a program level, that is how we work [...] if not everything is visible on the common backlog program and only visible in the XFTs backlog then you maybe having a mismatch." [OPO]*

Such potential *inconsistencies between different backlogs* as well as *lack of* their *transparency are a big challenge*. According to our interviewees, prioritization decisions need to be done on the program level. In contrast, information that is only available in the local backlog of a cross-functional team cannot be accessed and taken into consideration. Thus, if significant information is only available on the team's level and not visible on the program level, prioritization decisions cannot be optimal and mismatches will be the consequence. It is impossible to share all information (e.g. about decisions, new technology, dependencies) with other teams, product owners, and the whole organization. It is also very hard to understand the significance of information on the team level for prioritization. This potential mismatch makes it hard for the program board to establish a prioritization that teams will follow.

Planning Ability. Under the theme planning ability we discuss findings that either affect both estimation and prioritization, or that arise from translating estimations and prioritizations into a concrete plan. The planning ability in large-scale agile product development is according to our interviewees enabling to balance market priorities with the inflow of change requests and bug reports. Our interviewees mentioned two important goals: To be (i) less release-focused in their planning, thus supporting continuous deployment to customers, and (ii) to achieve a higher flexibility in their planning. For both goals, the existing challenges are impediments. Since the planning is so difficult in large-scale agile, there is resistance towards changing a plan or establishing it as a truly continuous activity.

Unclear requirements, one of the major challenges in large-scale agile planning, affect both estimation and prioritization. Our interviewees reported to be challenged to gain knowledge about the underlying user needs of a feature. This includes a potential lack of experience and knowledge about new features, starting with the area product owner.

Another challenge is the *unclear role of operational product owners* and our interviewees mention slightly different challenges in the two different products. In Product A, our interviewees expressed confusion about to what level teams should be involved in planning. In contrast, the responsibilities of operational product owners in Product B where clearer. They interacted quite naturally with informal leaders in the teams during planning, thus allowing involvement of the team, without distracting the team members too much from their development tasks. Accordingly, it is beneficial to share the plan with the whole team, without giving the team the formal responsibility to report on it.

Interviewees in both products agreed that balancing the *involvement of teams in large-scale agile planning* is challenging and that it is crucial to find a good process for their involvement. It is difficult for teams to engage in long-term planning beyond the next 18 month and while this might be necessary for large-scale agile development, our interviewees indicated that the teams do not benefit from participating in such long-term planning and do not understand why their participation should be necessary. While such a long-term plan is interesting to program leaders, program managers, and to the product line, teams should focus on producing results and cut the lead-time.

Finally, our interviews reveal technical dependencies as well as dependencies between hardware and software as a planning challenge. If known, they represent constraints on planning. However, often such technical dependencies are hidden, leading to duplicate work or waiting time. While such waste cannot fully be avoided during large-scale agile planning, approaches to mitigate its impact are needed.

4.2 Contextual Challenges

In addition to the general ability to estimate, prioritize, and plan, our data also revealed a number of challenges with respect of the context of planning, including *work environment*, *team build-up*, and *team spirit*.

Work Environment. The studied company arranges the work environment generally as *open space*, where different teams sit to carry out their daily work. While this facilitates information flow between teams, one team's daily meetings can *disturb other teams*, as for example shown in the following quote from one our interviews.

> *"...we have scrum meetings in open office space [...]. You kind of get disturbed when other teams are having their scrum meeting in the open setting. It is better [if] every team has their different rooms."[Dev.]*

Another issue mentioned by our interviewees is that sometimes other team members disturb them by walking into their teams to ask for help. While this is important inter-team communication, *by-passing the operative product owners* can be problematic when it happens too often or on non-trivial issues.

Team Build-Up. Capabilities and special knowledge of teams are crucial resource constraints for planning. According to our interviewees operative product owners and program leaders have specific views on the *capabilities of the team*. This can lead to additional pressure on teams, when they are expected to develop more than what they are capable of. Our interviewees pointed out that these different views on teams capability can lead to frustration, when teams feel they cannot live up to the demand of the operative product owner and the operative product owner feels maybe she has promised something to the area product owners and the teams cannot deliver what she has promised.

A common practice is to *move team members* to other teams that require additional resources (such as special knowledge). Our interviewees indicate difficulties in finding candidates to be moved between teams. Also, they mention doubts about the effectivity of this practice, since the team member to be moved does not possess deep knowledge about the target team and their context. Our interviewees claimed that instead *competence broadening* of established teams should be emphasized to address missing team capabilities. Such a solution of course implies a longer lead-time and our interviewees pointed out that it is challenging for them to learn new roles when they already are experts in other required roles.

Team Spirit. Our interviewees described, how team spirit starts to grow when team members have worked together and functioned successfully for some time. As a result, removing or adding new members to the team might decrease the spirit that has already been established within the team. As discussed above, some times people have to be moved between teams to provide teams with required resources. According to our data, removing team members from an established team destabilizes its spirit, which has been built over the period of close teamwork. In addition to that, the team spirit in the receiving team can also be impacted. Teams and team members adopt agile methods in different ways and some engineers are less open for the agile mindset because they have used the traditional method for a very long time and are accustomed to it, which can further impact the spirit of agile teams.

4.3 Ceremonial Agreement

In addition to technical abilities and context of planning, we discovered themes in our interview data that affect the room between those two domains: Ceremonial agreement allows a group of agile teams and product owners to align planning abilities with the teams' context. Efficient and effective information flows are necessary for keeping every employee aware about important decisions. According to our interviewees, it is however challenging to share knowledge about decisions within the large development context due to a *lack of suitable information channels*. Our interviewees said that they do not get updated on what (other) teams are doing due to insufficient time. If a product owner is responsible for several teams and these teams have their stand-up meetings at the same time, he needs to decide. But also the opposite can happen, when a team or an operative product owner have to interact with two area product owners who are typically very busy. In this situation, it is impossible to have frequent face-to-face meetings with them, resulting in asynchronous communication via email and social media. Such communication is not as effective as face-to-face communication and can result in long response times.

Coordination meetings (such as scrum-of-scrum (SoS)) are a potential solution, but were also criticized as *boring* or *too short* by our interviewees. They pointed out that in most of the SoS meetings it is difficult to have a thorough discussion and arrive at a good conclusion. Most of the times they have to close the meetings when they get into interesting technical discussion. One OPO mentioned that such discussions in the meetings might not be interesting to all participants.

While it is important not to by-pass the operative product owner when communicating with the team, this also introduces some indirection, e.g. between release leaders and the team. This requires building trusted relationships between release engineer, operative product owner, and team. A lot of such communication is the consequence of *inadequate anatomy of features*, i.e. *"the relation between different features and parts of features"*, as one of our interviewees put it. With other words, the way features are split up and assigned to sprint backlogs leads to dependencies between teams and creates the challenge of inter-team communication and coordination within the larger product portfolio. We found senior developers and product owners to rely on their *personal network* to coordinate across program boundaries:

"...I have a colleague that works as [...] operative product owner in other program and we try to collaborate between the programs and to align features for the customers and user experience". [OPO]

Thus, we conclude that typical agile ceremonies are well adopted locally within teams, but challenges remain largely on the levels of inter-team and inter-product communication across a portfolio of products.

"The biggest challenge I pick is the coordination of the feature portfolio, [...] on top of getting out features in our program fast and efficient, we need to collaborate on a portfolio basis to align the features over two programs". [OPO]

Again, our findings resonate with Sauer's recommendation to facilitate team spirit with opportunities for informal exchange, such as coffee breaks [14]. Ceremonial agreements should support large-scale agile planning in similar ways.

5 Discussion and Conclusion

Implications for Practice. From a practical point of view, we see two main advantages: First of all, it is necessary to understand which different themes actually affect large scale agile planning. Too often too much effort is spend on shallow opinions, which then become the base for future actions. By having the seven different themes thoroughly understood, actions can be taken that lead towards true improvements. One example is the thorough understanding of the theme 'Estimation Ability' where a team needs a number of practices in place to be able to manage its velocity. Secondly, and likely even more important, it is necessary to understand how the different themes impact each other. For instance, once a team has understood its velocity and can estimate properly, they can be part of larger planning game among many teams, where in the end solid prioritizations can be made in favor of having one complete release ready in time that matches a market request. Understanding these correlations between the themes helps industry to organize improvement initiatives in a way where it becomes obvious when there will be a true contribution to the product development.

Implications for Research. Our main contribution in this paper is the model derived from our exploratory case study (summarized in Fig. 1). This model includes the insight that a large-scale agile organization's ability of planning is not only depending on its teams' abilities or skill, but also on the context in which those teams operate. Ceremonies and practices on inter-team and inter-product level are currently missing and invite further research. Our model gives an overview of key aspects of collaborative planning in large-scale agile development. And we hope that others find this overview useful to focus their research. In particular, we would encourage constructive research to provide improvement for one or several aspects. Our vision is a collection of best, or at least good, practices for each area in out model.

Threats to Validity. We carefully reviewed the codes and themes generated by our research method, to ensure that our results are correctly derived from our data. It was beneficial, that we could bring both industrial and academic expertise together in these activities. Further, our qualitative investigation was carefully designed to align research method with research questions. Through reviews and pilot-interviews we made sure that participants of the study were able to understand and answer our questions, thus reducing the risk of misunderstanding and misinterpretation. Thus, we believe that we addressed internal and construct validity as well as reliability of the study in an adequate way. With our qualitative exploratory case study we did not aim for generalizability and external validity. Qualitative interviews and analysis are highly dependent on the researcher. To mitigate this threat to validity, we give a thorough description of context and procedures of our research in this paper. We are confident that repeating our study in a different, but comparable context will yield similar planning challenges of large-scale agile software development.

Outlook. When understanding themes and their correlation thoroughly, it is vital to get practices in place that embrace speed and responsiveness. These are the two key elements in agile development. Going forward, we see several different practices that could be further investigated: What methods can be used to improve team velocity? How can we organize work environments that facilitate a higher degree of responsiveness? Which ceremonies can be used to speed up the complete planning process? How can the planning process become more transparent? Are there any risks for planning too much? The potential of questions to continue to ask around large-scale agile planning is endless once the basic themes are understood and practiced to some level.

Acknowledgements. We thank our interviewees at Ericsson AB for their time and inspiring discussions. This work is partly funded by Software Center and Vinnova FFI project NGEA.

References

1. Leffingwell, D.: Scaling Software Agility: Best Practices for Large Enterprises. Addison-Wesley Professional, Upper Saddle River (2011)
2. Larman, C., Vodde, B.: Scaling Lean & Agile Development: Thinking and Organizational Tools for Large-Scale Scrum. Addison-Wesley Professional, Upper Saddle River (2009)
3. Bass, J.M.: Scrum master activities: process tailoring in large enterprise projects. In: Proceedings of 9th IEEE International Conference on Global Software Engineering (2014)

4. Paasivaara, M., Lassenius, C.: Scaling scrum in a large distributed project. In: Proceedings of International Symposium on Empirical Software Engineering and Measurement (ESEM) (2011)
5. Paasivaara, M., Heikkila, V.T., Lassenius, C.: Experiences in scaling the product owner role in large-scale globally distributed scrum. In: Proceedings of 7th IEEE International Conference on Global Software Engineering (ICGSE) (2012)
6. Abrahamsson, P., Salo, O., Ronkainen, J., Warsta, J.: Agile Software Development Methods: Review and Analysis (VTT publications), pp. 17–36 (2002)
7. Reifer, D.J., Maurer, F., Erdogmus, H.: Scaling agile methods. IEEE Softw. **20**(4), 12–14 (2001)
8. Cohen, D., Lindvall, M., Costa, P.: Agile software development. DACS SOAR Report, pp. 1–15 (2003)
9. Paasivaara, M., Durasiewicz, S., Lassenius, C.: Distributed agile development: using scrum in a large project. In: Proceedings of IEEE International Conference on Global Software Engineering (2008)
10. Dingsøyr, T., Moe, N.B.: Research challenges in large-scale agile software development. ACM SIGSOFT Software Engineering Notes **38**, 38–39 (2013)
11. Braun, V., Clarke, V.: Using thematic analysis in psychology. Qualitative Res. Psychol. **3**, 86–93 (2006)
12. Creswell, J.W.: Research Design: Qualitative, Quantitative, and Mixed Method Approaches. Sage Publications, Thousand Oaks (2009)
13. Petersen, K., Wohlin, C.: A comparison of issues and advantages in agile and incremental development between state of the art and an industrial case. J. Syst. Softw. **82**, 1479–1490 (2009)
14. Sauer, J.: Agile practices in offshore outsourcing–an analysis of published experiences. In: Proceedings of the 29th Information Systems Research Seminar in Scandinavia, IRIS, pp. 12–15 (2006)
15. Runeson, P., Höst, M.: Guidelines for conducting and reporting case study research in software engineering. Empirical Softw. Eng. **14**, 131–164 (2009)
16. Hennink, M., Hutter, I., Bailey, A.: Qualitative Research Methods. Sage, Thousand Oaks (2010)
17. Beck, K.: Extreme Programming Explained: Embrace Change. Addison-Wesley, Boston (1999)
18. Schwaber, K.: Agile Project Management With Scrum. Microsoft Press, Redmond (2004)
19. Daneva, M., Van Der Veen, E., Amrit, C., Ghaisas, S., Sikkel, K., Kumar, R., et al.: Agile requirements prioritization in large-scale outsourced system projects: An empirical study. J. Syst. Softw. **86**, 1333–1353 (2013)
20. Larman, C., Vodde, B.: Practices for Scaling Lean & Agile Development: Large, Multisite, and Offshore Product Development with Large-Scale Scrum. Pearson Education, Boston (2010)

The Lack of Sharing of Customer Data in Large Software Organizations: Challenges and Implications

Aleksander Fabijan[1(✉)], Helena Holmström Olsson[1], and Jan Bosch[2]

[1] Faculty of Technology and Society, Malmö University, Nordenskiöldsgatan 1, 211 19 Malmö, Sweden
{Aleksander.Fabijan,Helena.Holmstrom.Olsson}@mah.se

[2] Department of Computer Science and Engineering, Chalmers University of Technology, Hörselgången 11, 412 96 Göteborg, Sweden
Jan.Bosch@chalmers.se

Abstract. With agile teams becoming increasingly multi-disciplinary and including all functions, the role of customer feedback is gaining momentum. Today, companies collect feedback directly from customers, as well as indirectly from their products. As a result, companies face a situation in which the amount of data from which they can learn about their customers is larger than ever before. In previous studies, the collection of data is often identified as challenging. However, and as illustrated in our research, the challenge is not the collection of data but rather how to share this data among people in order to make effective use of it. In this paper, and based on case study research in three large software-intensive companies, we (1) provide empirical evidence that 'lack of sharing' is the primary reason for insufficient use of customer and product data, and (2) develop a model in which we identify what data is collected, by whom data is collected and in what development phases it is used. In particular, the model depicts critical hand-overs where certain types of data get lost, as well as the implications associated with this. We conclude that companies benefit from a very limited part of the data they collect, and that lack of sharing of data drives inaccurate assumptions of what constitutes customer value.

Keywords: Customer feedback · Product data · Qualitative and quantitative data · Data sharing practices · Data-driven development

1 Introduction

Traditional 'waterfall-like' methods of software development are progressively being replaced by development approaches such as e.g. agile practices that support rapid and continuous delivery of customer value [20]. Although the collection of customer feedback has always been important for R&D teams in order to better understand what customers want, it is today, when R&D teams are becoming increasingly multi-disciplinary to include all functions, that the full potential of customer data can be utilized [21]. In recent years, increasing attention has been put on the many different techniques that companies use to collect customer feedback. With connected products,

H. Sharp and T. Hall (Eds.): XP 2016, LNBIP 251, pp. 39–52, 2016.
DOI: 10.1007/978-3-319-33515-5_4

and trends such as 'Big Data' [1] and 'Internet of Things' [19], the qualitative techniques such as e.g. customer surveys, interviews and observations, are being complemented with quantitative logging and automated data collection techniques. For most companies, the increasing opportunities to collect data has resulted in rapidly growing amounts of data revealing contextual information about customer experiences and tasks, and technical information revealing system performance and operation.

However, and as recognized in recent research [8], the challenge is no longer about how to collect data. Rather, the challenge is about how to make efficient use of the large volumes of data that are continuously collected and that have the potential to reveal customer behaviors as well as product performance [1, 6, 7, 9]. Although having access to large amounts of data, most companies experience insufficient use of the data they collect, and as a result weak impact on decision-making and processes.

In this paper, we explore data collection practices in three large software-intensive companies, and we identify that 'lack of sharing' of data is the primary reason for insufficient use and impact of collected data. While the case companies collect large amounts of data from customers and from products in the field, they suffer from lack of practices that help them share data between people and development phases. As a result, decision-making and prioritization processes do not improve based on an accumulated data set that evolves throughout the development cycle, and organizations risk repetition of work due to lack of traceability.

The contribution of the paper is twofold. First, we identify that 'lack of sharing' is the primary reason for insufficient use of data and we provide empirical evidence on the challenges and implications involved in sharing of data in large software organizations. Second, and based on our empirical findings, we develop a model in which we identify what data is collected, by whom data is collected and in what development phases it is used. Our model depicts critical hand-overs where certain types of data get lost, and how this causes a situation where data does not accumulate and evolve throughout the development process. By capturing 'current state-of-practice', and by identifying critical hand-overs where data gets lost, the model supports companies in identifying what challenges they experience, and what implications this will result in. The awareness that the model helps create can work as valuable input when deciding what actions to take to improve sharing of data in large software-intensive organizations.

2 Background

2.1 Collection of Customer Feedback

In most companies, customer feedback is collected on a frequent basis in order to learn about how customers use products, what features they appreciate and what functionality they would like to see in new products [6, 5]. Typically, a wide range of different techniques are used to collect this feedback, spanning from qualitative techniques capturing customer experiences and behaviors [6, 7, 10], to quantitative techniques capturing product performance and operation [10–12]. While the qualitative techniques are used primarily in the early stages of development in order to understand the context in which the customer operates, the quantitative techniques are used post-deployment in order to understand the actual usage of products.

Starting with the pre-development stage, companies typically collect qualitative customer feedback using customer journeys, interviews, questionnaires and surveys [6, 7], forming the basis for the requirements generation [13]. At this stage, contextual information on the purpose of the product or a feature with functional characteristics and means of use are typically collected by customer representatives. Typically, this information is used to both define functional requirements as well as to form customer groups with similar needs and priorities, also known as personas [17].

During development, customer feedback is typically collected in prototyping sessions in which customers test the prototype, discuss it with the developers and user experience (UX) specialists, and suggest modifications of e.g. the user interface [6, 7, 14], As a result, developers get feedback on product behaviors and initial performance data. Customer feedback is typically mixed and consists of both qualitative information on e.g. design decisions and quantitative operational data [6].

In the post-deployment stage, and when the product has been released to its customers, a number of techniques are used to collect customer and product data. First, and since the products are increasingly being connected to the Internet and equipped with data collection mechanisms, operational data, and data revealing feature usage is collected [6, 14, 15]. Typically, this data is of quantitative type and collected by the engineers that operate the product and service centers that support it. Second, if customers generate incident requests and attach the product log revealing the state of the product, error message and other details. These are important sources of information for the support engineers when troubleshooting and improving the product [10]. Also, and as recognized in previous research [15, 16], A/B testing is a commonly deployed technique to collect quantitative feedback in connected products on which version of the feature offers a better conversion or return of investment. And although increasing amounts of data are being collected, very little is actually being used. The challenges in aggregating and analyzing this data in an efficient way prevent higher levels of the organization from benefiting from it [12].

2.2 Impact and Use of Customer Data

Companies operating within transportation, telecommunications, retailing, hospitality, travel, or health care industries already today gather and store large amounts of valuable customer data [19]. These data, in combination with a holistic understanding of the resources needed in customer value-creating processes and practices, can provide the companies that fully utilize it a competitive advantage on the market [18].

However, challenges with meaningfully combining and analyzing these customer data in an efficient way are preventing companies from utilizing the full potential from it [1, 8]. Instead of a complete organization benefiting from an accumulated knowledge, it is mostly only the engineers and technicians that have an advantage in using this data for operational purposes [12]. Higher levels in the organization such as product management or customer relationship departments need to find ways of better utilizing customer data in order to unlock its potential and use it for prioritization and customer value-actualization processes [18].

3 Research Method

This research builds on an ongoing work with three case companies that use agile methods and are involved in large-scale development of software products. The study was conducted between August 2015 and December 2015. We selected the case study methodology as an empirical method because it aims at investigating contemporary phenomena in their context, and it is well suited for this kind of software engineering research [22]. This is due to the fact that objects of this study are hard to study in isolation and case studies are by definition conducted in real world settings.

Based on experience from previous projects on how to advance beyond agile practices [3, 4], we held three individual workshops with all the companies involved in this research, following up with twenty-two individual interviews. We list the participants and their roles in Table 1.

Table 1. Description of the companies and the representatives that we met with.

Company and their domain	Representatives
Company A is a provider of telecommunication systems and equipment, communications networks and multimedia solutions for mobile and fixed network operators. The company has several sites and for the purpose of this study, we collaborated with representatives from one company site. The company has approximately 25.000 Employees in R&D. The participants marked with an asterisk (*) attended the workshop and were not available for a follow up-interview.	1 Product Owner 1 Product Manager 2 System Managers 2 Software Engineer 1 Release Manager 1 Area Prod. Mng.* 1 Lean Coach* 1 Section Mng.*
Company B is a software company specializing in navigational information, operations management and optimization solutions. Company B has approximately 3.000 Employees in R&D. All the participants attended the workshop and were interviewed.	1 Product Owner 1 System Architect 1 UX Designer 1 Service Manager
Company C is a manufacturer and supplier of transport solutions construction technology and vehicles for commercial use. The company has approximately 20.000 Employees in R&D. All the participants that attended the workshop were interviewed. In addition, one sales manager and one technology specialist wished to join the project at a later stage, and were interviewed.	1 Product Owner 2 Product Strategists 2 UX Managers 2 Function Owners 1 Feature Coord. 1 Sales Manager 2 Technology Spec.

3.1 Data Collection

During the group workshops with the companies, we were always three researchers sharing the responsibility of asking questions and facilitating the group discussion. Notes were taken by two of the researches and after each workshop, these notes were consolidated and shared to the third researcher and company representatives.

First, we conducted a workshop with an exercise with the post-it notes that build our inventory of the customer feedback techniques. Second, we held semi-structured group interviews with open-ended questions [2] during the workshop. These questions were asked by on of the researcher while two of the researchers were taking notes. In addition to the workshops, we conducted twenty-two individual interviews that lasted one hour in average, and were recorded using an iPhone Memo application. Individual Interviews were conducted and transcribed by one of the researchers. In total, we collected 13 pages of workshop notes, 176 post-it notes, 138 pages of interview transcriptions, and 9 graphical illustrations from the interviewees. All workshops and individual interviews were conducted in English.

3.2 Data Analysis

During analysis, the workshop notes, post-it notes, interview transcriptions and graphical illustrations were used when coding the data. The data collected were analyzed following the conventional qualitative content analysis approach where we derived the codes directly from the text data. This type of design is appropriate when striving to describe a phenomenon where existing theory or research literature is limited. Two of the researchers first independently and then jointly analyzed the collected data and derived the final codes that were consolidated with the third and independent researcher who also participated at the workshops. As soon as any questions or potential misunderstandings occurred, we verified the information with the other researcher and participating representatives from the companies.

3.3 Validity Considerations

To improve the study's construct validity, we conducted the exercise with the post-it notes and semi-structured interviews at the workshops with representatives working in several different roles and companies. This enabled us to ask clarifying questions, prevent misinterpretations, and study the phenomena from different angles. Next, we combined the workshop interviews with individual interviews. Workshop and interview notes were independently assessed by two researchers, guaranteeing inter-rater reliability. And since this study builds on ongoing work, the overall expectations between the researchers and companies were aligned and well understood.

The results of the validation cannot directly translate to other companies. However, considering external validity, and since these companies represent the current state of large-scale software development of embedded systems industry [3], we believe that the results can be generalized to other large-scale software development companies.

4 Findings

In this section, we present our empirical findings. In accordance with our research interests, we first outline the generalized data collection practices in the three case companies, i.e. what types of data that is collected in the different development phases, and by whom. Second, we identify the challenges that are associated with sharing of data in these organizations. Finally, we explore their implications.

4.1 Data Collection Practices: Current State

In the case companies, data is collected throughout the development cycle and by different roles in the organization. Typically, people working in the early phases of development collect qualitative data from customers reflecting customer environments, customer experience and customer tasks. The later in the development cycle, the more quantitative data is collected, reflecting system performance and operation when in the field. In Tables 2, 3 and 4, we illustrate the data collection practices, together with the customer feedback methods and types of data that different roles collect in each of the development stages.

Table 2. Customer data collection practices in the pre-development stage.

	Roles that collect customer feedback	Common customer feedback collection techniques	Common types of customer feedback collected
Pre-Development	Strategy specialists, Product managers, Product owners	Reading of industry press, Reading of published standards, Reading of internal reports, Reading customer visit reviews	Customer wishes, Short/Long market trends, Competitors ability of delivering the product
	Strategy specialists, Feature owners	Telephone interviews, Face-to-face interviews, Conducting group interviews	Existing product satisfaction, Future product specification, Personas and User Journeys

4.2 Data Sharing Practices: Challenges

Based on our interviews, we see that there are a number of challenges associated with sharing of data in large organizations. For example, our interviewees all report of difficulties in getting access to data that was collected by someone else and in a different development phase. Below, we identify the main challenges associated with sharing of data in the case companies:

Table 3. Customer data collection practices in the development stage.

	Roles that collect customer feedback	Common customer feedback collection techniques	Common types of customer feedback collected
Development	UX specialists, Software Engineers	System Usability Scale Form, Asking open ended questions, Demonstrating prototypes, Filming of users' product use	Acceptance of the prototype, Eye behavior and focus time, Points of pain, Bottlenecks and constrains, Interaction design sketches
	System managers, System architects, Software engineers	Consolidate feedback from other projects, Reading prototype log entries	Small improvement wishes, Configuration data, Product operational data

Table 4. Customer data collection practices in the post-deployment stage.

	Roles that collect customer feedback	Common customer feedback collection techniques	Common types of customer feedback collected
Post-Deployment	Release managers, Service managers Software engineers	Reading of customer reports, Analyzing incidents, Aggregating customer requests, Analyzing product log files	Number of incid. and req., Duration of incid. and req., Product operational data, Product performance data
	Sales managers	Reading articles in the media, Sentimental analysis Customer events participation, Reading industry press, Performing trend analysis	Opinions about the appeal of the product, Performance of the product, Business case descriptions

- ***Fragmented Collection and Storage of Data***

Individuals independently collect increasing amounts of customer feedback, analyze the data they obtained, and store their findings on local repositories. Although these findings are occasionally presented at meetings, the lack of transparency and tools prevents others in the organization to use and benefit from the data. With so many different roles collecting and storing data, systematic sharing across development phases becomes almost impossible. As a result, only those roles that work in close collaboration share data, and benefit from the analysis of this data. This situation is illustrated in the following quotes:

"... it is all in my head more or less." -Product owner, Company B

"Information exists but we don't know where it is."–UX Specialist from Company C

"I do not know everyone... So I contact only the person who is next in line." -Sales manager from Company C.

- ***Filtering of Customer Data***

People collect data, and share it only within the development stage they typically work in. For example, practitioners in the development phase actively exchange product log data, interaction design sketches, quality statistics and trouble reports. Similarly, those working in the post-deployment phase exchange release notes, business case descriptions and management system issues. Attempts to communicate the significance of customer feedback and their findings across development stages are typically unsuccessful. Feedback that is shared is filtered quantitative data.

"It is like there is a wall in-between. There is a tradition that we should not talk to each other." -Product Owner from Company C.

- ***Arduous to Measure Means Hard to Share.***

The only data that is successfully shared among people and development phases, is quantitative data representing those things that can be easily measured such as e.g. system performance and operation. The case companies are successful in sharing transaction records, incident figures, feature usage data and other technical feedback that can be easily measured. However, qualitative data such as user stories, feature purpose, or the intention of a certain requirement typically stay with the people that collected that feedback. As a result, and instead of benefitting from an accumulated set of data that evolves over time, companies run the risk of using fragmented data sets that misrepresent the customer and provides an insufficient understanding of what constitutes customer value.

"Maybe 10 % of information is shared. It is very difficult. It takes so much time, to, you need to write a novel more or less and distribute it" -Product manager from Company A.

4.3 Data Sharing Practices: Implications

Due to very limited amounts of data being shared among people and across the development phases, the case companies experience a number of implications. Below, we present the implications:

- ***Non-evolving and Non-accumulating Data.***

Although quantitative data describing operational and performance requirements is typically shared, the lack of qualitative information with the context describing where, how and why a certain feature or a product is needed and how it will be used cause discrepancies in understanding the overall purpose. As a result, the data forming customer knowledge across the development stages does not accumulate and evolve. Consequently, practitioners developing the product do not fully understand the overall purpose of the product or a feature under development and develop suboptimal products that can be different from the customer wishes.

> *"I think now a lot of thing are developed in a sub optimized way." -Technology Spec. from company C.*

> *"We get feature which is broken down and then this value somehow got lost when it was broken down, then it is harder to understand what they really need it for." –Software engineer from Company B.*

- ***Repetition of Work.***

Due to the lack of access to the qualitative feedback that is collected in the early stages of development, roles in later stages that seek contextual understanding of a feature are sometimes required to collect identical feedback to the one that was already collected. Consequently, resources are spent on repeating the work that has already been done once.

> *"You cannot build on what is already there since you don't know. You then repeat an activity that was already made by someone else." –UX specialist from Company C.*

- ***Inaccurate Models of Customer Value.***

Since the qualitative customer feedback is not shared across the development phases, companies risk to use only the available quantitative customer feedback to build or update the understanding of the customer. This results in inaccurate assumptions on what constitutes customer value. And as a consequence of using the feedback for prioritization on the product management level, projects that create waste risk to get prioritized.

> *"You think one thing is important but you don't realize that there is another thing that was even more important." -Technology Spec. from company C.*

- ***Validation of Customer Value is a "Self-Fulfilling Prophecy".***

Due to the fact that only quantitative customer feedback is exchanged across the development phases and development organization, companies risk to validate their products using only the effortlessly quantifiable feedback, and neglecting the rest. Instead of using the accumulated customer feedback and holistically asses their products, the validation of customer value becomes a "self-fulfilling prophecy" in that it focuses on developing and verifying things that can be quantified and provide tangible evidence.

We map the challenges with their implications for the companies and the products they develop, and summarize them in Table 5.

Table 5. The mapping of identified challenges to their implications.

Challenge	Description	Company implications	Product implications
Fragmented collection and storage of data	Sharing of data is limited across the development stages.	No evolving and accumulating of customer data and understanding.	Suboptimal products are being developed.
Filtering of customer data.	Only roles that work in close cooperation exchange feedback.	Inaccurate assumptions on customer value and repeating work.	Risk of developing wasteful features.
Arduous to measure means hard to share.	What can easily be measured and quantified is shared.	Validation of customer value is a "self-fulfilling prophecy".	Product maximizes partial models of customer value.

5 Discussion

Multi-disciplinary teams involved in the development of a software product are using customer feedback to develop and improve the product or a feature they are responsible for. Previous research [6, 8, 9] and our empirical findings show that companies collect increasingly large amounts of customer data. Both using the qualitative techniques are used primarily in the early stages of development [6, 7, 10] to construct an understanding of the customer and the context they operate in, and quantitative techniques that are used post-deployment to monitor the actual usage of products in the field [10–12]. And although companies gather and store large amounts of valuable customer data [19], challenges with meaningfully combining and analyzing it in an efficient way [1, 8] are preventing companies from evolving the data across the development stages and accumulating the customer knowledge.

5.1 The Model: From Quantifiable Feedback to Partial Customer Value

In response to the challenges and implications presented above, we illustrate our findings and challenges in a descriptive model on Fig. 1.

In the development process, the model advocates an approach in which an internal model of customer value in companies is being created. We illustrate that companies in fragments collect a complete understating of the customer and their wishes, however, benefit only from a part of the understanding.

In our model, we distinguish between three development stages, i.e. pre-development, development and post-deployment. Although we recognize that this is a simplified view, and that most development processes are of an iterative nature, we use these stages as they typically involve similar roles, techniques, and types of feedback collected.

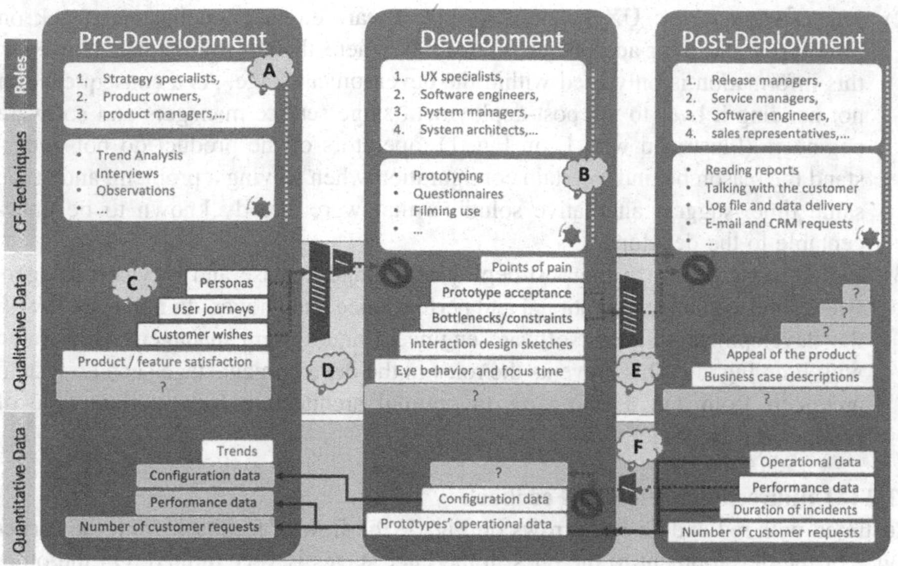

Fig. 1. Customer feedback sharing practices model.

On Fig. 1, we list a few roles that collect customer feedback (A) and different methods of how they perform the collection (B). Within each of the development stages we list the types of feedback being shared across the stages with a solid green lines and those that are not with a dashed red lines. Between development stages we identify three critical hand-over points where customer data that could and should get shared, dissipates. Instead of accumulating data being handed over, gaps across stages appear (illustrated with "?"symbols in blocks on Fig. 1).

5.1.1 The Vaporization of Customer Data.

We identify three critical hand-over blocks that cause data to disappear and prevent practicioners on project to build-on

(1) *The PreDev Block*: While there is extensive collection of qualitative customer feedback such as user journeys and product satisfaction surveys (Illustrated with C on Fig. 1), roles working in the pre-development stage do not sufficiently supply the development part of the organization with the information they collect. Qualitative data that would inform the development stage on the context of the product under development, how it is going to be used, and who the different user groups perishes in the hand-over process between product owners and managers on one side, and software engineers and UX specialist on the other (Illustrated with D on Fig. 1). Specifically, personas, user journeys and customer wishes are the types of feedback that should be handed over to the development stage, however, they are not. Consequently, the development part of the organization is forced to repeat collection activities in order to obtain this information when in need, or continue developing the product following only the specifications /requirements that were handed to them.

(2) *The DevOps Block*: UX specialists and software engineers collect feedback on prototypes and their acceptance, as well as where the constraints are. However, this information is only used within the development stage. As a consequence of not handing it over to the post-deployment stage service managers and software engineers (Illustrated with E on Fig. 1), operators of the product do not understand the reason behind a certain configuration when solving a problem, and at the same time, suggest alternative solutions that were already known to be unacceptable to the developers.

(3) *The OpsDev Block*: In the post-deployment stage, release and service managers collect and exchange operational and performance data, hover, do not share it with the development stage to software engineers and system managers. (Illustrated with F on Fig. 1). This prevents the roles in the development stage such as system architects from e.g. deciding on an optimal architecture for a certain type of product and customer size.

5.1.2 Unidirectional Flow of Feedback

Illustrated with red and dashed arrows on Fig. 1, the flow of feedback from the earlier stages of the development to the ones in the later stages is very limited. On the other hand, the flow of feedback from the later stages to the early ones is extensive. This both supports our finding about extensive sharing of quantitative data, which is typically available in the later stages, as well as implies that it is easier to share data about earlier releases of the software under development compared to sharing feedback about the current release. Validating the value of the current release is consequently done very late.

5.1.3 Shadow Representation of Customer Value

In the absence of the accumulated data being accessible and shared across the development stages (illustrated with missing data symbol "?" on Fig. 1), people in later stages base their prioritizations and decisions on shadow beliefs existing in the organization. Consequently, and instead of having a unique understanding of what constitutes customer value, individual development stages and roles prioritize based on their best intuition and shared quantitative data. If sharing of customer data in the direction towards the later stages is enabled, roles across the development stages will be able to conduct data-informative decisions. As seen in our findings, hazards of being purely quantitative data-driven are extensive. And with qualitative data being as accessible as quantitative, validation of customer data could be coherent, not a 'self-fulfilling prophecy' as it is today.

6 Conclusion

By moving away from traditional waterfall development practices and with agile teams becoming increasingly multi-disciplinary and including all functions from R&D to product management and sales [21], the role of customer feedback is increasingly gaining momentum. And although the collection of data has previously been identified as challenging, we show in our research that the challenge is not its collection, but rather how to share this data in order to make effective use of it.

In this paper, we explore the data collection practices in three large software-intensive organizations, and we identify that lack of sharing of data is the main inhibitor for effective product development and improvement. Based on our case study findings, we see that currently (1) companies benefit from a very limited part of the data they collect due to a lack of sharing of data across development phases and organizational units, (2) companies form inaccurate assumptions on what constitutes customer value and waste resources on repeating the activities that have already been performed, and (3) validation of customer in companies today is a "self-fulfilling prophecy" in that it focuses on quantifiable things that provide tangible evidence.

References

1. Chen, H., Chiang, R.H., Storey, V.C.: Business intelligence and analytics: From big data to big impact. MIS Q. **36**, 1165–1188 (2012)
2. Dzamashvili Fogelström, N., Gorschek, T., Svahnberg, M., et al.: The impact of agile principles on market-driven software product development. J. Softw. Maintenance Evol. Res. Pract. **22**, 53–80 (2010)
3. Olsson, H.H., Bosch, J.: From opinions to data-driven software R&D: a multi-case study on how to close the 'open loop' problem. In: 2014 40th EUROMICRO Conference on Software Engineering and Advanced Applications (SEAA), pp. 9–16 (2014)
4. Olsson, H.H., Bosch, J.: Towards continuous customer validation: a conceptual model for combining qualitative customer feedback with quantitative customer observation. In: Fernandes, J.M., Machado, R.J., Wnuk, K. (eds.) Software Business. LNBIP, vol. 210, pp. 154–166. Springer, Heidelberg (2015)
5. Von Hippel, E.: Lead users: a source of novel product concepts. Manage. Sci. **32**, 791–805 (1986)
6. Fabijan, A., Olsson, H., Bosch, J.: Customer feedback and data collection techniques in software R&D: a literature review. In: Fernandes, J.M., Machado, R.J., Wnuk, K. (eds.) Software Business. LNBIP, vol. 210, pp. 139–153. Springer, Heidelberg (2015)
7. Cockburn, A., Williams, L.: Agile software development: It's about feedback and change. Computer **36**, 39–43 (2003)
8. Bizer, C., Boncz, P., Brodie, M.L., Erling, O.: The meaningful use of big data: Four perspectives–four challenges. ACM SIGMOD Rec. **40**, 56–60 (2012)

9. Fabijan, A., Olsson, H.H., Bosch, J.: Early value argumentation and prediction: an iterative approach to quantifying feature value. In: Abrahamsson, P., et al. (eds.) PROFES 2015. LNCS, vol. 9459, pp. 16–23. Springer, Heidelberg (2015)
10. Bosch-Sijtsem, P., Bosch, J.: User involvement throughout the innovation process in high-tech industries. J. Prod. Innov. Manage. **32**(5), 793–807 (2014)
11. Olsson, H.H., Bosch, J.: Post-deployment data collection in software-intensive embedded products. In: Bosch, J. (ed.) Continuous Software Engineering, pp. 143–154. Springer, Heidelberg (2014)
12. Olsson, H.H., Bosch, J.: Towards data-driven product development: A multiple case study on post-deployment data usage in software-intensive embedded systems. In: Fitzgerald, B., Conboy, K., Power, K., Valerdi, R., Morgan, L., Stol, K.-J. (eds.) Lean Enterprise Software and Systems. LNBIP, vol. 167, pp. 152–164. Springer, Heidelberg (2013)
13. Sommerville, I., Kotonya, G.: Requirements Engineering: Processes and Techniques. Wiley, Chichester (1998)
14. Sampson, S.E.: Ramifications of monitoring service quality through passively solicited customer feedback. Decis. Sci. **27**(4), 601–622 (1996)
15. Bosch, J.: Building products as innovations experiment systems. In: Proceedings of 3rd International Conference on Software Business, Massachusetts, 18–20 June 2012
16. Kohavi, R., Longbotham, R., Sommerfield, D., Henne, R.M.: Controlled experiments on the web: survey and practice guide. Data Min. Knowl. Disc. **18**(1), 140–181 (2009)
17. Aoyama, M.: Persona-and-scenario based requirements engineering for software embedded in digital consumer products, pp. 85–94 (2005)
18. Saarijärvi, H., Karjaluoto, H., Kuusela, H.: Customer relationship management: The evolving role of customer data. Mark. Intell. Plan. **31**, 584–600 (2013)
19. Atzori, L., Iera, A., Morabito, G.: The internet of things: A survey. Comput. Netw. **54**, 2787–2805 (2010)
20. Rodríguez, P., Haghighatkhah, A., Lwakatare, L.E., Teppola, S., Suomalainen, T., Eskeli, J., Karvonen, T., Kuvaja, P., Verner, J.M., Oivo, M.: Continuous deployment of software intensive products and services: A systematic mapping study. J. Syst. Softw. (2015). http://www.sciencedirect.com/science/article/pii/S0164121215002812
21. Olsson, H.H., Alahyari, H., Bosch, J.: Climbing the "Stairway to Heaven", in software engineering and advanced applications (SEAA). In: 2012 38th EUROMICRO Conference on Software Engineering and Advanced Applications, Izmir, Turkey (2012)
22. Runeson, P., Höst, M.: Guidelines for conducting and reporting case study research in software engineering. Empir. Softw. Eng. **14**(2), 131–164 (2008)

TDDViz: Using Software Changes to Understand Conformance to Test Driven Development

Michael Hilton(✉), Nicholas Nelson, Hugh McDonald, Sean McDonald, Ron Metoyer, and Danny Dig

Oregon State University, Corvallis, USA
{hiltonm,nelsonni,mcdonalh,mcdonase,metoyer,digd}@eecs.oregonstate.edu

Abstract. A bad software development process leads to wasted effort and inferior products. In order to improve a software process, it must be first understood. Our unique approach in this paper uses code and test changes to understand conformance to the Test Driven Development (TDD) process.

We designed and implemented TDDViz, a tool that supports developers in better understanding how they conform to TDD. TDDViz supports this understanding by providing novel visualizations of developers' TDD process. To enable TDDViz's visualizations, we developed a novel automatic inferencer that identifies the phases that make up the TDD process solely based on code and test changes.

We evaluate TDDViz using two complementary methods: a controlled experiment with 35 participants to evaluate the visualization, and a case study with 2601 TDD Sessions to evaluate the inference algorithm. The controlled experiment shows that, in comparison to existing visualizations, participants performed significantly better when using TDDViz to answer questions about code evolution. In addition, the case study shows that the inferencing algorithm in TDDViz infers TDD phases with an accuracy (F-measure) of 87%.

Keywords: Test Driven Development · Software visualization · Development process

1 Introduction

A bad software development process leads to wasted effort and inferior products. Unless we understand how developers are following a process, we cannot improve it.

In this paper we use Test Driven Development (TDD) as a case study on how software changes can illuminate the development process. To help developers achieve a better understanding of their process, we examined seminal research [1–3] that found questions software developers ask. From this research, we focused on three question areas. We felt that the answers to these could provide developers with a better understanding of their process. We choose three

H. Sharp and T. Hall (Eds.): XP 2016, LNBIP 251, pp. 53–65, 2016.
DOI: 10.1007/978-3-319-33515-5_5

questions from the literature to focus on, and they spanned three areas: *identification*, *comprehension*, and *comparability*.

RQ1: *"Can we detect strategies, such as test-driven development?" (Identification)* [1]
RQ2: *"Why was this code changed or inserted?" (Comprehension)* [3]
RQ3: *"How much time went into testing vs. into development?" (Comparability)* [2]

To answer these questions, we use code and test changes to understand conformance to a process. In this paper, we present TDDViz, our tool which provides visualizations that support developers' understanding of how they conform to the TDD process. Our visual design is meant to answer RQ1-3 so that we ensure that our visualizations support developers in answering important questions about *identification*, *comprehension*, and *comparability* of code.

In order to enable these visualizations, we designed a novel algorithm to infer TDD phases. Given a sequence of code edits and test runs, TDDViz uses this algorithm to automatically detect changes that follow the TDD process. Moreover, the inferencer also associates specific code changes with specific parts of the TDD process. The inferencer is crucial for giving developers higher-level information that they need to improve their process.

One fundamental challenge for the inferencer is that during the TDD practice, not all code is developed according to the textbook definition of TDD. Even experienced TDD developers often selectively apply TDD during code development, and only on some parts of their code. This introduces lots of noise for any tool that checks conformance to processes. To ensure that our inference algorithm can correctly handle noisy data, we add a fourth Research Question.

RQ4: *"Can an algorithm infer TDD phases accurately?" (Accuracy)*

To answer this question, in this paper we use a corpus of data from cyber-dojo [1], a website that allows developers to practice and improve their TDD by coding solutions to various programming problems. Each time a user run tests, the code is committed to a git repository. Each of these commits becomes a fine-grained commit. Our corpus contains a total of 41766 fine-grained snapshots from 2601 programming sessions, each of which is an attempt to solve one of 30 different programming tasks.

To evaluate TDDViz, we performed a controlled experiment with 35 student participants already familiar with TDD. Our independent variable was using TDDViz or existing visualizations to answer questions about the TDD Process.

This paper makes the following contributions:

Process Conformance: We propose a novel usage of software changes to infer conformance to a process. Instead of analyzing metrics taken at various points in time, we analyze deltas (i.e., the changes in code and tests) to understand conformance to TDD.

TDD Visualization Design and Analysis: We present a visualization designed specifically for understanding conformance to TDD. Our visualizations

[1] www.cyberdojo.org.

show the presence or absence of TDD and allow progressive disclosure of TDD activities.

TDD Phase Inference Algorithm: We present the first algorithm to infer the activities in the TDD process solely based on snapshots taken when tests are run.

Implementation and Empirical Evaluation: We implement the visualization and inference algorithm in TDDViz, and empirically evaluate it using two complementary methods. First, we conduct a controlled experiment with 35 participants, in order to answer **RQ1–3**. Second, we evaluate the accuracy of our inferencer using a corpus of 2601 TDD sessions from cyber-dojo, in order to answer **RQ4.** Our inferencer achieves an accuracy of 87%. Together, both of these show that TDDViz is effective.

2 Visualization

2.1 Visualization Elements

TDD Cycle Plot. We represent a TDD cycle using a single glyph as shown in Fig. 1[a]. This representation was inspired by hive plots [4] and encodes the nominal cycle data with a positional and color encoding (red=test, green=code, blue=refactor). The position of the segment redundantly encodes the TDD cycle phase (e.g. the red phase is always top right, the green phase is always at the bottom, and the blue phase is always top left). The time spent in a phase is a quantitative value encoded in the area [5,6] of the cycle plot segment (i.e., the larger the area, the more time spent in that phase during that cycle). All subplots are on the same fixed scale. Taken together, a single cycle plot forms a glyph or specific 'shape' based on the characteristics of the phases, effectively using a 'shape' encoding for different types of TDD cycles. This design supports both *characterization* of entire cycles as well as *comparison* of a developer's time distribution in each phase of a cycle. We illustrate the shape patterns of various TDD cycles in the next section.

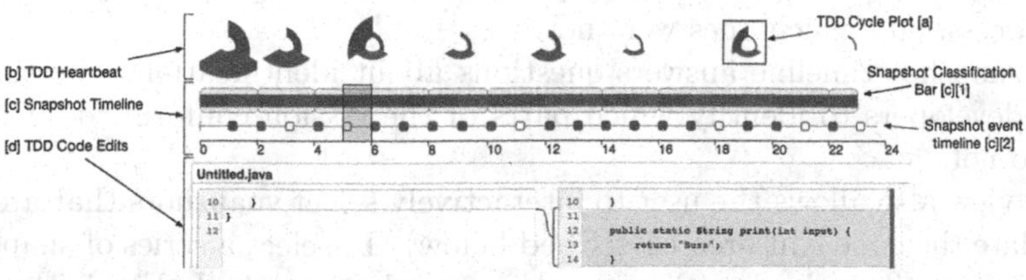

Fig. 1. Interactive visualization of a TDD session. The user can choose any arbitrary selection they wish. This example shows a session that conforms to TDD. Sizes in the TDD Heartbeat plot represent time spent in each phase. The different parts of the visualization have been labeled for clarity. [a] a TDD Cycle plot, [b] TDD Heartbeat, [c] Snapshot Timeline, [d] TDD Code Edits (Color figure online)

TDD Heartbeat. To support comparison of TDD cycles over time, we provide a small multiples view [7] that we call the TDD Heartbeat view. The TDD Heartbeat view consists of a series of TDD cycle plots, one for every cycle of that session (See Fig. 1, [b]) We call this the TDD heartbeat because this view gives an overall picture of the *health* of the TDD process as it evolves over time. This particular view supports the abstract tasks of *characterization* and *comparison*.

In particular, the user can compare entire cycles over time to see how they evolve, and she can characterize how her process is improving or degrading. For example, by looking at all the cycles that make up the TDD Heartbeat in Fig. 1, the user sees that for every cycle in this kata, the developer spent relatively more time writing production code than writing tests. They can also observe that the relationship between the time spent in each phase was fairly consistent.

Snapshot Timeline. The snapshot timeline provides more information about the TDD process, specifically showing all the snapshots in the current session. An example snapshot timeline is shown in Fig. 1[c]. The snapshot timeline consists of two parts, the snapshot classification bar (Fig. 1[c][1]) on the top, and the snapshot event timeline on the bottom (Fig. 1[c][2]). In the snapshot event timeline, each snapshot is represented with a rounded square. The color represents the outcome of the tests at that snapshot event. Red signifies the tests were run, but at least one test failed. If all the tests passed, then it is colored green. If the code and tests do not compile, we represent this with an empty white rounded box. The distance between each snapshot is evenly distributed, since the time in that phase is encoded in the TDD Cycle Plot.

The snapshot classification bar shows the cycle boundaries, and inside each cycle the ribbon of red, green and blue signifies which snapshot events fall into which phases. For example, in Fig. 1, snapshots 17–20 are all part of the same green phase. Snapshots 17–19 the developer is trying to get to a green, but they are not successful in making the tests pass until snapshot 20.

This view answers questions specifically dealing with how consistent coders followed the TDD process, what snapshots were written by coders using the TDD process, and which ones were not.

The snapshot timeline answers questions about identification. The timeline enables developers to identify which parts of the session conform to TDD and which do not.

This view also allows the user to interactively select snapshots that are used to populate the code edit area (described below). To select a series of snapshots, the user interactively drags and resizes the gray selection box. In Fig. 1, snapshots 5 and 6 are selected.

The snapshot timeline also answers questions dealing with comprehension. By seeing how TDDViz catagorizes a snapshot, a user can determine why selected changes were made. For example, Fig. 1 shows a selected snapshot which represents the changes between snapshots numbers 5 and 6. Since the selected changes are part of a green phase (as noted by the green area in the Snapshot Classification Bar), a user can determine that these were production changes to make a failing test pass. This can be confirmed by observing the code edits. This encoding supports the same questions as the cycle plot and heartbeat arrangement, but, it does so at a finer granularity, showing each individual test run.

TDD Code Edits. Figure 1[d] shows an example of a code edit, which displays the changes to the code between two snapshots. To understand the TDD process, a coder must be able to look at the code that was written, and see how it evolved over time. By positioning the selection box on the timeline as described above, a user can view how all the code evolved over any two arbitrary snapshots. The code edit region contains an expandable and collapsable box for each file that was changed in the selected range of snapshots. Each box contains two code editors, one for the code at the selection's starting snapshot, and one for the code at the ending snapshot.

Whenever the user selects a new snapshot range, these boxes dynamically repopulate their content with the correct diffs. There are additional examples of our visualizations on our accompanying web page http://cope.eecs.oregonstate.edu/visualization.html.

3 TDD Phase Inferencer

In order to build the visualizations we have presented thus far, we needed a TDD phase inference algorithm which uses test and code changes to infer the TDD process. Instead of relying on static analysis tools, we present a novel approach where the algorithm analyzes the changes to the code. We designed our algorithm to take as input a series of snapshots. The algorithm then analyzes the code changes between each snapshot and uses that information to determine if the code was developed using TDD. If the algorithm infers the TDD process, then it determines which parts of the TDD process those changes belong to.

3.1 Snapshots

We designed our algorithm to receive a series of snapshots as input. We define a *snapshot* as a copy of the code and tests at a given point in time. In addition to the contents of code and tests, the snapshot contains the results of running the tests at that point in time.

Our algorithm uses these snapshots to determine the developers' changes to the program. It then uses these changes to infer the TDD process. In this paper, we use a corpus of data where a snapshot was taken every time the code was compiled and the tests were run. It is important that the snapshots have this level of detail, because if they do not, we do not get a clear picture of the development process.

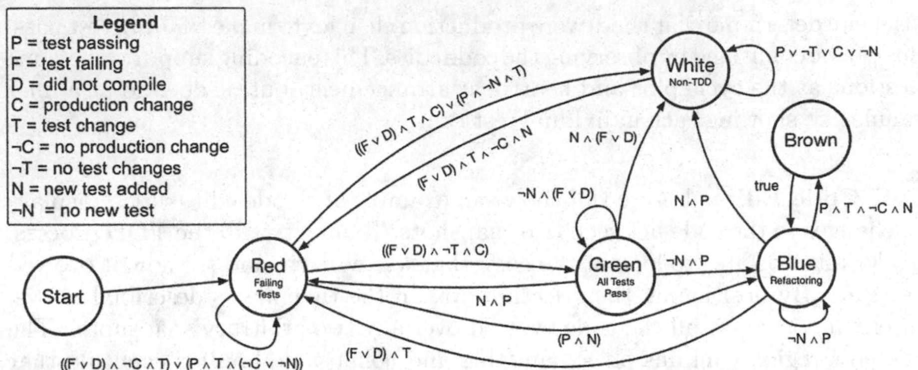

Fig. 2. State machine diagram of the TDD phase inference algorithm.

3.2 Abstract Syntax Tree

Since our inference algorithm must operate on the data that the snapshots contain, it is important to have a deeper understanding of code than just the textual contents. To this end, our inference algorithm constructs the Abstract Syntax Tree (AST) for each code and test snapshot in our data. This allows our inferencer to determine which edits belong to the production code and which edits belong to the test code. It also calculates the number of methods and assert statements at each snapshot. For the purposes of the algorithm, we consider code with asserts to be test codes, and code with no asserts to be production code. We consider each assert to be an individual test, even if it is in a method with other asserts. If a new assert is detected, we consider that to be a new test. All this information enables the algorithm to infer the phases of TDD. In our implementation of the algorithm in TDDViz, we use the Gumtree library [8] to create the ASTs.

3.3 Algorithm

We present the TDD phase inference algorithm using the state digram in Fig. 2. Our algorithm encodes a finite-state machine (FSM), where the state nodes are phases, and the transitions are guided by predicates on the current snapshot. We define each of the states as follows:

Red: This category indicates that the coder was writing test code in an attempt to make a failing test
Green: This category is when the coder is writing code in an attempt to make a failing test pass
Blue: This is when the coder has gotten the tests to pass, and is refactoring the code
White: This is when the code is written in a way that deviates from TDD
Brown: This is a special case, when the coder writes a new test and it passes

on the first try, without altering the existing production code. It could be they were expecting it to fail, or perhaps they just wanted to provide extra tests for extra security.

The predicates take a snapshot and using the AST changes to the production and test code, as well as the result of the test runs, compute a boolean function. We compose several predicates to determine a transition to another state. For example: in order to transition from green to blue, the following conditions must hold true. All the current unit tests must pass, and the developer may not add any new tests.

The transition requires passing tests, because if not, the developer either remains in the green phase or has deviated from TDD. No new tests are allowed because the addition of a new test, while a valid TDD practice, would signify that the developer has skipped the optional blue phase and moved directly to the red phase.

There are a few special cases in our algorithm. The algorithm's transition from Red to Blue is the case when a single snapshot comprised the entire Green phase, and therefore the algorithm has moved on to the blue phase. Another thing to note is that by definition, the brown phase only contains a single commit. Therefore, after the algorithm identifies a brown phase, it immediately moves back to the blue phase.

4 Evaluation

To evaluate the usefulness of TDDViz, we answer the following research questions:

RQ1. *Can programmers using* TDDViz *identify whether the code was developed in conformance with TDD? (Identification)*
RQ2. *Can programmers using* TDDViz *identify the reason why code was changed or inserted? (Comprehension)*
RQ3. *Can programmers using* TDDViz *determine how much time went into testing vs. development of production code? (Comparability)*
RQ4. *Can an algorithm infer TDD phases accurately? (Accuracy)*

In order to answer these research questions, we used two complementary empirical methods. We answer the first three questions with a controlled experiment with 35 participants, and the last question with a case study of 2601 TDD sessions. The experiment allows us to quantify the effectiveness of the visualization as used by programmers, while the case study gives more confidence that the proposed algorithm can handle a wide variety of TDD instances.

4.1 Controlled Experiment

Participants. Our participants were 35 students in a 3rd-year undergrad Software Engineering class who were in week 10 of a course in which they had used TDD for their class project.

Treatment. Our study consisted of two treatments. For the experimental treatment, we asked the participants to answer questions dealing with identification, comprehension, and comparability (RQ1–RQ3) by examining several coding sessions from cyber-dojo presented with our visualization. For the control treatment, we used the same questions applied to the same real-life code examples, but the code was visualized using the visualization[2] that is available on the cyber-dojo site. This visualization shows both the code, and the test results at each snapshot, but it does not present any information regarding the phases of TDD. We used this visualization for our control treatment because it is specifically designed to view the data in our corpus. Also, it is the only available visualization other than our own which shows both the code and the history of the test runs.

Experimental Procedure. In order to isolate the effect of our visualization, both treatments had the same introduction, except for when describing the parts of the visualizations which are different across treatments. Both treatments received the exact same questions on the same real-life data in the same order. The only independent variable was which visualization was presented to each treatment. We randomly assigned the students into two groups, one group with 17 participants and the other group with 18 participants. We then flipped a coin to determine which group received which treatment. We gave both treatments back to back on the same day.

Tasks. The experiment consisted of three tasks. To evaluate *identification*, we asked "Is this entire session conforming to TDD?" To evaluate *comprehension* we asked "Why was this code changed?" To evaluate *comparability* we asked "Was more time spent writing tests or production code?" For each task we asked the same question on four different instances of TDD sessions. The students were accustomed to using clickers to answer questions, and so for each task they answered questions through the use of their clickers. Each question was a multiple choice question.

Measures. The independent variable in this study was the visualization used to answer the questions. The dependent measure was the answers to the questions. For each of the three tasks we showed the subjects four different instances and evaluated the total correct responses against the total incorrect responses. We then looked at each question and compared the control treatment versus the experimental treatment. We used Fisher's Exact Test to determine significance because we had non-parametric data.

4.2 Controlled Experiment Results

Table 1 tabulates the results for the three questions. We will now explain each result in more detail.

[2] http://cyber-dojo.org/dashboard/show/C5AE528CB0.

Table 1. Results from controlled experiment.

	Identification		Comprehension		Comparability	
Treatment	Correct	Not correct	Correct	Not correct	Correct	Not correct
Control ($n = 18$)	37	34	24	48	23	49
Experimental ($n = 17$)	55	13	42	26	33	35

RQ1:*Identification.* When we asked the participants to identify TDD, we found that significantly more participants correctly identified TDD and non-TDD sessions using TDDViz than when using the default cyber-dojo visualization, as Table 1 shows (Fisher's Exact Test: $p<.0005$). This shows that our visualization does indeed aid in identifying TDD.

RQ2:*Comprehension.* When we asked participants why a specific code change had been made, we found that significantly more participants correctly identified why the code was changed when using TDDViz than when using the default cyber-dojo visualization (see Table 1: Comprehension, Fisher's Exact Test: $p<.0013$). They were able to identify if the given code was changed or inserted to make a test pass, make a test fail or to refactor.

RQ3:*Comparability.* When we asked our participants to compare the amount of time that went into writing tests vs. the time that went into writing code, the experimental participants were able to outperform the control group but only by a small margin. The difference was only just approaching significance (Fisher's Exact Test: $p<0.0578$). Additionally, as Table 1: Comparability shows, there were slightly more incorrect answers then correct answers for the experimental group. To answer this question, users had to mentally quantify whether the chart contained more red than green overall. In the future we plan on improving the visualization by providing a representation that provides a clear, numerical answer to this question.

4.3 Case Study

We now answer our fourth research question, which measures the accuracy of the TDD phase inference part of TDDViz, using a corpus of 2601 TDD sessions.

Corpus Origin. We use a corpus of katas that comes from cyber-dojo, a site that allows developers to practice and improve TDD by coding solutions to various katas.

Evaluation Corpus. To build our corpus we used *all* the Java/JUnit sessions as our evaluation framework currently only supports Java. Adding other languages would be straightforward, but is left as future work. This gives us a corpus of 2601 total Java/JUnit sessions.

We are using this corpus to evaluate our inferencer as all the sessions were attempted by people who had no knowledge of our work.

Corpus Preparation. We developed a Ruby on Rails application that allowed us to work with this corpus in an efficient manner. The raw data that we used to build the corpus consists of a repository and session data. The git repository contains commits of the code each time the coder pressed the "Test" button. This provides a fine-grained series of snapshots that allow us to evaluate the process used to develop the code. The session data contains meta-data files that track things such as when the session occurred, and what was the result of each compile and test run.

The Gold Standard. In order to evaluate our phase inferencer, we created a Gold Standard. The first two authors manually labeled 2489 snapshots with the TDD phase to which they belong.

We then graded our inferencer by comparing its results against the Gold Standard. In order to not bias the selection process, we randomly selected the sessions for our Gold Standard. To ensure that we were labeling consistently, we first verified that we had reached an inter-rater agreement of at least 85% between both of the authors that labeled the Gold Standard on 52 sessions (32% of the sessions).

Once we were convinced that we had reached a consensus among the raters, we divided the rest of the Gold Standard sessions up and rated them individually. We labeled a total of 2489 snapshots in our Gold Standard out of a corpus of 41766 snapshots in the corpus, which is 6% of the data. We labeled each snapshot as previously defined in Sect. 3.3.

Inference Evaluation. After we manually labeled each snapshot, we ran our inference algorithm against the sessions that compose the Gold Standard. We then compare the results of the algorithm at each snapshot and compare it against the labels that were assigned by hand. We next describe how we use this comparison to calculate precision and recall.

Accuracy. We calculate the accuracy of our inferencer by using the traditional F-measure, which considers both precision and recall. We compute precision and recall by first identifying $True$ and $False\ Positives$. If the inferencer identifies a snapshot to have the same category that it has in the Gold Standard, we consider this a $True\ Positive$. If the inferencer considers a snapshot to be in a different category than the Gold Standard, we consider this case to be a $False\ Positive$. A $False\ Negative$ is where a snapshot that should have been classified as one of the TDD phases was classified by the inferencer as white (non-TDD).

Once we calculated these for each session in the Gold Standard, we calculate precision and recall using the standard formulas. Next we calculated accuracy using the traditional harmonic mean of precision and recall.

4.4 Case Study Results

Precision. The Gold Standard contains 2489 snapshots. Of those, 2028 were correctly identified by the inferencer. This lead to a precision of 81%. The diversity of our corpus leads to a wide variety of TDD implementations, and there are quite a few edge cases. While our algorithm handles many of them, there are still a few edge cases that our algorithm cannot recognize in its current incarnation. These are cases that are hard even for human experts to agree upon.

Recall. Our Gold Standard contains 1517 snapshots that belong to one of the TDD phases (i.e., non-white phases). Of those, our inferencer correctly classified 1440, leading to a recall of 95%. Of the remaining 5 % missed cases, most of them arise because of difficulty identifying the template code the katas start with. This is an issue that can be easily solved in our future work.

RQ4:*Accuracy.* We calculate the accuracy using the F-measure. This gives us an accuracy of 87%. This shows that our inferencer is accurate and effective.

5 Related Work and Conclusions

Related Work. Multiple projects [9,10] detect the absence of TDD activities and give warnings when a developer deviates from TDD by identifying when a developer spends too much time writing code without tests. In contrast, TDDVIZ provides detailed analysis of the TDD phases, infers the presence or absence of TDD not based on time intervals between test runs, but on code and test changes. Thus, it is much more precise.

Several projects [11,12] infer TDD phases from low-level IDE edits. They all build on top of HackyStat [13], a framework for data collection and analysis. Hackystat collects "low-level and voluminous" data, which it sends to a web service for lexical parsing, event stream grouping, and development process analysis. In contrast to these approaches, by using AST analysis, TDDVIZ infers the TDD process without the entire stream of low-level actions.

TDD Dashboard[3] is a service offered by Industrial Logic, to visualize the TDD process. It is based on recording test and refactoring events in a IDE, but does not infer and visualize the phases of each cycle, thus enabling developers to answer questions on identification, comprehension, and comparability.

Conclusions. Without understanding there can be no improvement. In this paper we presented visualizations that enable developers to better understand the development process. To design these visualizations, we developed an inferencer that infers the TDD process with a novel use of code changes. We implemented the visualizations and the inferencer in a tool, TDDVIZ. We evaluated TDDVIZ using two complementary methods. We evaluated the visualization using 35 participants. We found that participants that used our visualization had significantly more correct answers when answering questions on identification, comprehension,

[3] https://ecoach.industriallogic.com/dashboard?team=il.

and comparability of code. We evaluated the TDD phase inferencer and showed that it is accurate and effective, with 81% precision and 95% recall.

Acknowledgements. We thank Mihai Codoban, Kendall Bailey and anonymous reviewers for their feedback on earlier versions of this paper. We thank Jon Jagger for making the TDD data available. We also thank Lutz Prechelt for his helpful and very thorough review. This work was partially funded through the NSF CCF-1439957 grant.

References

1. Zaidman, A., Van Rompaey, B., van Deursen, A., Demeyer, S.: Studying the co-evolution of production and test code in open source and industrial developer test processes through repository mining. Empir. Softw. Eng. **16**(3), 325–364 (2011)
2. Begel, A., Zimmermann, T.: Analyze this! 145 questions for data scientists in software engineering. In: ICSE 2014, June 2014
3. LaToza, T.D., Myers, B.A. Hard-to-answer questions about code. In: PLATEAU 2010, pp. 8:1–8:6 (2010)
4. Krzywinski, M., Birol, I., Jones, S.J.M., Marra, M.A.: Hive plots, rational approach to visualizing networks. Brief. Bioinform. **13**, 627–644 (2011). bbr069
5. Mackinlay, J.: Automating the design of graphical presentations of relational information. ACM Trans. Graph. (TOG) **5**(2), 141 (1986)
6. Munzner, T.: Visualization Analysis and Design. CRC Press, New York (2014)
7. Tufte, E.R., Graves-Morris, P.R.: The Visual Display of Quantitative Information, vol. 2. Graphics press, Los Angeles (1983)
8. Falleri, J.-R., Morandat, F., Blanc, X., Martinez, M., Monperrus, M.: Fine-grained and accurate source code differencing. In: ACM/IEEE International Conference on Automated Software Engineering, ASE 2014, Vasteras, Sweden, 15–19 September, pp. 313–324 (2014)
9. Mishali, O., Dubinsky, Y., Katz, S.: The TDD-guide training and guidance tool for test-driven development. In: Abrahamsson, P., Baskerville, R., Conboy, K., Fitzgerald, B., Morgan, L., Wang, X. (eds.) Agile Processes in Software Engineering and Extreme Programming. LNBIP, vol. 9, pp. 63–72. Springer, Heidelberg (2008)
10. Wege, C.: Automated support for process assessment in Test-Driven Development. dissertation, Universitat Tubingen (2004)
11. Wang, Y., Erdogmus, H.: The role of process measurement in test-driven development. In: XP/Agile Universe 2004 (2004)

12. Kou, H., Johnson, P.M., Erdogmus, H.: Operational definition, automated inference of test-driven development with zorro. Autom. Softw. Eng. **17**(1), 57–85 (2009)
13. Johnson, P.M.: Project hackystat: Accelerating adoption of empirically guided software development through non-disruptive, developer-centric, in-process data collection and analysis. Department of Information and Computer Sciences, University of Hawaii, vol. 22 (2001)

Minimum Viable User EXperience: A Framework for Supporting Product Design in Startups

Laura Hokkanen(✉), Kati Kuusinen, and Kaisa Väänänen

Department of Pervasive Computing, Tampere University of Technology, Korkeakoulunkatu 1, 33720 Tampere, Finland
{Laura.Hokkanen,Kati.Kuusinen,Kaisa.Vaananen}@tut.fi

Abstract. Startups operate with small resources in time pressure. Thus, building minimal product versions to test and validate ideas has emerged as a way to avoid wasteful creation of complicated products which may be proven unsuccessful in the markets. Often, design of these early product versions needs to be done fast and with little advance information from end-users. In this paper we introduce the Minimum Viable User eXperience (MVUX) that aims at providing users a good enough user experience already in the early, minimal versions of the product. MVUX enables communication of the envisioned product value, gathering of meaningful feedback, and it can promote positive word of mouth. To understand what MVUX consists of, we conducted an interview study with 17 entrepreneurs from 12 small startups. The main elements of MVUX recognized are Attractiveness, Approachability, Professionalism, and Selling the Idea. We present the structured framework and elements' contributing qualities.

1 Introduction

Global markets are being infiltrated by small startups with their innovative new products and business models. Software startups are characterized with scarce resources, little to none operating history, and time pressure [1]. One competitive advantage with startups compared to large organizations is their ability to move fast and adapt to changing circumstances [2]. However, as founding teams of startups often consist of only a few individuals, the team's skills are naturally limited. For the same reason, the primary business objective of startups is to survive [3]. To survive, startups need to make the most out of their limited resources. Customer development [4] and Lean startup method [5], that have been widely adopted and taught by accelerators and entrepreneurship programs [6], emphasize gathering fast feedback from customers, and testing product ideas with minimal product versions or Minimum Viable Product (MVP) as referred by Ries [5]. While Lean Startup has no scientific evidence for effectiveness in business creation, the method is influencing how entrepreneurs approach product development [6, 7].

While validating business potential with minimal product versions and real customers to minimize unnecessary risk, gathering useful feedback with early product

H. Sharp and T. Hall (Eds.): XP 2016, LNBIP 251, pp. 66–78, 2016.
DOI: 10.1007/978-3-319-33515-5_6

versions can be challenging. One challenge is that insufficient or disturbing user experience (UX) might reduce the user feedback and make the users concentrate mainly on the appearance of the user interface [8]. At the worst, poor UX can lead the user only to criticize the UX even if the product idea itself was good. [8] Benefits of delivering good UX from the earliest product version can be positive word of mouth advertisement [9], and users using the product for longer.

The goal of this paper is to identify and structure the UX elements that are essential when building early product versions in small software startups. To understand the elements of desirable UX of early product versions, we introduce the concept and framework of Minimum Viable User eXperience that aims at providing UX that enables users to understand and gain value already from the early product versions. Correspondingly, startup is then able to collect more meaningful feedback from potential customers over a longer period of time since users do not abandon the product.

In this paper, we report results of a two-phase interview study we conducted in Finland. In the first phase we interviewed 13 entrepreneurs from eight startups. All the startups were building, or had recently built, first versions of their products. Based on the analysis of these interviews, we created the initial MVUX framework. The framework is based on the assumption that MVUX is realized in the software being under development when (1) user can perform the core use cases to gain value, (2) basic hygiene factors for usability and appearance are in place, and (3) the startup is able to get enough of feedback and data to validate and further develop the product idea. To evaluate the MVUX framework, we then interviewed four entrepreneurs of four more startups, all having expertise in UX. Through the interviews, we answer the following research questions: (1) what are the goals and key elements of MVUX from the startups' perspective and (2) how can MVUX design framework help startups at the early phases of their product and business development.

The rest of this paper is structured as follows. Section 2 presents related work on characteristics of software startups and their ways of working, and UX practices. Section 3 presents context and methods of our study. In Sect. 4 we present the results of our study including the UX elements considered important by startups, as well as the results of the evaluation of the MVUX framework. Section 5 discusses the results and Sect. 6 presents the conclusions for the paper.

2 Related Work

2.1 Characteristics of Software Startups

Engineering and business concerns in software startups are more extensive than in established companies [2]. Those concerns include having scarce resources, being young and immature, operating with novel technologies in dynamic markets. Software startups are also influenced by divergent stakeholders such as investors, customers, partners, and competitors. [2] Also, customer-focused approach seems to be more crucial for small companies [2]: When the customer is happy with the software, it literally means more work and increased business opportunities for the small company as the happy customer wants more and is willing to recommend the software to others [10]. Because of unestablished customer base, such positive word of mouth and keeping the existing customers satisfied is essential for startups.

The professionalism of the entrepreneurs themselves often acts as a primary information source for startups due to unestablished stakeholder networks and customer base [3]. Moreover, people factors tend to be even more crucial for startups than for larger companies in the success or failure of the software [2]. Thus, the entrepreneur team is in a key role in keeping the startup focused and moving ahead [2]. For startups, short time to market is one of the most critical process goals [2]. Since a fundamental goal of a process is to describe the way an organization develops its software in a predictable and repeatable fashion, benefits of an established process do not meet essential needs of software startups [2, 3]. Therefore, startups require more informal and lightweight approaches.

New entrepreneurial practices Customer development [4] and Lean startup method [5] have been gaining attention in recent years. These practices emphasize that startups should concentrate on producing customer value and avoid wasteful activities, i.e. non-value adding activities. Although academic research on how well Customer development and the Lean startup method work is scarce, those methods have been widely adopted by incubators, accelerators and university entrepreneurship courses [6]. The Lean startup [5] suggests that by validating hypotheses of customer's problems startups find a problem/solution fit that indicates there is business potential in solving a specific problem with a particular solution. Once the problem/solution fit is established, the startup should validate what product suites to deliver the solution. For finding validation, startups should build minimum viable products (MVP) that are then tested with potential customers. An MVP should be built with as little resources as possible yet it needs to enable testing the current hypothesis. Furthermore, Ries [5] emphasizes that the key performance indicators need to be measured when "getting out of the building" with the MVPs. From these experiments, startup should gain validated learning [5]. This Build-Measure-Learn (BML) cycle should be continued until a product/market fit is found and startups should also be prepared to discard the MVPs if they do not measure up to validating sustainable business opportunity [5].

2.2 User Experience Work

UX is defined as "*a person's perceptions and responses that result from the use or anticipated use of a product, system or service*" [11]. Also, UX is often divided into practical-oriented and hedonic dimensions [12]. The first dimension includes aspects related to ease of use, productivity, and usability while the latter concentrates on users' emotions such as enjoyment and motivation. Regarding UX development in industry, companies in general tend to focus more on the practical qualities of UX while paying less attention to the hedonic ones [13].

UX design has roots in human-centered design (HCD) [11] that starts with thorough user research and design activities which are followed by design iterations. All in all, developing UX involves gaining understanding of the user and the context of use, designing and developing for good UX, and evaluating the resulting outcome [11].

While understanding users is considered important for startups [7], startups generally do not afford to follow rigorous methods for UX development. Research on UX development in startups is scarce. May [14] describes a case from applying lean methodology in a startup and recommends planning the UX activities in from early on. Klein [15] presents lightweight methods for UX work in lean startups. Finally, Hokkanen et al. [8] report that lack of UX expertise and time constrains hinder the startup from collecting useful feedback from users.

3 Methods, Research Context, and Participants

3.1 Course of the Study

To address our research goal of understanding which UX factors are essential when building early product versions in startups, semi-structured interviews were chosen as the data gathering method. The study was conducted in two phases. In the first phase we interviewed 13 entrepreneurs from 8 small startups in order to establish the MVUX framework. In the second phase, four entrepreneurs with UX expertise were interviewed to evaluate the created MVUX framework. Altogether, 12 interview sessions with 17 interviewees were conducted. All the interviews were conducted by one researcher and they lasted between 50–90 min. Interviews were audio recorded and transcribed for analysis. Participants were searched by going through Finnish startup incubator and accelerator programs. Some startups were recruited through directly contacting them based on their web page while others were recruited by advertising in the premises of one incubator program.

In the first phase, eight semi-structured interviews were conducted to understand the early design decisions and UX goals in startups. Initial results from these interviews, describing how startups start UX design, and what practices are beneficial at that stage, are reported in [7]. During the interviews, we introduced the general concept of MVUX to each interviewee. Participants were then asked to write down on a paper their goals and central elements for UX of their early product version intended to be deployed to users. Differences in UX goals between the earliest and complete product version were also shortly discussed. In all the interviews, focus was on UX related motivations and practices. However, activities such as product and business development were covered superficially to understand their impact on UX design.

In the second phase, four semi-structured interviews were conducted to evaluate the MVUX framework established based on the results of the first phase. The concept of MVUX was first discussed with the interviewee after which we presented them the initial MVUX framework. Then we asked questions about the interviewee's perception on the ability of the MVUX framework to cover the necessary UX elements without including unnecessary elements. In addition, we studied the usefulness of the framework by discussing with the interviewees how startups could utilize the MVUX framework while creating early product versions.

In both phases, analysis was done from the written transcripts utilizing iterative thematic coding. Main themes were established based on the interview questions while sub-themes emerged from the data. Terms the interviewees used to describe the goals and central elements of UX of the early product version were collected to construct the MVUX framework. Those terms were used as low-level elements on which the main elements of the framework were created using a bottom-up approach as follows. In total, 43 unique low-level elements were abstracted from the interview data. These low-level elements were divided into groups based on similarity to form mid-level elements of MVUX. Finally, mid-level elements were grouped based on similarity to determine the main elements of MVUX. In the grouping of elements both the term as well as the context in which the element was discussed was taken into consideration.

3.2 Participants

First Phase. Startups participating the first phase consisted of one to six person teams each creating one single software product (Table 1). In this paper, we number the startups from 'ST11' to 'ST18', to differentiate them from the startups that participated our previous study [8].

Table 1. Summary of startups and interviewees participating the first phase. Legend: CEO = Chief Executive Officer, UXD = User Experience Designer, B2B = Business to Business, B2C = Business to Consumer, SaaS = Software as a Service.

Startup	Interviewees	Company established	Size of startup	Product	Market
ST11	H01 (CEO)	2013	1	Online marketplace	B2B, B2C
ST12	H02 (CEO), H03	2014	6	Online marketplace	B2C
ST13	H04 (UXD)	2014	4	Online community and marketplace	B2B, B2C
ST14	H05, H06 (CEO)	2014	2	SaaS for pet owners	B2C
ST15	H07 (CEO), H08	2011	2	Automation software	B2B
ST16	H09 (CEO)	2014	5	Mobile sports application	B2B, B2C
ST17	H10, H11, H12	–	3	Mobile personal finances application	B2C
ST18	H13 (UXD)	2015	3	Mobile social application	B2C

Second Phase. In the second phase we interviewed four entrepreneurs of four other small startups to evaluate the MVUX framework created in the first phase (Table 2). H15 and H16 worked full time in startups, while H14 and H17 were employed also outside their startups. Interviewees H14, H15 and H16 worked as UX designers. H16 was the CEO of ST21, and worked also on product development. All the interviewees had been developing software products or services in startups.

Table 2. Participants of the second phase interviews.

Startup	Interviewee	Experience in entrepreneurship (Years)	Education
ST19	H14	3	Bachelor of Interactive Technology
ST20	H15	3	Bachelor of Arts and Media
ST21	H16	3	PhD, Interactive Technology
ST22	H17	2	Master of Science student, majoring in UX

4 Findings

4.1 Elements of MVUX

Those startups participating in the first phase were creating or had recently created limited versions of their product. UX goals of these product versions varied among startups depending on what they sought to achieve with the product version. Table 3 presents the hierarchical categorization of low-level elements mentioned by interviewees and then grouped to form mid-level elements, and how mid-level elemenst were further grouped to form the main elements of MVUX.

The most common goal was that the product UX should be intuitive to use (with six low-level elements). Furthermore, it was considered necessary to create a UI that was simple (5) and easy to use (5) to enable smooth start for the user. For the B2B case of ST15, in which the acceptance of end-users was important for convincing the pilot customer, H07 commented: *"The product had to be so easy to use that everyone would agree to start using it. That was the first requirement."* [H07] There was more diversity in how startups wanted the user to experience the product: humane (4), visual (5) or having a feel of novelty (3). Depending on the origin of the product idea, the early version of the product could also be built to fulfill the entrepreneur's needs. H06 from ST14 explained that their first version was developed to serve their own interests: *"We thought technical looking graphs would be cool and bring a sense of high-tech. [...] Then we realized normal people don't want to see that. You should have like soft high-tech. The high-tech Apple has, and not like laser beams."* [H06]

Hooking, or making the user to stay and want to come back was mentioned three times as well. These were related to needs to gain data that proved interest in the product, or showed how users behaved with the UI. Goals related to the product being functioning or technically working were mentioned three times. Depending on the product idea, communicating that the solution and application was credible (4) or efficient (3) was considered important by some startups (ST11, ST14, ST17) while for others it did not matter. For example, in the case of mobile personal finances application (ST17), it was crucial the product would be perceived as something the user can trust from early on.

Table 3. Elements of MVUX

Main element	Mid-level element	Low-level element
Attractive	Visual (5)	Visual (ST14)
		Visual experience (ST16)
		Good visual appearance (ST11)
		Modern visual appearance (ST13)
		Not technical looking (ST14)
	Humane (5)	Likable enough (ST12)
		Storytelling (ST13)
		Personal (ST17)
		Easy to approach (ST14)
		Cozy and warm (ST14)
	Novel (3)	Fresh (ST12)
		Differentiation from regular services (ST13)
		Strong colours to differentiate (ST11)
	Hooking (3)	Gamification (ST18)
		Hooking (ST13, ST18)
Approachable	Intuitive (6)	Familiar UI elements (ST13)
		Familiarity (ST14)
		Intuitive (ST17)
		No learning curve (ST18)
		Understandable (ST18)
		Explicit (ST16)
	Easy (5)	Easy to browse products (ST13)
		Easy to use (ST12, ST15, ST16, ST18)
	Simple (5)	Simple (ST12, ST14, ST15)
		Simple design (ST11)
		Minimal design (ST11)
Professional	Credible (4)	Premium (ST17)
		Reliable (ST11)
		Secure (ST17)
		Credible (ST11)
	Functioning (3)	Functioning (ST15)
		Smooth (ST17)
		Device independence (ST14)
	Efficient (3)	Compact (ST14)
		Fast (ST17)
		See by glancing (ST14)
Selling the Idea	Introducing the idea (5)	First impression (ST17)
		Introducing the idea (ST11)
		Example pictures (ST11)

(*Continued*)

Table 3. (*Continued*)

Main element	Mid-level element	Low-level element
		Lobbing (ST15)
		Solution (ST12)
	Building brand & fan base (4)	Traction (ST12)
		Exciting (ST12)
		Social (ST17)
		Word of mouth (ST12)

Being able to introduce the product idea and show the value in it was one of the mid-level elements abstracted from the low-level elements. Goals considering brand creation and getting fans for the product included four low-level elements. In case of ST11, starting to create positive word of mouth influenced how the UX was designed. H02 told that he would like users to see the product as exciting so that they would tell their friends about it.

4.2 MVUX Framework

The elements four main elements of MVUX are Attractiveness, Approachability, Professionalism and Selling the Idea. Classification of mid-level elements into these categories is demonstrated in Fig. 1. At the bottom of the Fig. 1 is Selling the Idea which is the main aim of MVUX since it offers the startup a possibility to get feedback from users who actually understand the product idea. The three other main elements

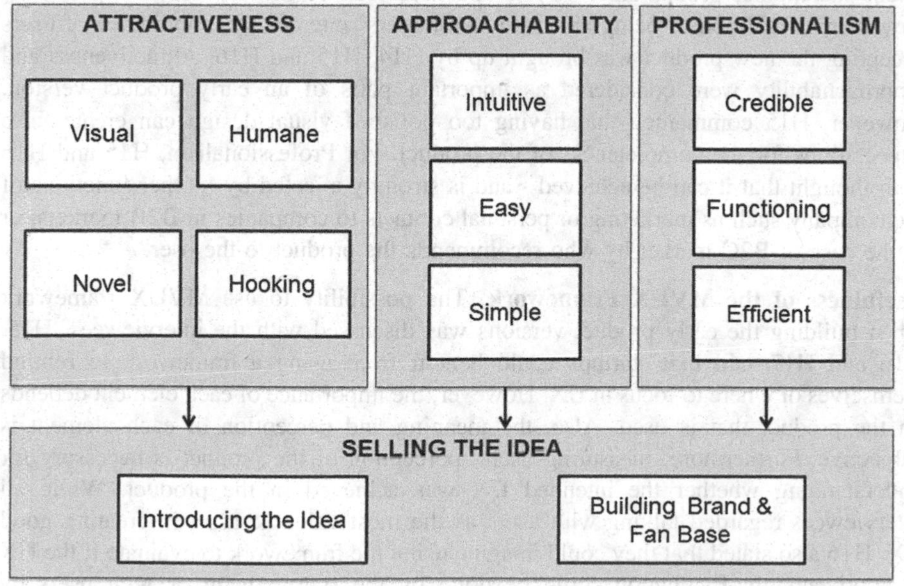

Fig. 1. MVUX framework for supporting early product development in startups.

(Attractiveness, Approachability, and Professionalism) create the foundation for the user to be interested in the product and to start using it. These three elements can also be seen affecting the user in different phases of getting to know the product. The first impression of the product is influenced by making the early product version attractive. With approachable elements, the usage is made easy and comfortable. Giving a professional image of the product, and the startup, is the result of a well-functioning, efficient product.

4.3 Validation of the MVUX Framework

Impressions on the MVUX Framework. Interviewees considered that the elements of the framework cover well the needs for UX in an early product version. H16 thought that having a framework to guide developing UX for new products in startups would be very useful. The importance of different elements was discussed with the interviewees. According to H14, the element Selling the Idea communicated that the attributes enabling to sell the product need to be taken into consideration also in UX design. In contrast, H15 felt that selling the product can be done by marketing it and thus it does not require having good UX or even the product itself in the beginning– even though building the planned product might then be too difficult for the startup team (H15). Optimization of internet marketing can help in introducing the idea and creating a (fan) community (H15).

Being able to communicate the value proposition of the company was mentioned by H14 as a critical part of the early phases of their startup, and this was mainly done with text on web pages. H16 mentioned that various means are required to convince different stakeholder groups since buyers and users can be in very different positions. However, in addition to being able to evoke buyers' interest, the importance of users accepting the new product was brought up by H14, H15 and H16. Attractiveness and Approachability were considered as important parts of an early product version. However, H15 commented that having too polished visual design can create false expectations for the completeness of the product. For Professionalism, H15 and H16 both thought that it can be achieved - and is strongly affected by – other functions of the company such as marketing or personal contacts to companies in B2B markets, or in the case of B2C market by who recommends the product to the user.

Usefulness of the MVUX Framework. The possibility to use MVUX framework when building the early product versions was discussed with the interviewees. H15, H16 and H17 said that startups could benefit from using a framework to remind themselves of where to focus in UX. However, the importance of each element depends on the product that is used. Also, the meaning and perception of each element is subjective. Furthermore, measuring users' perception of the product is necessary for understanding whether the intended UX was achieved in the product. While all interviewees regarded talking with users as the most valuable asset in creating good UX, H16 also stated that they could imagine using the framework to evaluate if the UX is good enough. Evaluation could be done by the startup team or with users by lightweight methods. To support the use of framework, H14, H16 and H17 thought that practical advice and examples would be needed to design graphical elements that support the wanted UX. However, graphical style was seen as something that can be easily created with existing tools for UI development as well as by utilizing image banks (H14, H15). H16 wished that the MVUX framework should indicate the iterative nature of creating products in startups. Also H14 and H15 mentioned iterative process – starting form early releases - to be essential for successful product development in startups.

5 Research Validity

Since our study was qualitative, we assess our research quality in terms of credibility, transferability, dependability, and conclusions confirmability [16].

Credibility. We identified no major threats to credibility. Since the participants themselves wrote down the elements they considered essential for the UX of early versions, the study is less prone to interpretation error. However, we did not discuss the MVUX framework with participants of the first phase to evaluate interpretation issues.

Regarding the **transferability** of the results to other contexts, our study was conducted with 12 small Finnish software startups. We consider that our descriptive findings are transferable to similar startups. However, as startups – to a certain degree – reflect the entrepreneurs themselves; personal characteristics may reduce the transferability of the results. In addition, when transferring the MVUX framework to other contexts, product type and the user must be considered. Transferability of the MVUX framework should be further analyzed with other startups.

Threats to **dependability** include that the studied startups did not form a random sample, instead convenience sampling was utilized. However, we utilized open sampling method in which new participants are recruited after interviewing the previous one to increase variation in the sample. Despite concentrating on Finnish startups, our study increases richness of related research that has been conducted, for instance, in Ireland [3] and in Ecuador [10].

Finally, threats to **confirmability** include that a single researcher planned, conducted and analyzed the study. The researcher, however, reflected with other researchers in every phase of the study. Finally, the MVUX framework was audited in a group of three researchers.

6 Discussion

Our contribution is in proposing a framework of UX elements that are essential to the early product versions startups create. Considering that the related research on startups in general and especially on their UX work is very limited, our study offers new insight both for the academia and for startups. In startups, the elements of MVUX could be used to guide the UX design of early product versions. Especially in the early phases, startups benefit from lightweight methods – such as promoted by [14] – and could also use MVUX framework to support the design decisions. However, further research should be done to understand and validate how MVUX can be used to support startups' UX strategy. Our initial validation shows that using MVUX framework with light-weight tools for implementing graphics design, and for measuring the perceived experience, would be beneficial in creating early product versions.

The goals and key qualities for UX of the early product versions had recurring themes from which we abstracted the elements of MVUX. Startups had different goals for what they wanted to achieve with their early product versions [7], and, accordingly, goals for UX varied. As reported in [7], startups also had different amounts of acquired understanding of their target users as well as previous validation of the product idea. This provided a wide scale of goals and qualities that reflected the different situations the startups were in. The four main elements of MVUX that we found are Attractiveness, Approachability, Professionalism, and Selling the Idea.

Based on our evaluation of MVUX framework with startup representatives that had expertise in UX, the MVUX framework covers the most important elements of UX in the early stages of startup's product development. However, the level of importance of different elements varies in products. Additionally, comparing the elements to our assumptions in the beginning of the study we can see how they are connected. We assumed that to communicate the product idea and UX well enough, the user should be able to perform the core use cases that answer to user's needs. Furthermore, we estimated the UX in these use cases should be at a satisfying level that does not disturb the user. These are in line with the elements Approachability and Professionalism that aim to provide trouble-free UX that shows the user that the product is trustworthy. Our third assumption for MVUX was that it needs to enable startup to gain feedback and data for validation and further development. This would be achieved through elements of Selling the Idea and Attractiveness. The element Attractiveness has a role in getting users interested in the product as well as hooking them to keep using the product. Selling the Idea part needs to be in place to raise interest in users, to communicate the product idea clearly, and to show how the product creates value to user so they will keep using the product. Implementation of elements of Attractiveness and Selling the Idea enables continuous data collection from longer usage as well as users being able to give feedback on the product idea while having no confusion on what the product is about. However, our initial assumptions did not emphasize the attractiveness and good visual design of the product, while the results of this study show that they are considered important in startups.

These results serve to create understanding of how UX should be taken into consideration when startups create their early product versions that are used by real user. Our study consisted of 12 Finnish-based companies so companies' motivations and goals are influenced by the Finnish business and startup culture. Furthermore, the end-users' preferred design elements may be influenced by the culture. Further research is needed to validate how well the discovered elements suit to the needs of startups and end-users in general.

7 Conclusions

In this paper we introduced the results of our two-phase interview study of 17 entrepreneurs from 12 startups. We presented the framework of Minimum Viable User eXperience (MVUX) that represents ways in which UX can be focused on already in early product versions. To gain value from building early product versions, MVUX enables the startup to collect meaningful feedback and data for validating and further developing the product idea. We abstracted the elements of MVUX through a bottom-up analysis of startups' goals and key elements for UX of early product versions. From these elements, a framework for supporting UX design in early product development was established. In the second phase of the study, the constructed framework was evaluated with experts of both entrepreneurship and UX. As a conclusion, we present the MVUX framework where the main elements of MVUX were defined as Attractiveness, Approachability, Professionalism and Selling the Idea.

References

1. Paternoster, N., Giardino, C., Unterkalmsteiner, M., et al.: Software development in startup companies: a systematic mapping study. Inf. Softw. Technol. **56**(10), 1200–1218 (2014)
2. Sutton, S.M.: The role of process in a software start-up. IEEE Softw. **17**(4), 33–39 (2000)
3. Coleman, G., O'Connor, R.: An investigation into software development process formation in software start-ups. J. Enterp. Inf. **21**(6), 633–648 (2008)
4. Blank, S.: Why the lean start-up changes everything. Harv. Bus. Rev. **91**, 63–72 (2013)
5. Ries, E.: The Lean Startup: How Today's Entrepreneurs Use Continuous Innovation to Create Radically Successful Businesses. Random House LLC, New York (2011)
6. York, J.L., Danes, J.E.: Customer development, innovation, and decision-making biases in the lean startup. J. Small Bus. Strategy **24**(2), 21–39 (2014)
7. Hokkanen, L., Kuusinen, K., Väänänen, K.: Early product design in startups: towards a UX strategy. In: Abrahamsson, P., et al. (eds.) PROFES 2015. LNCS, vol. 9459, pp. 217–224. Springer, Heidelberg (2015). doi:10.1007/978-3-319-26844-6_16
8. Hokkanen, L., Väänänen-Vainio-Mattila, K.: UX work in startups: current practices and future needs. In: Lassenius, C., Dingsøyr, T., Paasivaara, M. (eds.) XP 2015. LNBIP, vol. 212, pp. 81–92. Springer, Heidelberg (2015)

9. Füller, J., Schroll, R., von Hippel, E.: User generated brands and their contribution to the diffusion of user innovations. Res. Policy **42**, 1197–1209 (2013)
10. Sánchez-Gordón, M.-L., O'Connor, R.V.: Understanding the gap between software process practices and actual practice in very small companies. Softw. Qual. J. 1–22 (2015). Online First Articles (ISSN: 0963-9314 (Print) 1573-1367 (Online))
11. ISO: 9241-210:2010. Ergonomics of Human System Interaction-Part 210: Human-Centred Design for Interactive Systems. International Standardization Organization (ISO). Switzerland (2009)
12. Hassenzahl, M.: The interplay of beauty, goodness and usability in interactive products. Proc. HCI **19**(4), 319–349 (2004). Lawrence Erlbaum Associates
13. Väänänen-Vainio-Mattila, K., Roto, V., Hassenzahl, M.: Towards practical user experience evaluation methods. EL-C. In: Meaningful Measures: Valid Useful User Experience Measurement (VUUM), pp. 19–22 (2008)
14. May, B.: Applying lean startup: an experience report: lessons learned in creating & launching a complex consumer app. In: Agile Conference (AGILE), pp. 141–147. IEEE (2012)
15. Klein, L.: UX for Lean Startups: Faster Smarter User Experience Research and Design. O'Reilly Media Inc, Newton (2013)
16. Guba, E.G.: Criteria for assessing the trustworthiness of naturalistic inquiries. ECTJ **29**(2), 75–91 (1981)

Team Portfolio Scrum: An Action Research on Multitasking in Multi-project Scrum Teams

Christoph J. Stettina[1,2(✉)] and Mark N.W. Smit[2]

[1] Centre for Innovation, Leiden University, Schouwburgstraat 2, 2511 VA The Hague, The Netherlands
c.j.stettina@fgga.leidenuniv.nl

[2] Leiden Institute of Advanced Computer Science, Leiden University, Niels Bohrweg 1, 2333 CA Leiden, The Netherlands

Abstract. Multi-project agile software development is a relatively new area of research. While original Scrum caters to co-located teams working on a single project, multi-project Scrum teams are a day-to-day reality, especially in small organizations. Multitasking across projects is frequently associated with loss of effectiveness, but this assumption is not sufficiently supported by empirical evidence. In order to better understand the phenomenon, we review existing literature across scientific domains and execute an action research project. Our findings show that the Team Portfolio Scrum (TPS) practice designed to support multitasking across projects is perceived to be useful, but with an associated increase in overhead.

Keywords: Agile software development · Scrum · IT project governance · Project portfolio management · Task-switching · Multitasking

1 Introduction

Should agile teams work on multiple projects simultaneously? While Scrum provides an example of how to execute individual software projects outside of plan-driven bureaucracies, the search for new organizational forms continues [1].

Scrum has been widely associated to cater well for a sweet-spot of co-located project teams working on a single project, with a pre-defined project scope and budget [2,3]. In particular, it stresses the need for teams to work on a single product per sprint [4]. Nevertheless, working on multiple projects during each sprint is a common reality [5]. For example, small companies with a small contract value and a large customer base are likely to accept multiple projects at the same time. Also, projects can be simply too small to fully occupy a team for the duration of a sprint. However, despite common sense across practitioners and anecdotal evidence implying a decrease in efficiency, there is little empirical evidence on teams working on multiple projects in parallel and the impact of multi-tasking.

H. Sharp and T. Hall (Eds.): XP 2016, LNBIP 251, pp. 79–91, 2016.
DOI: 10.1007/978-3-319-33515-5_7

In this article we (1) review empirical evidence on multitasking and task switching across different scientific domains, (2) propose the practice of Team Portfolio Scrum (TPS) and the role of the Team Portfolio Owner to help lowering costs of task switching, and (3) execute an action research project to understand the challenges of its introduction in practice.

2 Background and Related Work

While our understanding of Scrum in individual projects is quite elaborate, there is comparably little research on agile methods in multi-project and multi-team organizations [1,6]. In particular, the majority of literature on agile software development assumes an environment where a software developer or team works on only one project at a time. While most reports advise this [7], there is little empirical evidence on agile teams working on multiple projects. To illustrate our case, Table 1 shows an overview of the agile methods discriminated by either a single team or multiple teams that are working on either a single project or multiple projects. In this paper we address the case of *Team Portfolio Scrum (TPS)*, the case where a single team works on multiple projects simultaneously.

In order to better understand the challenges of multitasking across different projects we will now review existing evidence across the fields of (1) software development, (2) psychology, and (3) management science.

Table 1. Overview of agile methods across different organizational contexts

	A single project/product	Multiple projects/products
Single team working on	*Scrum*	*Team Portfolio Scrum*
Multiple teams working on	*Program Management & Scrum*	*Portfolio Management & Scrum*

2.1 Software Development: Interruptions and Multiple Projects

Existing software development literature generally considers task switching to be a wasteful practice that should be prevented whenever possible [8–10].

Working on multiple software projects: A common argument against multi-project development is that projects produce a revenue stream for the company at the time of their completion. Finishing them sequentially maximises revenue, because most often the revenue diminishes over time [11]. Another argument is that switching between tasks (e.g., across projects) is considered as waste [9]. Concrete numbers on the waste are hard to find; practitioners claim a small production increase from going from one to two projects (70 % to 80 % effectiveness) and a steady decline in effective hours when adding more projects: 60 % with three, 45 % with four and 35 % with five simultaneous projects [8]. A study amongst 64 high tech firms suggests two simultaneous projects is optimal [12].

Task and resource allocation practices: A challenge frequently mentioned by practitioners is that a team working on multiple projects is burdened with making decisions on which project to prioritise. Lehto and Rautiainen [13] describe governance challenges identified in a middle-sized software company. The role of product owner was described as too much for 5 co-located teams and was divided into three roles with split responsibilities: Solution managers (commercial), product owner (technical), resource owner (resource). Nocks [14] describes the practice to create very small sprints that match the amount of work per project, but this is countered by the large overhead of meetings per Scrum sprint. Other sources [15] discuss the need to let the different project managers negotiate the time allocation, and the need for one person to manage the final priorities of the projects the team works on and call this a Product Owner. If a team works on multiple projects, the team should work from one backlog during the sprint, containing work items from multiple projects [16–19].

Interruptions in software development: Van Solingen et al. [20] found that every time a software developer is interrupted by others (e.g., individuals from other or own project team), it costs on average fifteen minutes to get back to focus on the task he/she was performing. Parnin and DeLine [21] found that besides the initial delay, the quality of code produced following an interruption is lower, which corresponds to the residual impact found by psychology studies.

2.2 Psychology: Interruptions and Task Switching

Experimental results on switching between simple tasks: Research has found that task switching is not simply a cost in time going from one task set to the other [22]. Instead, the impact of a task switch consists of three components [23]: (1) the passive removal of the previous task context, (2) preparation for the new task, and (3) a residual impact. The removal of a task's context and preparation for a new task constitute the primary costs measured between the execution of different tasks. The residual impact is measured as an increased response time and sometimes increased error rate.

Experimental results show consistently that switching is more difficult if a complex task is involved. Results are ambiguous for the comparison of switching from a simple to a complex task and vice versa. Some experiments show that switching from a simple task to a complex one has increased primary costs [24]. Others show that switch costs are mostly determined by the task that is switched from [22]. This suggests that the residual impact is mostly determined by the previous task and that the results for the primary costs are ambiguous. Further, it matters what kind of stimuli and responses both tasks consist of. In the case where there is no overlap at all in stimuli and responses, task switching costs have found to be zero [25]. The more the stimuli and responses overlap, the greater the impact of the task switch. Furthermore, it has been found that when performing two task switches shortly after each other, switching back to the first task has higher switch costs than switching to a third, unrelated task [26].

Complex tasks in knowledge work: Compared to the daily tasks of knowledge workers, the tasks in the controlled experiments performed by psychology researchers are of a very simple nature, even the more complex ones. This is of course to make them controllable and repeatable. With these simple tasks, switch costs are measured in order of milliseconds. The kind of real life switches that knowledge workers perform are several orders of magnitude more complex, how does the psychology research map to this?

Some researchers suggest the results for contrived tasks can be generalized to more complex tasks [26]. We found that in all studies using a combination of simple and complexer tasks, the latter had higher associated switch costs; this was found already as early as 1927 [27]. One can assume that the switch cost increases based on some function over the complexity of the task, however we could not find such a function. Some practitioner sources claim effects in the order of minutes which is an indication of such a function and the relation between task complexity and switch cost.

Task-switching between similar tasks is known to increase stress [28]. Possible causes might be increasing the number of deadlines because of working on more tasks and decreasing the time available to meet the deadlines because of decreased productivity. On the other hand, [29] found that people very commonly self-interrupt, which might be a form of self-protection, decreasing fatigue and increasing performance [30]. In general, there exist various opinions on the effects of stress on performance [31].

Interruptions, work contexts and office spaces: Interruptions are omnipresent in the work of knowledge workers. Mark et al. [32] report that a knowledge worker spends on average only 12 min uninterrupted in a work context. Another study found knowledge workers spend very little time in one context and are interrupted before completion 57 % of the time after which they tasks are resumed on average after 25 min [33]. Interruptions are often harmful, to a large degree because it takes time to get back into a task or project [34]. Tasks, when interrupted, take longer and have increased error rates [35]. However, interruptions do not necessarily imply a context switch. Interruptions that lead to a switch between working spheres (e.g., two unrelated projects) are in general far more disruptive than interruptions from within the same sphere [32]. Further, Mark et al. [32] show that while co-located individuals (e.g., in open offices) face more interruptions in general, distributed individuals feel more free to engage in interruptions on topics that are actually unrelated to their work [32].

3 Research Objectives

While existing literature recommends minimizing the amount of concurrent projects, this might not be feasible for small companies depending on a large number of clients. Especially small companies are likely to pursue many projects simultaneously to keep their customer base satisfied.

Based on existing empirical evidence we may conclude that: (1) working on multiple external projects increases interruptions and work pressure as team members have to deal with requests from multiple Product Owners, (2) such interruptions by Product Owners are expected to be far more disruptive compared to the more frequent interruptions by team members working in the same project context, (3) the context switching penalty of task switching decreases performance and lowers code quality, and (4) penalty largely depends on similarity and complexity of tasks.

Considering these facts we can assume that distraction, uncertainty and context switching are likely to increase especially if priorities across different projects are not clear. Literature suggests that teams working on multiple projects should work from one backlog during the sprint [16–19]. However, such task prioritization practices have been reported to be difficult to establish [13–15].

As such we pose the following research question: *What barriers can be met and what benefits can arise from introducing a task prioritization practice to support a team working on multiple projects in parallel?*

4 Research Method and Conduct

In order to appropriately understand the dynamics of small organizations pursuing multiple projects in context, a complex social phenomenon, we decided to conduct an exploratory action research in the context of a real organization. Action research (AR) is designed to create knowledge by organizational change through a collaboration between researchers and practitioners [36]. It does so by diagnosing the current state, bringing about guided changes and reflecting on the results to create theory.

To ensure a credible research approach we applied the five principles of Canonical Action Research [37], as follows: *1. Researcher-client agreement:* The research has been executed as part of a 2 year collaboration with the university. This ensured the collaboration of the company and provided the possibility to bring about change as part of daily routines as well as very frequent observations. *2. Cyclical process model:* We adopted the five-stage process model of Diagnosing, Action Planning, Action Taking, Evaluating and Specifying Learning. One full cycle was completed. *3. Theory principle:* The theoretical ambition is to understand task prioritization and coordination practices in agile teams. *4. Change through action:* We supported the case company throughout the entire project. The second author was a full-time employee at the company facilitating workshops and discussions. *5. Learning through reflection:* Throughout the project meetings and workshops have been initiated to stimulate discussions among developers and management by the second author.

Case selection: The study was performed at a Dutch software company building bespoke custom software for customers. The company consisted of about 20 employees, half of which were software developers. The company had two teams working for two or more Product Owners nearly all the time. A known challenge at the beginning of the research. The company had a flat structure, informal work environment and an open office space. Next to building custom websites for customers there are two in-house products. The team works on one of those products but a majority of the time is spent customizing the product implementation per customer. Greenfield development is rare. Maintenance is often urgent, with deadlines of one or two days being common. Work load was always high because of too few developers. The company has been endorsing Scrum from the beginning, however, struggled with its' implementation due to many parallel projects and customer requests.

Data collection and data sources: In order to build up an adequate understanding of the organization in context and throughout the action research project we used the following data sources:
Observations: While embedded within the company, the second author was able to observe the relevant practices at the company, including: (1) daily stand-ups, (2) portfolio meetings, (3) '*master stand-ups*', (4) planning sessions, and (5) development activities. We conducted structured observations on 41 occasions.
Semi-structured interviews: Next to informal discussions we conducted a total of 19 semi-structured interviews. Three types of interviews were executed: (1) Diagnosing and scoping, (2) mid-term, and (3) post-action interviews. The interviews were conducted with the management and development teams.
Questionnaires: We used bi-weekly questionnaires to create satisfaction graphs for involved practitioners over time (cf. [38]). The short questionnaires consisted of several questions using Likert-scales and open fields for additional remarks. Eight rounds of questionnaires have been collected with staff members.

Data analysis: In contrary to traditional passive qualitative research, the action itself provides a primary origin of interpretation [36]. To support the reflection among researchers and involved actors all observation notes, interviews and questionnaires were fully transcribed and used in discussions.

5 Action Research

5.1 Diagnosing

Diagnosing started in May 2013 and lasted until December. To understand the context, interviews were held with employees across all roles, resulting in a description of current roles and mapping of involved domains of practice. Generally the reported problems constituted a lack of structured process connecting the development to portfolio level decisions. On average the company has been working on two 'very small' projects and 30 to 40 'individual' to 'tiny' sized projects a year. When the company grew it became very difficult to keep an overview and coordinate these projects effectively. Further, the small teams were linked to multiple POs exposing them to discussions due to conflicting customer priorities.

During interviews and discussions with developers and management we identified a number of issues: *(1) Development staff is highly distracted, to a large degree caused by discussions with multiple POs. (2) Little connection of portfolio to strategy. Little coordination across the portfolio leading to suboptimal and unprofitable choices. Portfolio decisions are made by developers. (3) Poor knowledge management, resulting in overhead and posing a danger to project continuation. (4) Daily maintenance shifts help get maintenance tasks done while keeping most of the resources focused, however, overhead for working on unknown projects is high. (5) Hard to keep an overview and deliver work promised to clients.*

5.2 Action Planning

Following the diagnosis, management acknowledged that improvements were necessary. In discussions with all actors it became clear that a team having to deal with multiple POs does not work well because developers end up making decisions about portfolio priorities for a large part of their time. It was concluded that removing the portfolio decisions from the development staff and limiting interruptions of staff by management will likely reduce the distraction of team members and improve portfolio decisions. In early June 2014 an initial plan was developed based around the following proposals: (1) Introduce agile portfolio management, (2) introduce stable teams, (3) work with true Scrum sprints, limit task switching, and (4) improve company-wide knowledge management.

Based on that and hints found in practitioner's literature (cf. [39]), we designed the *Team Portfolio Scrum (TPS)* practice and the *Team Portfolio Owner (TPO)* role to support the implementation of portfolio management. TPS is based on a one week Scrum cycle including the usual Scrum practices (e.g., Sprint and review, daily stand-ups, retrospectives) in which the PO is replaced by the TPO. The practice follows characteristics of agile portfolio management [1] by (1) adding transparency of resources and work items through a Portfolio board, (2) close collaboration based on routines and artifacts enabling frequent feedback-loops across teams and management, (3) commitment to strategically managed portfolios, and (4) team orientation. In Table 2 we summarize the description and responsibilities of the new role.

5.3 Action Taking

Before introducing the TPO role, a portfolio team, a portfolio board and a team portfolio backlog were introduced. The TPO role was appointed from one of the three POs previously working with the team. On June 25 a workshop was held with the development team and management staff. Initial resistance arose among the developers as the goal was initially defined around increasing engineer productivity. In response the goal was rephrased to remove mid-sprint management interruptions and portfolio level responsibilities from the engineers.

Action taking began on June 30, 2015 with a reiteration of goals during a lunch presentation. The implementation of the practice was reflected throughout the project in Retrospective sessions staring on July 4. On August 15, 2014,

Table 2. The team portfolio owner role

Team Portfolio Owner:

Person responsible for the success a team's project portfolio. Analogously to a Product Owner, the Team Portfolio Owner (TPO) sets the priorities across projects during a Sprint. TPO shields team members from internal politics and different customers pushing project priorities

Responsibilities:

- Coordinates inter-project priorities with the team, portfolio team and customers
- Takes task switching penalties into account in discussions with the team and the Scrum Master
- Channels multiple projects into a single team backlog
- Guards inter-project priorities (1) when scope changes are needed (work taking longer/shorter or urgent other work, and (2) during the sprint planning meeting as the team negotiates work items
- Single channel of communication towards the team, lessening distractions (outwards communication is at the team's discretion)
- Attends the portfolio meetings to align priorities with company strategy
- Attends the daily stand-ups to keep up to date with the progress of the team

the team leader left the team for reasons unrelated to the project which had a big impact on the morale of the team as became visible in our satisfaction graphs. The action research continued with the practice being perceived as useful. The following time line outlines the execution of the project:

- **May 6, 2013:** Diagnosing: Scoping interviews
- **December 2, 2013:** Action Planning: Discussion of improvement initiatives
- **April 15, 2014**: Initial presentation of action plan to all employees
- **June 9, 2014:** Introduction of portfolio management (portfolio board)
- **June 24, 2014:** Preparation meeting with management and appointing TPO
- **June 25, 2014:** Workshop with development team and management
- **June 30, 2014:** Action Taking: Introduction of TPS practice
- **July 4, 2014:** Retrospective after first sprint
- **October 6, 2014:** End of Action Taking, beginning of evaluation
- **January 1, 2015:** Company wide implementation of TPS

5.4 Evaluating

The Team Portfolio Owner (TPO) role was adopted company-wide by our case company three months after the action research was completed. We consider this as an indicator for the success of the project. We now return to the research question in order to evaluate the action research.

Barriers to a team portfolio task prioritization practice: *Additional overhead:* In the case company, the hours of a manager, including the TPO, can not be billed to clients: *"As to whether it [the TPO role] is overhead, yes, per definition, because the work isn't billable to the client.* This is related to the way clients are billed at this company: actual booked development hours. Other methods exist that are much more suitable for Scrum [40]. However these methods assume one project per sprint. Billing might be a general problem for multi-project software development as is it hard to predict the proportions of the sprint for each customer in the face of scope changes.

High workload: The TPO reported his high workload at several occasions, especially towards the end of the action: *"..in the beginning I had much more time to do proper backlog management."*; *"it is extremely busy to fulfill this role."*

Benefits to a team portfolio task prioritization practice: *Better adherence to company strategy:* Due to the oversight the TPO can make better decisions in coordination across the entire portfolio. Yet, choosing the right projects can be difficult for a small company: *"For existing customers we basically have to do everything, we can't choose to not do a project. It is useful to decide on new customers though."*

Removing portfolio level decision making and conflicting decisions from multiple POs: This benefit of the introduced role functioned very well from the beginning, as confirmed by observations and multiple actors. Before introducing the practice, developers had to make decisions and were blamed for those. When asked about what to do when a task threatens achieving the sprint goals, a developer commented: *"I go directly to the TPO. The TPO manages what tasks get dropped. This works very well."*

Limiting interrupting requests from multiple POs: Before the change POs would often come to a developer's desk asking questions, planning work and lobbying for projects. As a developer comments: *"It is easier for developers to defend themselves.? and ?[the situation] improved. We have more breathing room because of the experiment. We can be more focused on software development."*

Specifying Learning. *Not more than one large context switch per day:* In our case organization the developers reported a benefit from the introduced TPS practice. However, also the number of parallel projects increased. Recommendations we found in literature deviate between two [12] parallel projects as an optimum, and not more than one large context switch per day - thus five projects per week. However, this largely depends on the homogeneity of the assignments. Here it is for the TPO and the team to discuss what a reasonable number of projects is according to: (1) familiarity with the project (architecture, code standards), (2) homogeneity (domain, application type), and (3) urgency.

TPO needs sufficient mandate: For fast resolving of issues, the TPO needs to have a complete mandate for choosing between the customers in the current sprint. A team member said at the beginning: *"The role itself has too much responsibility, at least too much for what the current TPO is mandated for.*

This adds a step between the management process: the team signals a problem to the TPO, the TPO needs to consult with the PO to make the decision. This means extra overhead for certain tasks. The TPO should define the priorities and shield the developers from the outside." The POs appreciated this delegation of responsibilities at later stages of the project: *"I liked it that the TPO could make the choices."*

Collaboration of TPO and POs: The introduction of the TPO role had a strong impact on the interaction of POs and teams. The POs had previously direct access to the teams, and had to go through the TPO as a *Master Product Owner* now. It took time to go through the TPO for planning or urgent maintenance: *"For me as a PO, the effect was that the planning was less fine grained, which was something I had to get used to since I'm a control freak. [About closing the scope] The smaller projects and maintenance are really hard to plan."*

TPO and the Portfolio Team: Knowing the inter-project priorities is very important for this role. The project portfolio board is the primary tool for the transfer of this information from the Portfolio Team to the TPO. Attending the Portfolio Management Meeting gives the TPO additional information and the possibility to discuss the priorities. The TPO said: *"The weekly portfolio management meeting is very important for this role."*

Limitations. There are two main limitations to this research: First, we present the results of a single action research study. Credibility of AR lies in knowledge generated and tested in practice [36]. Generalizations and external credibility from such AR studies depend on rich storytelling as well as application of AR guidelines such as CAR [37]. Second, with one developer leaving the team composition changed. This resource problem impacted the team, both in getting more work and lowering morale. However, many action research projects take an unpredicted course while still providing considerable scientific value [37].

6 Conclusions

In this paper we report on our experiences in introducing a task prioritization and coordination practice in Scrum teams executing multiple projects simultaneously. For teams operating in small companies such as the one presented here it is difficult to follow traditional Scrum as they are directly exposed to commercial pressure and customer needs. As such we address an under-researched scenario outside the *'agile sweet-spot'* [40] by linking Scrum to a portfolio management practice [1].

Despite the challenges encountered during this 17 months project, such as a team member leaving the team, the practice was perceived as useful by all participants and adopted company-wide after the project. The TPS practice helped our case organization to align tasks to strategy and limits interrupting requests to developers by appointing a dedicated Team Portfolio Owner.

To practitioners this paper provides the template of a concrete task prioritization practice, the barriers and benefits of its implementation. To academia, we contribute to understanding of new and more agile organizational forms. We add a literature analysis describing the existing body of knowledge on interruptions and task-switching across the domains of software development, psychology and management science. As such we lay the groundwork for further investigations to quantify the effects of task prioritization and coordination practices in Scrum.

Multitasking seems unavoidable. The presented practice helped to run more projects simultaneously, however, the involved actors should be aware that it comes at a high cost. Companies need to make good strategic choices regarding resources and their allocation to stay viable and sustainable.

Acknowledgments. We thank all the participants for generously contributing to this study.

References

1. Stettina, C.J., Hörz, J.: Agile portfolio management: An empirical perspective on the practice in use. Int. J. Proj. Manage. **33**(1), 140–152 (2015)
2. Azizyan, G., Magarian, M.K., Kajko-Matsson, M.: Survey of agile tool usage and needs. In: Agile Conference (AGILE 2011), pp. 29–38. IEEE (2011)
3. Kruchten, P.: Contextualizing agile software development. J. Softw.: Evol. Process **25**(4), 351–361 (2013)
4. Deemer, P., Benefield, G., Larman, C., Vodde, B.: The scrum primer (2010). http://assets.scrumtraininginstitute.com/downloads/1/scrumprimer121.pdf. Accessed 12 Aug 2014
5. Payne, J.H.: Management of multiple simultaneous projects: a state-of-the-art review. Int. J. Proj. Manage. **13**(3), 163–168 (1995)
6. Marchenko, A., Abrahamsson, P.: Scrum in a multiproject environment: An ethnographically-inspired case study on the adoption challenges. In: Conference of Agile, AGILE 2008, pp. 15–26. IEEE (2008)
7. Highsmith, J.: Agile Project Management: Creating Innovative Products. Pearson Education, Boston (2009)
8. Wheelwright, S.C.: Revolutionizing Product Development: Quantum Leaps in Speed, Efficiency, and Quality. Simon and Schuster, New York (1992)
9. Ikonen, M., Kettunen, P., Oza, N., Abrahamsson, P.: Exploring the sources of waste in kanban software development projects. In: 36th EUROMICRO Conference on Software Engineering and Advanced Applications (SEAA 2010), pp. 376–381. IEEE (2010)

10. Braun, E.: Lean/agile methods for web site development. Online-Weston Then Wilton **29**(5), 58 (2005)
11. Krebs, J.: Agile Portfolio Management. Microsoft Press, Richmond (2008)
12. McCollum, J.K., Sherman, J.D.: The effects of matrix organization size and number of project assignments on performance. IEEE Trans. Eng. Manage. **38**(1), 75–78 (1991)
13. Lehto, I., Rautiainen, K.: Software development governance challenges of a middle-sized company in agile transition. In: Proceedings of the 2009 ICSE Workshop on Software Development Governance, pp. 36–39. IEEE Computer Society (2009)
14. Nocks, J.: Multiple simultaneous projects with one extreme programming team. In: Agile Conference, 5 pp. IEEE (2006)
15. Wiseman, G.: Multiple projects, one agile team (2007). http://www.infoq.com/news/2007/12/multiple-projects-one-agile-team. Accessed 12 Aug 2014
16. Kathuria, M.: Happy marriage or divorce : What happens if single scrum team has to handle multiple projects (2013)
17. Levison, M.: Scrum on a small team with multiple "projects" (2013). https://groups.google.com/forum/#!topic/scrumalliance/8j-5V_Cl2aI. Accessed: 12 Aug 2014
18. Dinwiddie, G.: Combined backlog for multiple projects (2007). http://blog.gdinwiddie.com/2007/12/03/combined-backlog-for-multiple-projects/. Accessed 12 Aug 2014
19. Friedman, J.: Subprojects: Many projects, one team; one project, many teams (2013). http://blog.assembla.com/AssemblaBlog/tabid/12618/bid/98674/Space-Manager-Many-projects-one-team-One-project-many-teams.aspx. Accessed 16 Jan 2015
20. Van Solingen, R., Berghout, E., Van Latum, F.: Interrupts: just a minute never is. IEEE Softw. **15**(5), 97 (1998)
21. Parnin, C., DeLine, R.: Evaluating cues for resuming interrupted programming tasks. In: Proceedings of the SIGCHI Conference on Human Factors in Computing Systems, pp. 93–102. ACM (2010)
22. Wylie, G., Allport, A.: Task switching and the measurement of switch costs. Psychol. Res. **63**(3–4), 212–233 (2000)
23. Meiran, N., Chorev, Z., Sapir, A.: Component processes in task switching. Cogn. Psychol. **41**(3), 211–253 (2000)
24. Mayr, U., Kliegl, R.: Task-set switching and long-term memory retrieval. J. Exp. Psychol. Learn Mem. Cogn. **26**(5), 1124–1140 (2000)
25. Waszak, F., Hommel, B., Allport, A.: Task-switching and long-term priming: Role of episodic stimulus-task bindings in task-shift costs. Cogn. Psychol. **46**(4), 361–413 (2003)
26. Mayr, U., Keele, S.W.: Changing internal constraints on action: the role of backward inhibition. J. Exp. Psychol.: Gen. **129**(1), 4 (2000)
27. Jersild, A.T.: Mental set and shift. Arch. Psychol. **14**, 81 (1927)
28. Wetherell, M.A., Carter, K.: The multitasking framework: the effects of increasing workload on acute psychobiological stress reactivity. Stress Health **30**(2), 103–109 (2014)
29. Lenox, T., Pilarski, N., Leathers, L.: The effects of interruptions on remembering task information. Inf. Syst. Appl. Res. **5**(4), 11 (2012)
30. Keick, K.E.: Cosmos vs. chaos: Sense and nonsense in electronic contexts. Organ. Dyn. **14**(2), 51–64 (1985)

31. Diamond, D.M., Campbell, A.M., Park, C.R., Halonen, J., Zoladz, P.R.: The temporal dynamics model of emotional memory processing: a synthesis on the neurobiological basis of stress-induced amnesia, flashbulb and traumatic memories, and the yerkes-dodson law. Neural Plasticity **2007**, 1–33 (2007)
32. González, V.M., Mark, G.: Constant, constant, multi-tasking craziness: managing multiple working spheres. In: Proceedings of the SIGCHI Conference on Human Factors in Computing Systems, pp. 113–120. ACM (2004)
33. Mark, G., Gonzalez, V.M., Harris, J.: No task left behind?: examining the nature of fragmented work. In: Proceedings of the SIGCHI Conference on Human Factors in Computing Systems, pp. 321–330. ACM (2005)
34. Czerwinski, M., Horvitz, E., Wilhite, S.: A diary study of task switching and interruptions. In: Proceedings of the SIGCHI Conference on Human Factors in Computing Systems, pp. 175–182. ACM (2004)
35. Eyrolle, H., Cellier, J.M.: The effects of interruptions in work activity: Field and laboratory results. Appl. Ergonomics **31**(5), 537–543 (2000)
36. Greenwood, D.J., Levin, M.: Introduction to Action Research: Social Research for Social Change. SAGE publications, Thousand Oaks (2006)
37. Davison, R., Martinsons, M.G., Kock, N.: Principles of canonical action research. Inf. Syst. J. **14**(1), 65–86 (2004)
38. Stettina, C.J., Heijstek, W., Fægri, T.E.: Documentation work in agile teams: The role of documentation formalism in achieving a sustainable practice. In: AGILE 2012, pp. 31–40. IEEE, Washington, DC (2012)
39. Singerman, D.: How does scrum work when you have multiple projects? (2009). http://stackoverflow.com/questions/412525/how-does-scrum-work-when-you-have-multiple-projects/413061\#413061. Accessed 12 Aug 2014
40. Hoda, R., Kruchten, P., Noble, J., Marshall, S.: Agility in context. In: Proceedings of the ACM International Conference on Object Oriented Programming Systems Languages and Applications, OOPSLA 2010, pp. 74–88. ACM, NY, USA (2010)

Quality Assurance in Scrum Applied to Safety Critical Software

Geir K. Hanssen[1(✉)], Børge Haugset[1], Tor Stålhane[2], Thor Myklebust[1], and Ingar Kulbrandstad[3]

[1] SINTEF ICT, Strindveien 4, 7465 Trondheim, Norway
{Geir.K.Hanssen,Borge.Haugset,Thor.Myklebust}@sintef.no

[2] NTNU, Sem Sælandsvei 9, 7491 Trondheim, Norway
stalhane@idi.ntnu.no

[3] Autronica Fire and Security AS, Haakon VII's Gate 4, 7041 Trondheim, Norway
Ingar.Kulbrandstad@autronicafire.no

Abstract. Various agile methods have several quality assurance mechanisms embedded in the process itself, without any explicit QA role. In principle, the team takes care of quality assurance during sprints and as part of daily stand-ups, sprint reviews and retrospectives. We have defined SafeScrum, a variant of Scrum with some additional XP techniques that can be used to develop safety-critical software and have the software certified according to the IEC 61508 standard. This imposes a load of additional requirements on the process. In a recent industrial case, we have experienced that the quality assurance mechanisms in Scrum becomes insufficient. We have therefore analyzed the standard, consulted an independent assessor and worked with the Scrum team to identify necessary additional tasks for a team-internal QA role to be added to the SafeScrum process.

Keywords: Safety critical software · Scrum · Safescrum · IEC61508 · Quality assurance

1 Introduction

Agile software development methods and in particular variants of Scrum, often in combination with XP techniques, has had a large uptake in the software industry over the past decade. One of the many aspects of Scrum and similar approaches is that quality assurance is embedded in the process itself, and not explicitly documented. A Scrum team is supposed to be self-sustained, not having to rely on an external quality management or assurance function like a QA manager or QA department. The latter has been a typical role in line organizations doing plan-based development [19, 20]. First of all, a Scrum project enforces visibility and has frequent evaluation of status, progress and problems, which is used to re-plan and improve the project based on the most recent and updated knowledge. Scrum also has dedicated activities for managing quality issues with both the product under development and the process itself; each short work-period, or sprint, concludes with a sprint review and potentially also a retrospective. The former evaluate the results so far and the latter evaluates the process itself to identify

H. Sharp and T. Hall (Eds.): XP 2016, LNBIP 251, pp. 92–103, 2016.
DOI: 10.1007/978-3-319-33515-5_8

improvement needs and opportunities. Scrum also strongly emphasizes frequent interaction with the customer or the problem owner, and XP stresses continuous and frequent testing. This is necessary to ensure that the functionality as well as the quality of the system meets requirements and expectations. In short– Scrum can be seen as a combined and self-sustained planning, development, *and* quality assurance process, although lacking traceability.

Scrum was initially designed for small development projects with small self-managed teams, solving small-scale problems. Research from the past decade provides examples that this works well and that Scrum projects are more effective and flexible than plan-driven projects [4]. However, the trend in the software industry today is that Scrum is being used in increasingly more complex settings. We see cases where globally distributed Scrum teams collaborate in developing large software systems [6]. We also see that Scrum is being used for development of safety-critical systems, which have to comply with strict quality and safety standards [5, 14, 18].

This trend of increasing complexity means that the core principles of self-sustained, multi-disciplinary, and self-managed teams are challenged. In this paper, we look into how this development affects the embedded quality assurance function in Scrum. We base our analysis and discussion on an ongoing industry case where a Scrum team develops a high-integrity fire and gas detection system where the goal is to achieve a SIL3 (SIL: Safety Integrity Level) rating according to the IEC61508 standard [7]. The Scrum process used by the team is adjusted and continuously refined to match the requirements of the IEC61508 standard; we name this variant SafeScrum [18] (see Sect. 4 for more details).

In the following, we present some background on the inherent challenges when developing and certifying safety-critical systems, on how SafeScrum can be adapted to support this process and the role of quality management and assurance. We then look into our case to show how this is being done in practical terms before we use our insights from the case to discuss how Scrum can be enforced to manage quality in high complexity settings.

2 Quality Assurance in Agile Software Development

Mnkandla and Duolatzky gives a thorough discussion of the use of the term quality [11]. Most of the definitions identified by the two authors have a production focus and are not relevant for development. The concept of quality– software or otherwise – is defined by ISO 9000 as "the totality of characteristics of an entity that bear on its ability to satisfy stated and implied needs". According to this definition, the main concept of quality is to make the customer happy. Deliver a quality product thus means to deliver a product that is according to the customer's specified and implied requirements. Sticking with older definitions – e.g., quality is conformance to specifications – ignore the customer and is not a smart move in a competitive industry.

Inherent in the plan-driven approach to software development is the idea that all requirements are known at the start of the project. With faster innovation, more rapid requirement changes, and more volatility allowed in the prioritized tasks, this idea is void. Plan-driven development creates a significant risk that the users' requirements remain unclear or that important opportunities for innovation are missed. The problem is that up-front requirements become increasingly irrelevant as the pace of innovation quickens and customers' expectancy to fit-for-use rises. Consequently, the discrepancy between software practice, end-users and traditional requirements specification widens. Requirements that are out of sync with real needs has been claimed as a common cause of terminated IT projects [13].

Agile development attempts to allow for frequent updates of the requirements as the customer's needs and problem understanding develop over time, thus increasing the probability of delivering improved product quality.

3 Safety Critical Software Development

A system is defined as safety-critical if a failure may result in death or severe injury to people, loss or severe damage to property, or harm to the environment. Examples of such systems are fire alarm systems (failing to sound an alarm may cause casualties) or railway signaling systems (signal error may lead to collisions etc.). Safety critical systems are found in almost all parts of our daily lives, from transportation, to energy systems, in medical devices etc. Traditionally, such systems have been hardware reliant, but as hardware has become more powerful, flexible and programmable, the trend is that larger parts of the total system are implemented in software, meaning that the software complexity is growing. For example, the top-notch fighter plane of the forties, the Spitfire, had zero lines of code. Today, the F-35 fighter has about 8 million lines of code where most of them comprise what could be defined a safety critical system [10].

Safety critical systems may be classified with a SIL value, defining the level of performance of the safety function of the system, or in other words, how likely the system is to operate as intended. The classification of levels varies between different standards, but for IEC61508, which is relevant to our case, SIL is divided from 1 to 4 where SIL 4 is the highest safety integrity level.

In order to use a safety critical system, the customer needs a certificate. A "software certification demonstrates the reliability and safety of software systems in such a way that it can be checked by an independent authority with minimal trust in the techniques and tools used in the certification process itself" [3]. The certificate is an independent document that ensures that the system operates as specified and according to the safety standard. This introduces the role of the assessor, an independent third party with the responsibility of assessing and eventually certifying that the development process leading to the system is compliant with the requirements in the standard. It is important to understand that a standard like IEC 61508 mainly has requirements for the *process*. As stated in the introduction: "This International Standard sets out a generic approach for all safety lifecycle activities for systems comprised of electrical and/or electronic and/or programmable electronic (E/E/PE) elements that are used to perform safety functions." E.g., the section on architecture contains material on ***how*** to select architecture but no material on ***what*** the architecture should look like.

In practical terms, the standard is a list of good software engineering practices [15]. These must be followed or argued irrelevant. The designated SIL determines which requirements that are recommended or highly recommended. The assessor bases the assessment on proof of compliance, which are various types of information showing how requirements have been met. Providing such documentation imposes a large extra effort on the development project and in some cases it may actually constitute up to 50% of the total development cost [14].

Looking back at the past decades, we see that the development process of safety critical systems is optimized for hardware development, where design decisions have to be made early and locked prior to implementation to avoid late change in design, which may impose very high costs. Normally some variant of the V-model is used to guide design, implementation, testing and validation.

As shown in Fig. 1, integration and validation testing is done on the right side of the V–meaning that a large part of the code-related documentation is made *after* coding. While a natural approach for most hardware development, this may impose problems for an agile software development project. Here, new or changed requirements will often lead to changes in the low-level design, which may then lead to changes in the code. In these cases, it is important to have well-documented code plus traceability from requirements, via architecture and design down to code.

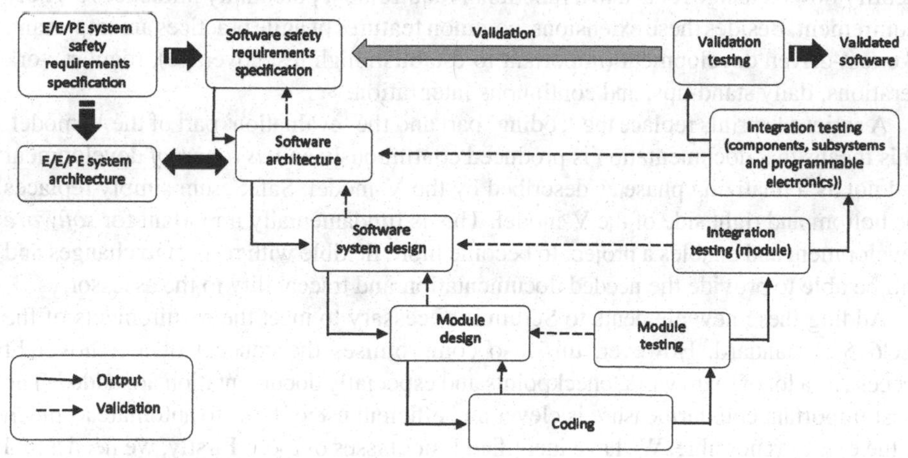

Fig. 1. The V-model

During software development is it important to control size and complexity. Complexity is obvious – high complexity hinders understanding and can thus lead to errors. However, experience shows that sheer size also will create problems for developers since a large code volume makes it difficult to keep the overview, which again leads to coding errors.

4 SafeScrum – Agile Development of Safety Critical Software

SafeScrum is a variant of the well-known and extensively used Scrum development model [16] where some additional elements are added to be able to fulfill the process requirements from the IEC61508 standard [18]. Based on a thorough investigation of the requirements in the standards part 3 which defines the software part of the total system [14], we propose a set of extensions to make Scrum applicable to development of safety critical software. Firstly, there are two backlogs, one for functional requirements and one for safety requirements. Functional requirements may change frequently whilst safety requirements normally are stable and even reusable between projects and products. Relationships between these are maintained to keep track of which safety requirements that are affected by which functional requirements. Secondly, SafeScrum needs to be a traceable process. All decisions and changes throughout development must be documented, stored and made available to the assessor. The same goes for code reviews where all remarks and how they were resolved needs to be kept track of. Thirdly, each sprint encompasses a validation of the safety of the present system. As part of the sprint review of each sprint, the product backlog may be updated. In cases where a change is considered to affect the safety of the system, a change impact analysis (CIA) [17] is done – and documented. Here the two backlogs come in handy as a mean to identify how a change related to a functional requirement potentially influences a safety requirement. Besides these extensions, common features of agile practices are important, like test-driven development (important to establish high test coverage), regular work iterations, daily stand-ups, and continuous integration.

A series of sprints replace the 'coding' part and the 'evaluation' part of the V-model. This means that documentation is produced continuously and *as a part of* development and not as a finalizing phase as described by the V-model. SafeScrum simply replaces the bottom and right side of the V-model. This is fundamentally important for *software* development and enables a project to become more flexible with respect to changes and still be able to provide the needed documentation and traceability to the assessor.

Adding these new elements to Scrum is necessary to meet the requirements of the IEC61508 standard. However, this also compromises the concept of a lightweight process as a lot of extra work, checkpoints and especially documentation are added. The most important countermeasure is clever and efficient use of tools to automate as much of the extras as possible. We have identified four classes of tools. Firstly, we need a tool to support process and workflow management, like defining, assigning and following up tasks, their responsibilities and order, etc. Put simply, this is a tool to automate the Scrum board. Secondly, we need tools to establish and maintain traceability of requirements, tests and code. Even a small project will generate large amounts of information, which requires tool support. Thirdly, we need dedicated tools for managing information like design, code and architectural documentation. Fourthly, we need tools to support code quality assurance, which is particularly important with respect to IEC61508. This includes test coverage analysis, static code analysis and test automation. There are plenty of tools to choose from and many of them are flexible and can be combined and linked to create a tool chain to support the SafeScrum process. The IEC61508 standard has requirements to tools and should be checked (IEC61508-3, Sect. 7.4.4, and table A3). The walkthrough of our case will provide concrete examples of such a tool chain (Fig. 3).

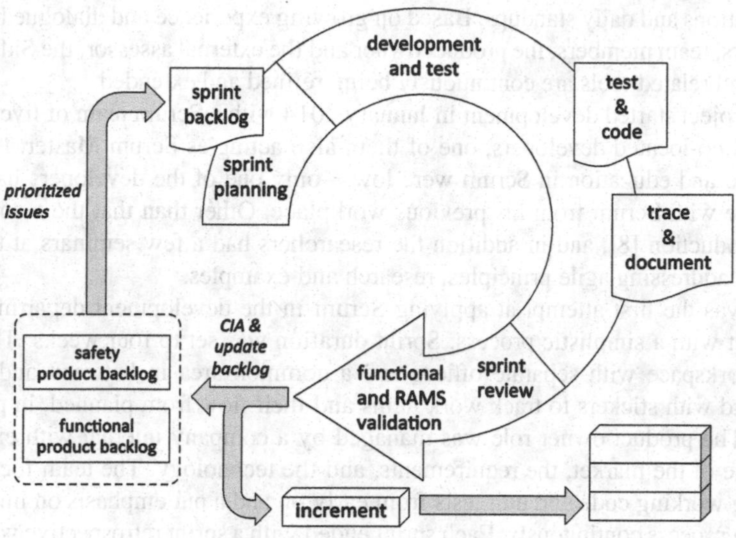

Fig. 2. The SafeScrum model

5 A SafeScrum Case

The authors have been working with Autronica Fire & Security for about two years in order to detail and trial the SafeScrum process in a real SIL3 industrial case. This collaboration is part of a large R&D project, partly funded by the Research Council of Norway. The collaboration is organized as an action research project [2] and the case being described here shows some of the findings, so far. All data are collected, managed and reported according to a joint R&D contract.

Autronica Fire & Security [1], with 380 employees, is an internationally leading provider of fire and gas detection systems. A large part of the business is offshore installations at oilrigs and ships where demands for safety performance are high. Our case is a project developing new software for a fire detection system, SIL 3.

The authors have followed the case project from the start and collected data in the form of 1) observations of sprint review and planning meetings (11), 2) analysis of documentation like project plans and requirements documents, and 3) interviews and discussions with the Scrum team and related roles. This also includes the assessor (a TÜV organization), which has been asked to comment on our development process (SafeScrum). This dialogue has been important to ensure that the development process and the documentation it produces meet the expectations and is aligned with the IEC61508 standard. The product being developed by the case project itself is however not yet certified – the completion is still some years ahead. In addition to this participative role in the shaping of SafeScrum, the researchers also made an analysis of the standard to identify any issues with respect to using an agile method [18]. Such issues were discussed with the Scrum team to ensure compliance. The SafeScrum process has emerged through practice. It started out by using only a few fundamental principles, like short iterations and daily standups. Based on growing experience and dialogue between researchers, team members, the product owner and the external assessor, the SafeScrum process and related tools are continuously being refined and extended.

The project started development in January 2014 with a Scrum team of five experienced and co-located developers, one of them also acting as Scrum Master. Previous experience and education in Scrum were low – only one of the developers had some experience with Scrum from his previous workplace. Other than that the team read a basic introduction [8], and in addition the researchers had a few seminars at the case company, addressing agile principles, research and examples.

This was the first attempt at applying Scrum in the development department and started out with a simplistic process. Sprint duration was set to four weeks. The team shared workspace with separate offices and a common area in between and used a whiteboard with stickers to track work items and their flow from planned, in progress to done. The product owner role was managed by a company internal with extensive knowledge of the market, the requirements, and the technology. The team focused on producing working code and unit tests from early on and a put emphasis on improving the Scrum process continuously. Each sprint ended with a sprint retrospective where the process was evaluated by the team, adjustments were made and new tools were trialed and added/removed as needed.

After a few sprints, Jira was introduced to manage the workflow and thus replaced the manual scrum board. RMsis, a plug-in for Jira, was used to establish traceability of the requirements management process. Confluence was used to support team collaboration and to document the sprints, e.g. by storing memos from sprint reviews. Stash and Git was used to manage software version control and code reviews and Bamboo was used for continuous builds, tests and release management. Doxygen was used for maintaining design and code documentation. In addition, a set of tools was used for additional quality assurance; Gtest and Gmoc were used to manage unit tests, Squish Coco was used for code coverage analysis and QAC/QACPP for static code analysis.

In total, these tools constitute a tool-chain where some of the tools are linked and operate as a greater whole. In particular, Jira serves as a hub in the tool chain. There are many alternative tools and ways of composing them, but in our case, this setup enables the Scrum team to be both agile and to automate many of the additional requirements imposed by the IEC61508 standard. Figure 3 shows how the tools are inter-related.

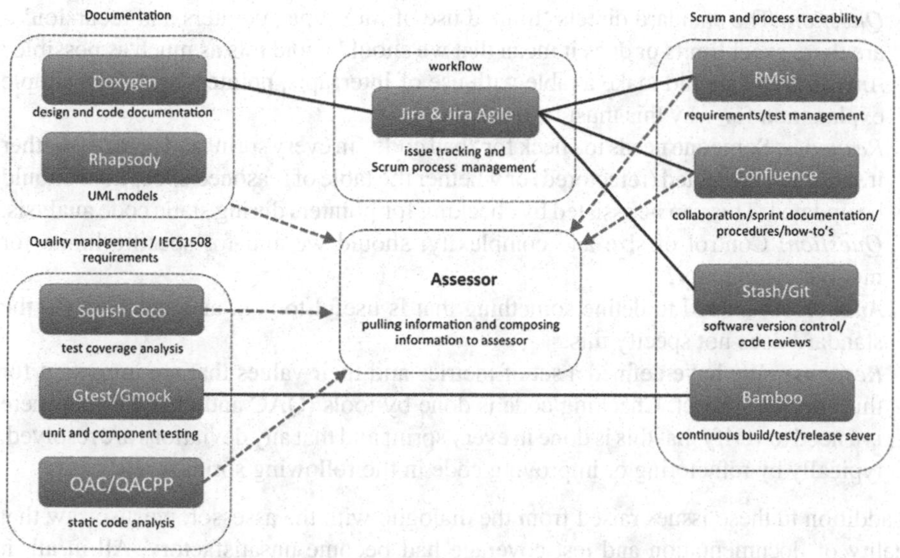

Fig. 3. The tool-chain supporting the SafeScrum process

6 The Need for Extra Attention to Quality Management

The shaping and introduction of SafeScrum at the case company has been done step by step and by building on growing experience. The described process extensions and the tool chain made the team able to produce and maintain the information required to achieve a SIL3 certificate. However, after a few months, and sprints, of operation we saw that this also puts a burden on the team, and in particular on the Scrum master who spent an increasingly large amount of time making sure that development was compliant with IEC61508. Some corrective actions were made but there was a concern that some glitches happened. It was also not clear what the most important considerations to make were. In short, the project needed some clarification on quality assurance, and asked the researchers for assistance.

This led us to consult the assessor to clarify his expectations for QA on three topics:

1. *Question:* Traceability of safety related requirements: Is it sufficient to have a trace between documents or should it be possible to trace issues down to sections, pages, or lines in the text?

   Answer: The assessor requires a link between requirements and tests, e.g. by referring to unique requirements ID in test cases.
   Response: This level of trace is handled by a dedicated requirements management tool, RMsis, linking requirements to tests that validates them, as well as linking requirements and tests to design and code. However, we have identified a need to manually verify that this is done correctly and to make necessary corrections. The QA role shall continuously verify that traceability is kept up to date and verify that all steps of the process are done.

2. *Question:* The standard directs 'limited use of interrupts, pointers and recursion' – are there exact limits or does it mean that we should avoid this as much as possible? *Answer:* You should make a table with use of interrupts, pointers etc. and a simple explanation for why this must be used.
   Response: Someone needs to check for "bad code" in every sprint and decide whether it should be corrected (refactored) or whether the table of reasoned exceptions should be updated. This can be assisted by checking for pointers during static code analysis.
3. *Question:* Control of size and complexity: should we aim for specific limits for module complexity?
   Answer: You need to define something that is useful to you, and argue why – the standard does not specify this.
   Response: We have defined a set of metrics and their values that are important for this specific project. Checking code is done by tools (QAC and QACPP) but there is a need to verify that this is done in every sprint and that any deviations are resolved, typically by refactoring or improving code in the following sprint.

In addition to these issues raised from the dialogue with the assessor, we also saw that quality of documentation and test coverage had become unsatisfactory. All in all, it became obvious that the self-regulating quality mechanisms in Scrum were overloaded and that there was a need to strengthen the QA function. A dedicated QA function is a necessary part of SafeScrum, but it is important to remember that the entire team still has a large responsibility for QA as well. The team plays an important role e.g. in retrospectives to continuously improve the development process and in resolving issues that are identified by the QA-role.

7 Shaping an Embedded QA Role in SafeScrum

Using the insights described above, the researchers, the Scrum team and the product owner had a series of meetings to define a specific QA role in SafeScrum to alleviate the problems. The traditional approach in this and similar organizations would be to place the QA role as a specialized function in the line organization, outside the project. We decided, however, to add the QA role to the Scrum team to be close to the activities and to the information needed to execute quality assurance. This adds to the principle of cross functional teams [12] in Scrum. We are also considering making this a rotating role to make it a shared responsibility and to share the workload. We need a QA log to trace findings, decisions, corrective actions, and the follow up/results of these. In our case, Confluence is a good tool to establish this log. We have identified four tasks:

QA Task 1: Check Code Metric Values for New or Changed Code: Neither the IEC61508 standard nor the assessor provide directions on specific metrics and limits to monitor at the component level. We have consulted the research literature [9] and used Minitab to analyze data from code from previous projects at the case company to define the following metrics and limits: (1) number of static paths – STPTH: 250, (2) McCabe's cyclomatic number – STCYC: 15, (3) number of parameters – STPAR: 5, (4) function call count – STSUB: 13, (5) maximum nesting of control structures – STMIF: 5, (6) number of executable lines – STXLN: 70, and (7) Myer's value – (STMCC): 10.

QAC is used to analyze new and changed code to produce values for the metrics. This is done at the end of each sprint. The metrics are displayed, together with their defined maximum values in a radar plot. It is thus easy to if there are metrics that are exceeding their defined limits. If the values are inside their limits, QA will accept the code. If one or more values are outside their limits, the code is presented by QA in the sprint review meeting where the team decides to either accept the violation or plan refactoring. If the violation is accepted, a brief explanation must be added to the log and potentially also in the code (required by the standard). If the violation is unacceptable, the team needs to define a new task in Jira to refactor the code.

QA Task 2: Check Documentation Coverage: Check new/changed code to ensure proper inline documentation and documents in Doxygen. This has to be done manually. In case of missing or poor documentation, the QA-log should be updated and the findings should be discussed in the sprint review meeting to decide how to resolve it (giving a task to someone in the team). This check could be done at the end of each sprint.

QA Task 3: Check Test Coverage: Check for code coverage using Squish Coco. The QA log should be updated with references to uncovered code. This could be checked by the end of each sprint. Uncovered code should be discussed at the sprint review meeting and the team should define corrective actions, like defining tasks to produce tests. According to the standard, the coverage should be at least 99%.

QA Task 4: Check Requirements-Task-Code Traceability: For new requirements, tasks, and code check that 1) requirements (RMsis) is linked to issues (e.g. in Jira), and 2) that code (e.g. Stash) is linked to issues (e.g. Jira). The QA role should control consistency at the end of the sprint and the team should resolve any identified issues immediately. The IEC61508 standard provides a set of explicit requirements for traceability; see table A.4 – Software design and development – detailed design, and table A.5 – Software design and development – software module testing and integration. We consulted the assessor about a definition of 'module' and its size (LOC). He referred to part 7, chapter C.2.9: *"a software module should have a single well-defined task or function to fulfill."* The assessor recommended 1000 LOC as an upper limit. In cases where the limit is exceeded it should be explained and documented.

The tasks have been defined to be as simple and inexpensive as possible, partly by using the tool chain that already is in place. The goal is to not add more work to the process ceremony than strictly needed, but to use the QA role to simplify the sprint reviews so that they are not bogged down with unimportant details. So far, this is done by letting the QA close issues that have low risk and complexity on his own in advance of the sprint retrospective, where the whole team participates. This reduces the time spent on unimportant decisions and helps the team focus on difficult tasks where a joint evaluation and decision is needed.

There should be a list of which criteria's the team members shall have done before the issue can be set as resolved and the QA needs to check that they have been fulfilled (not do them himself). The project should also create a list of which criteria's where the QA can close an issue without any further investigation. Only QA or the team can move an issue from resolved status to closed status. Closed issues cannot be changed.

8 Conclusions

After around two years of shaping and using SafeScrum we see that the inherent quality assurance mechanisms in Scrum are not sufficient to meet the demands imposed by the IEC61508 standard. We have consulted the assessor to ensure a proper match with the standard and shaped a new role to Scrum.

Developing safety critical solutions using SafeScrum, calls for a lot of extra attention, ceremony and documentation, which initially may be seen as a threat to the ability to be agile [13]. However, we see that the iterative nature of Scrum with frequent breaks between the sprints in addition to the tool chain we have put into use makes it possible to manage quality assurance internally in the team without adding too much extra work.

As part of further work we will look into opportunities to streamline and perfect this new role as it is vital to maintain an efficient SafeScrum process and to meet the requirements of the IEC61508 standard and the assessors expectations. One viable step would be to add tool support to assist the QA role in order to collect and analyze quality information with less effort and with more precision. The authors have been involved in the U-QASAR FP7 EU project, which has developed a tool that serves as a central quality dashboard consolidating quality information in a unified overview. We will look into integrating this with the tool chain as a new tool for the team and the QA role.

Acknowledgements. This work was partially funded by the Norwegian research council under grant #228431 (the SUSS project) and the EU FP7 project U-QASAR (grant agreement no. 318082). Research has been done in collaboration with Autronica Fire & Security AS. We are grateful for valuable input from the external assessor.

References

1. Camarinha-Matos, L.M., Afsarmanesh, H. (eds.): Collaborative Networked Organizations: A research agenda for emerging business models, 1st edn, p. 346. Springer, Heidelberg (2004)
2. Davison, R.M., Martinsons, M.G., Kock, N.: Principles of canonical action research. Inf. Syst. J. **14**(1), 65–86 (2004)
3. Denney, E., Fischer, B.: Software certification and software certificate management systems. In: NASA Ames Research Center (2005)
4. Dingsøyr, T., Dybå, T., Moe, N.B.: Agile Software Development: An Introduction and Overview, in Agile Software Development. Springer-Verlag, Heidelberg (2010)
5. Fitzgerald, B., Stol, K.-J., O'Sullivan, R., O'Brien, D.: Scaling agile methods to regulated environments: an industry case study. In: Proceedings of the 2013 International Conference on Software Engineering. IEEE Press (2013)
6. Hanssen, G.K., Smite, D., Moe, N.B.: Signs of agile trends in global software engineering research: A tertiary study. In: Proceedings of International Conference on Global Software Engineering (ICGSE). IEEE, Helsinki (2011)
7. IEC, 61508: 2010 Functional Safety of Electrical/Electronic/Programmable Electronic Safety-related Systems (E/E/PE, or E/E/PES)
8. Kniberg, H.: Scrum and XP from the Trenches - How we do Scrum. Enterprise Software Development Series, Plesa, D. (ed.) InfoQ. 131 (2007)
9. Krusko, A.: Complexity analysis of real time software – using software complexity metrics to improve the quality of real time software. In: Department of Numerical Analysis and Computer Science, Royal Institute of Technology (KTH): Stockholm, Sweden, p. 97 (2004)
10. Martin, L.: A Digital Jet for the Modern Battlespace (2015). http://www.f35.com/about/life-cycle/software
11. Mnkandla, E., Dwolatzky, B.: Defining agile software quality assurance. In: International Conference on Software Engineering Advances, IEEE (2006)
12. Moe, N.B., Dingsøyr, T., Dybå, T.: A teamwork model for understanding an agile team: A case study of a Scrum project. Inf. Softw. Technol. **52**(5), 480–491 (2010)
13. Myklebust, T., Stålhane, T., Hanssen, G., Wien, T., Haugset, B.: Scrum, documentation and the IEC 61508-3:2010 software standard. In: International Conference on Probabilistic Safety Assesment and Management (PSAM). PSAM, Hawaii (2014)
14. Myklebust, T., Stålhane, T., Hanssen, G.K., Wien, T., Haugset, B.: Scrum, documentation and the IEC 61508-3:2010 software standard. In: Proceedings of Probabilistic Safety Assessment & Management conference (PSAM12). Self-published, Oahu, USA (2014)
15. Myklebust, T., Stålhane, T., Haugset, B., Hanssen, G.K.: Using a goal-based approach to improve the IEC 61508-3 software safety standard. In: Proceedings of the Twenty-Third Safety-Critical System Symposium, Bristol, UK, 3rd-5th February 2015
16. Schwaber, K., Beedle, M.: Agile Software Development with Scrum. Prentice Hall, New Jersey (2001)
17. Stålhane, T., Hanssen, G.K., Myklebust, T., Haugset, B.: Agile change impact analysis of safety critical software. In: Bondavalli, A., Ceccarelli, A., Ortmeier, F. (eds.) SAFECOMP 2014. LNCS, vol. 8696, pp. 444–454. Springer, Heidelberg (2014)
18. Stålhane, T., Myklebust, T., Hanssen, G.K.: The application of Scrum IEC 61508 certifiable software. In: Proceedings of ESREL. Helsinki, Finland (2012)
19. Talby, D., Keren, A., Hazzan, O., Dubinsky, Y.: Agile software testing in a large-scale project. IEEE Softw. **23**(4), 30–37 (2006)
20. Vaibmu. QA role in Agile Teams (2013). http://www.uqasar.eu/qa-role-in-agile-teams/

Flow, Intrinsic Motivation, and Developer Experience in Software Engineering

Kati Kuusinen[1(✉)], Helen Petrie[2], Fabian Fagerholm[3], and Tommi Mikkonen[1]

[1] Tampere University of Technology, Tampere, Finland
{kati.kuusinen, tommi.mikkonen}@tut.fi
[2] University of York, York, UK
helen.petrie@york.ac.uk
[3] University of Helsinki, Helsinki, Finland
fabian.fagerholm@helsinki.fi

Abstract. Software developers are both users of development tools but also designers of new software systems. This dual role makes developers special users of work-related software. To increase the understanding of developers as users and to evaluate the ability of common measurement scales to address developer experience, we conducted a survey measuring developers' flow state, intrinsic motivation and user experience. Scales used were the Short Dispositional Flow Scale, items from the Intrinsic Motivation Inventory, the Short AttrakDiff-2, and our own DEXI scale. 57 developers from 25 countries responded and results indicate that intrinsic motivation and autotelic experience are significant predictors of developers' UX whereas hedonic, pragmatic, and general quality are not. In addition, developers' needs are characterized by efficiency, informativeness, intuitiveness, and flexibility of the tool.

Keywords: Software development · User experience · Developer experience · Development tools · Integrated development environments · Human factors

1 Introduction

Software engineering (SE) is a professional human activity that demands numerous skills and qualities from developers. Technical skills are needed to create the code that builds the software, while social skills are needed to be able to collaborate with other developers and to communicate with stakeholders. SE is an endeavor which builds complex systems that realize user and business requirements in technologically sophisticated manners. Considering the challenges of SE, the user experience (UX) of developers is an area that has been very little studied. Developers are users of multi-faceted development tools such as integrated development environments (IDEs). Yet little is known about how these tools support developers in their demanding activities and the nature of their UX with such tools.

IDEs are commonly used tools in SE, and are applications used for composing, compiling and debugging program code [1]. IDEs also manage dependencies among different packages and modules, control builds, and provide linking to other tools such

H. Sharp and T. Hall (Eds.): XP 2016, LNBIP 251, pp. 104–117, 2016.
DOI: 10.1007/978-3-319-33515-5_9

as those for requirements management or test environments. Consequently, IDEs play a major role in making developers productive and feel comfortable during their daily activities. Yet despite their important role, little is known about how these tools support developers and the nature of UX with such tools. While it may be overreaching to conclude that happy developers are better at their work [2], both happiness and motivation have been connected with raised productivity [3]. Mood influences developers' performance on programming tasks [4], and happiness has been found to have productivity benefits [5].

Although qualities of both developers and development work have been studied, developers have rarely been investigated as users of development tools. As developers are users of IDEs, all that is true of any user according to UX definitions (e.g. [6]), should apply also to developers. However, the dual role of developer as both users of systems and developers of systems makes them special: besides being IDE users, developers should be able to understand the human user to be able to fulfill their needs with the software under development. A concept of developer experience (DX) has been suggested to address the particularities to SE [7]. The concept of DX is influenced by the concept of UX [7]. Moreover, DX consists of aspects related to cognition, affect, and intention and an understanding of the concept should help practitioners in improving development environments with respect to developers' needs, perceptions and feelings [7].

In this paper we address DX in terms of the experienced state of flow, intrinsic motivation (IM) and UX. Our goal is to determine the core concepts and predictors of DX related to IDE usage in order enable improvement of IDEs to improve developers' IM towards their work and their ability to experience flow (deep, focused, rewarding concentration) during their work. Our assumption is that these factors both make developers' work more enjoyable and increase their productivity. To this end, we conducted a survey of developers' experiences of software development using a particular IDE, Qt Creator. We used the Short Dispositional Flow Scale (SDFS-2) [8], parts of Intrinsic Motivation Inventory (IMI) [9], and a UX scale consisting of the Short AttrakDiff-2 [10] and our own DEXI scale. We ran multiple linear regression analyses to investigate whether these scales can significantly predict developers' ratings of overall UX (OUX) and the IDE's ability to fulfill their needs (need fulfillment score, NFS). Moreover, we address the impact of perceived choice of Qt Creator since it often is the employer who decides which tools are used. Finally, we present best qualities and areas for improvement in the IDE as assessed by the respondents. Our contributions include increased understanding of developers as users, and core UX concepts related to DX and developers' needs related to IDEs.

The rest of the paper is structured as follows: the next section presents the background and related work followed by the research methodology. Then the results section presents the linear regression analyses on the scales' ability to predict OUX and NFS, the impact of perceived choice on DX, and the core qualities of IDEs. We discuss our results and threats to validity. Finally, we present concluding remarks.

2 Background

Motivation and Flow. One of the current influential theories of motivation is self-determination theory developed by Deci and Ryan [11]. They distinguish between intrinsic (IM) and extrinsic motivations (EM). IM refers to engaging in a task because of it is inherently pleasurable and satisfying, whereas EM refers to engaging in a task because of its outcomes, the task is used as a means to lead to the outcome [11]. In contrast, flow refers to a state of concentration so focused that it amounts to absolute absorption in an activity [12]. Applicable to both work and leisure [13], flow builds on IM and internal reward over the achievement rather than on external goal or recognition. Its effect can be characterized as being totally focused on a particular task at hand, so that the person becomes fully immersed in a feeling of energized focus, full involvement, and enjoyment in the process of the activity. While immersed, three conditions have to be met to achieve a flow state [14]: (1) One must be involved in an activity with a clear set of *goals and progress*; (2) The task at hand must have clear and immediate *feedback*; (3) One must have a good balance between the perceived *challenges* of the task at hand and their own perceived *skills*, so that there can be confidence in one's ability to complete the task at hand.

User Experience. Commonly, UX is understood as subjective, context-dependent, and dynamic [15]. It is affected by user's expectations, needs and motivation, as well as system characteristics such as purpose and functionality, and the context of use including physical, organizational and psychological aspects [6]. The hedonic-pragmatic model of UX divides user experience into a hedonic or non-utilitarian dimension and a pragmatic or instrumental dimension [16]. Hassenzahl [16] further divides the hedonic into two sub-dimensions of identification and stimulation while the pragmatic/instrumental dimension relates to usability and usefulness.

Software Engineering. The core of software development is writing program code that constructs the running software; this demands the ability to concentrate and work alone for many hours [17]. Moreover, programming work requires a logical mind and the ability to pay attention to details [17]. Developers need to be analytical, capable of making decisions, independent, creative, tenacious, and be able to tolerate stress [18]. Although programmers tend to be introverted, sensing, and thinking [17], social skills are crucial in their work: developers' interpersonal and communication skills have been considered even more important than their technical skills for project success [19]. Due to the complex nature of software development, specialized tools are used. One of the most general tools that are used to create programs is an IDE, which offers numerous features. A sophisticated IDE, extended with plugins, may manage dependencies among different packages and modules, control complex builds, and provide linking to other tools such as requirements management or test environment. Thus, the IDE acts as an interface between the developer and the computing infrastructure that is needed for creating, configuring, and managing complex applications as well as their source code and build environment.

IDEs have two main productive goals: increasing developer speed and reducing the number of errors made by developers [1]. As IDEs are a main tool in software development, they also play a major role in making developers productive and comfortable in their work. Moreover, IDEs are a key aspect in developer experience (DX), a concept that encompasses developer's perceptions of their work and phenomena related to it such as cognitive, motivational, affective, and social aspects. For example, memory overload is a limiting factor for programmers, especially for beginners who have not yet developed strategies to relieve it [20]. Modern development environments provide many aids to programmers, but the same challenges are still present. Cognitive factors also concern larger structures in software development, such as methods and processes, but research on this aspect is scarce.

Developer Experience and Motivation. The concept of DX aims to provide an intuitive abstraction of the huge variety and quantity of human factors that influence developers and the outcomes of SE [7]. While UX considers the context of use of a system, DX considers the context of software development, including aspects beyond software tools, such as development processes, modeling methods, and other means of structuring SE tasks. Some of these aspects are embedded in tools such as IDEs while others are part of organizational practices. The software development activity and environment differ in significant ways from other information-intensive activities and environments. For example, software development requires a nested understanding: developers use software to build further software that is to be used by users to accomplish their particular tasks. Also, developers frequently configure and extend their tools, in effect continuously developing both the development environment and the end product at the same time.

Developer motivation is as another important factor in SE. The majority of studies on motivation in SE report that developers are distinct from other occupational groups with respect to motivation [3]. "The work itself" is the most commonly cited motivator, but there is a lack of detail regarding what aspects of the work is motivating, how motivational processes occur, and the outcomes of motivating developers [3, 21]. Investigations also show the importance of considering affective aspects of SE. The presence and variation of developers' emotions over time has been documented [22]. Programming is influenced by mood [4], and happiness has been found to have productivity benefits [2]. This underlines the importance of considering affective aspects both for purposes of well-being and outcomes.

3 Method

Our research goal is to increase understanding of DX. We aim to clarify how flow, IM, and UX are intertwined in software development. This will enable improvement of development tools to better support developers' ability to experience flow in their work and to enhance developers' IM towards their work. Our hypothesis is that these factors make developers' work more enjoyable and increases their productivity.

In this paper we address the following research questions:

1. Can we predict the developers' overall UX with the IDE and its ability to fulfill their needs from their sense of flow in their work and their IM?
2. Can we predict the developers' overall UX with the IDE and its ability to fulfill their needs from their assessment of the practical, hedonic, and general quality of the IDE?
3. What kind of impact does perceived choice have on developers' assessments?
4. How do developers describe the best qualities of the IDE and those that need improvement in relation to UX vocabulary?

We conducted a survey measuring developers' self-reported experiences of software development activities when using Qt Creator, a cross-platform IDE including a code editor, graphical user interface editor, compiler, visual debugger, and version control. Our survey consisted of the following three scales: (1) the Short Dispositional Flow State Scale (SDFS-2) [8] used in its entirety, (2) parts of the Intrinsic Motivation Inventory (IMI) [9] including questions related to interest/enjoyment, perceived competence, effort/importance, and perceived choice, and (3) a UX scale consisting of the short version of the AttrakDiff-2 (SAD-2) [10] used in its entirety and our own Developer Experience Scale (DEXI). The scales, except DEXI, were selected because they are widely used and validated. They are also short enough to be combined in a single survey. DEXI was created to address characteristics of software development.

Respondents also rated the overall UX (OUX) of the IDE and its ability to fulfill their needs (NFS) as follows: (1) OUX: "How would you rate the overall user experience of Qt Creator?" (from 1 = bad to 7 = good). (2) NFS: "How well does Qt Creator respond to your needs?" (ranging from 1 = not at all to 7 = completely). We also asked respondents to describe the qualities of the IDE on two open-ended questions: (1) "In your opinion, what are the best qualities of Qt Creator?" and (2) "How could Qt Creator better support your development work?". Finally, we collected demographic information, including the country they were based in, age, experience of software development (in years), experience of using Qt Creator, developer role, size of the organization they are working for, their operating system and target platforms, and used license type of Qt Creator.

Dispositional Flow State Scale (SDFS-2). We measured the frequency with which developers experience different dimensions of flow during software development activities with Qt Creator using the Short Dispositional Flow State Scale (SDFS-2) [8], with Likert items (from 1 = never to 7 = always). The SDFS-2 measures nine dimensions of flow, each with one item (Table 1). In addition to the SDFS-2 items, an additional item measured the experience of frustration: "I feel frustrated".

Intrinsic Motivation Inventory (IMI). Since the original IMI is long and repetitive, we used a shortened version as recommended [23] (Table 2) with selected items from the following IMI subscales: interest/enjoyment (the actual self-report measure of IM), perceived competence, effort/importance, and perceived choice. Framing of the question and assessment scale was according to the IMI. Thus, the question was as follows: "*For each of the following statements, please indicate how true it is for you, using the following scale*" (from 1 = not at all true to 7 = very true).

Table 1. SDFS-2 scale. Dimensions of state of flow and related survey items [8]

Flow dimensions	SDFS-2 item
Challenge-skill balance	I feel I am competent enough to meet the high demands of the situation
Action awareness	I do things spontaneously and automatically without having to think
Clear goals	I have a strong sense of what I want to do
Unambiguous feedback	I have a good idea while I am performing about how well I am doing
Concentration on task	I am completely focused on the task at hand
Sense of control	I have a feeling of total control
Loss of self-consciousness	I am not worried about what others may be thinking of me
Transformation of time	The way time passes seems to be different from normal
Autotelic experience	The experience is extremely rewarding

Table 2. Selected subscales and survey items of IMI [9]

Subscale	Survey item
Interest/enjoyment	I enjoy software development work very much
	I think software development is a boring activity
	I enjoy using Qt Creator very much
Perceived competence	I am satisfied with my performance at software development
	I am pretty skilled in software development
	I am pretty skilled in using Qt Creator
Effort/Importance	It is important to me to do well in software development
Perceived choice	I use Qt Creator because I have no choice

UX Scales. We used the short version of AttrakDiff-2 (SAD-2) [10]. It contains four items (word-pairs) for both practical (PQ) and hedonic quality (HQ) of UX, and one each for measuring goodness and beauty (general UX quality, GQ). In addition, we formed our own DEXI scale for measuring additional aspects of UX. We selected DEXI items from the following sources: AttrakDiff [16], the dataset of a meta-study of often used UX items [24], and concepts that have been used to describe DX [7]. We used the structure and wording of AttrakDiff in DEXI. We aimed at construct a scale that would be relevant to software development. We selected 5 items (PQ1– PQ5) measuring pragmatic UX quality (difficult/easy to learn; inflexible/flexible; limited/extensive; uninformative/informative; inefficient/efficient) and 6 items (HQ1–HQ6) measuring hedonic (non-utilitarian) quality (discouraging/motivating; suppresses/promotes creativity; decreases/increases respect; unenjoyable/enjoyable; separates me from others/brings me closer to others; uninvolving/engaging). One item (GQ-1) measured general quality (not recommendable/recommendable).

Procedure. A web survey was organized with the Qt Company, the provider of Qt Creator. The survey had a front page presenting informed consent statements adopted from World Health Organization's template for qualitative studies [25]. We instructed only those who had been using the IDE to respond, and to respond only once. A global online developer community and Twitter were used to target users of the IDE. Although the survey was distributed globally, the main interest of the IDE provider was in Middle European market. The survey was available for the respondents for four weeks. Participants' median completion time was 9 min (M = 17, SD = 31).

Participants. Participants were developers using Qt Creator in their work. In total, 57 developers responded from 25 different countries. Respondents' countries were: France: 8; Germany: 7; Italy: 5; Norway: 4; Austria, Australia, Finland, Switzerland, and United States: 3; Russia and Sweden: 2; Algeria, Andorra, Bulgaria, Brazil, Belarus, Czech Republic, Denmark, Indonesia, India, Iran, Poland, Slovenia, Ukraine, and United Kingdom: 1. The average age of respondents was 35 years (SD: 10). Respondents had on average 8 years (SD: 5) of working experience in software development. 86.0 % of respondents had been using Qt Creator for over a year, 12.3 % for over a month but less than a year, and 1.8 % had used it several times. 42.1 % of the respondents considered themselves as front-end developers, 21.1 % as back-end developers, 19.3 % as architects, and 17.5 % considered themselves as other types including either a combination of these roles, or hobbyist, teacher, or researcher. Considering the size of organization where they worked, 22.8 % were individual developers, 19.3 % worked for micro businesses (employing ten people or less), 19.3 % worked for small companies (over ten but less than hundred employees), 24.6 % worked for middle-sized companies (100–1000 employees), and 14.0 % worked for large enterprises employing more than 1000 people. Approximately half the respondents (49.1 %) used Linux as their primary development platform, while 28.1 % used MS Windows and 21.1 % OS X. Most of the respondents (91.2 %) developed desktop software, 40.3 % developed mobile software, and 25.6 % developed embedded software (multiple choices were possible on this question). Free software licenses were used by 75.4 % of respondents, while the rest (24.6 %) used commercial licenses. Demographic variables were not significant predictors of any of the studied variables.

4 Results

Predicting Overall UX and Needs Assessment from Sense of Flow and Intrinsic Motivation. Four multiple linear regressions investigated whether the items of the measures of flow (SDSF-2) and intrinsic motivation (IMI) significantly predicted the respondents' ratings of overall UX (OUX) with the IDE and its ability to meet their needs (NFS).

OUX could be predicted significantly from the SDSF-2 scale (see Table 3). However, only one of the SDSF-2 items was a significant individual predictor, the autotelic experience item, ("the experience is extremely rewarding"). OUX could also be predicted from the IMI scale with two of the items being significant individual predictors, both interest/enjoyment items: "I enjoy software development work very much" and "I enjoy using Qt Creator very much".

Table 3. Survey scales/items that significantly predicted OUX and NFS scores. Legend: "UX scales" refers to SAD-2 and DEXI together.

Overall UX (OUX)	Needs Assessment (NFS)
SDFS-2 (F = 3.44, df = 10, p < 0.005)	**SDFS-2 (F = 4.48, df = 10, 46, p < 0.001)**
The experience is extremely rewarding (t = 2.85, p < 0.01)	The experience is extremely rewarding (t = 2.27, p < 0.05)
	I have a feeling of total control (t = 2.80, p < 0.01)
IMI (F = 6.72, df = 8, 48, p < 0.001)	**IMI (F = 9.04, df = 7, 49, p < 0.001)**
I enjoy software development work very much (t = 2.29, p < 0.05)	I think software development work is a boring activity (t = 2.26, p < 0.05)
I enjoy using Qt Creator very much (t = 5.01, p < 0.001)	I enjoy using Qt Creator very much (t = 5.62, p < 0.001)
UX scales (F = 9.80, df = 3, p < 0.001)	**UX scales (F = 6.24, df = 3, p < .01)**
General quality (GQ) (t = .129, n.s.)	General quality (GQ) (t = .48, n.s.)
Hedonic quality (HQ) (t = 2.00, p = 0.05)	Hedonic quality (HQ) (t = .16, n.s.)
Practical quality (PQ) (t = .556, n.s.)	Practical quality (PQ) (t = 1.49, n.s.)

Need fulfillment (NFS) could also be predicted from the SDSF-2. Two individual items were significant individual predictors: the autotelic experience item ("the experience is extremely rewarding") and the sense of control item ("I have a feeling of total control. NFS could also be predicted from the IMI scale. Two items were significant predictors: "I think software development work is a boring activity" and "I enjoy using Qt Creator very much".

Predicting Overall UX and Needs Assessment from Practical, Hedonic, and General UX Qualities. When comparing the assessments of quality types, general quality had the highest mean assessment score while the hedonic had the lowest. The difference is statistically significant: The null hypothesis that "the median difference between measurements of PQ, GQ, and HQ, pairwise, is zero" was rejected as follows: between measurements of practical and general quality Z = −3.333, p < .01. between measurements of hedonic and practical quality Z = −4.171, p < .001; between hedonic and general quality Z = −5.590, p < .001. Thus, the GQ assessment was significantly higher than assessment of PQ and HQ.

The overall UX rating, OUX, could be predicted significantly from PQ, GQ, and HQ together (see Table 3). However, only HQ was on the borderline of being a significant predictor.

NFS could be predicted significantly from PQ, GQ, and HQ together (see Table 3). However, none of the quality types were significant predictors.

Perceived Choice. The use of work-related tools can be mandatory since often the employer is the one who selects the tools to be used [24]. We measured perceived choice of use with the IMI scale question "I use Qt Creator because I have no choice". It had significant negative correlation with both OUX and NFS (r = −.380, and r = −.370, respectively, p < .01 for both). Thus, developers who perceived high level of choice in use of the IDE assessed OUX and NFS higher than developers who perceived their use of the IDE as mandatory. In addition, developers with low perceived choice enjoyed using the IDE less; there was a moderate negative correlation between perceived choice and the IMI item "I enjoy using Qt Creator very much" ($r = -.534$, $p < .001$). Enjoyment on the IMI scale measures motivation and thus we can conclude that developers with lower perceived choice were less motivated towards using the IDE compared to those with high perceived choice. Developers with low perceived choice also felt frustrated more often ($r = .519$, $p < .001$). Finally, there was a significant negative correlation between the perceived choice and challenge-skill balance in using the IDE ($r = -.296$, $p < .05$).

Since developers with low perceived choice enjoyed using the IDE less than others, we also address here correlations between the motivation towards using the IDE ("I enjoy using Qt Creator very much") and other measures. There was a significant correlation between motivation towards using the IDE and both NFS and OUX ratings ($r = .682$, and $r = .639$, respectively, $p < 0.001$ for both). On the SDFS-2 items, developers who enjoyed using the IDE also experienced a significantly higher sense of control ($r = .548$, $p < .001$) and considered the experience significantly more rewarding ($r = .539$, $p < .001$). They also felt frustration significantly less ($r = -.498$, $p < .001$). In addition, developers who enjoyed using the IDE considered themselves significantly more skilled in using the tool ($r = .400$, $p < .01$).

Best Qualities of the IDE and Opportunities for Improvement. Respondents considered efficiency, flexibility, informativeness and intuitiveness the best qualities of Qt Creator and flexibility, informativeness, and reliability required improvement the most (see Fig. 1) [26]. Thus, although the IDE was considered both flexible and informative, these were also areas that required improvement the most. It might indicate that these concepts are focal for an IDE. In contrast, developers considered efficiency as one of the best qualities most often (38 % of respondents mentioned it), and it rarely was considered as subject for improvement. However, reliability was rarely mentioned as good quality, whereas 36 % of the respondents considered Qt Creator should be more reliable, mostly in terms of stability and faultlessness.

The category of efficiency includes mainly items related to the IDE being fast and efficient to use. Flexibility is the ability of an IDE to respond to developers' needs such as being customizable, scalable, extensive, compatible, or complete. Informativeness was most often related to the presentation of code and text editors, for instance, to intelligent code completion and text highlighting. It was also related to the quality and presentation of information in different built-in tools such as the debugger. Reliability addresses the robustness, stability, faultlessness, and recoverability of the IDE. Intuitiveness is related to the IDE being simple, intuitive, understandable, intelligent, and sensible. Clarity includes such items as clean, unbloated, uncluttered, light, and well-structured. Value was described with the following words: good, great, awesome, best, and free. Aesthetic design was related to the screen layout and the outlook and visual design of the IDE. Empowerment means the ability of the IDE to support developers' work and respect the variety of tasks they have. Finally, approachability was mentioned as creating friendly atmosphere and making the developer to feel at home.

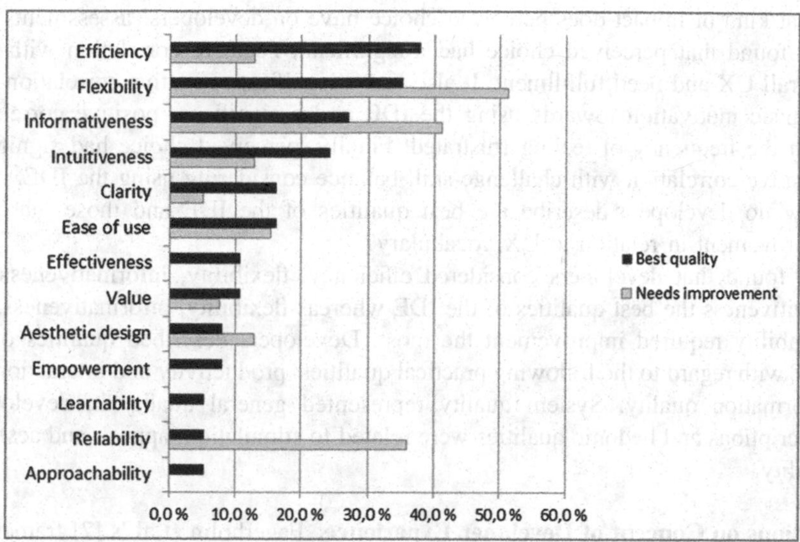

Fig. 1. Best qualities of Qt Creator and those that need improvement as reported by respondents. Percentage of respondents (N = 45) per category.

Of the UX qualities identified efficiency, effectiveness and learnability are productivity factors. Ease of use and intuitiveness relate to interaction quality whereas informativeness and reliability relate to information and system quality, respectively. Empowerment, approachability, and aesthetic design are hedonic qualities related to stimulation, appeal and aesthetic quality, respectively [16].

5 Discussion

Based on the responses of 57 developers from 25 countries, who responded to the survey, research questions are answered as follows:

1. Can we predict the developers' overall UX with the IDE and its ability to fulfill their needs from their sense of flow in their work and their intrinsic motivation?
   We found that autotelic experience and intrinsic motivation (IM) towards both software development and the IDE were significant predictors of developers' overall UX. Need fulfillment could be predicted from the aforementioned autotelic experience item and sense of control and from intrinsic motivation.
2. Can we predict the developers' overall UX with the IDE and its ability to fulfill their needs from their assessment of the practical, hedonic, and general quality of the IDE?
   We found that practical, hedonic, and general quality together were significant predictors of overall UX. None of the qualities alone significantly predicted overall UX. However, hedonic quality was on the borderline of being a significant predictor ($p = .05$). Practical, hedonic, and general quality together were also significant predictors of need fulfillment. However, none of the qualities alone was a significant predictor of need fulfillment.

3. What kind of impact does perceived choice have on developers' assessments?
   We found that perceived choice had a significant negative correlation with both overall UX and need fulfillment. It also had a significant negative correlation with intrinsic motivation towards using the IDE and a significant positive correlation with the frequency of feeling frustrated. Finally, perceived choice had significant negative correlation with challenge-skill balance considering using the IDE.
4. How do developers describe the best qualities of the IDE and those that need improvement in relation to UX vocabulary?
   We found that developers considered efficiency, flexibility, informativeness and intuitiveness the best qualities of the IDE whereas flexibility, informativeness, and reliability required improvement the most. Developers described qualities of the IDE with regard to the following practical qualities: productivity and interaction and information quality. System quality represented general quality in developers' descriptions and hedonic qualities were related to stimulation, appeal, and aesthetic quality.

Reflections on Concept of Developer Experience. Fagerholm et al.'s [7] framework of DX addresses the concept in terms of factors related to the perception of development infrastructure, feelings towards work, and the value of the developer's contribution. They relate cognition to the perception of infrastructure, affect with feelings towards the work, and intention (conation) with the value of contribution. In our study, the IDE itself represents the development infrastructure and cognition, affect and intention were addressed with regard to it. Our results indicate that developers also address the infrastructure via intention and affect. Their IM was towards both the use of the IDE and the development work. Some developers described the best qualities of the IDE with affection. In addition, the overall UX assessment of developers seemed to be affected more by the hedonic than pragmatic quality of the IDE since the mean value of the hedonic aspect of UX (HQ) was on the borderline of being a significant predictor of overall UX ($p = 0.05$) whereas the overall UX could not be predicted from the practical or general quality. Thus, our results suggest that Fagerholm et al. over emphasized the cognitive approach of developers towards the development infrastructure. Moreover, the developers' intrinsic motivation also seems to focus on using the IDE while Fagerholm et al. associate it with the developer's contribution. However, the IDE is used to create a contribution and thus our study cannot separate motivation towards development work itself and motivation towards the software under development.

Threats to Validity. We studied only one IDE and thus some of our results might be specific to that. We also had a relatively limited number of respondents (57). In the future, other IDEs and development work in general should be studied. We did not control multiple answering of the questionnaire but asked developers to respond only once. However, we consider the likelihood of multiple answering small. Since the invitation to participate was sent to an online developer community and Twitter, only developers who use those channels could participate, thus limiting the population of developers we sampled from. However, we found no significant difference between developers who were recruited via the online community and those contacted via Twitter. In addition, demographic variables were not significant predictors of any of the studied variables.

6 Conclusions

We have presented results of software developers' sense of flow, their intrinsic motivation (IM) and developer experience (DX) in the context of software engineering. We conducted a survey study on developers using Qt Creator as their development environment. We aimed to clarify how flow, IM, and UX are intertwined in software development. Our final goal is the improvement of development tools to better support developers' ability to experience flow – deep, focused, rewarding concentration in their work – and to enhance developers' IM towards their work. Our hypothesis was that these factors make developers' work more enjoyable and increase their productivity. Our results suggest that IM and sense of flow are significant predictors of DX. IM towards both development work itself and using the IDE significantly predicted DX. Moreover, we found perceived choice of use a significant predictor of both developers' assessment of UX and need fulfillment. Perceived choice also affects developers' IM towards using the IDE and their sense of frustration during development tasks. Thus, developers' motivation is affected both by tool selection and qualities of development tools. Further studies are needed to address their impact on developers' productivity.

Our work examined DX mainly in relation to the key development tool, the IDE. Considering the central role of the IDE in developers' daily activities, it can be expected that results considering developers' experiences while using the IDE play a prominent role also for DX in general. In relation to the concept of DX, our paper contributes to increased understanding of its key factors and its relation to UX, IM, and the flow state experience.

References

1. Muşlu, K., Brun, Y., Holmes, R., Ernst, M.D., Notkin, D.: Speculative analysis of integrated development environment recommendations. ACM SIGPLAN Not. **47**(10), 669–682 (2012)
2. Graziotin, D., Wang, X., Abrahamsson, P.: Happy software developers solve problems better: psychological measurements in empirical software engineering. PeerJ **2**(1), e289 (2014)
3. Beecham, S., Baddoo, N., Hall, T., Robinson, H., Sharp, H.: Motivation in software engineering: A systematic literature review. IST **50**, 860–878 (2008)
4. Khan, I.A., Brinkman, W.-P., Hierons, R.M.: Do moods affect programmers' debug performance? Cogn. Technol. Work **13**(4), 245–258 (2011)
5. Graziotin, D., Wang, X., Abrahamsson, P.: Software developers, moods, emotions, and performance. IEEE Softw. **31**(4), 24–27 (2014)
6. Hassenzahl, M., Tractinsky, N.: User experience - A research agenda. BIT **25**(2), 91–97 (2006)
7. Fagerholm, F., Münch, J.: Developer experience: Concept and definition. In: Proceedings of the International Conference on Software and System Process, pp. 73–77. IEEE Press (2012)
8. Jackson, S.A., Martin, A.J., Eklund, R.C.: Long and short measures of flow: the construct validity of the FSS-2, DFS-2, and new brief counterparts. JSEP **30**(5), 561 (2008)
9. Ryan, R.M.: Control and information in the intrapersonal sphere: An extension of cognitive evaluation theory. J. Pers. Soci. Psychol. **43**, 450–461 (1982)
10. Hassenzahl, M., Diefenbach, S., Göritz, A.: Needs, affect, and interactive products–Facets of user experience. Interact. Comput. **22**(5), 353–362 (2010)
11. Deci, E., Ryan, R.M.: Self-determination theory. Handbook of theories of social psychology. SAGE, Los Angeles (2012). ISBN 9780857029607
12. Csikszentmihalyi, M.: Flow: The psychology of optimal experience, vol. 41. HarperPerennial, New York (1991)
13. Csikszentmihalyi, M., LeFevre, J.: Optimal experience in work and leisure. J. Pers. Soc. Psychol. **56**(5), 815–822 (1989)
14. Csikszentmihalyi, M., Abuhamdeh, S., Nakamura, J.: Flow. In: Elliot, A. (ed.) Handbook of Competence and Motivation, pp. 598–698. The Guilford Press, New York (2005)
15. Law, E.L.-C., Roto, V., Hassenzahl, M., Vermeeren, A.P.O.S., Kort, J.: Understanding, scoping and defining user experience: a survey approach. In: Proceedings SIGCHI Conference on Human Factors in Computing Systems (CHI 2009), pp. 719–728. ACM (2009)
16. Hassenzahl, M.: The interplay of beauty, goodness and usability in interactive products. Proc. HCI Lawrence Erlbaum Associates **19**(4), 319–349 (2004)
17. Capretz, L.F., Ahmed, F.: Making sense of software development and personality types. IT Prof. **12**(1), 6–13 (2010)
18. Acuna, S.T., Juristo, N., Moreno, A.M.: Emphasizing human capabilities in software development. Softw. IEEE **23**(2), 94–101 (2006)
19. Lee, D., Trauth, E., Farwell, D.: Critical skills and knowledge requirements of IS professionals: a joint academic/industry investigation. MIS Q. **19**(3), 313–340 (1995)
20. Anderson, J.R., Jeffries, R.: Novice LISP Errors: Undetected losses of information from working memory. Hum. Comput. Interact. **1**, 107–131 (1985)
21. Franca, A.C.C., Gouveia, T.B., Santos, P.C.F., Santana, C.A., da Silva, F.Q.B.: Motivation in software engineering: A systematic review update. In: Proceedings Evaluation and Assessment in Software Engineering (EASE), pp. 154–163 (2011)

22. Shaw, T.: The emotions of systems developers: an empirical study of affective events theory. In: Proceedings Computer Personnel Research: Careers, Culture, and Ethics in a Networked Environment, SIGMIS CPR 2004, pp. 124–126. ACM (2004)
23. McAuley, E., Duncan, T., Tammen, V.V.: Psychometric properties of the intrinsic motivation inventory in a competitive sport setting: a confirmatory factor analysis. Res. Q. Exerc. Sport **60**, 48–58 (1989)
24. Sundberg, H.-R.: The importance of user experience related factors in new product development – Comparing the views of designers and users of industrial products. In: 23rd Nordic Academy of Management Conference, 12-14 August 2015, Copenhagen, Denmark (2015)
25. World Health Organization, Informed consent form template for qualitative studies. http://www.who.int/rpc/research_ethics/informed_consent/enTools
26. Kuusinen, K.: Software developers as users: Developer experience of a cross-platform integrated development environment. In: Product-Focused Software Process Improvement (PROFES 2015), pp. 546–552. Springer International Publishing (2015)

Minimum Viable Product or Multiple Facet Product? The Role of MVP in Software Startups

Anh Nguyen Duc(✉) and Pekka Abrahamsson

Department of Computer and Information Science (IDI), NTNU, 7491 Trondheim, Norway
{anhn, pekkaa}@ntnu.no

Abstract. Minimum viable product (MVP) is the main focus of both business and product development activities in software startups. We empirically explored five early stage software startups to understand how MVP are used in early stages. Data was collected from interviews, observation and documents. We looked at the MVP usage from two angles, software prototyping and boundary spanning theory. We found that roles of MVPs in startups were not fully aware by entrepreneurs. Besides supporting validated learning, MVPs are used to facilitate product design, to bridge communication gaps and to facilitate cost-effective product development activities. Entrepreneurs should consider a systematic approach to fully explore the value of MVP, as a multiple facet product (MFP). The work also implies several research directions about prototyping practices and patterns in software startups.

Keywords: Prototype · MVP · MFP · Software startups · Software development · Empirical study · Exploratory case study

1 Introduction

Software industry has witnessed a growing trend of software products developed by software startups, often newly created companies with little operating history aiming at high-growth software products. Different from established companies, startups typically deal with identifying and implementing a product that delivers actual customer value [1]. Recent methodological approaches for startup product development, i.e. Lean startup [3] or new product development processes [2] emphasize the ability to learn about actual problems from early customers and the speed of learning. According to Lean Startup [3], every startup should start with building a Minimum viable product (MVP), and use it to validate their hypotheses about customer needs.

MVPs, defined as products with just enough features to gather validated learning about the products, is a major focus in early stages. It plays an important role not only for a startup team, but also the startup's external stakeholders, such as potential users, investors and mentors. Nowadays, MVP is a key artifact to be shown in a meeting with an investor. There are several different types of MVPs, varied by development efforts, their purposes and stages they often occur [3]. For instance, a landing page, as one

H. Sharp and T. Hall (Eds.): XP 2016, LNBIP 251, pp. 118–130, 2016.
DOI: 10.1007/978-3-319-33515-5_10

MVP, can be quickly created to communicate the product proposals to public. A single feature prototype, as another MVP, might take several months for construction and integrate into final product. Besides, different MVPs might be used to serve the same purpose, for instance, to communicate with investors.

It is little known about how MVPs are used after their creation, from both community of practitioners and researchers. Given the importance of MVPs for early stage startups, we are interested in understanding how the MVP is used in software startups:

"RQ: How are MVPs used in early stage software startups?"

We argued that from an engineering perspective a MVP shares a lot of characteristics with a software prototype. Prototyping has a long history in Software Engineering (SE) research, as an essential part of water fall life cycle [5]. However, in SE research, there is little discussion about prototypes in the context of software startups [6, 7]. In this paper, we discussed about the usage of MVP in the relation to prototype's characteristics. We also argued that MVPs has been used to communicate with external stakeholders, such as investors and early customers. Information System (IS) has a theory to explain about how an artifact was used to communicate among different communities with different expertise [8]. Therefore, we utilized the boundary spanning theory to initiate and to capture the MVP usage.

The paper is organized as follows; firstly we presented backgrounds about MVPs, software prototype and boundary spanning theory (Sect. 2). Then, we described our research approach and case description (Sect. 3). After that, the qualitative findings are presented (Sect. 4). Finally, we discussed the reflections of study, threats to validity (Sect. 5), conclusion and future work (Sect. 6).

2 Background

2.1 Classification of MVPs and Prototypes

Eric Ries initiates the classification of MVP types [3], which are discussed among the community of practitioners, including:

- Explainer video: a short animation that explains what your product does and why users should buy it. The video is often simple, lasts for 30 s to few minutes.
- Landing page: a web page where visitors "*land*" after clicking a link from an e-mail or another type of a campaign. A landing page is used to quickly communicate the startup proposals, to diffuse objections, and to call the visitors to action.
- Wizard of Oz: an user interface that looks like a real working product, but the actual business process is manually carried on. The purpose of this MVP is to demonstrate the complete job done by the product.
- Concierge MVP: a manual service that consists of exactly the same steps users would go through with the product.
- Piecemeal MVP: similar to Wizards of Oz MVP, however, execution of the tasks is done by using existing tools.
- Mockup MVP: such as, paper prototype and wireframe, was representative of product user interface without any functionality.

- Public project proposal: Kickstarter and other crowdsourcing sites allow for users to pre-purchase the product and provide a great way to raise money for initial orders.
- Single feature MVP: a prototype that implements the most important function of the product.
- Rip off MVP: a successful product to get feedback, then pivot in a different direction.

The term "prototype" is also often used in startup context as an interchangeable term with MVP. There are different types of software prototypes often used in early phases of software development, such as throwaway, or rapid prototype, which consumes very little efforts with minimum requirement analysis to build a prototype [9]. Another type of prototype is evolutionary prototype, which bases on building actual minimal functionality in the beginning [9]. Last but not least, incremental prototype refers to building multiple functional prototypes of the various sub systems and then integrating all the available prototypes to form a complete system [9]. In this paper, we use the above categories to differentiate and discuss about different type of MVPs during earl-stage software startups.

2.2 Theory of Boundary Spanning

To explain the roles of MVPs and prototypes, we borrow the theory of boundary spanning across boundaries in software startups. From the view of knowledge management, most innovation happens at the boundaries between specialized pools of knowledge [8, 10, 11]. Three types of knowledge boundary is commonly mentioned in IS literature:

- A syntactic knowledge boundary occurs when there is a lack of a shared syntax and creates the concern that information may not be processed properly across a given boundary [8]. For instance, entrepreneurs use business terms that make developers do not understand.
- A semantic knowledge boundary occurs when a common syntax is present, different interpretations of the common syntax make communication and collaboration difficult [8]. For instance, a designer might think about artistic mindset while a developer think of software architecture when talking about design thinking.
- Pragmatic knowledge boundary occurs when a common interest has to be achieved when participants negotiate with each other on the scope [8], consequences and conflict solutions of knowledge delivery, i.e. developers and entrepreneur do not share common interests, i.e. a clash of interests occurs.

Boundary artifact is used to cross these different types of knowledge boundaries [10]. The theory states that an artifact only helps bridging knowledge boundaries if it qualifies as a boundary object, which is described as an artifact that "*sits in the middle*" of diverse knowledge groups, establishing a "*shared and sharable*" context for distributed problem solving. These artifacts need to be "*both plastic enough to adapt to local needs and constraints of the several parties employing them, yet robust enough to maintain a common identity across sites*" [11].

3 Research Approach

3.1 Study Design and Case Selection

We conducted this study by using a multiple-case study design [12]. As shown in Fig. 1, we adopted a mixed approach of deductive and inductive research. The initial observations about MVP usage were extracted from Case B and abstracted by using classification from software prototyping and theory of boundary spanning. The initial themes were used to guide the analysis of interview transcripts later. The final thematic scheme of significant MVP usage was extended from all five case studies.

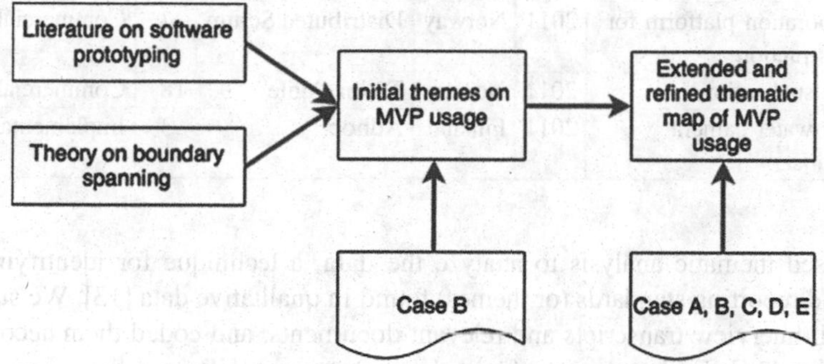

Fig. 1. Research approach

These cases describe startups from the seed-stage to the early growth-stage i.e. from ideas to prototypes and operating products. For concealment the startups are not named in this paper, but are instead referred to as Company A, B, C, D and E, as described in Table 1. The cases are selected by using our industrial network, using three selection criteria: (1) companies have at least three people and first paying customer, (2) companies have at least six months operations, (3) and companies have performed some types of software development. The industry domain varies from retail, marketing to construction. Cases come from Italy, Norway and Finland with company size vary from three to 18 full-time employees. Most cases have been operated mainly by self-funding. Business models include both Business-to-Business (B2B) and Business-to-Customer (B2C). All of the investigated startups were founded by experts in software development.

3.2 Data Collection and Analysis

Methodological triangulation in data collection is implemented by using documents, interviews and observation. Business documents, such as business model canvases and full description of business plan was exposed to the research team as a preliminary step prepared for interviews. Interview is our primary source of information. In most of the cases, we conducted multiple interviews with their CEOs, CTOs and co-founders. The interviewees were asked questions about (1) realization of business idea (2) pivot practices (3) product design and development. Observation is useful to understand how

MVPs and prototypes were implemented and used in the working environment. In Case B, the author participated in five weekly meetings. In Case A, the CEO has provided a narrative description of the startup process and observations from that.

Table 1. Startup case demographic

Id	Product	Year	Loc.	Dev. approach	# Ppl.	Latest Stage
A	Online photo marketplace	2012	Italy	Lean startup, Tailor Agile	6	Implementation
B	Marketplace for food hub	2015	Norway	Adhoc	3	Conceptualization
C	Collaboration platform for construction	2011	Norway	Distributed Scrum	4	Commercialization
D	Sale visualization	2011	Norway	Tailor Agile	18	Commercialization
E	Under water camera product	2011	Finland	Adhoc	3	Implementation

We used thematic analysis to analyze the data, a technique for identifying, analyzing, and reporting standards (or themes) found in qualitative data [13]. We started by reading all interview transcripts and relevant documents, and coded them according to open coding [14]. Each segment of text that expresses MVPs and the usage of these MVPs or prototypes were labeled with an appropriate code. The MVPs were later classified into the MVP types, prototype types and boundary spanning types, if relevance. The emerged MVP usages were compared across interviews and finally merged into a final thematic map.

4 Result

4.1 Types of MVPs

Table 2 summarizes different types of MVP used in our cases. According to the data, software startups adopted several types of MVPs in early stages. Landing page were used by all cases, often during the product development or close to the product launch. Different types of mockups were used extensively during early stages. For example, Case B used a wireframe tool called JustInMind, as the major tasks in the beginning of their project. In Case C, paper prototypes were used during most of all customer meeting. Except Case C, all of our cases started early with developing the first most important feature of their product. Other types of MVPs, such as Concierge MVP, Wizard of Oz and Picemeal MVP were also used in some cases. In the next sections, we described three main roles of these MVPs, which are design artifact, boundary spanning object and reusable artifact.

Table 2. Prototyping approaches in our cases

	Cases				
	A	B	C	D	E
Types of prototype					
Landing page	X	X	X	X	X
Mockup MVP	X	X	X	X	X
Single feature MVP	X	X		X	X
Concierge MVP				X	
Explainer video			X		
Wizard of Oz		X			
Piecemeal MVP			X		

4.2 MVP as a Design Artifact

Table 3 describes the themes that were grounded from interviews, As a design artifact, a MVP facilitates the visualization of ideas, the reflection on architectural design and the innovation process.

Table 3. Data grounded themes on prototype usage

	Companies				
	A	B	C	D	E
MVP as a design artifact					
Visualizing design idea	X	X	X	X	X
Reflection on architectural design		X	X		X
Facilitation of creativity		X		X	
Clarifying mismatches on user expectation	X	X			X
MVP as a boundary spanning artifact					
Bridge between Business mind vs. Technical mind	X	X			X
Bridge between Entrepreneur team vs. End user		X	X		
Bridge between Entrepreneur team vs. Investors			X	X	X
MVP as a reusable artifact					
Documentation	X	X	X		
Growth hacking mechanism		X		X	
Bootstrapping tool	X	X	X	X	X

Visualizing Design Idea: As a rapid prototype, MVP is a mean to travel from idea to real product. In Case B, paper-based UI prototypes were used during brainstorming sections when the team virtually meets. The CEO mentioned, "*Each of us has our own design version of [Product name], when [CTO name] describes his idea about sharing meals among students ... We start sketching the workflow and the app UI right away ...*".

The practice is also found in Case C and D, for example, "*During the design meeting, the team worked together in the a collaborative mockup prototyping tool. The team members continued giving inputs to refine the prototype.*", mentioned by the CEO of Company C.

Initial ideas and prototypes can vary, hence, cross-check during prototyping phase is often necessary. For non-technical founders, visualizing their thoughts is important to provide inputs for technical design: "*I have many great ideas, but I have no idea if they can be implemented. Building a prototype at least allows me and also others in my team to ask the right questions... Visions and theory are notoriously hard to implement. A prototype has to be real enough to be convincing, without looking like science fiction.*" (CEO of Company C).

Reflection on Architectural Design: MVP prototyping process is where product design is reflected and revised. In Case B, mockup MVPs were created by the CEO to capture the idealization phase. Meanwhile, the architecture of a product was initiated by the CTO. The mockup MVP and architectural design was started at the same time and gradually became two separate tasks that reflect business requirements and technical insights. After talking to early customers, the MVP was updated according to new requirements. Consequently, the MVP became a batch of new inputs for the final product architecture: "*From looking at the MVP you can see that the options for taken-away or eat-with-host is not there in our workflow. I will update it in the next meeting ...*" (CTO of Company B). It is also similarly mentioned in Case E, while the CTO reflected on how they had changed the code structure based on early feedback from early stage working prototypes: "*Refactoring is not too big an issue compared to benefits of early releases...*" (CTO of Company E).

Facilitation of Creativity: MVP, as a rapid prototype, is more important than idealization phase, as it gives the balance between realistic and futuristic design. In Case B, the process of finalizing a product idea has a typical path of a new product development process [2]. Several ideas were discussed from the beginning, such as mood tracking, event scheduling, e-receipt and food sharing. After many internal discussions, the focus is to create a platform that facilitates gathering with friends by sharing food. Diverged from theory, idea screening and concept testing was not really distinguished and occurs iteratively in Case B. As ideas could come from all team members, to illustrate a given concept, the CTO created a small prototype to convince other team member. From experience of a serial entrepreneur, making a concrete visualization of an idea will make his/herself and other team member easier to evaluate the innovative characteristics of the product: "*When initiating in my mind, the idea sounds great. When putting it into paper, it looks similar to existing products that I know.*" (CEO of Company D).

Realize Prototype-User Expectation Mismatch: MVP is also appeared as a part of Lean startup approach to adjust the problem-solution fit. Some MVP, i.e. single feature MVP is the latest point in time where disagreement, misalignment and different perspectives are harmonized for the sake of the project success. For example, in Company E, the CEO mentioned: "*Real-life use cases give always nasty surprises compared to the lab environment. In my case, river-side installations in our case are fairly challenging. The deployed version gives much lesson to learn*".

4.3 MVP as a Boundary-Spanning Object

The interview data revealed that MVPs facilitate bridging knowledge gap between the entrepreneur team and external stakeholders, i.e. customers, mentor, vendor and investor.

Bridge between Business mind vs. Technical mind: MVP is used to communicate about technical detail and business idea, which often is the case of early stage startups. In Company B, a syntactic boundary occurred during an early stage of team formation by a lack of the consistent use of technical terms. A mockup MVP was used to facilitate common language: "*She is very sharp about business and finance stuffs, but it takes a long discussion to explain her about the importance of having flexible product design ...*" (CTO of Company B). The gap also occurs in case the product is technically complicated, as described in Company E. Technical details was too much to verbally explain in our interview, which can lead to a threat of synaptic knowledge gaps. The CTO decided to use a paper architectural diagram to hide some of the technical details, but still convey the product ideas and good level of technology. In Company A, we found a quote presenting a semantic knowledge boundary between the CEO and a developer: "*I asked the guy (developer) to create a registration page and he has done a complicated page with all the detail ... I only need a very simple login function ...*" The CEO mentioned that if a paper description was given, the mis-interpretation might not be there.

Bridge between Entrepreneur team vs. End users: As mentioned in [3], MVP is used to validate if the entrepreneur's ideas are the same with end user's expectation. In Company B, the idea was to develop a platform for sharing food and food-based social gathering. Presenting the ideas to people without showing a MVP was quite difficult: "*We have done interviews with some friends ... by explaining key concepts like cuisine, Airbnb of food, ... which is not effective*" (CEO of Company B). Rapid prototypes, such as landing page and explainer video were proposed to communicate to a large amount of audiences: "*As a suggestion for the next entrepreneurs, one things we should do from the beginning is to create a landing page. It is always difficult to follow up after interviews if you do not have a link for them*" (CTO of Company B).

In Company C, the product serves for construction tenants, the CEO had stayed in customer organization for a period to understand gaps in the current work culture and process. At the beginning, without a MVP, the CEO had a hard time to convince customers about the benefits of her product. Syntactic knowledge gap was the barrier when the CEO needed to learn about their language. The one-feature MVP was used to show practical use of her solution: "*We work with a customer organization, learn how they have worked with the current solutions and describe our proposal via the prototype. It is hard for them to realize the benefit without concrete examples...*" (CEO of Company C).

Bridge between Entrepreneur team vs. Investors: knowledge gaps were observed not only within internal members, but also between entrepreneur teams and external stakeholders, such as vendor and investors. MVPs were used in Case E to support communication and negotiation beyond the team boundary: "*A three-dimensional* *prototype is always better than just a documented specification when negotiating contracts for manufacturing, support, and marketing. As a startup, you need all the leverage you can get" (CTO company E).* In Company C, MVPs were used to reduce misunderstanding between entrepreneur team and outsourcing vendor. The CEO of Company C mentioned that mockup MVP is the major mean to communicate with the development team in India: "*I can't seat here and write about hundred page features and that not sure everyone understands.*"

Observations from investor pitches in Company B suggest that MVP is always recommended in any pitches and be a part of evaluation criteria. This is also mentioned by CEO of Company D: "*It is important to show investors that you are committed, and past the idea stage. Without a prototype, most professional investors won't take you seriously.*" While most of investors have certain knowledge about technology and the domain, the threat can be eliminated is the pragmatic knowledge gap. The presentation can be more interesting with demonstration, and attracting interest of investors.

4.4 MVP as a Reusable Artifact

Aligned with bootstrapping approaches of many software startups, MVPs need to be useful in many purposes. Even for a throw-away prototype, it can be used later in the startup processes for other purposes.

Documentation: MVP is a way to document project progress and technical documents. In Company B, a wireframe is implemented using JustInMind, with concepts of layers, reusable objects and screen scenarios. The tool also provides a function to generating html versions with textual descriptions. In Company C, single feature MVP is made in a self-explained and changeable manner. It is also included architectural decisions and instruction for further extension. Besides, each prototype is an important milestone marker to quickly keep track on pivoting: *"it doesn't matter how certain you are about your solution; it probably will take several changes soon. It's much easier to pivot the pre-production prototype than to dispose of unsellable inventory... We can later understand why we have changed from that prototype.*"

Growth Hacking Exploration: Prototyping is the phase where growth hacking can be experienced. Growth hacking techniques help to increase the amount of users, often require the knowledge about both marketing and software development. In Company B, one of the early discussions was on what type of MVPs should be used in the current stage. After consulting with mentors, the team decided to use a mockup MVP that is hosted in a public server for having better reach: *"We decided to use a mockup MVP, it is hosted in Google web server. The link was attached to our online questionnaire so we can reach more people than going to each individual interview"*. In Company D, video was used in early stage to explain the concepts to large amount of customers without going into detail of sale and marketing terms. When the first one-feature MVP is available, it is freely offered to some organizations as beta testing.

Bootstrapping Mechanism: MVP is an economical approach of having a product, which is demonstrable to investors and early customers. In Company E, both software and hardware technology is needed in the product. They adopted multiple iterations to gradually improve quality and performance of the product. It is mentioned that prototype reduces cost of final product development: "*One purpose of the long prototyping process is that we can better learn about the technology. Once technical uncertainties are clear, we can start again much faster with a clean product.*" (CTO of Company C).

For startup generally, time means wasting opportunities, and would be come competitor's advantage. In Company D, the CEO suggested that "*Don't spend your whole development budget, before finding that you need another iteration.*" Company D composed of all technical members from the beginning: "*You could say that we have followed the Lean startup, the first MVP we have at December 2012 when we was in [Incubator place] ... We focus on the development of the MVP from Day one" (CEO of Company C).* With heavily focus on product development, they implemented the strategies that making different prototypes of the same domain area. These MVPs later can be (partly) reused by integrating into another product. CEO of Company A mentioned:" *In reality, the process of designing, building, and validating a prototype does dramatically reduce the risk, and allows everyone to hone in on the real costs of going into production".*

5 Discussion

As a central part of build-measure-learn, Eric Ries emphasized the main role of MVP as an artifact for customer validation [3]. Based on five case studies, we found that MVPs could be useful for a startup as a design artifact, a boundary spanning artifact and a reusable artifact. The process from business ideas to a launching product consists not only loops but also parallel branches. When market validation and product design tasks are carried on at the same time, certain types of MVPs would play a role of mutual adjustment between input from customers and product design. In many cases, we observed the benefits of having MVPs on final product development, such as increase feedback quality and reachability.

Adoption of MVP might be influenced by many contextual factors. We discussed about one most relevant factor, which is product development methodology. In our cases, Agile development is the most viable processes for software startups (in Case A, B, C, and D). In this context, fast releases with an iterative and incremental approach shorten the time from idea conception to production. The continuous integration might be the impetus for popular adopting evolutionary prototypes and single-feature MVP in our cases (Company A, B, D, E). However, the prototyping process might be hindered by other business and technical factors, leading to the inappropriateness of Agile principles sometimes during the startup process. In Company A and D, the evolutionary prototypes were implemented quite early and quickly during the process. While in Company E, the prototype is evolved gradually over months, due to the technical complexity of the product.

Reflecting on boundary spanning theory [10, 11, 13], we observed all three types of knowledge boundary within a startup team and also between the team and external stakeholders. MVP has been shown as an effective tool to break all these gaps. Syntactic knowledge boundary was found between the CEO and a customer when explaining the product. It seems that syntactic boundary is not the main issues in our startup cases. The reason may due to the nature of products (for wide range of users in Company A and B), the familiarity of the CEO with the industry (Company C) and the familiarity with some customers in the field (Company C, D and E). Semantic boundary was found in a conversation between CEO and a developer, which can be observed more within an entrepreneurial team. We have not found much evidence about the boundary with mentors or investors, but it might happen as well. Pragmatic boundary seems to be the most important issues among the team members and between the team and investors. This can because of the divergence of entrepreneurial team in term of startup goals and motivation over time (Company A), or pitch and presentation skill to attract interest from investors and customers (Company B). We observe at least in these cases that MVPs play the role of bridging these gaps.

Our research revealed different ways that MVPs can be used to support startup business activities. However, they are not equally perceived among all startups. For instance, only in Case B most of the MVP usages were identified. Moreover, tactics with using MVP are arbitrary and there is no systematic approach to fully utilize the benefit of MVP. For practitioners, we suggested that the development of MVP should consider the ability to communicate among different stakeholders, to facilitate the design and to save business and product development costs. In short, MVP should be developed as a Multiple Facet Product (MFP).

There are several threats to validities worth to discuss [15]. One internal threat of validity is the bias in data collection, as data might not represent the comprehensive story. An important issue is related to the fact that the limited number of interviews might not represent the complete scenarios in our context of study. In order to mitigate this threat we selected CTO and CEO as interviewees, who have the best understanding about their startups. We also use other types of data sources to increase our understanding about the cases. With Company A and Company B, we also acted as the startup team members, which enables a lot of insights beyond interviews. Another internal threat of validity is about how reliable the reported cases are. This is ensured as two of the authors have not only theoretical background about software startups but also hand-on experience.

A construct threat of validity is a possible inadequate description of constructs. During the coding of interview transcripts, we adopted explanatory descriptive labels for theoretical categories, to capture the underlying phenomenon without losing relevant details. An external threat of validity is the representativeness of our selected cases. As discussed earlier, the sample is collected from European technical-founded bootstrap startups. A startup from USA or America, and a startup with different financial models might introduce other MVP usage patterns. For more thorough understanding and generalization of the results, a large pool of startups with variety profiles should be included. All of the cases are small startups under development seeking for seed funding. Besides, the startup decisions on MVP might be influenced by individual personalities.

6 Conclusions

The study of five startups reveals some insights for prototyping approaches in software startups. We found that MVP is also be used as a MFP, where it supports the design process, bridges communication gaps and facilitate the cost-saving activities. When market validation and product design tasks are carried on at the same time, certain types of MVPs would play a role of mutual adjustment between input from customers and product design. MVPs were used to bridge knowledge gaps between entrepreneurs and developers, customers, investors. Particularly, we illustrate how three types of knowledge boundaries have been resolved using MVPs.

So far, we have explored the stated research questions through a multiple case study. Our next step in the research is to include different types of software startups. Possible sequences of MVPs to be developed were initially observed in Company B and Company C. Future study will explore in-depth about MVP development processes in other cases. Another research topic is to understand how software prototype practices fit into Agile development context. Last but not least, OSS adoption has been essential for product development in startup. The question would be in which way startup companies can really benefit from adopting OSS.

References

1. Paternoster, N., Giardino, C., Unterkalmsteiner, M., Gorschek, T., Abrahamsson, P.: Software development in startup companies: A systematic mapping study. Inf. Softw. Technol. **56**(10), 1200–1218 (2014)
2. Coleman, G., O'Connor, R.: An investigation into software development process formation in software start-ups. J. Enterp. Inf. Manage. **21**(6), 633–648 (2008)
3. Ries, E.: The lean startup: How today's entrepreneurs use continuous innovation to create radically successful businesses. Crown Business, New York (2011)
4. Khurum, M., Fricker, S., Gorschek, T.: The contextual nature of innovation - An empirical investigation of three software intensive products. Inf. Softw. Technol. **57**, 595–613 (2015)
5. Sommerville, I.: Software Engineering, 9th edn. Pearson Education, Harlow, England (2010)

6. Bosch, J., Holmström Olsson, H., Björk, J., Ljungblad, J.: The early stage software startup development model: A framework for operationalizing lean principles in software startups. In: Fitzgerald, B., Conboy, K., Power, K., Valerdi, R., Morgan, L., Stol, K.-J. (eds.) LESS 2013. LNBIP, vol. 167, pp. 1–15. Springer, Heidelberg (2013)
7. Lindgren, E., Münch, J.: Software development as an experiment system: A qualitative survey on the state of the practice. In: Lassenius, C., Dingsøyr, T., Paasivaara, M. (eds.) XP 2015. LNBIP, vol. 212, pp. 117–128. Springer, Heidelberg (2015)
8. Carlile, P.R.: A pragmatic view of knowledge and boundaries: Boundary objects in new product development. Organ. Sci. **13**, 442–455 (2002)
9. Floyd, C.: A systematic look at prototyping. In: Budde, R., Kuhlenkamp, K., Mathiassen, L., Zullighoven, H. (eds.) Approaches to Prototyping, pp. 1–18. Springer, Heidelberg (1984)
10. Tushman, M.L., Scanlan, T.J.: Boundary spanning individuals: their role in information transfer and their antecedents. Acad. Manage. J. **24**, 289–305 (1981)
11. Bowker, G., Star, S.L.: Sorting Things Out: Classification and Its Consequences. MIT Press, Cambridge, MA (1999)
12. Yin, R.K.: Case Study Research: Design and Methods (Applied Social Research Methods), 5th edn. SAGE Publications Inc, Thousand Oaks (2014)
13. Strauss, A., Corbin, J.: Basics of Qualitative Research Techniques and Procedures for Developing Grounded Theory. 2nd edition (1998)
14. Boyatzis, R.E.: Transforming qualitative information: thematic analysis and code development. Sage Publications, Thousand Oaks (1998)
15. Runeson, P., Höst, M.: Guidelines for conducting and reporting case study research in software engineering. Empirical Softw. Eng. **14**(2), 131–164 (2009)

On the Impact of Mixing Responsibilities Between Devs and Ops

Kristian Nybom(✉), Jens Smeds, and Ivan Porres

Faculty of Science and Engineering, Information Technologies,
Åbo Akademi University, Vesilinnantie 3, 20500 Turku, Finland
kristian.nybom@abo.fi

Abstract. Many software engineering organizations around the world are adopting DevOps. One of the goals of DevOps is to foster better collaboration between development and operations personnel, in order to improve organizational efficiency. Since DevOps is lacking a common definition, there are several approaches to adopt it, and organizations largely need to determine how to apply DevOps for themselves. In this paper, we present results from a case study in which a software organization adopts DevOps. The focus of this research is to study the impact of mixing the responsibilities between development and operations engineers. We interviewed 14 employees in the organization during the study, and results indicate several benefits of the chosen approach, such as improved collaboration and trust, and smoother work flow. This comes at the cost of a number of complications, such as new sources for friction among the employees, risk for holistically sub-optimal service configurations, and more.

Keywords: DevOps · Software process improvement · Adoption benefits and challenges

1 Introduction

DevOps has in recent years gained interest in the software and service development industry, and its adoption rate is expected to grow over the coming years [1]. DevOps addresses the challenge of what is often described as a gap between development and operations personnel. The gap is reduced through a combination of processes, cultural enhancements, and supporting technologies. More specifically, DevOps encompasses automation for reducing manual effort and improving stability, continuous feedback using metrics for improving software development processes, and a culture of collaboration and information sharing between teams [2]. However, the term "DevOps" is still an ambiguous concept and is lacking a standard definition [3–5]. While the purpose of DevOps is clear, organizations adopting DevOps must interpret and define what DevOps means to them.

The fact that DevOps is lacking a standard definition implies that there is no simple approach to follow when adopting DevOps in an organization. Adopting DevOps may thus not be a straightforward task since it may require that an

H. Sharp and T. Hall (Eds.): XP 2016, LNBIP 251, pp. 131–143, 2016.
DOI: 10.1007/978-3-319-33515-5_11

organization introduces process, personnel and technological changes and innovations. Since DevOps focuses on principles for software and service development, rather than specifying exactly how to implement DevOps, it means the path to a successful DevOps adoption is unique to each organization [6]. Therefore, we feel that it can be beneficial to learn from the successes and challenges experienced during previous DevOps adoptions when planning new DevOps initiatives.

In this article, we present how a particular organization adopted DevOps and what the impact was of this adoption from the perspective of engineers. In particular, we study the impact of mixing responsibilities between development and operations personnel, and how this affects the culture, tools and work practices. The study was carried out by interviewing both development ("Devs") and operations ("Ops") personnel before the start of the DevOps adoption and six months into the adoption.

2 Background: Approaches to DevOps Adoption

DevOps is commonly viewed as a professional movement that emphasizes communication, collaboration and integration between software developers and IT operations, see e.g. [7]. According to Willis [8], DevOps is comprised of four key aspects: *culture*, *automation*, *measurement* and *sharing*. In our previous work [9], we described DevOps as a number of *engineering process capabilities* supported by certain cultural and technological *enablers*. According to this definition, the capabilities define processes that an organization should be able to carry out, while the enablers support efficient work execution of these processes.

Common to most definitions of DevOps is that one of the main goals behind it is to tackle the problem of having development and operations teams in functional silos (see e.g. [10]) – a problem which is often present in non-DevOps software development organizations. The teams are in functional silos when there is little support for communication and collaboration between them in order to make releases. Breaking down the silos improves the development cycle, by bringing Devs and Ops closer to each other, allowing the organization to produce more production-ready code and deliver better services more frequently. Breaking down existing silos is, however, a non-trivial task, and it is tightly coupled with improvements in work processes, culture, and technology.

Focusing on concrete actions that address the problem of bringing Devs and Ops closer to each other, three possible but distinct approaches are to

1. Mix responsibilities: assign both development and operations responsibilities to all engineers, or
2. Mix personnel: increase communication and collaboration between Dev and Ops, but keep existing roles differentiated, or
3. Bridge team: create a separate DevOps team that functions as a bridge between Devs and Ops

Which approach to use may be difficult to decide on. An argument for following Approach 1 (mix responsibilities) lies in the concept of *Infrastructure as Code*. What this concept refers to is that the infrastructure for deploying software is fully automated, and is controlled by code. As mentioned in [11]:

> "If infrastructure is code, then almost by definition, infrastructure becomes to some degree a function of development, or at least so hard to separate from development that the distinction becomes almost irrelevant."

Assuming that infrastructure is code, this statement suggests that Approach 1 (mix responsibilities) is a natural approach, because Ops will be involved in Dev tasks by developing the infrastructure together with the Devs.

As for Approach 2 (mix personnel), it is stated in [12] that creating cross-functional teams is a good approach when adopting DevOps. These teams should consist of Devs, testers, Ops personnel and others, and then each of them would contribute code to a shared repository. In this way, the Dev and Ops responsibilities are maintained, but communication and collaboration is promoted. It is also mentioned in [12] that although promoting communication and collaboration is key, training for Devs and Ops on the responsibilities of other departments can be very beneficial for communication.

In a blog post [10], Jez Humble strongly states that Approach 3 (bridge team) should not be followed when adopting DevOps, since a separate DevOps team will not break any silos, but instead create new ones. Nevertheless, [13] reports that DevOps departments are a growing trend, and that according to their survey, more than 90 percent of those working in DevOps departments are in companies with medium to high IT performance.

3 Research Questions and Study Design

We consider that there is a need for empirical studies describing how DevOps is being adopted in different organizations and for the benefits and drawbacks of adopting DevOps. In this article, we decided to focus on the DevOps approach based on mixing responsibilities, and left studies of other approaches for future work. The main research question is as follows

RQ What may happen when mixing responsibilities between developers and operations teams in an existing organization?
RQ.a How does this approach affect the culture?
RQ.b How does this approach affect the tooling?
RQ.c How does this approach affect the ways of working?

This research was done as a longitudinal case study: we observed an organization as the phenomenon happened. For collecting data for the study, we used semi-structured interviews of company employees. For selecting the organization for the case study, we had the following two criteria:

1. Before the start of the DevOps adoption, there has to be clearly separated roles between Devs and Ops in the organization
2. The organization chooses Approach 1 as part of their DevOps adoption

The selected organization was an international IT company with a long history and over 1000 employees, which develops both software and services for customers. The case organization contains several organizational units, each having their own R&D teams. These units are combined by a separate operations unit.

This study was carried out in one of the organizational units, which develops and operates in the cloud services area. That unit was also the only unit in the organization that was actively adopting DevOps. Motivations for the adoption were to make software deployments faster and more frequent, to share knowledge between development and operations, and to keep deployment costs low.

A total of 14 experienced employees were selected by the company so they would represent different work areas, e.g. development, quality assurance, operations, and management. Their familiarity with DevOps prior to the study varied from understanding the basics of the concept to having previous professional experience of successfully adopting DevOps.

We conducted two rounds of interviews. The first interviews were conducted in the end of May 2014. Before the interviews, the participants were informed about the study, that the interviews will be recorded and that the answers will be handled anonymously. The interviews lasted roughly 45 min on average. An interview guide containing a broad field of questions was used for the semi-structured interviews. The purpose of the first round of interviews was to get an overview of the organization, of their processes, of the daily work, and of employees' expectations and concerns regarding their DevOps adoption. The recordings of the interviews were transcribed, coded and analyzed, and some results from that round have been reported in [9].

The second round of interviews were conducted in October 2014, and followed the same procedure as the first round. The questions for the second round were designed based on the results from the first round, and many of them were angled to expose changes since the first round. Other topics covered were related to the software development processes, relationship between development and operations, teamwork, employees' feelings (such as pressure, impact and importance regarding his/her work), how the DevOps adoption had proceeded along with expectations and concerns, views on the management, and the DevOps aspects of automation and familiarity with others' work.

The recordings from the second round were transcribed. Thereafter they were coded separately by two of the researchers to make sure that no relevant information would be missed, and to reduce the risk of researcher subjectivity influencing the codes. The researchers used slightly different approaches to code the material. The first coding approach was as follows. First, the transcripts were read though and summarized to obtain a quick overview of the subjects discussed in the interviews. Then, the transcripts were read through in detail with the researcher identifying, assigning, comparing and adjusting codes according to the content. Finally, the transcripts and the corresponding coding were read through once more from the start to check and make some final adjustments to the codes.

A second coding approach was to use pre-defined codes according to the research questions in this article. While reading through the transcripts and assigning content to the codes, different subjects discussed during the interviews were simultaneously identified. A second round of coding was then done within each of the pre-defined codes, using the identified subjects as pre-defined sub-codes. This resulted in detailed codes for each research question. The researchers then individually identified what was perceived as beneficial or challenging from both coding approaches. The individual lists were then compared, discussed and merged into our final list of outcomes. The results presented in this article are based on the second round of interviews.

4 Results

Before presenting the outcomes of the interviews, it is worth mentioning that the organizational structure, or more specifically, the fact that operations were attending the products for all the different organizational units, had an impact on several of the things mentioned below. Most notably, this resulted in operations having limited possibilities in taking on development responsibilities. Another fact to notice is that only one of the organizational units were actively adopting DevOps, while the other units were not, resulting in a difficult situation for operations: depending on which unit they were attending, they needed to work according to a specific pattern.

In the following we use the terms "Dev" and "Ops" to describe engineers with previous experience and responsibilities within software and service development and operations respectively.

4.1 Impact on Culture

A New Source for Friction. In order to enable Devs to deal with operations tasks, it was necessary to give administration rights to Devs to different environments. Based on the comments from the employees, it was evident that gaining access served as a cause for friction and mistrust. It was also mentioned that the process for obtaining access was long and tedious.

The long process also had negative implications on the work efficiency, because employees often realized too late that they needed the access, causing extra delays. The decision process for who was granted the access was also described as unfair. Some employees mention that access seem to have been granted based on shown interest rather on experience and knowledge. Devs also complained about Ops getting access faster than Devs. This made them angry and irritated.

An Eye-Opening Experience. Mixing the responsibilities of Devs and Ops was considered educating for the Devs. In the organization, the Devs had been developing various tools for their operations personnel to use for a long time, but only now with the DevOps adoption initiative did they get to see how their own tools were working.

Seeing the operations side also surprised the Devs in the sense that they now realized how far from production ready their software usually was, although it had passed all the tests in their own environment.

Through teaching others and learning from others, Devs and Ops were beginning to trust each other more. The increased level of trust was accompanied with stress relief, specifically for operations personnel as they could trust Devs to do part of the operations tasks. As a consequence, knowledge about operations tasks and problems were increased among the Devs. This lead to Devs starting to improve test environments to better correspond with production environments, while also contributing to increased collaboration between Devs and Ops.

Learning how to do operations tasks was not straightforward for everyone. Some employees mention it being extremely challenging, and that they did not see the point in having Devs do tasks which other more proficient employees do better. The complications in learning how to do operations tasks resulted in a certain reluctance in learning new things among the Devs. These Devs mentioned that they would prefer having the distinction between Devs and Ops more clear, implying that the mixing of responsibilities were not to their liking. Additionally, learning how to do upgrades was considered time consuming, but on the positive side, it had also revealed flaws in the upgrade processes. Devs mentioned the greater need for knowledge and expertise, since they now were responsible for everything and consequently needed to know every technology used. This was visible as mixed feelings among the Devs.

Shared Responsibilities. The view on how responsibilities were shared varied. Devs largely felt that responsibilities were shared, and if something went wrong, it was everybody's fault, while some Ops felt that Devs were somewhat unaccountable, specifically when it came to fixing problems late in the evenings. Their opinion was that Devs wanted to decide on everything, how the product is designed, how it is deployed, etc., without involving operations personnel. Then at the end of regular office hours, Devs would not care anymore and would want Ops to take care of it.

Employees agreed that within development, the responsibility of deploying software was shared among the Devs. They mentioned that whenever someone had problems with deploying software, they simply needed to shout it out, and everyone was alert and helping that person if needed.

Improved Collaboration. Mixing the responsibilities brought Devs and Ops closer to each other. Employees mentioned that Devs and Ops now collaborate on different tasks, since they now realize the importance of collaboration. Everyone agreed that collaboration between Devs and Ops is good on an individual level, and to some extent also on team level, but some employees called on the support from managers to further improve collaboration by providing more reasons for collaboration. It was mentioned that through the improved collaboration, it was easier to get things moving forward, since Devs could discuss directly their issues with Ops personnel, which is much faster than having to contact managers to get the issues solved.

On the other hand, Ops felt uneasy about Devs coming into their domain, and mentioned that adjusting to this takes time. Additionally, the closer collaboration and specifically keeping Devs and Ops synchronized was described being time consuming. It was argued that, although individual, the work space affects the level of collaboration to some degree, since long walking distances might imply a threshold for going to talk to some other person.

Through the collaboration, both Devs and Ops had become more trusting and understanding towards the other. Ops had seen that Devs can do the operations tasks without jeopardizing service stability and Devs had realized what Ops have to struggle with in order to deploy their software.

4.2 Impact on Internal Development Tools

Awareness of Tool Quality. As mentioned earlier, Devs had been developing tools for their operations personnel, and now that Devs were dealing with operations tasks, they were using their own tools. Devs mentioned that they were now experiencing the flaws and problems that the tools had, something which Ops had been aware of all the time. But now that Devs were using their own tools, and since they were not accustomed to having poor solutions, they were putting extra effort into creating very good tools for deployment. Development of these improved tools was performed in collaboration with Ops.

Deployment Risks. Previously operations was the place where the entire service stack came together, where all problems materialized, and where decisions were made which affected the entire service stack. Since Devs had been given the power to deploy their own product, there was some concern that they could make decisions that would be optimal for their specific product, while unknowingly disregarding the impact of their decisions on the remaining service stack. The main risk identified was that problems caused by these kinds of decisions are realized too late.

Identified Tooling Obstacles. It was mentioned that the many environments and many ways of upgrading different services creates an obstacle for full automation. Ops mentioned that automatic reactions to various glitches that may occur cannot be defined. Ops always have to investigate those problems manually. These problems were partially realized by Devs too. They perceived deployment as being time consuming and requiring significant effort, and while they technically could create scripts that would deploy everything, the real problem was to create scripts that recover from glitches. Another concern mentioned was that without automation, configuring all the different environments correctly is error-prone, specifically when there is a change in configuration. The Devs felt that it is easy to forget to align the configurations across all the different environments.

4.3 Impact on Ways of Working

Added Responsibilities. According to the chosen DevOps adoption approach, Devs were now responsible for performing upgrades on certain production environments. These environments were pre-staging environments, in the sense that they were mostly for internal users. A so called build master role was introduced among the Devs, which would rotate within the team on a weekly basis. In addition to doing the upgrades, the build master was also required to debug and investigate the production environment.

Devs mentioned that getting used to the build master role, and focusing on it was demanding – it is easy for Devs to start working on something else as soon as they have completed their task as build master, even though they noticed something that should be fixed.

Benefits of Having Administration Rights. The perceived benefits of Devs having access to different environments were manifold. Getting e.g. statistics from the production environments was described being considerably easier through the granted access, making work much smoother. Devs mentioned that it also allows better debugging, because Devs do not need to ask Ops for help anymore. It is faster, and more thorough, because Ops do not always have time to delve into the problems. On the other hand, this is time away from feature development. Ops also said that they had many times received help from Devs in problematic situations, making their work easier.

Common Ways of Working. Employees mentioned that the mixing of responsibilities puts higher requirements on common work practices and technical solutions between Devs and Ops. Without this, a risk identified was that Devs create tools specific for only their own unit's needs rather than having common solutions for all the organization. They mentioned that the upper management needs to push for common solutions in order to avoid this situation. They also mentioned that without strong management, the increased freedom among the Devs may result in a chaotic working environment, where everyone is doing as he or she pleases.

A concern was that even though access had been granted to Devs and employees had new responsibilities, work was done quite far in the same way as earlier. Other concerns among the Ops were that with added responsibilities and granted access for the Devs, Ops responsibilities had changed towards support, and that Devs were making decisions without consulting Ops.

Devs occasionally dealing with operations tasks was mentioned to have negative implications on the employees' work flow, as they caused complicated context switches. They said that it is easy to switch between tasks when they are within the same area, but switching between development and operations tasks is complicated. These context switches were perceived as frustrating.

Concerns with Mixed Responsibilities. Several concerns in the chosen approach of adopting DevOps were also discussed. It was mentioned that people like to do what they are used to doing. Thus, introducing operations tasks to Devs was perceived as complicated, and Devs would try to avoid them. Devs were used to making their own engineering decisions, but this was described as problematic, since they now created their own solutions also for operations tasks, instead of learning from others and reusing common solutions.

The combined effort of Devs and Ops was described having its own complications, because more people making changes to configuration and software leads to an increase in the probability of error, simply because the tools and processes for performing such changes have not emerged. To cope with this situation, employees felt that there is a great need for guidance, and will for involvement from everyone, so that they can agree on a common approach.

Devs doing operation tasks was experienced both positively and negatively. Some people loved having control over the entire delivery chain, while others wondered why not more experienced people could take care of the deployment. Several employees felt, however, that the chosen approach of mixing responsibilities was the wrong approach for doing DevOps. A perceived problem was that technical systems were tied to specific APIs and then Devs and different development teams were given too much freedom in choosing their own way of doing things. With many such development teams, a risk mentioned was that the organization ends up with many ways of working, causing lack of synergy.

5 Discussion

The results from the interviews indicate several beneficial aspects when mixing responsibilities between Devs and Ops. Devs have seen what work is required in order to deploy their software, which is educating for them. In addition to allowing them to develop more production ready code, it also reveals problems and flaws in some of the tools they have developed for the Ops. As a consequence, Devs are now putting more effort into developing better tools, which is done in collaboration with Ops. This clearly shows a benefit of learning about responsibilities of other teams. When Devs learn what happens with their code after it is developed and tested, they can exploit this knowledge for producing better code in the future. Unfortunately, corresponding benefits for the operations personnel were not revealed, because they were unable to take on development responsibilities. This was mainly due to the organizational structure, which required the operations teams to deal with software from all the organizational units.

Both the collaboration and trust between Devs and Ops is improved through the mixed responsibilities. Instead of contacting managers to solve problems, employees can discuss directly with personnel from the other team which is much faster. Ops have realized that Devs can deal with the operations tasks they are assigned with, without jeopardizing the stability of the service. Devs, on the other hand, have seen what Ops have to go through in order to deploy their software. This weakens the silo structure between the Devs and Ops, and the teams are effectively collaborating more. The weakened silos also inspire employees for even more collaboration, and some employees said that they would want the managers to give them even more reasons for collaboration. Thus, mixing the responsibilities seems to weaken the silos, as Devs and Ops are encouraged, and even required, to communicate and collaborate more.

Giving administration rights to Devs was seen as beneficial in many ways. Devs get statistics from production environments making work smoother, they can fix errors more easily than previously, and fixing errors is more thorough and efficient. The drawback is that all of this is time away from feature development.

The chosen adoption approach was not without complications. Surprisingly, getting administration rights was described as a source for friction, since employees felt that administration rights were not granted on a fair basis. Dealing with operations tasks was far from an easy task for several Devs, and because of this, the opinion of having separate responsibilities was strengthened among them. The organizational structure prevented Ops to fully take part in the DevOps adoption, since they already had their hands tied with operations tasks for other organizational units. We believe that this fact also partially prevented the teams from developing common ways of working, since Ops also had to work with other units that were not adopting DevOps. The concerns associated with taking on operations tasks among the Devs are a natural reaction. It is understandable that they wonder why they have to deal with operations tasks when there already is more proficient personnel to deal with those tasks. In general, a certain reluctance towards the adoption of DevOps was observed.

Devs having the power to deploy their own software was repeatedly mentioned as dangerous because this could potentially damage the entire service stack in the organization. The reason is that Devs were not aware of software developed in other organizational units, and consequently were configuring their software without those in mind. This presents a risk with the adoption approach, because if other organizational units had had similar power, it could have produced a chaotic end result, where all units would create their own solutions. With a lack of collaboration, communication and shared work practices and goals between Devs and Ops, this risk is further strengthened. To improve the situation, management could actively try to improve inter-team relations in order to facilitate communication to ensure that information spreads across teams. Automation could also assist in solving this problem to some degree.

Creating fully automated deployment tools was mentioned being a necessity for a well-functioning DevOps implementation. With the many different environments and many ways of upgrading, employees were of the opinion that automatic reactions to various glitches that may occur cannot be defined. Consequently, a large effort was continuously put into configuring and upgrading software, and employees called for a holistically well-functioning deployment tool chain. The effort required to put into this also had other implications, since it required Devs to make complicated context switches between development and operations tasks. Better automation could have assisted with the context switches, improving the work flow of the employees.

When both Devs and Ops independently make changes to configuration and software, there is a greater probability of error, as long as the tools and processes for performing such changes are not improved. This clearly shows the need for developing common ways of working and improving the automation.

It is clear from the respondents that what DevOps means to the organization should be clearly communicated to the employees in order to support a successful adoption. Currently, Devs felt that DevOps mostly meant that they get additional operations tasks to deal with once in a while, and when they are completed, they go back to developing. Clearly, this view is counterproductive for improving collaboration between the teams, and to avoid this, guidance and instructions are a necessity.

Had a third round of interviews been performed later into the adoption process, it is likely that the collaboration between the teams had been further improved, and that DevOps had stabilized more. When the second round of interviews was performed, however, employees were still adapting to the new responsibilities. Since people change slowly, it is not surprising to see certain instability, uncertainty, and reluctance among the employees.

6 Conclusions

This paper describes phenomena that arose when mixing responsibilities between developers and operations personnel in an organization when adopting DevOps. The results are from a case study, in which a software organization adopting DevOps was studied. The case organization consisted of several organizational units and a separate operations unit. In the organization only one organizational unit was adopting DevOps, which impacted the results in the sense that operations were not fully able to participate in the adoption.

The results indicate several benefits of the mixed responsibilities. Collaboration and trust were improved between Devs and Ops, and seeing what the other team has to deal with was very educating, helping employees in their work. Through increased collaboration, the work flow was described as smoother and faster as compared to earlier. Since Devs were dealing with operations tasks, they realized problems and flaws in the tools that they had earlier developed for operations, and Devs were now working on improving the tooling.

Several complications with the chosen adoption approach were also revealed. As Devs had the power to configure and deploy their own software, a major concern was that they would create solutions that were optimal for their software, while unknowingly disregarding the impact this had on the remaining service stack. The lack of common ways of working between Devs and Ops reinforced this concern. Dealing with new responsibilities among the Devs was considered challenging by many, and even strengthened their opinion of having separate responsibilities. Because of the challenging operations tasks, Devs realized the importance of having automated infrastructure, but accomplishing this was described as being extremely complicated in the case organization.

Finally, the study reveals the need for a strong management when adopting DevOps, since Devs and Ops need to develop common goals, practices of deploying, and approaches to technical solutions. The management also needs to clearly communicate to the employees what DevOps means to the organization, so that the personnel will realize the reason for the adoption, and the requirements and benefits of it. Automation of the infrastructure is of key importance, specifically when Devs are given the responsibility of configuring and deploying their own software.

The results indicate that when operations work with several organizational units, it is challenging to adopt DevOps in only some of those units. Thus, the overall organizational structure may impact the DevOps adoption process.

Acknowledgements. This work has been partially supported by the Digile Need for Speed program and funded by Tekes, the Finnish Funding Agency for Technology and Innovation.

References

1. Gartner, Inc.: Gartner says by 2016, devops will evolve from a niche to a mainstream strategy employed by 25 percent of global 2000 organizations. http://www.gartner.com/newsroom/id/2999017. Accessed 23 February 2016
2. Babar, Z., Lapouchnian, A., Yu, E.: Modeling DevOps deployment choices using process architecture design dimensions. In: Ralyté, J. (ed.) PoEM 2015. LNBIP, vol. 235, pp. 322–337. Springer, Heidelberg (2015). doi:10.1007/978-3-319-25897-3_21
3. Hüttermann, M.: DevOps for Developers, 1st edn. Apress, Berkely (2012)
4. Roche, J.: Adopting devops practices in quality assurance. Commun. ACM **56**(11), 38–43 (2013)
5. Capgemini, Devops - the future of application lifecycle automation, December 2014. https://www.capgemini.com/resources/devops-the-future-of-application-lifecycle-automation. Accessed 17 December 2015
6. Virmani, M.: Understanding devops & bridging the gap from continuous integration to continuous delivery. In: 2015 Fifth International Conference on Innovative Computing Technology (INTECH), pp. 78–82, May 2015
7. New Relic, What is devops'? http://newrelic.com/devops/what-is-devops. Accessed 18th December 2015
8. Willis, J.: What devops means to me, July 2010. http://www.getchef.com/blog/2010/07/16/what-devops-means-to-me/. Accessed 3 December 2014
9. Smeds, J., Nybom, K., Porres, I.: DevOps: a definition and perceived adoption impediments. In: Lassenius, C., Dingsøyr, T., Paasivaara, M. (eds.) XP 2015. LNBIP, vol. 212, pp. 166–177. Springer, Heidelberg (2015)

10. Humble, J.: There is no such thing as a "devops team", October 2012. http://continuousdelivery.com/2012/10/theres-no-such-thing-as-a-devops-team/. Accessed 17 December 2015
11. Riley, C.: Do, should developers own infrastructure? June 2015. http://devops.com/2015/06/25/doshould-developers-infrastructure/. Accessed 17 December 2015
12. Wade, E.: In devops culture, communication, collaboration are key. https://www.veracode.com/blog/2015/07/devops-culture-communication-and-collaboration-are-key. Accessed 27 December 2015
13. Puppet Labs, New Relic and Thoughtworks, "2014 state of devops report" (2014). http://puppetlabs.com/sites/default/files/2014-state-of-devops-report.pdf. Accessed 23 February 2016

Arsonists or Firefighters? Affectiveness in Agile Software Development

Marco Ortu[1], Giuseppe Destefanis[2(✉)], Steve Counsell[2], Stephen Swift[2], Roberto Tonelli[1], and Michele Marchesi[1]

[1] DIEE, University of Cagliari, Cagliari, Italy
{marco.ortu,roberto.tonelli,michele}@diee.unica.it
[2] Brunel University, Uxbridge, UK
{giuseppe.destefanis,steve.counsell,stephen.swift}@brunel.ac.uk

Abstract. In this paper, we present an analysis of more than 500 K comments from open-source repositories of software systems developed using agile methodologies. Our aim is to empirically determine how developers interact with each other under certain psychological conditions generated by politeness, sentiment and emotion expressed within developers' comments. Developers involved in an open-source projects do not usually know each other; they mainly communicate through mailing lists, chat, and tools such as issue tracking systems. The way in which they communicate affects the development process and the productivity of the people involved in the project. We evaluated politeness, sentiment and emotions of comments posted by agile developers and studied the communication flow to understand how they interacted in the presence of impolite and negative comments (and *vice versa*). Our analysis shows that "firefighters" prevail. When in presence of impolite or negative comments, the probability of the next comment being impolite or negative is 13 % and 25 %, respectively; *ANGER* however, has a probability of 40 % of being followed by a further *ANGER* comment. The result could help managers take control the development phases of a system, since social aspects can seriously affect a developer's productivity. In a distributed agile environment this may have a particular resonance.

Keywords: Agile · Data mining · Human aspect

1 Introduction

The study of emotions and psychological status of developers and people involved in the software-building system is gaining the attention of both practitioners and researchers [12]. Feldt et al. [8] focused on personality as one important psychometric factor and presented initial results from an empirical study investigating the correlation between personality and attitudes to software engineering processes and tools.

Software is a complex artefact which requires sharing of knowledge, team building and exchange of opinion between people. While it has been possible to

H. Sharp and T. Hall (Eds.): XP 2016, LNBIP 251, pp. 144–155, 2016.
DOI: 10.1007/978-3-319-33515-5_12

standardise classical industrial processes (e.g., car production), it is still difficult to standardise software production. Immateriality plays a major role in the complexity of software and despite attempts to standardise the software production process, software engineering is still a challenging and open field. There are too many constraints to take into account. Developers build an artefact that will be executed on a machine; software metrics, design patterns, micro patterns and good practices help to increase the quality of a software [4,6], but developers are humans and prone to human sensitivities. Coordinating and structuring developer teams is a vital activity for software companies [17] and dynamics within a team have a direct influence on group success; on the other hand, social aspects are intangible elements which, if monitored, can help the team in reaching its goals. Researchers are increasingly focusing their effort on understanding how the human aspects of a technical discipline can affect the final results [3,7,11].

Open-source development usually involves developers that voluntarily participate in a project by contributing with code. The management of such developers could even be more complex than the management of a team within a company, since developers are not in the same place at the same time and coordination becomes more difficult. The absence of face-to-face communication mandates the use of mailing lists, electronic boards, or specific tools such as Issue Tracking Systems. Being rude when writing a comment or replying to a contributor can affect the cohesion of the group and the successfulness of a project; equally a respectful environment is an incentive for new contributors joining the project [13,20,24].

In this paper, we empirically analyze more than 500 K comments from Ortu et al. [17] to understand how agile developers behave when dealing with polite/impolite or positive/negative (sentiment) issue comments. We empirically built three Markov chain models with states for politeness (polite, neutral, impolite), sentiment (positive, neutral, negative), and emotions (joy, anger, love, sadness). We aim to answer the following questions:

- Do developers change behaviour in the context of impolite/negative comments?
- What is the probability of shifting from comments holding positive emotions to comments holding negative emotion?

The remainder of this paper is structured as follows: In the next section, we provide a summary of related work. Section 3 describes the dataset used for this study and our approach/rationale to evaluate affectiveness of comments posted by developers. In Sect. 4, we present the results and elaborate on the research questions we address. Section 5 discusses the threats to validity. Finally, we summarize the study findings in Sect. 6.

2 Related Work

Several recent studies have demonstrated the importance and relationship of productivity and quality to human aspects associated with the software development process. Ortu et al. studied the effect of politeness [16] and emotions [15] on the time required to fix any given issue. The authors demonstrated that emotions did have an effect on the issue fixing time. Research has focused on understanding how the human aspects of a technical discipline can affect final results [3,7,11], and the effect of politeness [14,23,25]. The Manifesto for Agile Development indicates that people and communications are more essential than procedures and tools [2]. Several recent studies have demonstrated the importance and relationship of productivity and quality to human aspects associated with the software development process. Ortu et al. studied the effect of politeness [16] and emotions [15] on the time required to fix any given issue. The authors demonstrated that emotions did have an effect on the issue fixing time. Steinmacher et al. [22] analyzed social barriers that obstructed first contributions of newcomers (new developers joining an open-source project). The study indicated how impolite answers were considered as a barrier by newcomers. These barriers were identified through a systematic literature review, responses collected from open source project contributors and students contributing to open source projects. Rigby et al. [20] analyzed, using a psychometrically-based linguistic analysis tool, the five big personality traits of software developers in the Apache httpd server mailing list. The authors found that the two developers that were responsible for the major Apache releases had similar personalities and their personalities were different from other developers. Bazzelli et al. [1] analyzed questions and answers on stackoverflow.com to determine the developer personality traits, using the Linguistic Inquiry and Word Count [19]. The authors found that the top reputed authors were more extroverted and expressed less negative emotions than authors of down voted posts. Gomez et al. [9] performed an experiment to evaluate whether the level of extraversion in a team influenced the final quality of the software products obtained and the satisfaction perceived while this work was being carried out. Results indicated that when forming work teams, project managers should carry out a personality test in order to balance the amount of extraverted team members with those who are not extraverted. This would permit the team members to feel satisfied with the work carried out by the team without reducing the quality of the software products developed.

Compared to the existing literature, the goal of this paper is to build Markov chain models which describe how developers interact in a distributed Agile environment evaluating politeness, sentiment and emotions. Such models provide a mathematical view of the behavioural aspects among developers.

3 Experimental Setup

3.1 Dataset

We built our dataset from fifteen open-source, publicly available projects from a dataset proposed by Ortu et al. [18]. We selected the fifteen projects with the highest number of comments (from December 2002 to December 2013), from those projects which had a significant amount of activities in their agile kanban-boards. The projects were developed following agile practices (mainly continuous delivery and use of kanban-boards). Table 1 shows summary project statistics.

Table 1. Selected project statistics

Project	# of comments	# of developers
HBase	91016	951
Hadoop Common	61958	1243
Derby	52668	675
Lucene Core	50152	1107
Hadoop HDFS	42208	757
Cassandra	41966	1177
Solr	41695	1590
Hive	39002	850
Hadoop Map/Reduce	34793	875
Harmony	28619	316
OFBiz	25694	578
Infrastructure	25439	1362
Camel	24109	908
ZooKeeper	16672	495
Wicket	17449	1243

3.2 Affective Metrics

Henceforward, we consider the term "affective metric" as a definition indicating all those measures linked to human aspects and obtained from text written by developers (i.e., comments posted on issue tracking systems). This study is based on the affective metrics (sentiment, politeness and emotions) used by Ortu et al. [15].

Sentiment. We measured sentiment using the SentiStrength[1] tool, which is able to estimate the degree of positive and negative sentiment in short texts, even for informal language. SentiStrength, by default, detects two sentiment polarizations:

- Negative: -1 (slightly negative) to -5 (extremely negative)
- Positive: 1 (slightly positive) to 5 (extremely positive)

The tool uses a lexicon approach based on a list of words to detect sentiment; SentiStrength was originally developed for the English language and was optimized for short social web texts. We used the tool to measure the sentiment of developers in issue comments.

Politeness. To evaluate the level of politeness of comments related to a given issue, we used the tool developed by Danescu et al. [5]; the tool uses a machine

[1] http://sentistrength.wlv.ac.uk.

learning approach and calculates the politeness of sentences providing, as a result, one of two possible labels: polite or impolite. The tool also provides a level of confidence related to the probability of a politeness class being assigned. We considered comments whose level of confidence was less than 0.5 as neutral (the text did not convey either politeness or impoliteness). For each comment we assigned a value according to the following rules:

- Value of +1 for comments marked as polite;
- Value of 0 for comments marked as neutral (confidence level<0.5);
- Value of -1 for comments marked as impolite.

For each issue in our dataset, we built a temporal series of comments, and using the two tools we assigned a value of politeness and sentiment for each comment in the series. Next, for each issue, we calculated, starting from the first comment posted, the probability of having a polite/impolite/neutral following comment (for politeness), and a positive/neutral/negative comment (for sentiment). We thus calculated the probability of shifting from "polite" to "neutral" and *vice versa*; from "polite" to "impolite" and *vice versa*; finally, from "neutral" to "impolite" and *vice versa.*

Emotion. The presence of emotion in software engineering artifacts have been analysed by Murgia et al. [13]. Ortu et al. [15] provided a machine learning based approach for emotion detection in developers' comments. We used the emotion detection tool provided by Ortu et al. [15] to detect the presence of *SADNESS*, *ANGER*, *JOY*, *LOVE* and *NEUTRAL.*

3.3 Affective Markov Chains

Markov Chains (MC) have been used to model behavioural aspects in social sciences [10,21]. A Markov chain consists of K states and is a discrete-time stochastic process, a process that occurs in a series of time-steps in each of which a random choice is made.

We built a MC for each affective metric: sentiment, politeness and emotion. Figure 1 shows the steps in building the politeness MC as an example for an issue report in which three developers posted five comments. As a first step, we used the politeness tool [5] to label each comment as *POLITE*, *IMPOLITE* or *NEUTRAL.* Next we collected the politeness labels of the issue report, considering the set of labels as a politeness sequences of N-1 pair-wise politeness-transitions ([P,N,I,I,P] in the example), where N is the number of comments in the issue report.

In this example, the issue report has 4 transitions: polite-neutral, neutral-impolite, impolite-impolite and impolite-polite. Finally, we counted the frequency of each politeness-transition obtaining the corresponding MC. In our example, if we consider the *POLITE* state, we have two transition, P-P and P-N; hence, the transition from *POLITE* to *IMPOLITE* state will have a probability of 0 and the transitions to *POLITE* and *IMPOLITE* state probability 0.5.

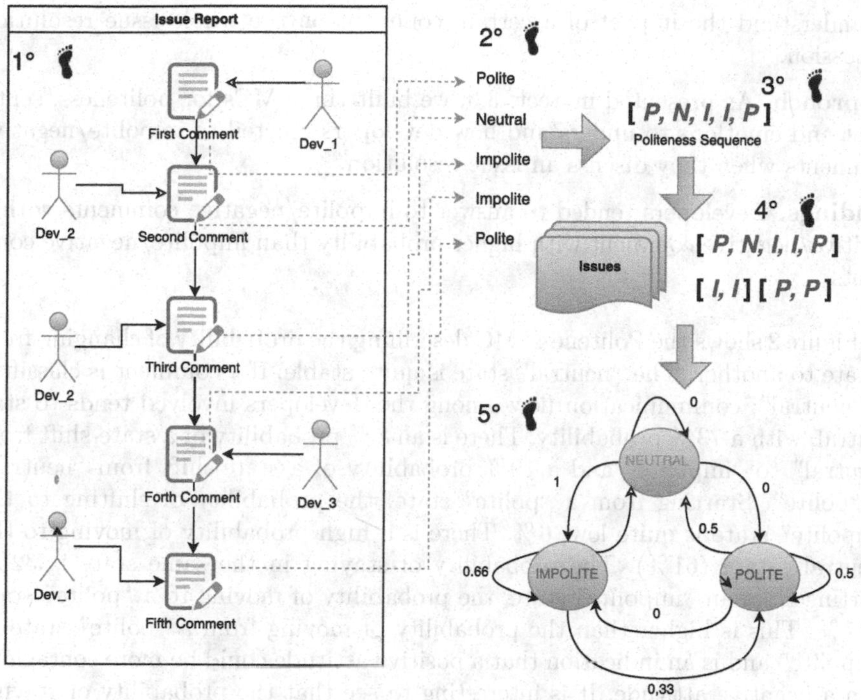

Fig. 1. Politeness' Markov's chain schema

The MC for sentiment is built in a similar way to the politeness MC. The MC which models emotion transitions is slightly different; however, a comment can be polite, impolite or neutral when considering politeness, but it might contain more than one emotion. We used the emotion classifier proposed by Ortu et al. [15] to analyze each comment and to attribute to it: Anger, Sadness, Joy and/or Love. For example, if a comment is labeled as containing *ANGER* and *SADNESS* and the next labeled as containing no emotion (*NEUTRAL*), then we consider two transitions *ANGER-NEUTRAL* and *SADNESS-NEUTRAL*.

4 Results and Discussion

4.1 Do Developers Change Behaviour in the Context of Impolite/Negative Comments?

Motivation. Existing research has already explored links between productivity (as measured by issue fixing time) and discrete emotions, sentiment and politeness [13,15]. The dynamic of an issue resolution involves complex interactions between different stakeholders such as users, developer and managers. A model able to describe such interactions could inform in the decision making process. The underlying assumption is that a model of social interaction can be used to understand the impact of a certain comment on the whole issue resolution discussion.

Approach. As presented in Sect. 3.3, we built three MCs for politeness, sentiment and emotions to understand how developers reacted to impolite/negative comments when they discuss an issue resolution.

Findings. Developers tended to answer to impolite/negative comments with a positive/negative comment with higher probability than impolite/negative comments.

Figure 2 shows the Politeness' MC describing the probability of changing from a state to another. The "neutral" state is quite stable. If a comment is classified as "neutral", communication flow among the developers involved tends to stay neutral, with a 73 % probability. There is an 8 % probability of a state-shift from "neutral" to "impolite" and a 19 % probability of a state-shift from "neutral" to "polite". Starting from a "polite" state, the probability of shifting to the "impolite" state is quite low, 6 %. There is a high probability of moving to the "neutral" state (61 %). The probability of staying in the same state is 32 %. Starting from an "impolite" state, the probability of moving to a "polite" state is 17 %. This is higher than the probability of moving from a "polite" state to "impolite" and is an indication that a positive attitude could be more contagious than a negative attitude. It is interesting to see that the probability of staying in an "impolite" state is only 13 % (far lower than the probabilities of staying in both "neutral" and "polite states), and that there is a 70 % of probability of a shift from "impolite" to "neutral".

Figure 3 shows the Sentiment MC which describes the probability of changing from one state to another.

The "neutral" state in this case is also quite stable. If a comment is classified as "neutral", communication flow among developers tends to stay neutral, with a 60 % probability. There is a 16 % probability of a state-shift from "neutral" to "negative" and a 24 % probability of a state-shift from "neutral" to "positive".

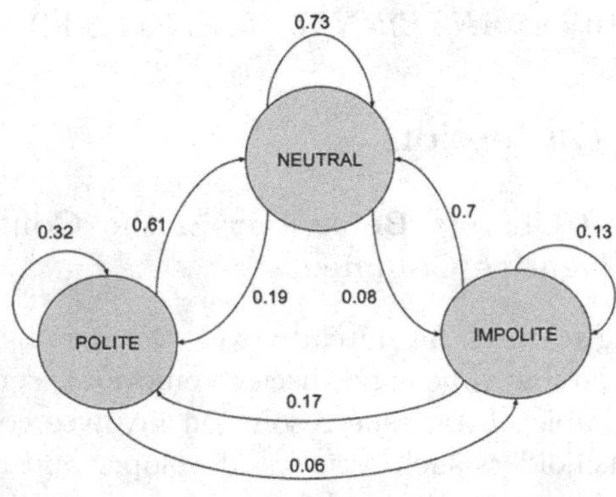

Fig. 2. Politeness MC

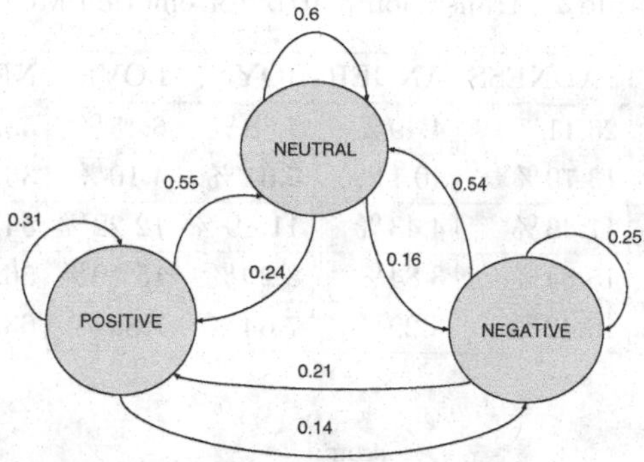

Fig. 3. Sentiment MC

Starting from a "positive" state, the probability of a shift to the "negative" state is 14 %. The probability of a move to the "neutral" state is 55 %. The probability of staying in the same state is 31 %. From a "negative" state, the probability of moving to a "positive" state is 21 %. In this case, the value is higher than the probability of moving from a "positive" state to a "negative" one. The probability of staying in a "negative" state is 25 % (also lower than the probabilities of staying in both "neutral" and "positive" states), and that there is a 54 % probability to shift from "negative" to "neutral".

4.2 What is the Probability of Shifting from Comments Holding Positive Emotions to Comments Holding Negative Emotion?

Motivation. The first research question showed how agile developers tended to respond more positively than negatively when considering politeness and sentiment. It is interesting to analyze if the same behaviours occur for emotions.

Approach. We built the MCs for emotions as presented in Sect. 3.3 to analyze the probabilities of shifting from an emotion to another when developers communicate.

Findings. Negative emotions such as *SADNESS* and *ANGER* tend to be followed by negative emotions more than positive emotion are followed by positive emotions. Table 2 shows the emotion transitions matrix. As for previous MCs, the numbers represent the probability of a comment containing emotion X being followed by a comment containing emotion Y (e.g., a comment expressing *SADNESS* has a probability of 0.26 of being followed by another *SADNESS* comment).

As confirmed by other studies [13], most of the comments expressing emotion are likely to be followed by *NEUTRAL* comments, with the exception of *ANGER*. Figure 4 is a graphical representation of the portion of Table 2 for the *ANGER* emotion showing it has probability of 0.4 of being followed by an *ANGER* comment against probability of 0.36 to be followed by a *NEUTRAL*

Table 2. Transiction matrix for emotion MC

	SADNESS	ANGER	JOY	LOVE	NEUTRAL
SADNESS	26.11 %	4.49 %	7.88 %	6.45 %	55.08 %
ANGER	13.79 %	40.11 %	5.61 %	4.10 %	36.39 %
JOY	17.46 %	4.43 %	11.89 %	12.22 %	54.00 %
LOVE	15.84 %	3.84 %	8.29 %	15.59 %	56.44 %
NEUTRAL	16.42 %	4.29 %	7.64 %	7.80 %	63.85 %

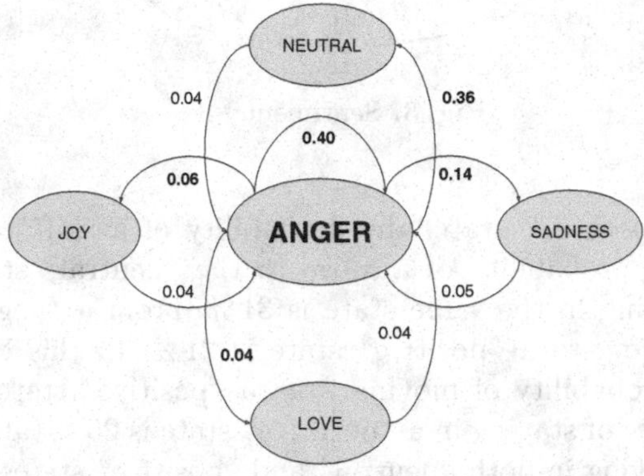

Fig. 4. Anger Markov chain. For simplicity only edges from/to ANGER are diplayed

comment. This represents an interesting finding which seems consistent with the common experience: negative emotions are more contagious than positive emotions.

5 Threats to Validity

Several threats to validity need to be considered. Threats to external validity are related to generalisation of our conclusions. With regard to the system studied in this work, we considered only open-source systems and this could affect the generality of the study; our results are not meant to be representative of all environments or programming languages. Commercial software is typically developed using different platforms and technologies, with strict deadlines and cost limitations and by developers with different experience. Politeness, sentiment and emotions measures are approximations given the challenges of natural language and subtle phenomena like sarcasm. To deal with these threats, we used SentiStrength form measuring sentiment, Danescu et al.'s politeness tool [5] and Ortu et al. [15] for measuring politeness. This is a threat to construct validity. Threats to internal validity concern confounding factors that could influence the obtained results. Since the comments used in this study were collected over an extended period from developers unaware of being subject to analysis, we are confident that the emotions we mined are genuine. This study is focused on text written by agile developers for developers. To correctly depict the affectiveness embedded in such comments, it is necessary to understand the developers' dictionary and slang. This assumption is supported by Murgia et al. [13] for measuring emotions. We are confident that the tools used for measuring sentiment and politeness however are equally reliable in the software engineering domain as in other domains.

6 Conclusions and Future Work

This paper presented an analysis of more than 500 K comments from open-source issue tracking system repositories. We empirically determined how agile developers interacted with each other under certain psychological conditions generated by politeness, sentiment and emotions of a comment posted on a issue tracking system. Results showed that when in the presence of impolite or negative comments, there is higher probability for the next comment to be neutral or polite (neutral or positive in case of sentiment) than impolite or negative. This fact demonstrates that developers, in the dataset considered for this study, tended to resolve conflicts instead of increasing negativity within the communication flow. This is not true when we consider emotions; negative emotions are more likely to be followed by negative emotions than positive. Markov models provide a mathematical description of developer behavioural aspects and the result could help managers take control the development phases of a system (expecially in a distributed environment), since social aspects can seriously affect a developer's productivity. As future works we plan to investigate possible links existing between software metrics and emotions, to better understand the impact of affectiveness on software quality.

Acknowledgement. The research presented in this paper was partly funded by the Engineering and Physical Sciences Research Council (EPSRC) of the UK under grant ref: EP/M024083/1.

References

1. Bazelli, B., Hindle, A., Stroulia, E.: On the personality traits of stackoverflow users. In: 2013 29th IEEE International Conference on Software Maintenance (ICSM), pp. 460–463. IEEE (2013)
2. Beck, K., Beedle, M., Van Bennekum, A., Cockburn, A., Cunningham, W., Fowler, M., Grenning, J., Highsmith, J., Hunt, A., Jeffries, R., et al.: Manifesto for agile software development (2001)
3. Brief, A.P., Weiss, H.M.: Organizational behavior: affect in the workplace. Annu. Rev. Psychol. **53**(1), 279–307 (2002)
4. Concas, G., Destefanis, G., Marchesi, M., Ortu, M., Tonelli, R.: Micro patterns in agile software. In: Baumeister, H., Weber, B. (eds.) XP 2013. LNBIP, vol. 149, pp. 210–222. Springer, Heidelberg (2013)
5. Danescu-Niculescu-Mizil, C., Sudhof, M., Jurafsky, D., Leskovec, J., Potts, C.: A computational approach to politeness with application to social factors. In: Proceedings of ACL (2013)
6. Destefanis, G., Tonelli, R., Tempero, E., Concas, G., Marchesi, M.: Micro pattern fault-proneness. In: 2012 38th EUROMICRO Conference on Software Engineering and Advanced Applications (SEAA), pp. 302–306. IEEE (2012)
7. Erez, A., Isen, A.M.: The influence of positive affect on the components of expectancy motivation. J. Appl. Psychol. **87**(6), 1055 (2002)
8. Feldt, R., Torkar, R., Angelis, L., Samuelsson, M.: Towards individualized software engineering: empirical studies should collect psychometrics. In: Proceedings of the International Workshop on Cooperative and Human Aspects of Software Engineering, pp. 49–52. ACM (2008)
9. Gómez, M.N., Acuña, S.T., Genero, M., Cruz-Lemus, J.A.: How does the extraversion of software development teams influence team satisfaction and software quality?: A controlled experiment. Int. J. Hum. Capital Inf. Technol. Professionals (IJHCITP) **3**(4), 11–24 (2012)
10. Jordan, M.I.: Learning in Graphical Models. NATO ASI Series, vol. 89. Springer, Heidelberg (1998)
11. Kaluzniacky, E.: Managing Psychological Factors in Information Systems Work: An Orientation to Emotional Intelligence. IGI Global, Hershey (2004)
12. Ke, W., Zhang, P.: The effects of extrinsic motivations and satisfaction in open source software development. J. Assoc. Inf. Syst. **11**(12), 784–808 (2010)
13. Murgia, A., Tourani, P., Adams, B., Ortu, M.: Do developers feel emotions? An exploratory analysis of emotions in software artifacts. In: Proceedings of the 11th Working Conference on Mining Software Repositories, MSR 2014, pp. 262–271. ACM, New York (2014)
14. Novielli, N., Calefato, F., Lanubile, F.: Towards discovering the role of emotions in stack overflow. In: Proceedings of the 6th International Workshop on Social Software Engineering, pp. 33–36. ACM (2014)
15. Ortu, M., Adams, B., Destefanis, G., Tourani, P., Marchesi, M., Tonelli, R.: Are bullies more productive? Empirical study of affectiveness vs. issue fixing time. In: Proceedings of the 12th Working Conference on Mining Software Repositories, MSR 2015 (2015)
16. Ortu, M., Destefanis, G., Kassab, M., Counsell, S., Marchesi, M., Tonelli, R.: Would you mind fixing this issue? An empirical analysis of politeness and attractiveness in software developed using agile boards. In: Lassenius, C., Dingsøyr, T., Paasivaara, M. (eds.) XP 2015. LNBIP, vol. 212, pp. 129–140. Springer, Heidelberg (2015)

17. Ortu, M., Destefanis, G., Kassab, M., Marchesi, M.: Measuring and understanding the effectiveness of JIRA developers communities. In: Proceedings of the 6th International Workshop on Emerging Trends in Software Metrics, WETSoM 2015 (2015)
18. Ortu, M., Destefanis, G., Murgia, A., Marchesi, M., Tonelli, R., Adams, B.: The JIRA repository dataset: Understanding social aspects of software development. In: Proceedings of the 11th International Conference on Predictive Models and Data Analytics in Software Engineering, p. 1. ACM (2015)
19. Pennebaker, J.W., Francis, M.E., Booth, R.J.: Linguistic Inquiry and Word Count: LIWC 2001, vol. 71. Lawrence Erlbaum Associates, Mahway (2001)
20. Rigby, P.C., Hassan, A.E.: What can OSS mailing lists tell us? a preliminary psychometric text analysis of the apache developer mailing list. In: Proceedings of the Fourth International Workshop on Mining Software Repositories, p. 23. IEEE Computer Society (2007)
21. Snijders, T.A.: The statistical evaluation of social network dynamics. Sociol. Methodol. **31**(1), 361–395 (2001)
22. Steinmacher, I., Conte, T.U., Gerosa, M., Redmiles, D.: Social barriers faced by newcomers placing their first contribution in open source software projects. In: Proceedings of the 18th ACM Conference on Computer Supported Cooperative Work & Social Computing, pp. 1–13 (2015)
23. Tan, S., Howard-Jones, P.: Rude or polite: do personality and emotion in an artificial pedagogical agent affect task performance? In: Global Conference on Teaching and Learning with Technology (CTLT 2014) Conference Proceedings, p. 41 (2014)
24. Tourani, P., Jiang, Y., Adams, B.: Monitoring sentiment in open source mailing lists - exploratory study on the apache ecosystem. In: Proceedings of the 2014 Conference of the Center for Advanced Studies on Collaborative Research (CASCON), Toronto, ON, Canada, November 2014
25. Tsay, J., Dabbish, L., Herbsleb, J.: Lets talk about it: Evaluating contributions through discussion in github. In: FSE. ACM (2014)

Insights into the Perceived Benefits of Kanban in Software Companies: Practitioners' Views

Muhammad Ovais Ahmad(✉), Jouni Markkula, and Markku Oivo

M-Group, University of Oulu, Oulu, Finland
{Muhammad.Ahmad, Jouni.Markkula, Markku.Oivo}@oulu.fi

Abstract. In the last decade, Kanban has been promoted as a means for bringing visibility to work while improving the software development flow, team communication and collaboration. However, little empirical evidence exists regarding Kanban use in the software industry. This paper aims to investigate the factors that users perceive to be important for Kanban use. We conducted a survey in 2015 among Kanban practitioners in the LeanKanban LinkedIn community. The survey results consist of 146 responses from 27 different organisations, with all respondents being experienced in using Kanban. The results show that practitioners perceived Kanban as easy to learn and useful in individual and team work. They also consider organisational support and social influence to be important determinants for Kanban use. Respondents noted various perceived benefits for using Kanban, such as bringing visibility to work, helping to reduce work in progress, improving development flow, increasing team communication and facilitating coordination. Despite the benefits, participants also identified challenges to using Kanban, such as organisational support and culture, difficulties in Kanban implementation, lack of training and misunderstanding of key concepts. The paper summarises the results and includes a discussion of implications for effective deployment of Kanban before describing future research needs.

Keywords: Kanban · Lean · Agile · Use · Adoption

1 Introduction

In the last two decades, Agile and Lean approaches have gained wide acceptance in the software industry. In this realm, Kanban emerged in 2004 with a strong practitioner-driven support movement [3, 4], and today, Kanban is increasingly adopted to complement Scrum and other Agile methods. Kanban tends to focus on fast production, rapid and continual user feedback and interaction [1].

Used for controlling the logistical chain from a production point of view, Kanban was developed and applied in the Japanese manufacturing industry in the 1950s [1]. Kanban's success in the manufacturing industry has convinced software engineers to adopt this approach, with practitioner-driven support furthering this trend. In 2004, David Anderson introduced Kanban to a small IT team at Microsoft, aiming to help the team members visualise their work and put limits on their work in progress (WIP). Kanban has five underlying principles [7], the so-called Kanban properties [10]: *visualise the workflow, limit work in progress, measure and manage flow, make process policies explicit and use models to recognise improvement and opportunities.*

H. Sharp and T. Hall (Eds.): XP 2016, LNBIP 251, pp. 156–168, 2016.
DOI: 10.1007/978-3-319-33515-5_13

The motivation behind visualisation and limiting WIP was to identify the constraints of the process and to focus on a single item at a time. Additionally, instead of pushing work on to software developers, Kanban promotes a pull approach: when a team member finishes an existing task, he or she automatically pulls the next item to begin work. In brief, Kanban aims to provide visibility to the software development process, communicate priorities and highlight bottlenecks [5]. This process results in a constant flow of releasing work items to customers, as the developers focus only on a few items at a given time [6]. The proliferation of Kanban in software engineering boomed after the publication of key books. These seminal books included David Anderson's *Kanban* [10], which introduces the concept of Kanban in systems and software development, and Corey Lada's *Scrumban* [23], which discusses the fusion of Scrum and Kanban. The key motivation for Kanban use involves a focus on flow and the omission of the obligatory iteration cycles in Scrum.

Kanban has received considerable attention from some organisations; others remain reluctant to adopt it. So far, there have been few scientific studies [1, 6, 33] addressing Kanban usage in software organisations, and none of the existing studies report on practitioners' perceptions of it. Earlier Kanban studies report a number of challenges in its use and adoption, such as organisational, social and technical issues. These studies introduce Kanban as a new way to develop software and systems. Research is still required to identify factors that might influence its effective usage in organisations. Therefore, this study aims to investigate factors that practitioners deem to be important in Kanban use. Conducted in 2015, the study includes Kanban practitioners from the LeanKanban LinkedIn community. LeanKanban is one of the biggest social media communities of professionals who use Kanban at their organisations.

The remainder of the paper is organised as follows. Section 2 explains the research strategy and data collection method, while Sect. 3 provides the results. Section 4 presents validity threats before moving into Sect. 5, which concludes the paper with recommendations for future research.

2 Research Strategy and Methods

In this section, we first introduce the theoretical model adopted as a basis for designing the empirical research. The discussion continues with the survey design and data collection process.

2.1 Theoretical Model

As shown in Fig. 1, we adopted Dybå et al. [8] model which is an extension of Riemenschneider et al. [9] research model in order to explore practitioners' perceptions regarding Kanban use.

Riemenschneider et al. [9] explain software developers' acceptance of methodologies by comparing five well-known and established theoretical models: the Technology Acceptance Model (TAM), TAM2 (an extension of TAM), Perceived Characteristics of Innovating, Theory of Planned Behaviour and Model of Personal

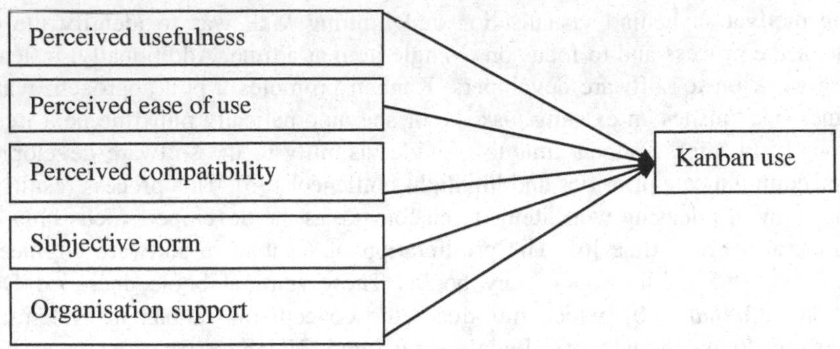

Fig. 1. Conceptual model

Computer Utilisation. Dybå et al. [8] extend Riemenschneider et al.'s [9] work by incorporating measures of organisational support. The model derives its theoretical foundations by combining prior research in technology acceptance [11, 12, 17] with aspects of innovation diffusion theory [16] as well as empirically-tested research on software developers' acceptance of methodologies [9]. The model contains five constructs: perceived usefulness, perceived ease of use, perceived compatibility, subjective norms and organisational support.

Perceived usefulness is defined as the degree to which a person believes that using a particular system will enhance his or her job performance [9], which is similar to Rogers' [16] perceived relative advantage [15]. Software developers generally receive reinforcements for good performance through raises, promotions and bonuses. In this study, perceived usefulness with respect to Kanban implies that a user believes that there is a positive user-performance relationship. The existing research provides evidence that perceived usefulness affects behavioural intention and actual use [9, 11–13, 17]. This pattern has also been confirmed within the software engineering domain [9]. **Perceived ease of use** refers to the degree to which a person believes that using a particular system will be free of effort [9]. Riemenschneider et al. found that ease of use played an insignificant role in software developers' acceptance of methodologies [9]. However, perceived ease of use recurs in several studies as a significant determinant of adoption behaviour [9, 12, 17, 19]. In this regard, compared to other Agile methods, Kanban is perceived to be easier to use and less complex. According to Rogers, **perceived compatibility** refers to the degree to which an innovation is perceived as being consistent with the existing values, needs and past experience of potential adopters [16]. Rogers further proposes that compatibility positively relates to the diffusion of innovations [16], making it a significant factor in explaining software developers' acceptance of methodologies [9, 30]. Thus, a positive perceived compatibility may lead to favourable attitudes toward Kanban use. **Subjective norms** represent the degree to which software developers believe that others who are important to them think that they should use Kanban. This factor implies that the perceived social pressure to perform the behaviour will influence a person's intentions [3], and some studies indeed demonstrate its importance [9, 13, 17, 18]. Thus, there is reason to believe that peers may influence Kanban use. Research has also noted the importance of **organisational support,** the degree to which change agents promote or support efforts, as a factor in explaining an innovation's rate of adoption [14, 16, 29]. Studies therefore suggest that there is reason to believe that organisational support assists in Kanban use.

2.2 Survey Design and Data Collection

Sampling and Population: For the study, we targeted a global population of Kanban practitioners, sending out the survey to a Kanban practitioners group on LinkedIn, administered by LeanKanban Incorporated. The population includes approximately 2000 software industry practitioners using Lean and Kanban in their work.

Prior to administration, we pre-tested the survey with three experts from the software industry and three researchers. On the basis of this feedback, we revised the statements to have clearer wordings. At the beginning of the survey, participants were provided information about the purpose of the research and its benefits as well as information about the researchers. After revision, the survey was launched and remained open for one and a half months, between 20 June and 20 July 2015. During that time, 148 responses were received. Two of these responses were discarded because the participants were not using Kanban. These omissions left us with a total of 146 responses, forming the data for analysis. The survey consisted of three sections:

Demographics: This part captured information about the respondents in terms of their organisations, Kanban experience and type of training received.

Factors affecting Kanban use: The factors affecting Kanban-use questions were based on previous studies [8, 9], but adapted to the particular context of this study. All of the variables related to the model's five factors were measured using a five-point Likert-type scale, ranging from 1 (strongly disagree) to 5 (strongly agree). Survey questions are provided in the Appendix.

Benefits and challenges of using Kanban: Questions regarding Kanban benefits were formulated based on previous studies [1, 6]. A five-point Likert-type scale was used to ask the respondents to rate the significance of particular benefits to their organisations. Further, in open-ended questions, the respondents could explain the obtained benefits and challenges faced in Kanban use.

The data analysis was conducted through descriptive statistics. Before the analysis, the reliability of the factor construct measurements were analysed with Cronbach's alpha.

3 Results

The collected data set included 146 responses: 92 were from North America, 22 from Europe, 4 from Australia, 1 from South Korea and 1 from Russia. 26 respondents did not specify their country. The majority of the respondents came from North America (62.9 %). The respondents were from 27 different organisations, but 17 of the respondents failed to specify their organisations.

Most of the organisations were involved in software (n = 115) or IT services (n = 13). Other represented industries included telecommunication (n = 1) and hardware manufacturing (n = 1). Sixteen of the respondents did not identify their company's primary business. Most respondents belonged to big organisations (72.6 %, more than 250 employees); the rest worked for middle size (11 %, number of employees between "50–249") and small (13.7 %, number of employees between "10–49") organisations. Very small organisations or start-ups with 10 or less employees represented 2.7 % of the population.

Respondents' main organisational roles involved work for software development teams (n = 63) and first-level management (n = 33). Table 1 presents the respondents' Kanban training type, and Table 2 illustrates their level of Kanban knowledge.

Table 1. Respondents Kanban training

Training type (n = 146)	Freq.	Percentage
No training	10	2
Self-studying	26	18.5
Peer mentoring	22	38.4
1–4 days training	61	28.8
More than 4 days training	27	18.5

Table 2. Responds Kanban knowledge

Knowledge level	Freq.	Percentage
Novice	3	2
Advance beginner	27	18.5
Competent	56	38.4
Proficient	42	28.8
Expert	18	12.3

The majority of the respondents received (n = 88) Kanban training ranging in duration from 1–4 days (n = 61) to more than 4 days (n = 27). Only 10 respondents had no formal training but gained familiarity with Kanban. Most respondents use Kanban on most or all organisation projects (68.8 %). 23.9 % have used it for a few projects, and only 8.2 % have used it on an experimental basis.

We performed a reliability analysis to test the reliability of scale constructs [27] using Cronbach's alpha, which measures the internal consistency of the factor measured by different variables. Table 3 demonstrates that the reliability of the factor measurement is high; the Cronbach alpha value varied between 0.763 for subjective norms and 0.941 for perceived usefulness.

Attitudes towards Kanban are quite positive among Kanban users, with an average of around 4 for all variables related to perceived ease of use, perceived usefulness and perceived compatibility. Perceptions of subjective norms and organisational support appear to be somewhat lower, with averages of 3.7 and 3.6, respectively.

The high average for **perceived ease of use** variables indicates that Kanban practitioners have a positive attitude towards using Kanban because it does not require a great deal of mental effort to learn, and it is easy to use in their work. Previous studies have reported similar findings regarding software development methodologies [9, 13].

The respondents perceived that **Kanban is useful** in terms of improving their job performance, productivity and quality of work. This finding aligns with prior research [9, 13]: when new methodologies and practices are perceived as enabling job

Table 3. Results of the factors affecting Kanban use

Constructs (n = 146)	Variables	Mean	Median	Reliability α	Type
Perceived ease of use	Easy to learn	4.2	4.0	0.793	High reliability
	Does not require a lot of mental effort	3.6	4.0		
	Clear and understandable	4.1	4.0		
	Easy to use	4.0	4.0		
Perceived usefulness	Useful in my job	4.3	5.0	0.941	Excellent reliability
	Improves my job performance	3.9	4.0		
	Increases my productivity	3.8	4.0		
	Enhances the quality of my job	3.8	4.0		
	Makes it easier to do my job	4.0	4.0		
	Overall using Kanban is useful in my job	4.2	4.0		
Perceived compatibility	Compatible with all aspects of my work	3.9	4.0	0.880	High reliability
	Fits well with the way I work	4.0	4.0		
	Compatible with the way our team organises work	4.0	4.0		
Subjective norms	People who influence my work think that I should use Kanban	3.7	4.0	0.763	High reliability
	Co-workers think that I should use Kanban	3.7	4.0		
Organisational support	Specialised Kanban training is available	3.5	4.0	0.809	High reliability
	Written Kanban instructions are available	3.5	4.0		
	Management provides necessary help and resources	3.7	4.0		

performance, they are more likely to be used and adopted. Respondents **perceived Kanban as compatible** with how they organised their individual and team work. Previous empirical studies have verified the importance of perceived compatibility in development methodologies [9, 13, 30]. The emphasis on teamwork in software development creates social pressure on individuals. Kanban software development teams emphasise collaborative work, which may bring about social pressure at the individual level. Therefore, practitioners are more likely to adopt Kanban when the **subjective norms** for use are strong. Some studies have found subjective norms to be significant [9, 20], while others found them to be insignificant [8, 13]. In this study, the participants' responses were positive in regards to subjective norms. The respondents were also positive in their responses regarding **organisational support**. They noted that their organisations provide necessary resources to support Kanban use, including training and written Kanban guidance documents. The literature shows that organisational support, such as external training and consultation, plays an important role in the use of Agile methodologies [20]. Training brings fresh perspectives to software industry practitioners while enabling their use of Kanban. Studies suggest that training positively affects individuals' beliefs about the perceived compatibility of an innovation [20, 31]. Because methodology training is the key to successful implementation [28], Kanban adoption is more likely to be successful with organisational support.

3.1 Kanban Benefits

As presented in Fig. 2, the Kanban practitioners rated the significance of particular benefits [1, 6]. Respondents further explained their obtained Kanban-use benefits with the help of open-ended questions.

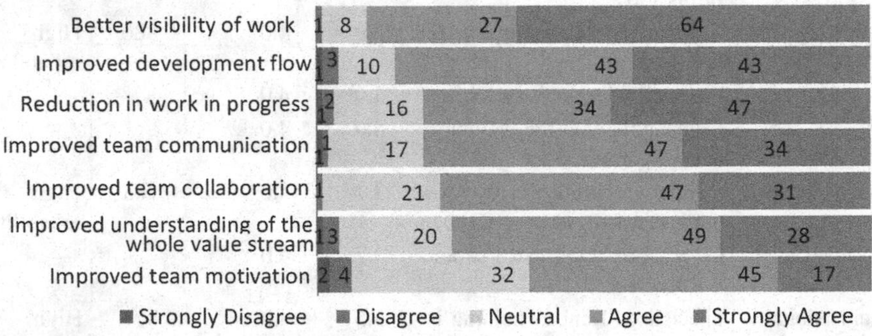

Fig. 2. Kanban benefits (Color figure online)

The top two benefits were improved visibility of work and improved development flow, findings verified in previous studies [1, 3, 5, 6, 10]. Respondents elaborated as follows:

> *"The most important benefit is how the visualization of your workflow increases the need for continuous improvement".*
> *"Kanban provides a very large increase in the ability to identify and minimize impediments as well as allow the team to self-swarm and work to bring resolution to potential trouble areas".*
> *"Benefits from Kanban include quicker identification of issues, bottlenecks, etc., of our processes, thus creating performance evaluation, control and continuous improvement opportunities for our development teams".*

The third identified benefit of Kanban is that it helps to reduce WIP. It forces team members to work on a limited number of tasks at a given time, which reduces their mental stress and leads to faster completion of tasks. Respondents further explained as follows:

> *"Working on one story at a time reduces the stress".*
> *"Limiting work in progress makes it much easier for the team leaders to see what is happening in the team at any given moment in time. Before with a large amount of WIP, it was very hard to*

keep track of who was working on what and how each of our feature groups were progressing. Also, limiting WIP and focusing on our oldest stories has helped us to dramatically control our cycle time".

When WIP limits are reduced, the teams work on smaller chunks that can be completed more easily, a finding also reported in previous studies [1, 3, 5, 6, 10]. A respondent expressed his or her team experience as follows: "[*With Kanban, it is*] *easier to get smaller work items done. We had the problem that smaller items didn't get worked on because the development team only concentrated on the larger products as directed by the product team. By splitting large work items up into smaller* [*pieces*] *we could get the smaller work items through as well*".

Finally, Kanban helps to improve communication and collaboration inside the teams and with related stakeholders. The respondents explained that Kanban "*improves communication with the customers and other stakeholders, helps to collaborate and find solutions, improves the knowledge about the processes collecting data and using metrics*". The teams work collaboratively on tasks and find solutions for any impediments, which is a sign of team self-organisation.

3.2 Challenges in Kanban Use

In an open-ended question, respondents shared challenges in using Kanban in their organisation. These challenges are organised in three main categories.

Lack of proper training and misunderstanding of Kanban is a major challenge in its use. Surprisingly, the respondents demonstrated positive attitudes towards organisational support variables in the adopted research model. This finding could be due to the fact that respondents mentioned that co-workers usually teach Kanban's key concepts and ways of working within organisations. This mentoring process can transfer bad habits and misunderstandings of Kanban's key concepts. One respondent explains, "*It (Kanban) is mostly taught through peer reviews and co-workers. If a set of people have a bad habit, that habit is often duplicated by those they train*".

Other respondents made these statements:

"*Kanban is very often misinterpreted and seen only as having work items visualised and progressed through on a board*".
"*The biggest challenge I face is the lack of knowledge and understanding about what Kanban really is and the technical aspects of how to do it. Many people think they know but they really don't know anything about it. So demystifying it for them has been an on-going and challenging issue*". Interestingly, similar challenges have been reported in earlier studies [1, 5, 6, 25].

Organisational culture and mind set is the second major challenge mentioned by respondents. They noted that management is quite busy and fails to devote attention to improving work processes. Further, there is mind-set challenge because managers prefer to use traditional methods, resisting the new way of working. Similar to other Agile methods, Kanban faces challenges in organisational culture and people's mind-sets [1, 5, 6, 25]. Respondents mentioned the following:

"*Time is not reserved for improving ways of working*" "*People and management are too busy to improve, resulting in not caring about process management methods. Some managers still prefer Microsoft projects and traditional methods*".

Silos are created by top management and defended by middle management. Upper management seems hesitant to adopt Kanban".
Many people are resistant to change; there is a lack of proper culture and management involvement and commitment".

Difficulties in Kanban implementation can be linked to a number of other challenges. For example, the respondents noted that there was a lack of proper planning before introducing Kanban to teams. With poor planning, the teams found it difficult to determine and respect WIP limits. They also found it challenging to work with remote offices and to see the big picture of work when broken down into smaller pieces. These challenges were expressed in these statements:

"Work is broken down into smaller pieces, which make it more difficult to see the big picture".
"After a period of time, we need to level set to get back on WIP limit awareness and Kanban board protocol. It is challenging to determine correct WIP limits. Stories are often so closely related that developers are conflicting with each other, resulting in difficult merges, etc. Developers have no power to change the process. When work is impeded, it's unclear what the impeded developer is supposed to do. Kanban slows everything down for the sake of providing information".

Again, earlier studies confirm these findings [1, 5, 6, 25, 28].

4 Validity Threats

In this study, we considered threats to validity throughout the research process by following the guidelines outlined by Runeson and Höst [26]. With online surveys, there is always a risk that questions may be misunderstood. To reduce this risk, we pre-tested the survey with three experts from the software industry and three researchers. It is important to take in consideration that this study is not empirically validating the adopted model. There could be other factors which are affecting Kanban actual use.

The survey was posted on LinkedIn; there was no control for the researchers with respect to external validity (i.e., the general applicability of the results). What can be observed is that the respondents come from various sectors, such as software companies, telecommunication services and hardware manufacturing companies. It is important to note that the study subjects were individuals who represented different organisations. Therefore, it would have been impossible for a single person to answer on behalf of the whole organisation. Additionally, respondents' positions and roles vary within the organisations. Respondents in different organisational positions may have divergent views about the organisational practices and varying knowledge about Kanban, factors that could affect the reliability of the results to some degree. The respondents that opted to answer are more positive towards Kanban use; it may cause positive bias in the study.

We intentionally selected the LeanKanban LinkedIn community to obtain an appropriate data sample because the community has an understanding of Kanban and its use at work. LinkedIn professional are considered groups to be a good source of data collection for researchers and practitioners from all seniority levels [32].

5 Conclusion and Future Work

This research sought to explore the factors that practitioners consider to be important in the use of Kanban. It also investigated participants' perceived Kanban benefits and challenges. The study indicates that perceived usefulness, perceived ease of use, perceived compatibility, subjective norms and organisational support can play important roles in Kanban use. Kanban practitioners find it easy to learn and use in their individual and team work. They also believe that Kanban is compatible with their work and useful in terms of improving job performance, productivity and quality.

In general, it is important for managers to monitor and evaluate innovation factors, such as perceived usefulness and perceived compatibility. Such monitoring will help to sustain effective Kanban use while enabling recognition of any need for change. Higher management support remains vital to Kanban initiatives in order to sustain visible benefits throughout the organisation.

The results show three primary benefits of using Kanban: improved visibility of work, stronger development flow and reduced WIP. The respondents expressed that starting to use Kanban at work is not a straightforward process; rather, it requires convincing managers, developers and trainers. Kanban practitioners also reported three main challenges in Kanban use: organisational culture and mind set; lack of training and misunderstanding of Kanban; and difficulties in Kanban implementation.

In the future, similar studies are needed in different regions and countries. Such studies would enable comparison of the latest trends in Kanban use and adoption around the globe. Additionally, future qualitative studies should focus explicitly on issues and problems.

Acknowledgments. We would like to thank the participants and companies who take part in this study. This research was carried out within the DIGILE Need for Speed program, and partially funded by Tekes (the Finnish Funding Agency for Technology and Innovation). We would like to thank LeanKanban incorporated and the participating companies.

Appendix: Operationalization of Constructs

See Table 4.

Table 4. Likert scales.

Constructs	Questions
Perceived ease of use	I find Kanban easy to use
	I find Kanban useful in my job
	I find Kanban clear and understandable
	Learning to use Kanban was easy for me
	Using Kanban does not require a lot of mental effort
Perceived usefulness	Using Kanban increases my productivity
	Using Kanban makes it easier to do my job
	Using Kanban improves my job performance
	Using Kanban enhances the quality of my job
	Overall, using Kanban is useful in my job
Perceived compatibility	Kanban fits well with the way I work
	Kanban is compatible with all aspects of my work
	Kanban is compatible with the way our team organize work
Subjective norm	People who influence my work think that I should use Kanban
	Co-workers think that I should use Kanban
Organisational support	Specialized training concerning Kanban is available to me
	Written instructions concerning Kanban are available to me
	Management provides the necessary help and resources to enable people to use Kanban
Kanban benefits	Using Kanban reduced work in progress
	Using Kanban improved team motivation
	Using Kanban improved development flow
	Using Kanban improved team collaboration
	Using Kanban improved team communication
	Using Kanban improved understanding of the whole value stream
Open ended question	Please describe, what other benefits are obtained with Kanban use
	Please describe, what do you consider as the main challenges of Kanban in your organisation

References

1. Al-Baik, O., Miller, J.: The kanban approach, between agility and leanness: a systematic review. Empirical Softw. Eng. **20**(6), 1–37 (2014)
2. Liker, J.: The Toyota Way. McGraw-Hill, New York (2004)
3. Hiranabe, K.: Kanban applied to software development: From agile to lean, InfoQ. http://www.infoq.com/articles/hiranabe-lean-agile-kanban. Accessed 4 May 2015

4. Shalloway, A., Guy, B., Trott, R.J.: Lean-agile Software Development: Achieving Enterprise Agility. Pearson Education, Boston (2009)
5. Ahmad, M.O., Markkula, J., Oivo, M., Kuvaja, P.: Usage of Kanban in software companies: an empirical study on motivation, benefits and challenges. In: Proceedings of 9th International Conference on Software Engineering Advances (2014)
6. Ahmad, M.O., Markkula, J., Oivo, M.: Kanban in software development: a systematic literature review. In: Proceedings of IEEE 39th Euromicro SEAA (2013)
7. Boeg, J.: Priming Kanban: A 10 Step Guide to Optimizing Flow in Your Software Delivery System, 2nd edn. Trifork, Amsterdam (2012)
8. Dybå, T., Moe, N.B., Mikkelsen, E.M.: An empirical investigation on factors affecting software development acceptance and utilization of Electronic Process Guides. In: Proceedings of Software Metrics, 10th International Symposium (Metrics 2004), pp. 220–231 (2004)
9. Riemenschneider, C.K., Hardgrave, B.C., Davis, F.D.: Explaining software developer acceptance of methodologies: a comparison of five theoretical models. IEEE Trans. Softw. Eng. **28**(12), 1135–1145 (2002)
10. Anderson, D.: Kanban – Successful Evolutionary Change for Your Technology Business. Blue Hole Press, Sequim (2010)
11. Davis, F.: Perceived usefulness, perceived ease of use, and user acceptance of information technology. MIS Q. **13**(3), 318–339 (1989)
12. Davis, F., Bagozzi, R., Warshaw, P.: User acceptance of computer technology: a comparison of two theoretical models. Manage. Sci. **35**(8), 982–1003 (1989)
13. Hardgrave, B.C., Johnson, R.A.: Toward an information systems development acceptance model: the case of object-oriented systems development. IEEE Trans. Eng. Manage. **50**(3), 322–336 (2003)
14. Iivari, J.: Why are CASE tools not used? Commun. ACM **39**(10), 94–103 (1996)
15. Moore, G.C., Benbasat, I.: Development of an instrument to measure the perceptions of adopting an information technology innovation. Inf. Syst. Res. **2**(3), 192–222 (1991)
16. Rogers, E.M.: Diffusion of Innovations, 4th edn. The Free Press, New York (1995)
17. Venkatesh, V., Davis, F.: A theoretical extension of the technology acceptance model: four longitudinal field studies. Manage. Sci. **46**(2), 186–204 (2000)
18. Taylor, S., Todd, P.: Understanding information technology usage: a test of competing models. Inf. Syst. Res. **6**(2), 144–176 (1995)
19. Adams, D.A., Nelson, R.R., Todd, P.A.: Perceived usefulness, ease of use, and usage of information technology: a replication. MIS Q. **16**, 227–247 (1992)
20. Chan, F.K., Thong, J.Y.: Acceptance of agile methodologies: A critical review and conceptual framework. Decis. Support Syst. **46**(4), 803–814 (2009)
21. Wang, X., Conboy, K., Pikkarainen, M.: Assimilation of agile practices in use. Inf. Syst. J. **22**(6), 435–455 (2012)
22. Kniberg, H., Skarin, M.: Kanban and scrum – Making the most of both, InfoQ (2010)
23. Ladas, C.: Scrumban – Essays on Kanban Systems for Lean Software Development. Modus Cooperandi Press, Salt Lake City (2009)
24. Middleton, P., Joyce, D.: Lean software management: BBC Worldwide case study. IEEE Trans. Eng. Manage. **59**(1), 20–32 (2012)
25. Rodríguez, P., Markkula, J., Oivo, M., Turula, K.: Survey on agile and lean usage in Finnish software industry. In: Proceedings of the ACM-IEEE International Symposium on Empirical Software Engineering and Measurement, pp. 139–148. ACM (2012)
26. Runeson, P., Höst, M.: Guidelines for conducting and reporting case study research in software engineering. Empirical Softw. Eng. **14**(2), 131–164 (2009)
27. Kline, P.: The Handbook of Psychological Testing. Routledge, London (1999)

28. Roberts, T.L., Hughes, C.T.: Obstacles to implementing a system development methodology. J. Syst. Manage. **47**(2), 36–40 (1996)
29. Nerur, S., Mahapatra, R., Mangalaraj, G.: Challenges of migrating to agile methodologies. Commun. ACM **48**(5), 73–78 (2005)
30. McManus, J.: Team agility. Comput. Bull. **45**(5), 26–27 (2003)
31. Agarwal, R., Prasad, J.: A field study of the adoption of software process innovations by information systems professionals. IEEE Trans. Eng. Manage. **47**(3), 295–308 (2000)
32. de Mello, R.M., da Silva, P.C., Travassos, G.H.: Investigating probabilistic sampling approaches for large-scale surveys in software engineering. In: Proceedings of 11th Workshop on Experimental Software Engineering (2014)
33. Ahmad, M.O., Kuvaja, P., Oivo, M., Markkula, J.: Transition of software maintenance teams from Scrum to Kanban. In: 49th Hawaii International Conference on System Sciences (2016)

Key Challenges in Software Startups Across Life Cycle Stages

Xiaofeng Wang[1](✉), Henry Edison[1], Sohaib Shahid Bajwa[1], Carmine Giardino[1], and Pekka Abrahamsson[2]

[1] Free University of Bozen-Bolzano, Piazza Domenicani 3, 39100 Bolzano, Italy
xiaofeng.wang@unibz.it

[2] Norwegian University of Science Technology, 7491 Trondheim, Norway
http://www.unibz.it
http://softwarestartups.org

Abstract. Software startups are challenging endeavours, with various road blocks on their path to success. The current understanding of the challenges that software startups may encounter is very limited. In this paper, we use the research framework of learning and product development stages to analyse the key challenges that software startups have to deal with at different life cycle stages, from problem definition to solution validation and from concept to mature product. Based on an analysis of the empirical data collected by a large survey of 4100 startups, we find out that what perceived as biggest challenges by software startups do vary across different life cycle stages. Building product is the biggest obstacle for software startups, even though its significance decreases when the learning focuses of the startups move from problem to solution and their products mature. Business related challenges such as customer acquisition and scaling are more noticeable at the later stages. Our study raises the awareness of these challenges and suggests to tackle right challenges at the right time.

Keywords: Software startups · Challenges · Learning · Product development stages · Building product

1 Introduction

Startups are newly created companies that aspire to grow fast in extreme uncertainty. They are considered one of the key drivers of economic growth [1]. But what is also often underlined is the alarmingly high failure rate of startups. Sixty percent of startups do not survive in the first five years, whilst seventy five percent of venture capital funded startups fail [2]. This demonstrates that startups are very challenging endeavours. It is especially true for software startups. According to Sutton [3], software startups are characterized by little or no operating history. Most of them are young and immature. There is a serious lack of time and resource. Moreover, they are subject to multiple influences from an environment that is extremely dynamic, unpredictable and even chaotic.

H. Sharp and T. Hall (Eds.): XP 2016, LNBIP 251, pp. 169–182, 2016.
DOI: 10.1007/978-3-319-33515-5_14

A good understanding of the challenges that software startups have to cope with can help entrepreneurs to be better prepared when confronted by them, and to overcome them eventually.

However, the current Software Engineering (SE) literature offers very limited understanding of the challenges in the context of software startups. A very few number of studies have investigated them in specific areas such as decision making [4], or user experience design [5]. A broader view has been taken in our previous study [6], which examines the key challenges emerging from different areas of early stage software startups. What left unexplored are the challenges faced by software startups at later stages, and how the challenges differ across a startup life cycle. Based on this observation, our study aims at offering a complete and comprehensive understanding of the key challenges in software startups. To this end, we adopted the research framework of learning and product development stages to analyse the key challenges faced by software startups. The main research question asked in our study is:

RQ: what are the key challenges faced by software startups at different learning and product development stages?

To answer the research question, we draw upon the empirical data obtained from a large-scale survey of worldwide software startups conducted between 2013 and 2014. The responses from 4100 software startups were included in the data analysis. The main results of our study is a comprehensive list of challenges faced by software startups at different stages and the contextual understanding of them in terms of learning and product development stages.

The rest of the paper is organized as follows: in Sect. 2, the related work are presented drawing upon relevant software engineering and business literature. Section 3 provides more details on the survey. It is followed by the presentation of the findings in Sect. 4, which are further discussed in Sect. 5, together with the reflection on the limitations of the study. The paper is summarized in Sect. 6 outlining the future research.

2 Literature Review

2.1 Challenges in Software Startups

As Bosch et al. [4] point out, in order to understand the many challenges that software startups face, there is need to understand what a software startup is. An increasingly accepted definition of startup is from Ries [7], a human institution designed to deliver a new product or service under the conditions of extreme uncertainty. This definition highlights the characteristic of no or limited history that a software startup has [3], and the chaotic environment it operates in. However, the definition does not emphasize the intention of a startup to find a scalable and sustainable business model [8], which is a key distinguishing characteristic from established small businesses.

There are few studies that investigate the challenges faced by software startups in SE research field [9,10], due to the nascent nature of software startup as a research area. One study that touches upon the challenges in early-stage startups is Bosch et al. [4]. One of the two research questions the study explores is what are the typical challenges when finding a product idea worth scaling. They conducted qualitative interviews with the practitioners in nine startup companies. The interviewees confirm that it is very difficult to know how to work in a straight forward manner in early stage startups, and that decision-making support is limited. However no other challenges have been mentioned and the focus of the study itself is less on investigating the challenges and more on developing a methodology to support multiple product ideas being investigated in parallel.

Another study is focused on the specific challenges software startups confront with respect to user experience design, an increasingly important aspect of software engineering. Based on an interview study with eight startups on their approaches to user experience work, Hokkanen and Väänänen-Vainio-Mattila [5] discover several user experience related challenges, including collecting meaningful information from users or customers, applying right method for collecting user feedback, and approaching right set of users.

Our previous study [6] investigated the key challenges faced by software startups at early stages. By "early stage" we mean "from idea conceptualization to first time to market". Based on a survey study, a list of top 10 challenges were identified: thriving in technology uncertainty, acquiring first paying customers, acquiring initial funding, building entrepreneurial team, delivering customer value, managing multiple tasks, defining minimum viable product, targeting a niche market, staying focused and disciplined, and reaching the break-even point. These challenges are further classified into product, market, finance and team categories. A case study of two software startups is also presented in the paper, to provide a richer understanding than that allowed by a ranking list only. Since the focus of the study is limited to early stage software startups, a complete picture of the challenges faced by software startups at different stages is missing. The study presented in this paper is a continuation of [6] and intends to fill the observed knowledge gap.

2.2 Startup Life Cycle Stages

Learning is a crucial aspect and element for any startup, as emphasized by the Lean Startup methodology [7]. According to Ries [7], startups do not exist to "make stuff". They exist to "learn how to build a sustainable business". The process of learning can be divided into four stages in accordance to the customer development process [8]: defining or observing a problem; evaluating the problem; defining a solution; and evaluating the solution. It is worth emphasizing that the learning stages are not linear. Startups need to go through multiple build-measure-learn loops to find their sustainable business models.

On the other hand, a startup goes through a product development process in parallel [8], which can be further divided into the following stages: concept, in development, working prototype, functional product with limited users, functional product with high growth, and mature product. While the learning process is engaged in customer-centric activities mainly happening outside the building, product development is focused on the product-centric activities that are taking place internally. As contended by Blank [8], for a startup to succeed, the two processes must remain synchronized and operate in concert.

In this study, we adopt both learning and product development stages as the perspectives on the life cycle of a software startup, and use them to systematically analyse the perceived challenges.

3 Research Approach

This study is based on a large survey that was employed to explore different aspects of software startups. For the purpose of this study, we only used a subset of the questions in the whole survey. These questions are composed of three parts. In the first part, the respondents were asked to provide background information about their startups, including the principal business domains, the countries they work in, and their roles within their startups. The second part is composed of the questions related to the learning stages and product development stages. Each question should be answered with a single choice from a set of predefined options as described in Sect. 2.2. In the third part, the participants were asked to provide three most significant challenges they perceived recently when working on their startups, ranked as biggest, second biggest and third biggest. Each question in this part should also be answered with a single choice from a set of predefined challenges. To obtain the set of challenges, various online forums related to entrepreneurship were searched. However, one open option was given when each challenge question was asked. If a respondent could not find a suitable option from the list, there was a possibility to specify a different challenge. The list of survey questions relevant to this study can be found in Appendix A.

In total 8240 responses were received. We went through a more strict data cleaning process than that employed in our previous study [6] in order to ensure the quality of the data to be used in the analysis phase. First of all, we filtered out the responses that missed the values in the fields related to learning stage, product development stage and perceived biggest challenge. The data in these fields are mandatory for us to conduct further analysis. Since the unit of analysis is software startup company, we removed the data points which either did not provide startup names or entered suspicious names, such as “balh”, “ABC”, “name”, etc. Secondly, we identified the companies that have multiple responses in the survey, and kept the response from the most senior role of the company based on the assumption that he/she would have a more holistic view of the company. If the roles of the respondents were not provided, we took the last entered entry from the same company. To further clean the data, we removed the responses which did not confirm that the startups in question were still in operation at the time the survey was answered, since the challenges were about those “recently” faced by the startups. If a startup was no more in operation, the answer about the challenges may not be as recent as requested. Last but not least, we removed what we considered “outlier” responses and data points showing some abnormal patterns. As a result, the total sample size was reduced to 4100.

To answer the research question, what are the key challenges faced by software startups at different learning stages and product development stages, we examined the frequency at which each challenge was perceived by the respondents based on the learning stages and product development stages their startups are at. To determine if the challenges perceived by the startups are related to the stages they are at, we formulated the following hypotheses that need to be tested:

H1: There are differences between learning stages regarding the challenges perceived by software startups.

H2: There are differences between product development stages regarding the challenges perceived by software startups.

Since the stages (both learning stages and product development stages) and challenge are categorical variables, to test the relatedness between two categorical variables, Pearson Chi-square test is a suitable statistics. We also checked the expected frequency counts of the cross-tabulation fed into the tests, to make sure that the validity requirements of Chi-square test are met, e.g., no more than 20 % of the cells containing the frequency counts less than 5, and none containing 0 value. We used statistics software package R for both frequency counting and running Chi-square tests.

4 Results

4.1 Background of the Sampled Software Startups

Except the 487 responses that did not reveal locating countries, 3613 sampled software startups come from seventy three countries around the world. Not surprisingly, the majority are located in the United Stages (51.3 %), followed by countries such as Canada (4.98 %), United Kingdom (3.44 %), Israel (2.83 %), Australia (2.61 %), Germany and India (both 2.07 %). The business domains that these startup companies operate in are very diverse and there is no dominant one emerging from the data. The example domains include travel, art and gifts, fashion, e-commerce, social network, idea management, event management, social advertising, project and task management, mobile and social games, luxury hobbies, real estate, e-learning, financial services, health care, etc. The types of software these startups develop are shown in Fig. 1.

The typical team size in these software startups is less than 10 people. The most common team sizes are 2 persons (16.3 %), 3 persons (15.6 %), 4 persons (12.2 %), 5 persons (10.6 %) and also, as one respondent put it, "One man army" (9.88 %). In contrast to the very small team sizes, it is interesting to see that the respondents used more than 200 different terms to describe the roles they are playing in their startups. The most frequently mentioned roles are "CEO" (2710), followed by "CTO" (459) and "Engineer" (171). Apart from the traditional chief officer titles, there are also "CXO" (Chief user eXperience Officer), "COO" (Chief Operation Officer), "CPO" (Chief Product Officer), etc. Some interesting titles reflect the characteristics of entrepreneurs, such as "All the hats", "jack of all trades", "General Specialist", "do-it-all", "all-in-one", "all rounder", or

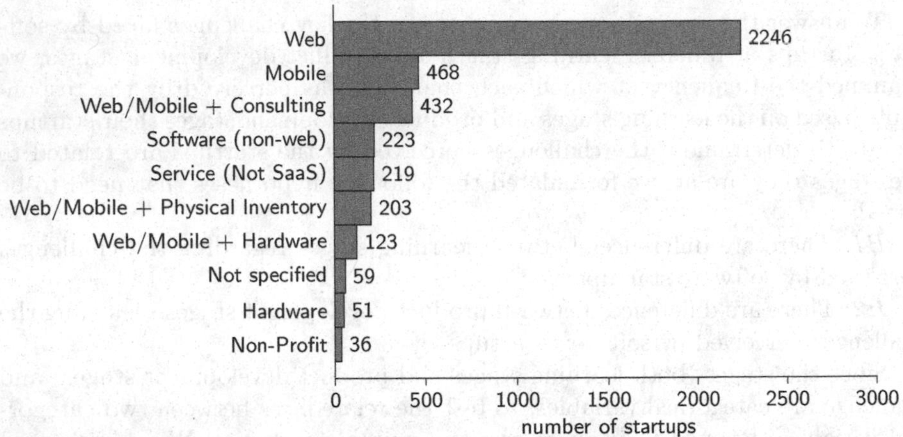

Fig. 1. The types of software applications developed by the startups

"we dont have defined roles". Others expose nicely the role a founder plays, e.g., "visionary", "Chief Visionary", "Chief cook and dish washer", "motivator", or "guy that does stuff".

4.2 Key Challenges Across Life Cycle Stages

The sampled software startups are scattered at the different life cycle stages. As shown in Table 1, in terms of product development stages, the majority are working on either prototypes or functional products with limited users. Only less than 3 % of the startups consider their products mature. In terms of the learning stages, most consider they are in the stage of either validating problems or defining solutions.

Table 1 shows the distribution of sampled software startups across learning stages and product development stages. The biggest percentage are the startups at the stage of defining the solutions and working on functional product with limited users. Two startups are at the problem definition stage but already working on either functional product with high growth or mature product. It might be that the two data points are not valid, or the two startups are truly outliers.

Table 2 lists the challenges perceived by the sampled software startups. It shows that *building product* is the biggest challenge for 859 startups, the second biggest for 560 and the third biggest for further 327. In total 1746 startups consider it a key challenge. *Customer acquisition*, *funding* and *building the team* are the following big concerns of more than a thousand of startup companies each. In contrast, *legal* and *regulations* are perceived as challenges by least startups in the sample.

Figure 2 (generated from the frequency table in Appendix B) depicts how the software startups at one learning stage perceive their biggest challenges differently

Table 1. Distribution of software startups across learning and product development stages

	Problem definition	Problem validation	Solution definition	Solution validation	Total
Concept	113 (2.76 %)	187 (4.56 %)	118 (2.88 %)	23 (0.56 %)	441
In development	74 (1.80 %)	366 (8.93 %)	331 (8.07 %)	35 (0.85 %)	806
Working prototype	32 (0.78 %)	337 (8.22 %)	358 (8.73 %)	53 (1.29 %)	780
Functional product with limited users	3 (0.07 %)	295 (7.20 %)	1038 (25.32 %)	275 (6.71 %)	1611
Functional product with high growth	1 (0.02 %)	14 (0.34 %)	124 (3.02 %)	202 (4.93 %)	341
Mature product	1 (0.02 %)	11 (0.27 %)	40 (0.98 %)	69 (1.68 %)	121
Total	224	1210	2009	657	4100

*The percentages are cell percentages.

than those at another learning stage. As shown in Fig. 2, *building product* as the most frequently perceived biggest challenge is clearly visible, even though the percentage of software startups decreases while the learning stage is advancing.

Another key challenge, the importance of which declines, is *minimum viable product.* it starts as the third most frequently perceived big challenge at the first learning stage - problem definition. In the solution validation stage, instead, it gives way to other challenges which are much less perceived at the first learning stage, such as *critical mass, leadership & team alignment, over capacity/too much to do*, and *revenue. Staying focused & disciplined* shows a similar pattern to *minimum viable product.*

It is interesting to compare the pair *problem solution fit* and *product market fit.* It can be observed that the first fit is a much more perceived challenge than the second at the first learning stage. However its percentage decreases while the startups are focused more on the second fit in later learning stages.

On the contrary, the percentage of software startups that perceive *customer acquisition* as the biggest challenge increases along the learning stages. For the software startups at the solution validation stage, *customer acquisition* exceeds *building product* noticeably and becomes the biggest challenge for the majority startups at this learning stage. Similarly, *partnership* and *scaling* are not perceived as the biggest challenges by the software startups at the first learning stage. They are perceived so by the startups at later learning stages, especially *scaling*, the significance of which increases greatly at the last stage.

The percentage change of *funding* takes a different shape. It is perceived as crucial in the first learning stage, but becomes much more noticeable in the problem validation and solution definition phases. Instead, its significance drops back a bit at the solution validation stage. The percentage of *building the team* challenge does not reveal any obvious pattern of change. Even though fluctuating visibly, it remains as a significant concern across the learning stages. The change

Table 2. Overview of key challenges perceived by software startups

	No. of software startups that perceive			
	As 1st challenge	As 2nd challenge	As 3rd challenge	Total
Building product	859	560	327	1746
Customer acquisition	678	454	324	1456
Funding	526	393	420	1339
Building the team	317	394	293	1004
Business model	282	345	250	877
Over capacity/Too much to do	262	309	289	860
Revenue	150	202	326	678
Minimum viable product	130	218	260	608
Staying focused & disciplined	248	191	152	591
Product market fit	151	186	193	530
Critical mass	161	162	132	455
Scaling	92	107	176	375
Problem solution fit	95	100	100	295
Leadership & team alignment	60	99	111	270
Partnership	44	71	114	229
Legal	35	56	61	152
Regulations	10	27	28	65

of *business model* does not follow any particular pattern either. However it is visible that the percentage of the startups perceiving it as the biggest challenge drops significantly from the first learning stage to the rest of the learning process. *Legal* and *regulation* remain as the least perceived challenges across the learning stages.

Figure 3 (based on a frequency table similar to the one in Appendix B, with product development rather than learning as the stage) depicts how the software startups at one product development stage perceive their biggest challenges differently than those at another product development stage. The challenges in Fig. 3 show less regular patterns when the stages are more granular. But some similar tendencies are still observable, such as *building product* decrease vs. *customer acquisition* increase. There are a couple of noticeable differences. One is the percentage change pattern of *funding*. Even though the significance drops as in the learning stage figure, it is more significant at the early stages of product development, especially at the development and prototyping stages, which is understandable since the companies have no products to sell therefore need funding to sustain the product development. Another notable difference is that *legal* as the biggest challenge is not perceived by any of the startup companies with mature products.

To test the hypotheses that there are differences between different learning stages (H1) and product development stages (H2) regarding the challenges perceived by the software startups, we run the Chi-square tests on the datasets (see Appendix B as an example). The results are shown in Table 3. With p-value $<$ 0.0001, H1 and H2 are supported with high confidence. We repeated the Chi-square tests on the second and third biggest challenges perceived by the software startups at different stages of learning and product development. They are also significantly related to the learning and product development stages. Therefore H1 and H2 are supported again by taking into account the second and third biggest challenges.

5 Discussion

Table 2 adds more perceived big challenges to the list reported in [6]. The new entries are *revenue*, *scaling*, *problem solution fit*, *leadership & team alignment*, *partnership*, *legal* and *regulations*. Among them only *problem solution fit* is clearly a concern more relevant to early stage startups [11]. In comparison to the key challenges in early stage software startups reported in our previous study [6], the list of top ten challenges in Table 2 does not differ much[1]. The only change is that *revenue*, in the place of *critical mass*, becomes one of the top ten key challenges across the stages. The little variance between the two lists can be explained by the fact that the sample used in this study, even though including all stages of software startups, is skewed towards early stage startups. Table 1 shows that the majority of the startups in the sample are at early stages (at the first four stages of product development).

Our study results demonstrate that *building product* is the biggest challenge faced by software startups at all stages, not just those at an early stage as shown in [6]. Along the same line of argument in [6], this finding is consistent with the generally innovative nature of software startups who are often chasing new technological changes and disrupting the software industry. Therefore they need to deal with cutting edge technology and apply innovative tools and techniques, which renders product development challenging endeavours.

With an extremely small p-value (<0.0001), the hypotheses H1 and H2 are supported, which means that what are perceived as the biggest challenges by software startups do vary across different learning as well as product development stages. Even though it is difficult to declare a global change pattern based on Figs. 2 and 3, it is noticeable that the significance of product and finance related challenges, such as *building the product*, *minimum viable product* and *funding*, decreases when learning and product development progress. In comparison, market related challenges such as *customer acquisition* and *scaling* become increasingly perceivable. This is hardly surprising since the main focuses and tasks of startups shift along their life cycles, so do the concerns and challenges entrepreneurial teams have to tackle. The picture is less clear when people and team related challenges are concerned, including *building the team* and *stay focus & disciplined*. There is no detectable overall tendency. This is somehow contradictory to our expectation that the more advanced startups are, the more stable and better jelled entrepreneurial teams are, and therefore the less people and team related challenges are perceived.

[1] The names of the challenges reported in [6] were the adapted versions of the ones reported in this paper. The purpose of the adaptation was to better reflect the characteristics and focus of early stage software startups.

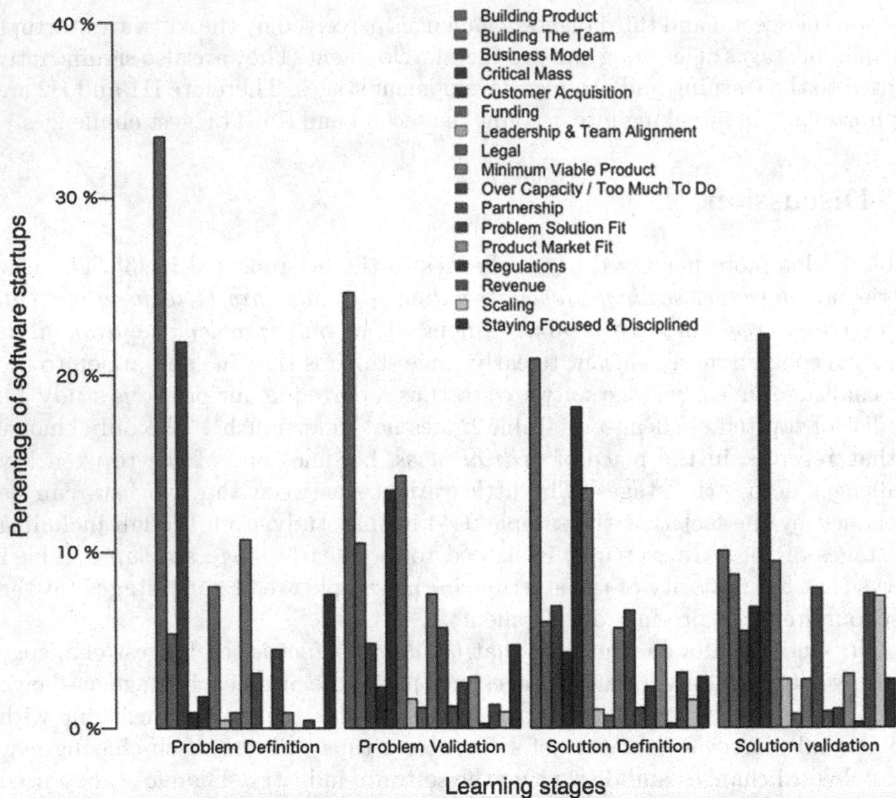

Fig. 2. Distribution of software startups in terms of the biggest challenge per learning stage

Table 3. Chi-square test results

	H1(learning stages)	H2(product development stages)
X-squared	506.9612	943.4645
df(degree of freedom)	48	80
p-value <	0.0001	0.0001

In addition, our data analysis reveals that, in a few software startups, learning and product development stages are not synchronised (e.g., as shown in Table 1), or they are dealing with challenges that are either too early or too late to confront in terms of what need to be learnt or what need to be developed, e.g., confronting *product market fit* at the problem definition phase (the first learning stage), or still tackling *problem solution fit* when the product is already mature. As argued in [11], investing on product market fit strategies prematurely given that users are not yet sold on the product can be a crucial failure factor. On the other

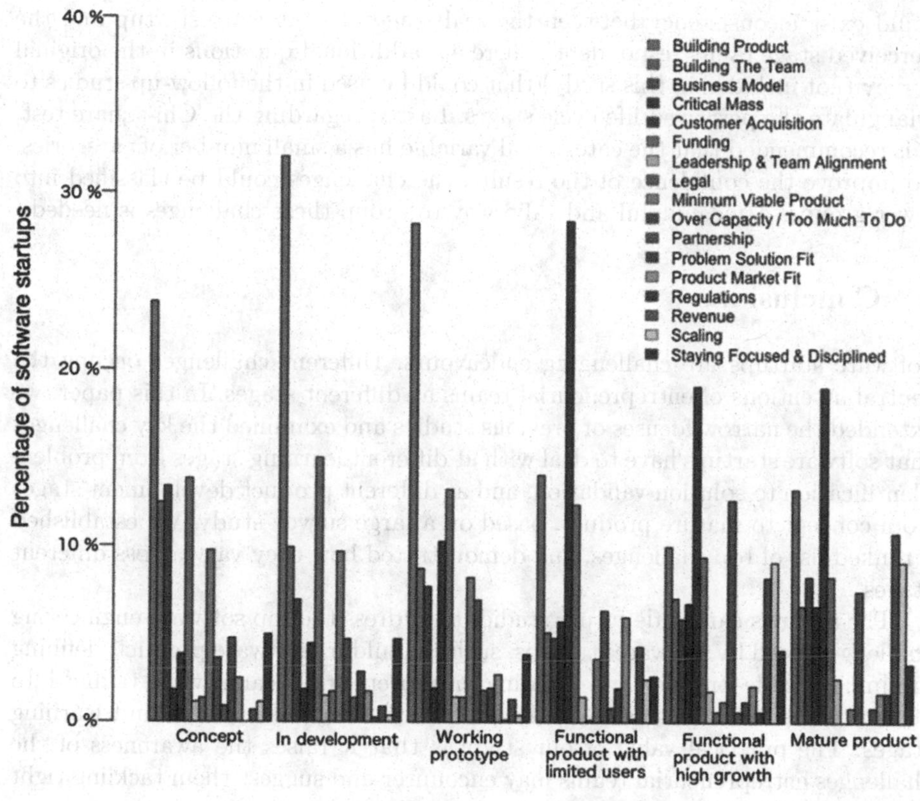

Fig. 3. Distribution of software startups in terms of the biggest challenge per product development stage

hand, having already a mature product is a huge waste if the problem solution fit is not reached.

Regarding the limitations of the study, one limitation lies in the set of predefined challenges used in the original questionnaire design. It is not based on existing literature due to the scarcity of related studies. The challenges were obtained through searching various online entrepreneurship forums. They need scientific evidence to support their validity. The fact that most survey respondents selected from the predefined set to certain extent demonstrates that these challenges are relevant and significant. Of course, the fact that no meaningful new challenges were identified in addition to the predefined list may also due to the questionnaire design. A more flexible design would encourage respondents to express the challenges in their own words, even though it means much more effort needed for data analysis. Another limitation of the study is that the life cycle stages of the software startups in the survey were chosen by the respondents, therefore were based on their opinions rather then objective evidences. There could exist inconsistency between the real stage of a software startup and the perceived stage by its respondent. There are additional questions in the original survey (not included in this study) that could be used in the follow-up studies to triangulate the perceived life cycle stages. Lastly, regarding the Chi-square test, it is recommended that the categorical variable has a small number of categories. To improve the confidence of the results, the challenges could be classified into fewer groups. A meaningful and valid way to group these challenges is needed.

6 Conclusions

Software startups are challenging endeavours. Different challenges occupy the central attentions of entrepreneurial teams at different stages. In this paper, we extended the narrow focuses of previous studies and examined the key challenges that software startups have to deal with at different learning stages from problem identification to solution validation, and at different product development stages from concept to mature product, based on a large survey study. We established a ranked list of top challenges, and demonstrated how they vary across different stages.

The findings can guide future studies to address the top software engineering challenges faced by software startups, such as building software product, defining minimum viable product and building entrepreneurial team, while taking into account contextual factors, e.g., the product development stages and learning stages. The practical value of our study is that it raises the awareness of the challenges entrepreneurial teams may encounter and suggest them tackling right ones at the right time.

The survey data provides a snapshot of the challenges faced by different software startups at different stages. A longitudinal study of different challenges faced by same companies at different stages would validate the findings from this study and provide richer contextual understanding of these challenges. It is also interesting to understand the uniqueness of the software startup challenges and their significance in comparison to other types of startups or new product development endeavours in general. Further more, future studies can investigate the potential linkage between the misalignment of learning and product development stages and startup failure.

Appendice

Appendix A Key Survey Questions

Category	Question
Demographic questions	Name of Your Startup
	Web Site
	Did you fill out the survey for a company that is still operating?
	Which best describes your role on the team?
	What kind of startup are you a part of?
	How many products do you have?
	What market are you tackling?
	What is the total size of your team?
Questions related to startup stages	What's the stage of your learning process?
	What's the stage of your primary product?
Questions related to challenges	What has recently been your startup's biggest challenge?
	What has recently been your startup's second biggest challenge?
	What has recently been your startup's third biggest challenge?

Appendix B Challenges Perceived by Software Startups at Different Learning Stages: Frequency Table

	Problem definition	Problem validation	Solution definition	Solution validation
Building product	75 (33.48 %)	298 (24.63 %)	420 (20.91 %)	66 (10.05 %)
Customer acquisition	4 (1.79 %)	163 (13.47 %)	365 (18.17 %)	146 (22.22 %)
Funding	18 (8.04 %)	173 (14.30 %)	273 (13.59 %)	62 (9.44 %)
Building the team	12 (5.36 %)	127 (10.50 %)	121 (6.02 %)	57 (8.68 %)
Business model	49 (21.88 %)	58 (4.79 %)	139 (6.92 %)	36 (5.48 %)
Over capacity/Too much to do	7 (3.13 %)	69 (5.70 %)	134 (6.67 %)	52 (7.92 %)
Revenue	1 (0.45 %)	16 (1.32 %)	63 (3.14 %)	50 (7.61 %)
Minimum viable product	24 (10.71 %)	92 (7.60 %)	114 (5.67 %)	18 (2.74 %)
Staying focused & disciplined	17 (7.59 %)	57 (4.71 %)	58 (2.89 %)	18 (2.74 %)
Product market fit	2 (0.89 %)	35 (2.89 %)	94 (4.68 %)	20 (3.04 %)
Critical mass	2 (0.89 %)	28 (2.31 %)	86 (4.28 %)	45 (6.85 %)
Scaling	0 (0 %)	11 (0.91 %)	32 (1.59 %)	49 (7.46 %)
Problem solution fit	10 (4.46 %)	31 (2.56 %)	47 (2.34 %)	7 (1.07 %)
Leadership & team alignment	1 (0.45 %)	20 (1.65 %)	21 (1.05 %)	18 (2.74 %)
Partnership	0 (0 %)	15 (1.24 %)	23 (1.14 %)	6 (0.91 %)
Legal	2 (0.89 %)	14 (1.16 %)	14 (0.70 %)	5 (0.76 %)
Regulations	0 (0 %)	3 (0.25 %)	5 (0.25 %)	2 (0.30 %)

*The percentages are column percentages.

References

1. Dishman, L.: The state of the american entrepreneur in 2015. http://www.fastcompany.com/3046773/hit-the-ground-running/the-state-of-the-american-entrepreneur-in-2015. Accessed 15 Oct 2015
2. Nobel, C.: Why companies fail-and how their founders can bounce back. Working Knowledge, Harvard Business School, Boston. http://hbswk.hbs.edu/item/6591.html (2011). Accessed 29 Aug 2013
3. Sutton, S.M.: The role of process in software start-up. IEEE Softw. **17**(4), 33–39 (2000)
4. Bosch, J., Holmström Olsson, H., Björk, J., Ljungblad, J.: The early stage software startup development model: A framework for operationalizing lean principles in software startups. In: Fitzgerald, B., Conboy, K., Power, K., Valerdi, R., Morgan, L., Stol, K.-J. (eds.) LESS 2013. LNBIP, vol. 167, pp. 1–15. Springer, Heidelberg (2013)
5. Hokkanen, L., Väänänen-Vainio-Mattila, K.: UX work in startups: Current practices and future needs. In: Lassenius, C., Dingsøyr, T., Paasivaara, M. (eds.) XP 2015. LNBIP, vol. 212, pp. 81–92. Springer, Heidelberg (2015)
6. Giardino, C., Bajwa, S.S., Wang, X., Abrahamsson, P.: Key challenges in early-stage software startups. In: Lassenius, C., Dingsøyr, T., Paasivaara, M. (eds.) XP 2015. LNBIP, vol. 212, pp. 52–63. Springer, Heidelberg (2015)
7. Ries, E.: The Lean Startup: How Today's Entrepreneurs Use Continuous Innovation to Create Radically Successful Businesses. Crown Business, New York (2011)
8. Blank, S.: The Four Steps to the Epiphany. CafePress, San Mateo (2005)
9. Paternoster, N., Giardino, C., Unterkalmsteiner, M., Gorschek, T., Abrahamsson, P.: Software development in startup companies: A systematic mapping study. Inf. Softw. Technol. **56**(10), 1200–1218 (2014)
10. Klotins, E., Unterkalmsteiner, M., Gorschek, T.: Software engineering knowledge areas in startup companies: A mapping study. In: Fernandes, J.M., Machado, R.J., Wnuk, K. (eds.) ICSOB 2015. LNBIP, vol. 210, pp. 245–257. Springer, Heidelberg (2015)
11. Giardino, C., Wang, X., Abrahamsson, P.: Why early-stage software startups Fail: A behavioral framework. In: Lassenius, C., Smolander, K. (eds.) ICSOB 2014. LNBIP, vol. 182, pp. 27–41. Springer, Heidelberg (2014)

Experience Reports

Mob Programming: Find Fun Faster

Karel Boekhout(✉)

Haarlem, The Netherlands
karel@boekhout.org

Abstract. The Mob Programming technique proves to be an effective learning instrument with a group of less experienced developers. It is also used to explore topics outside of just software development.

This paper describes how, with a set of weekly Mob Programming sessions, the teams as a whole and all its individuals have grown much faster than they could have done otherwise. They improved their coding skills, mastery of tools, involvement in Scrum ceremonies, estimation skills, process modeling (!) and learned to be much more self-sufficient.

This didn't happen without plenty of experimentation, and some dead ends. I will describe the different approaches we tried, how we ended up with a surprisingly strict process for our mobbing sessions, and how acceptance was easier with a team that had fewer ingrained habits of work.

Keywords: Learning · Pairing · Mob Programming · Discovering unknown territories

1 Introduction

It started with two teams that needed to improve their skills in many different areas but with very little support available to get them there. No seniors, no training, and a single, non-technical, coach trying to help them.

Having been impressed by the Mob Programming [3] session at XP2015 in Helsinki, I started an experiment to see whether that technique could help us accelerate the learning process. We tried Mob Programming for a period of two months, with one full day of mobbing a week. It proved to be a great experience for both the teams as well as for this coach, albeit one with a steep learning curve.

In this experience report, I show the effects mobbing had on different aspects of our work. How the adoption of the practice was different between two differently structured teams. What we did to make it work, and how mobbing was particularly effective in supporting learning and discovery in both technical skills as team maturity.

2 Situation

This experiment happened in a small department of a company (consisting of 18 people, 14 developers in 3 teams) based in Rijswijk, The Netherlands. The main period of the experiment was in the summer of 2015, fresh after the inspiration from the XP2015 conference in Helsinki.

H. Sharp and T. Hall (Eds.): XP 2016, LNBIP 251, pp. 185–192, 2016.
DOI: 10.1007/978-3-319-33515-5_15

The experiment involved two teams within the company: a junior team (let's call them team Red), and a less junior team of developers (team Yellow). The junior team, the Reds, consisted entirely of young programmers with no previous work experience as developers. There was no senior developer available to guide them, and we needed some way to accelerate their learning process. The Yellow team was also very junior but had some programming experience, some from working at another company.

This isn't a group who by themselves who would scout the outer limits of IT innovation, so I didn't expect them to be eager to try Mob Programming out. The reception was not even lukewarm; I would have to earn my pay to get this accepted.

3 Introduction of Mob Programming to Teams

I started out by showing Woody Zuill's video 'A Day of Mob Programming' [4] to the whole group. I explained that even I, a non-developer, had had a lot of fun participating in a session of Llewellyn Falco and that I would like to try it with the teams.

I told them I thought it would be fun, and mentioned similarities I saw with some of the online games that I knew the junior team members liked playing in their own time. These games are high paced shoot-'m-ups, in which they acted as a team with a lot of online communication, and I hoped the similarities would spark an interest.

A second argument was, via feedback in the retrospectives the teams had raised, that there was lot of difference in the skill level and use of tools between the team members, regardless of seniority and time with the company. Everyone agreed that it would be in the interest of the teams, the individuals and the company to spread those skills more evenly. I emphasized how Mob Programming could help us achieve this.

Still, the first reactions were lukewarm. Even while stressing that the goal was learning and not delivery, people were complaining about the apparent lack of efficiency. A senior colleague, who was not part of these teams but influential in the company, openly said he would dislike working on a daily basis as was shown in the video. I stressed that if people liked this way of working we could do it more often, but that it was not my goal to make this the new default way of working in the office. In the end, I decided to just try.

4 Experiments

As part of the series of Mob Programming sessions, we continuously adapted our way of working. When you're doing hourly retrospectives, the rate of change can be very high. In the following Sect. 1 describe some of the larger, and more important, changes that happened, and the process we ended up with.

4.1 Room Setup

We went through a few iterations before we arrived at a room setup that worked for us. Starting by just using the big screen we use for giving demo's in the main team room, we quickly found that the screen was too small, and it was hard to get everyone a position near enough to it, due to all the desks. Distractions were also an issue, with many interruptions from outside the team, and simply from people's workstations (see Fig. 1).

Fig. 1. First try: mobbing in the team room

Fig. 2. Second attempt: training room in conference-inspired setting

Fig. 3. The final setup: comfort and proper lighting

At the company we have a room designed for training. In this room we were somewhat more isolated from interruptions. The room has a projector and a big monitor for presentations. We quickly discovered that the resolution of the projector was too low and not clear enough. A good high resolution projector is the most optimal solution. We had to use the big monitor.

The setup in the training room initially resembled the setup used in the XP2015 conference setting that I participated in. We rearranged the tables to create one central table, directly in front of the monitor, with a keyboard, mouse and one laptop. We arranged some chairs in a semicircle around that driver position, and simply switched places (see Fig. 2).

We still found issues with this setup. The simple chairs, though good enough for a short mobbing session at a conference, wouldn't do for sitting on all day. So we decided to use proper office chairs, and have everybody move around keeping their chair to save time and avoid continuously fiddling with the chair configuration (see Fig. 3).

Lighting also turned out to be important; if there's too much, it makes it hard to read the screen. But when it's too dark the bright screen strains the eyes too much. By switching to a side-wall for the screen we could alleviate that particular issue.

4.2 Cycle Time

Copying Woody's video, we started with a rotation of 10 min. Unfortunately, it seemed that every change of driver and navigator became an interruption and it took the team time to get back in focus on the problem at hand. There was clearly no sign of flow.

A tip I got from Llewellyn Franco at Agile 2015 [1] proved to be very important: lower the rotation cycle from 10 to 4 min. By rotating so quickly, the switch has to go smoothly, so that you really need to make sure the workspace is good, you have a good timer and most important, that everybody is fully involved all the time. After a while, Team Red slowed to 5 min, and declared this the sweet spot for them.

4.3 Structured Breaks

Full involvement all the time can be exhausting. It's worth noting that more mature teams might experience Mob Programming less stressing than Pair Programming, due to breaks in the rotation. However, in this situation the primary goal was not delivering software, but focus was on learning though training.

So I made sure that every hour there was a 5–10 min break after the retrospective where people weren't allowed to be behind the screen. Even then a full day can feel like a marathon. The biggest advantage of a full day, was that you can do a full Sprint and finish work in one day, which people found fulfilling.

4.4 A Sprint a Day Keeps the Coach Away

I emphasized that the Mob Programming days were an experiment with the focus on learning, rather than delivering. Apparently I was a little bit too effective with the emphasis on learning and creating an environment of not delivering.

The sessions were not always happening with the full attention of everyone in the team. The results were incomplete and would bleed over into additional work outside of the mob, and inside of the containing, normal sprint. Reflecting on this, we decided to put a little more focus on the mobbing day, and have a clear goal of taking a small story and having it deployed to production. I called this the 'sprint in a day', and it did put the whole process in a pressure cooker.

The structure of that single-day-sprint was as follows:

- the team picks a user story during the planning session, taking into consideration that it had to be possible to finish the story in one day,
- the day starts with a tasking session, where the team does a breakdown of all the tasks needed to deliver the user story,
- then hourly cycles of development, which each ended in a retro and break,
- at the end of the day, the user story would be deployed to production
- the retro for the last hourly cycle is extended, looking back at the last hour and the whole day,
- the day is closed by making the retro report together as a mob,
- and we clean up the room before we leave.

Giving ourselves this goal of completing the work had, perhaps predictably, an immediate effect. The first time the whole team stayed for an additional two and a half hours to deploy. Thus, they decided in the retro that perhaps more automation in the deployment process would not be a bad idea. It also raised awareness in the team about the advantages of small stories.

4.5 Hourly Retrospectives

Already mentioned above, a core practice for our teams were the hourly retrospectives. With our focus on team learning, the most important outcome of the mob was in learning how to improve.

An hourly retro needs to be short and to-the-point. We started with a simple positive/negative items system, and made sure this was visualized on our daily scrum board. Here's an example of an early Task & Retro board (see Fig. 4):

Fig. 4. An early task and retro board - notice the focus on the hourly retro

The basis of the board is the horizontal axis for the hourly blocks. Every hour the corresponding column is used. The top part for positive feedback (e.g. "We chose a good user story to work on"), the lower part for the improvements (e.g. "tests fail").

The left of the board is a basic scrum (ToDo/In Progress/Done) board, turned on its side, where we kept track of the tasks for the day's story.

As we refined the retro, we changed the board from having distinct sections for positive and negative points to one where we have a gradual scale from top to bottom, inspired by the happiness metric [2].

In the example below (Fig. 5), note the trend towards negativity as the day progresses, undoubtedly influenced by the lack of progress on the tasks shown in the task board on the left.

In the next example (Fig. 6), a board from team Red, we do see a clear upward trend in day. The team has further extended the board by adding a task burn-up chart.

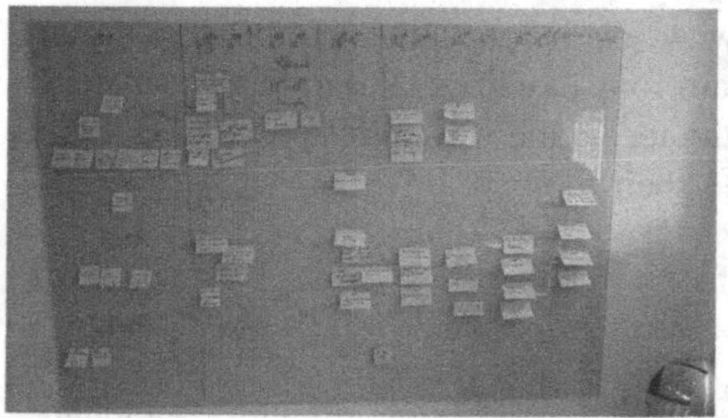

Fig. 5. An incremental improvement to the retro board: a gradual scale of positive to negative

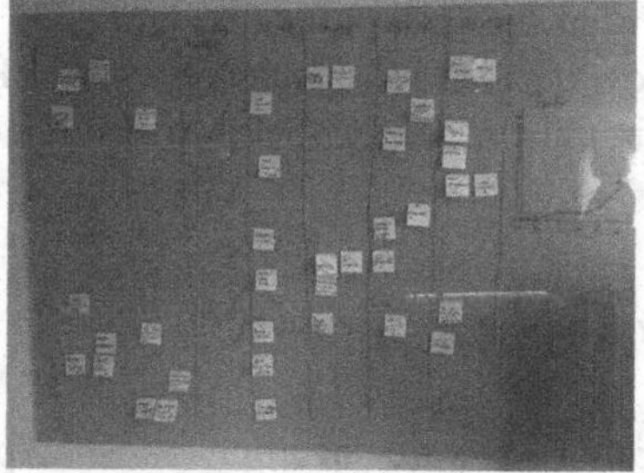

Fig. 6. A more upward trend of the day, in both retro-points and task burn-up

Retrospectives are also put in Confluence. Easier to read, for reference, and as this is done as a Mob at the end of the day, it is another moment where the retro points are digested by the team. Additionally, actions for the next session are added as tasks.

4.6 A Special Mob: Process Flow

In one of our mobbing sessions it turned out that the story required the creation of a process flow. As no-one in the team had any experience in this area, this was a session where the coach (who used to be a process manager in a previous life) took on the role of navigator for the start of the session. It was interesting to see that, even though whiteboard drawings and Visio diagrams were the output instead of Java code, the same effects occurred as with other techniques: after a while our process manager could see that the basic skills had landed, and he could step back and let others take on the navigator role.

5 Acceptance

Team Red, our junior team, embraced Mob Programming the most. They've indicated that they don't want to work this way all week, because they had to do an individual study as well, and time spent in the mob meant less time to prepare for their OCA and OCP exams. But, even after the initial 8 sessions of our summer experiment, the team continues to have regular mobbing days.

On the other hand, Team Yellow, the less junior team, disliked the experiment, didn't like the working in a group, and kept saying that they thought it was inefficient, no matter how much I made clear that this wasn't a consideration. So they stopped after only 3 attempts at mobbing.

A few months after they had stopped, team Yellow needed to work in a new technical domain, with some pressure on learning this domain quickly due to a new project that they had landed. Team Yellow then decided to split in two groups, both addressing a particular area. Although they didn't do the strict rotation, the interaction (with driver/navigator roles, frequent updates in group and between the two groups) was clearly reminiscent of the setup they had experienced a few months earlier while mobbing.

In an unexpected late update, only a few weeks before finalizing this paper team Yellow decided independently to Mob Program for a day to tackle a difficult user story. My initial conclusion that they had rejected the technique was premature: they did find value in mobbing and added this new tool to their toolbox.

6 Team Growth

Learning software development is the primary goal for our group of junior developers. They were already delivering demos weekly, proving they understood the studied chapters in their books. Working in a mob with their peers accelerated everything, from exchanging coding practices to learning to have an opinion and to share or even defend it.

For instance, one day Team Red discovered that the training room was not available, so they decided to move to the boardroom. With unfavorable light conditions and table arrangement, they themselves decided the room as unfit and changed to a better room. All without any intervention of the coach, something that would be unthinkable a few weeks earlier.

Team Red started to identify user stories that were suitable for Mob Programming and those which were not, in light of the very short cycle and strict rhythm. The characteristics of these stories proved to be mainly how clear the goal was and whether enough contextual information was available. Basically, they were finding shortcomings previously undetected in the Backlog. This dramatically improved the interactions with the Product Owner and within the team during the regular refinement sessions.

Having to finish a story at the end of the day, the Yellow team noticed *together* that deployment to production took far too much time. Since they had the rule in place that everyone stayed until the day was closed with deploying the user story, it felt even longer. This drastically changed their attitude to deployment automation.

A set of scripts had been disabled in Jenkins, because it gave too many errors. To speed up the deployment process the team had to re-enable the scripts and fix the problems. The process went down from 40 min to 10.

With both teams lacking experience in Pair Programming, I made sure that the rules for Mob and Pair Programming were almost the same. So basically we do Mob Programming, but if the group consists of only two people we call it Pair Programming. Many people would perhaps dislike this approach, but after the experiment the result is that people more often choose to do Pair Programming than before. I am positive that with additional exposure they will reach a point where a more relaxed approach to pairing will also work for them.

Overall, the level of discipline/cadence/structure went up for both teams, while at the same time the evaluations during the retrospectives were more positive and productive.

The Red team is now very mature and self-sufficient in their day to day processes. Though they still need support on technical issues, they only need help from a scrum master when they run into conflicts or other situations that have a need for more life and work experience.

7 Conclusions

I can state that because of these weekly Mob Programming days, the team as a whole and all its individuals have grown much faster than they could have done otherwise. Not only did they improve their coding skills, they improved in many other aspects, such as their requirements process, deployment procedures, appreciation for focus, and perhaps most important of all, their much higher degree of self-sufficiency. Learning would have been quicker and more directed with a senior as part of the team, but they progressed greatly, even on their own.

As a coach, I had my own learning experience. The difference in reaction between the teams indicates that a different approach might be more effective with more senior people. Perhaps that is not surprising. We all get more set in our ways the longer we are used to our particular habits. The experience for me as a coach has resulted in lessons learned I'll take into my next Mob Programming experiments. And those will certainly happen!

Acknowledgements. First I like to thank the teams at Qualogy Solutions for being my test subjects. Woody Zuill and Llewellyn Franco deserve credit for inspiring me, in their sessions and through their ideas, to conduct this experiment. Many thanks go to Wouter Lagerweij, for encouraging me to submit this report and helping me clean up the mess afterwards. Final thanks go to Joseph Yoder, for shepherding me through the process. His knowledge of the process and interest and enthusiasm for the subject helped me greatly.

References

1. Falco, L.: Group Learning. Today's exercise: Unit Testing (session at Agile 2015)
2. Kniberg, H.: What is Crisp (on The Happiness Metric) http://blog.crisp.se/2010/05/08/henrikkniberg/what-is-crisp
3. Zuill, W.: Mob Programming: A Whole Team Approach, experience report at Agile (2014). https://agile2014.sched.org/event/1exPSc0/mob-programming-a-whole-team-approach-woody-zuill
4. Zuill, W.: A Day of Mob Programming. https://www.youtube.com/watch?v=p_pvslS4gEI

Agile Testing on an Online Betting Application

Nuno Gouveia(✉)

Blip (Betfair), Rua Heróis e Mártires de Angola, n°59 4°, Porto, Portugal
nuno.estrada@blip.pt

Abstract. Agile development with continuous integration and constant releases is only sustainable followed by a rock solid quality process. At blip/betfair we work very hard to build and continuously improve our quality process to provide at the same time a unique reliability experience to our customers and new features fast. Three major components of this process are: **Mind maps** to help us learn more about our product and represent our knowledge about it in a structure way, **Exploratory Testing** that must be free and creative and happen as soon as possible in the process to allow fast feedback cycles and **CI pipelines** with high levels of automation testing to avoid regression. Agile development with continuous integration and constant releases is only possible with a rock solid quality process.

Keywords: Agile · Testing · Mind maps · Exploratory tests · Continuous integration · Quality

1 Introduction

Before joining Blip in July 2013, all I knew about Agile was based on articles or conversations with other people. After two and a half years of experience, where I have had the freedom to decide the best way to do my job, I feel that my perception about quality in agile environments has evolved a lot. This report shares my journey from learning the existing quality process for the *Exchange Desktop* project, to helping improve it to its current state.

1.1 Background

Blip is part of the *Betfair Group plc*, one of the biggest and most successful online betting companies in the world, being the largest internet betting exchange, and also has a strong position in the traditional online bookmaking business. The growth of the online gambling market in the recent years has led to an increase in the number of online betting websites. This generates a fierce competition for market share which in turn increases the pressure for the companies to be more innovative and to release new features fast in order to draw the attention of as many users as possible. At Blip, the way we deal with this pressure is to use agile methodologies (mostly Scrum) and continuous integration.

H. Sharp and T. Hall (Eds.): XP 2016, LNBIP 251, pp. 193–200, 2016.
DOI: 10.1007/978-3-319-33515-5_16

Although we need to deliver new features fast, our main concern when it comes to the continuous integration of our products is **quality**. Despite being considered an "entertainment" product, our applications deal with an extremely sensitive subject for our customers: their money. With this in mind we dedicate a lot of time to the development of a strong quality process that gives us the confidence to release our products frequently. This process is in constant evolution with the input from Delivery Managers and Developers but primarily from Quality Analysts.

We work mainly with the most popular agile methodology Scrum, in multidisciplinary teams of around 5–7 people, which includes the quality analysts (usually one for each team/we don't have a separate quality department). This integration of quality analysts into the teams means that different projects have different realities and in most cases, the project teams have the freedom to tailor their quality process according to their needs. For this reason, I will only refer to the quality process for the project that I have worked on, for the past 2,5 years, the *Exchange desktop* product that has 2 on-going projects: the *Sports Site Web* (SSW), a Java-based (backend) desktop app, and the *Exchange Desktop Site* (EDS), a newer (1,5 years), Angular-based desktop app.

I will focus on three different subjects within our quality process - *Mind mapping*, *Exploratory Testing* and *Continuous integration pipeline* - and try to describe their evolution over the time I have been in the company.

2 Mind Mapping

2.1 Early Days and Old Process

Back in 2013 when I joined Blip, mind maps were not a part of our quality process. As this was my first full time job as a Quality Analyst (in my previous job, testing was just a small part of my tasks), I started by learning the current process from other QA's from the project. As we work in Scrum with two weeks sprints, the QA process is tightly connected with our Scrum process.

As in most Scrum teams, the first interaction that a QA had with any user story was in the **grooming** ceremony. In this ceremony the Product owner explained the user stories in the backlog to the team. The QA, like any team member, tried to understand any possible flaws with the specification and make sure it was ready to be played. Before the team estimated the user story, it was common for the QA to discuss with the team a general idea of the strategy to test the user story, with special focus on the kind of automated regression tests that could be done. This helped the team estimate the user story with a bit more detail. This part of the process is still in use nowadays, as we feel it works well.

In the beginning of a **sprint** the first goal of the QA was to define test cases (this would happen before any real testing with the application). So for every user story the QA would do the following tasks:

1. Study the user story in more detail with special focus on its acceptance criteria,

2. Create test cases in our agile management tool (*AMT*) for all the scenarios that we would test **manually** as well as different input combinations for the scenarios to validate the acceptance criteria, and
3. Create test cases for all the scenarios that would be automated as regression tests.

Applying this process to all the user stories would usually take at least the first couple of days of the sprint. After a user story was implemented, the QA would test it in a development environment following the test cases that had previously been defined, trying to find bugs. We understood later that doing so was quite restrictive, limiting our creativity and exploration. Our test activities mostly followed the "scripts".

2.2 The Introduction of Mind Maps

In late 2013, one of the more senior QA's shared a new technique he had learned to help him explore the user stories and create a visual representation of our knowledge about a product feature, **mind maps**. This idea blew my mind completely and I immediately started thinking how we could use this in our process. On the following sprint I started experimenting with this idea and created mind maps to help me in my testing strategy for every user story. The use of this technique had a huge and instantaneous impact in the way I worked. Since then, the way we use mind maps has gone through different stages. I will now explain what happened and what we learned along the way.

2.3 Mind Maps for Test Scenarios

The very first thing I tried to do was to use the mind maps to replace step 2 of our process, which was the one I thought was the most inefficient. So instead of documenting every scenario that I was going to test with in different test cases in our *AMT*, I would create a mind map with all that information and attach that single mindmap to the user story. This was helpful at first because it was a much more visual way to represent that information than in separate test cases and it was more practical to use when I was testing the user story, executing those scenarios. Besides using the mind maps to guide me as I was testing the user story, I also started ticking off as complete the different scenarios and steps as I tested them in the app. I would later insert this updated mind map to the respective user story as a test result. This could be used as historical data to be consulted in the future if necessary. After some sprints following this method I realized that all this test result information was useless because nobody really needed it. Not me, not my delivery manager, not the other QA's. So as a good Agile practitioner I stopped doing it because it wasn't adding any value. I also stopped creating mind maps for test scenarios as I started observing that having all those predetermined test scenarios wasn't really helping me find many bugs and was having the same impact in testing that step 2 previously had.

2.4 Mind Maps to Represent User Stories

Around the time I was struggling with the route to pursue next with the mind maps, Michael Bolton came to Blip for the *Rapid Software Testing* workshop. We talked a lot about exploration, experimentation and learning. One technique exhaustively used during the workshop was precisely using mind maps to learn and explore the features and characteristics of a product. This inspired me to use mind maps in the same way, to learn more about the product instead of representing testing scenarios as I was doing before.

I decided from that point on to try to represent the information on the user stories in a more structured way. Instead of mapping scenarios, I started mapping the different components of the module (or small section) that was being implemented and think about the different states that each component could have. Instead of replacing step 2 of the process, this new method helped me with the step 1 - learning as much as possible about the user story. Later, after the team had implemented the user story, I used the mind map that I had created to help me with my exploratory tests. At this point, and with the new concepts about exploration we had learned in the workshop, we (the QA's on the project) decided to drop step 2 of our process, as we understood that it wasn't adding value and didn't really help us discover many bugs when we were testing. This meant that the only test cases that we defined in our *AMT* were those defined in step 3, the ones that would be automated as regression tests.

2.5 Repurposing Mind Maps - The Oracles Breakthrough

Usually when implementing a new module, the work is divided into several user stories. Instead of creating one mind map for each user story, we started creating a single mind map for the entire module and updating it in every user story. These mind maps also included things common to the entire module like the visual specs or google analytics events that would be fired on specific actions. Figure 1 shows one our mind maps.

This process was working fine, but I realized we had a problem: we were creating all these mind maps for every user story and modules and they were very useful while we were testing. But after that, they were stored in a folder and they were never used again. We understood that this was quite wasteful because we had so much valuable information being basically thrown away after the first utilization.

Linking Everything. What I started doing was linking everything. At this point we had a mind map for each module but they were disconnected. So we created a "root" mind map that would reference all the different modules and pages we have in our application. Through this "root" mind map, anyone could access any mind map of any module in a few clicks. For some modules there were more levels of maps. In some cases we can have a module that has different implementations according to the sport we are in (e.g., market header for football, tennis, volleyball, etc.) and in those cases there will be a mind map

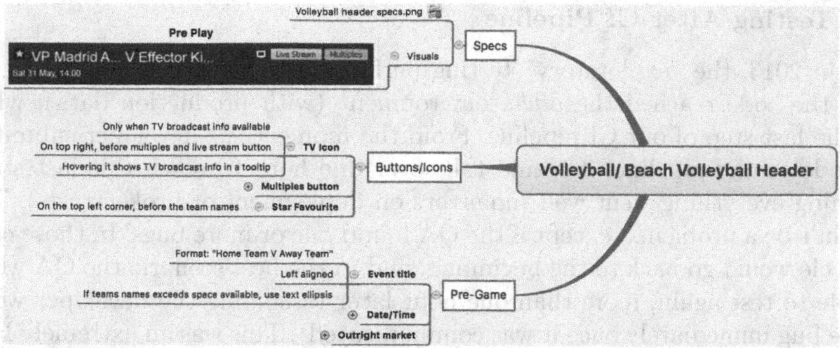

Fig. 1. A simplified version of an actual mind map for the volleyball implementation of the *Sports Header* module

for each of those implementations and one "super" mind map that links all of them together. For more complex modules, we may have the mind map of the module which has "sub" mind maps for different areas or sections of the module.

This concept of linking mind maps really revolutionized the way we used this tool. Most importantly it helped us create something that was missing in our project: a high level vision of our product. Using this powerful tool, we centralized all the relevant information about our product that would otherwise be scattered all around our *AMT*. Mind maps started being used not just by testers but also by product owners, developers or any other person who wants to understand the expected behaviour of any module in our application. We would often see someone asking a question like: "Is this module supposed to appear in this page?" or "Do you remember the rules for this module we implemented a few months ago?" being answered two or three clicks after opening the root mind map. Now we can confidently say that this tool is in fact an **Oracle** for the behaviour of our application.

3 Exploratory Testing

Exploratory testing in its essence has been used in Blip for many years, but it wasn't always called that. Two and a half years ago, the term we used for the tests that were performed by the QA's when a user story was implemented, was *Manual Testing.* Only later, around the same time we started using mind maps, we started using more consistently the term Exploratory testing, which is now completely rooted in our testing vocabulary.

Exploratory testing at Blip has evolved a lot over the years. We made many improvements like introducing new testing techniques we learned or stopping specifying the test cases (for "manual" testing) beforehand, to allow us to explore and experiment with more freedom, without a predetermined script. Those were improvements but the aspect of exploratory testing that I want to talk about is not so much **how** we do it, but **when** we do it.

3.1 Testing After CI Pipeline

Back in 2013, the "exploratory" testing performed by the QA's only happened when the code reached the *alpha* environment (with production data), which was the last step of our CI pipeline. From the moment the developer submitted the code to the pipeline, it would take over one hour to reach this last stage, assuming everything went well (no errors on deployment or broken tests). This wouldn't be a problem... except if the QA found one or more bugs! In those cases the cycle would go back to the beginning, and in the best scenario the QA would be able to test again, more than one hour later (assuming the developer would fix the bug immediately once it was communicated). This was an extremely large feedback cycle and had a huge impact in the amount of time it took to get a user story in front of the Product Owner, and so we decided to change that.

3.2 Setting the Local Environment

Our strategy was to make sure that we as QA's would have the same local environment that developers use to test their code. This way, when development is ready, we simply have to checkout the code from the remote repository and run it on our machines. We always have to make sure that this code is also updated with the latest version of the *master* branch, so that we don't test the new user story on an outdated version of the site.

This process allows us to have the user story in our hands faster as we don't have to wait that it reaches the *alpha* environment. It also allows us to reduce drastically the time for the feedback cycle of any bug that is found - once we find it we can communicate it to developer and after he/she fixes it, we have it again in our hands seconds later.

After the exploratory testing is finished, the code is then submitted to our CI pipeline and once it reaches the *alpha* environment, we perform some sanity tests on the feature just to make sure everything is ok, and then we send it to our PO.

This change we implemented may seem small, but it had a huge impact on the lead time of our user stories and allowed us to have them much earlier in front of our PO for approval. Feedback is an essential part of agile development, especially from the "client" (our PO in this case). The sooner it happens, the better.

4 Continuous Integration Pipeline

Continuous Integration has been present at Blip for a long time now.

Our CI pipelines are a central piece of our quality process because they are the ones that allow us to continuously integrate our code while making sure that no regression has happened in our applications.

Each project at Blip has its own CI pipeline and as in other components of the quality process, it is normal that each project adopts its own strategy for that too.

For the Exchange desktop product we have two ongoing projects, and therefore two pipelines, one for the SSW project and other for the EDS project. In the SSW project we are currently only doing maintenance work, so the pipeline structure hasn't changed in a long time, as well as the test suites that run in it. On the contrary, the EDS project is our currently most active project, which means that has a continuously improving pipeline, both from the regression testing suites and from the pipeline structure itself. For those reasons I will focus on describing the EDS pipeline.

4.1 EDS Pipeline Structure

Figure 2 shows an example of a build in our pipeline.

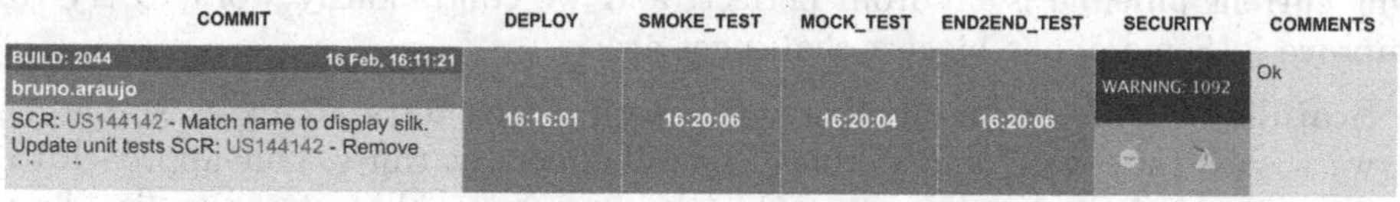

Fig. 2. Example of a build in our EDS pipeline. It shows all the steps: commit, deploy, smoke test, mock test and end2end test which were all successful

When a commit is made to the *master* branch, a new build is generated, triggering the first step of the pipeline.

1. **The first step** of our pipeline basically generates an *RPM* for that version of the code and runs our *unit test* suite against it. The unit tests suite is our largest test suite (over 2000 tests) for obvious reasons: it allows us to evaluate the correctness of each function in the code and with a very low execution time (under 16 s). Coverage can be a misleading metric, but we try to use it as a rule to have at least 80 % branch coverage in our *unit test* suite. After this step the build is ready to be installed in any environment;
2. **The second step** is to deploy our build to our *alpha* test environment. This environment uses production data and can be used both for exploratory testing and automated regression testing. Once this step is completed, the following three steps start simultaneously. They are our UI test automation suites and run against the *alpha* test environment. They used to run sequentially, but now they run in parallel saving a lot of time, specially when all the tests pass.
3. **The third step**, executes our **Smoke test** suite. It runs tests with barely any interaction with the page aside from the assertions themselves (or expectations as we call it) which makes the tests quite fast. This suite is quite small representing roughly **10 %** of our regression strategy.
4. **The fourth step**, runs the **Mock test** suite. These are simulation tests, where we control all the responses from the services, testing mainly two different situations: the modules in isolation (testing all their components and their possible states) and more complex situations that generated or could

generate critical defects. These are the most stable tests once they are not subject to possible service failures and we have total control over the data that is shown on the page. This suite represents around **60 %** of our regression strategy.

5. **The fifth step** executes the **End2End test** suite. These tests represent more "real" scenarios that usually interact with several different modules of the application, not making use of any mocked data. These tests are great to test the integration between modules but are always held hostages of the data that is available in production. This suite represents the remaining **20 %** of our regression strategy.

4.2 Current Challenges

Our current pipeline is far from perfect, and we continuously work to try to improve it. Some of our biggest challenges are:

- **Stability** - This is our number one priority. Our tests aren't as stable as we wished they were, and we have some flakiness at times. Our approach to improve this issue has been to tackle the most unstable tests first, disabling and fixing them. We are making some progress but we still have some tests (the ones in worst shape) that show a failure rate of around 13 % which is not that good.
- **Speed** - The entire pipeline, from the first to the last step takes about 19 min. We are always concerned about this, because we don't want our pipeline to become a delivery bottleneck for our User stories, and as we grow our codebase, the number of regression tests keeps increasing. Our latest improvements were to use as much parallelization as possible: our functional test suites (steps 3 to 5) run simultaneously as well as the suites themselves also parallelize their tests, using a *selenium grid*.

Acknowledgements. First and foremost I would like to thank Blip for being an amazing company that provides a fail-safe environment and for always encouraging us to find better ways to do things. I'd also like to thank my colleagues in my project in particular to the *Avengers* team for always welcoming change and personally to Pedro Tavares who mentored me in my early days at Blip and introduced me to the mind maps concept. Finally I would like to thank my shepherd Rebecca Wirfs-Brock for her thoughtful guidance that made this report possible.

Pause, Reflect and Act, the Pursuit of Continuous Transformation

Sandeep Hublikar(✉) and Shrikanth Hampiholi(✉)

CISCO Video Technologies India Pvt. Ltd., Bangalore, India
{sahublik, shampiho}@cisco.com

Abstract. Organizations take up agile transformation as silver bullet for all their business problems, but the fact is transformation journey is an eye opener to discover the real problems which were previously unnoticed. The authors were part of such a journey. It's easy to reap the obvious benefits of agile, but difficult to sustain and solve systemic obstacles like long build time, complex code base and legacy architecture that become a way of life over a long period of time. Here we describe the challenges we faced in sustaining our transformation beyond early victories and our efforts towards identifying and solving systemic obstacles across the organization by setting up an effective CI environment and addressing top people issues.

Keywords: Transformation · Agile · Sustenance · Scaling

1 Introduction

Video Business Unit (BU) in Cisco is a leader in Pay TV technology provider powering over 50+ Pay TV Service Providers and close to 80 million subscribers worldwide (and growing). It operates in cable, IP, mobile, terrestrial and satellite TV space. The BU has about 700 Engineers organized into more than 100 teams working on more than 40 projects based on a single code base. The authors of this paper are part of one project performing the role of Scrum master and Architect, additionally they are also part AGILE champions team responsible for deployment for AGILE practices across organization.

2 Background

CISCO Video Business unit, in order to position itself as the leading next generation broadcast platform, had to solve business challenges such as:

1. Disruptive technologies evolving in the Pay TV business
2. The need of employees to focus and have fun at work.
3. Improve predictability to launch a complex feature to our customers.

We had to change and change quickly to maintain and extend our competitive advantage.

H. Sharp and T. Hall (Eds.): XP 2016, LNBIP 251, pp. 201–208, 2016.
DOI: 10.1007/978-3-319-33515-5_17

Our legacy organization structure reflected our system architecture, where Teams were structured by components and subsystems, there were teams responsible for integration of these components and testing and validation responsibility was owned by a specialized team.

Analysis had repeatedly shown that multiple mutual dependencies and hand-offs between different teams slowed down deliveries, developers didn't feel responsibility for integration and testing which lead to late identification of defects and developers worked in silos which lead to local optimization instead of global optimization in terms of number of defects and performance.

After careful consideration and planning the agile transformation initiative was launched in year 2013. Once the decision was made the organization structure was changed to one suitable for Scrum [1]. Component teams were replaced by self-contained cross-functional feature development teams working from the common project code base (Grandmaster trunk). Developers, Testers, Integrators roles were all renamed to single role of developers. Similarly project leadership structure of Team Managers, Component Managers, Software Project Managers and Line Managers were replaced by Project Leadership Team (PLT) comprising of Product Owner (PO), Scrum Master (SM), Engineering Manager (EM) (Developers reported to EM) and Architect. Each of the 40+ projects was assigned their own Leadership team.

The first wave of agile transformation started to address problems of long requirement cycle and slow time to market. We focused on challenges of learning scrum practices, building CI machinery and cultivating a culture of delivering shippable code every sprint. In practice the customer deployed the software in field every quarter, the focus was to demonstrate and allow the customer to test and give early feedback on a sprint by sprint basis.

It was very challenging yet very interesting journey with a lot of opportunities on the way, a lot of learning and successful results. Slowly customers were acknowledging their happiness courtesy of the improved quality and on-time deliverables.

3 Ground Reality

Any transformational journey is a work in progress; either we keep improving or we start declining. Two years into the journey around middle of 2015 our transformation had hit a plateau and inefficiencies were creeping back in the organization.

Motivation levels were somewhat low thanks to some unresolved systemic obstacles like

- Long build times.
- Attrition of Subject Matter Experts with knowledge of Stack.
- Long learning curves for new comers due to complex codebase.
- Dependencies between different parties like driver providers, box manufacturers and chipsets vendors.
- Strict Definition of Done (DOD) without adequate supporting infrastructure.
- No safety net in terms automated test suite to avoid regression.
- Scalability and flexibility challenges in legacy architecture..

There were strong indications that at this rate, the transformation would fizzle out within a few quarters.

During a brain storming session involving the project leadership teams along with coaches and directors, metaphors were used to obtain a "pulse" or sentiment of the developers. One of the activities was to portray the biggest challenge being faced in our journey. Participants created an animal named ELIGA with small body and big/sharp teeth. (ELIGA is nothing but AGILE reversed). If not tamed at the earliest, this monster had the potential to eat and destroy whatever we had achieved so far (Fig. 1).

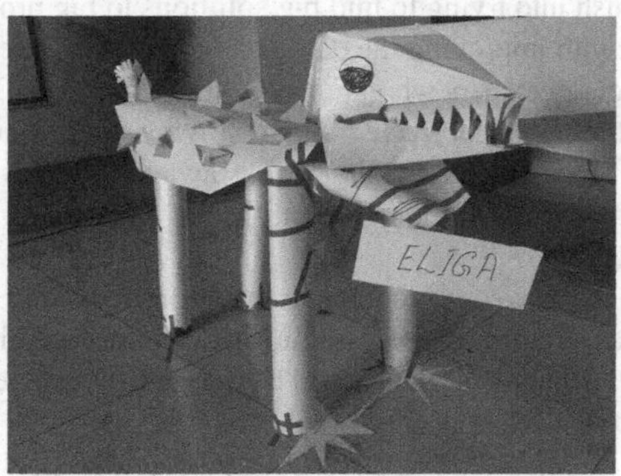

Fig. 1. ELIGA, an AGILE eating Monster

Since the start of journey we had learnt that multiyear timeframe is required for consistent sustainable agile transformation [2]. As transformation evolves business dynamics might change but organization would have embraced business agility.

Over a period, on time delivery of projects with agreed scope became priority over agile transformation. Secondly teams that were used to work in their own component specialization felt taxed in the new organization structure of self-sufficient cross functional teams.

Overall there was overwhelming consensus that over time the visible benefits of agile reaped by organization were going down.

4 Moving Forward

Multiple retrospections in the project leadership teams and feedback received from customers as well as developer community made it amply clear that periodic reinforcement of agile way of working for all stakeholders and executive commitment was a must for sustained transformation.

As a result we established an action team of about 10 people comprising Directors, Scrum Masters and coaches and put together a plan to re-energize and reestablish the organizational commitment to continuous transformation, thus BU wide *transformation 2.0* program was started. The authors of this report were part of the leadership team and active agile evangelists in the organization.

We evaluated Scaled Agile Framework (SAFe®) as most of projects were inter-linked and stacked on top of legacy projects. While SAFe® had its own merits we decided not pursue it as it didn't suit our context of running multiple independent projects on a common code base nor we were willing to invest in such large scale adoption again. We were practicing traditional scrum [1] in pockets and were quite happy with it.

We learnt that one of the better ways to solve the problems of the large program was by getting better at solving smaller, more focused problems. Interactions with industry practitioners and coaches had indicated that typically many large companies/accounts rush into trying to find big solutions to big problems, because they were not comfortable with improving the day-to-day activities, operational choices and obstacles which impact developers who are really doing the work. Becoming skillful at identifying small but obvious obstacles and resolving them had higher chance of resulting in the larger obstacles eventually fading away.

We wanted to find answers to the question: "What *does a happy organization look like and how do we get there?"*

In pursuit of finding answers to the above question a Vision Statement of the BU emerged which read as "Happy People, Engineering Better Solutions, Everyday"

We believed that a happy organization is the one where teams would deliver releases on time without stretching over weekends by:

(a) Ensuring that an employee is motivated in their day to day work.
(b) Manager is actively interested in employee's development.
(c) Project Leadership team actively participates in Sprint Ceremonies.
(d) Building skills for technical excellence (Engineering Excellence).
(e) Directors actively attending sprint demos and appreciating team's Contribution.
(f) Creating atmosphere of fun by celebrating small success

5 Action Plan

We had a series of workshops with the directors and leadership teams of all 40 + projects to identify the areas to focus in the near future and prioritize the epics to work on. The broad themes picked were "Code Quality" and "Employee Engagement". These two epics were picked as priorities because these were major pain points and fixing them as fundamental for achieving further progress in transformation 2.0 (Fig. 2)

Some of the pain points with "Code Quality" were

- Frequently failing builds.
- Long cycle time to identify and fix regressions.
- Staying on Code repository branches for longer time due to release pressures.
- Long build time.

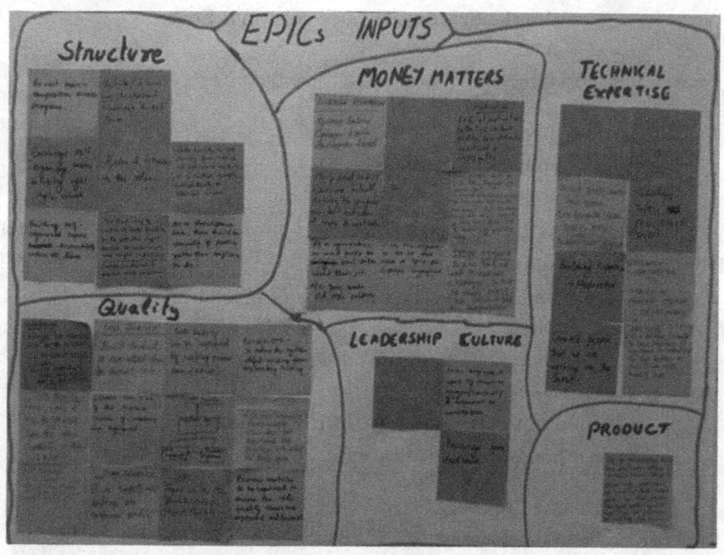

Fig. 2. Raw feedback as captured from the transformation 2.0 workshop

Some of the pain points with "Employee Engagement" were

- High attrition rate.
- Low scores and comments in engagement surveys.
- Lack of career path and role clarity.
- Lack of management involvement in project life cycle.

From these broad themes ten epics (Table 1) were derived and each epic had a sponsor who along with her core team ensured, supported and facilitated the implementation of the epic across organization. Each sponsor put together their own core teams (members of project leadership teams) who were passionate to work on the selected epics and to take the execution forward.

In the subsequent workshops, we arrived at plan to implement the epics across all customer projects, since each of the 40+ projects worked with their own backlog, each of the user stories from the epic became part of all the individual project backlogs. Respective product owners prioritized these user stories along with other user stories so that teams could plan in advance for the upcoming sprints without jeopardizing deliverables.

Epics ranging from infrastructure improvements like CI/CD to people centric improvements like Engagement and Leadership accountability were identified.

Table 1. Selected Themes split into Epics

Theme	Epic	Sponsor
Code Quality	Stable Code grandmaster main	Engineering Director 1
	Continuous Integration	
	Continuous Deployment	
	Building stack expertise	
Employee Engagement	Frequent interaction of Directors with scrum teams.	Engineering Director 2
	Participation in sprint ceremonies.	
	Proactive communication and timely resolution of obstacles.	
	Organize various forums to discuss issues common across organization	
	Monthly meeting with PO/SM/EM/Architects	
	Open house meetings in shorter groups	

Ways of working were agreed to drive these EPICs across the projects

1. Epic Sponsors would work with the core team to define and prioritize the user stories.
2. The sponsor and core team would work with the project leadership teams to drive the implementation in two week sprints.
3. Deploying the EPICS in projects was an added responsibility of the CORE team in addition to their regular project leadership work.
4. Release Demo to demonstrate what was the shift brought by these epics to be conducted at the end of 8 weeks.

6 Results

The Goal was to ensure everybody took steps together so that the positive change was felt uniformly across the whole system. This was one of core learning's from earlier transformation.

The table below summarizes the results we managed to achieve in the EPICs Chosen (Table 2).

Table 2. Status of epics so far achieved

	CODE QUALITY	EMPLOYEE ENGAGEMENT
Planned	• Reduce Build Time. • Reduce Mean Time Between Failures (MTBF). • Improve success rate of builds. • Improve code coverage in sanity testing.	• Informal interactions of Directors with the team. • Director's participation in Sprint demos. • Timely resolution of obstacles. • Periodic project retrospective across organization.

(*Continued*)

Table 2. (*Continued*)

	CODE QUALITY	EMPLOYEE ENGAGEMENT
Achieved	• Build time reduced from 48 Min to 23 Min. • MTBF reduced from many days to 24 h. • Build Success Rate increased to 80 %. • Sanity test Coverage increased to 96 %.	• Regular formal one to one discussions between Directors and engineers. • Obstacle boards in Directors office. Directors pro-actively seeking acknowledgement of resolutions from submitters. • Reduced number of spill over user stories.
Challenges faced	• Ownership of build failures and identification of culprit check-in • Team capacity to take up transformation 2.0 user stories.	• Project Leadership and accountability. • Detecting and Measuring RACI matrix [3]. • Shielding Developers from Customer escalations.
Future Goal	• Reducing MTBF to 2 h. • Developer level Ownership of build failures and fixing. • Improve Sanity to cover 100 %. • Focus on reducing regressions. • Double the number of builds per day on CI System.	• Lower attrition rate. • Better scores and comments in surveys. • Happier faces around. • Developers approaching execs more often.

7 What We Learned

While it was very easy and straight forward to realize initial benefits of AGILE, beyond a point complacency sets in and its difficult to identify and improve unless there is a drive from top management. We also observed that the business continuity takes a front seat compared the commitment towards transformation which requires extreme courage and ability to take hard decisions that might be easy to take but are hard to live with. During the transformation journey it was very evident that it is far easier to implement and solve systemic obstacles than changing people mindset. Eg. It was easy to improve the CI/CD system as compared developing expertise or making people take ownership and being accountable.

Participation of people across the organization itself is a challenge when people are not clear of what the benefit to them is, even after lot of planning and persuasion, significant number of people in leadership team felt that there was no need for transformation 2.0 as we had improved on quality and timeliness of deliverables, also among the people who actively participated[1] there was a skew towards Scrum Masters and Engineering managers (Fig. 3).

[1] The figures show percentage of leadership team only as developers were not part of the transformation 2.0 driving committee.

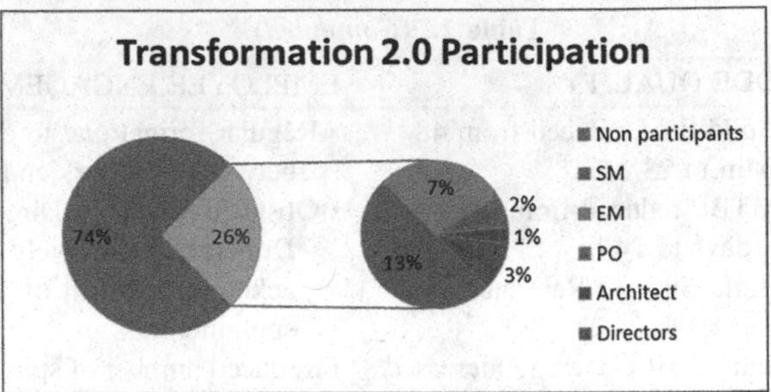

Fig. 3. Transformation Participation profile

Acknowledgements. We would like to thank CISCO for providing opportunity to contribute to agile transformation. We would like to thank colleagues for sharing agile learning's which have inspired this paper. We would also like to thank Ken Power for helping us to understand and appreciate rigor involved in submission of experience reports and thus helping us to prioritize. Last, but certainly not least, we would like to thank our experience report shepherd Maria Paasivaara for her gentle but firm guidance in shaping this experience report. *Thanks Maria for all the help. It probably couldn't have come together without you!*

References

1. CISCO Agile Play book
2. Large scale Agile Transformation at Danske bank, Innovate (2013)
3. Effective Project Management: Traditional, Agile, Extreme. Chapter 2, Robert K. Wysocki
4. Agile Product Development at Cisco. http://www.cisco.com/c/dam/en/us/products/collateral/customer-collaboration/unified-contact-center-enterprise/agile_product_development.pdf

Smoothing the Transition from Agile Software Development to Agile Software Maintenance

Stephen McCalden[1], Mark Tumilty[1], and David Bustard[2(✉)]

[1] Kainos, Belfast BT7 1NT, UK
{S.McCalden,M.Tumilty}@kainos.com
[2] Ulster University, Coleraine BT52 1SA, UK
dw.bustard@ulster.ac.uk

Abstract. Kainos is a software company based in Belfast, Northern Ireland. As well as bespoke development, its work includes service contracts for the maintenance of software created elsewhere. This type of work is challenging because of the knowledge transition involved. The experience reported here is of tackling such projects in a way that integrates with the agile processes of the client. Background on agile practice in Kainos is discussed before focusing on a specific project for the UK Government Cabinet Office.

Keywords: Agile software development · Development-maintenance transition · Scrum · Kanban · Case study

1 Introduction

Kainos [1] is a public limited software company, established in 1986 and based in Belfast, Northern Ireland. It develops information technology solutions for businesses and organizations, particularly in the public, healthcare and financial services sectors. The company also provides consulting and support services. Kainos has offices in the UK, Ireland, Poland and the US, operating across Europe, the Middle East, Africa and North America. It has grown rapidly in recent years, with employee numbers of 260 in 2010, 350 in 2012, and now over 750 in 2015, of whom approximately 490 are engaged in development and 95 in service support (maintenance).

Roughly, three-quarters of the work in the Service Support Department is concerned with software developed by the company. There are several major projects, however, where development took place elsewhere. In such cases, there is a significant challenge in taking on the software in a way that is relatively seamless for the client. The central concern is knowledge acquisition, with the goal being to build an understanding of all aspects of the software without any adverse effect on the service provided in the transition period.

The paper focuses on the situation where a client has had an agile way of working during development and wishes to work with Kainos using the same process during maintenance. The experience of a specific project with the UK Government Cabinet Office is described. This is preceded by background information on agile practices within Kainos.

H. Sharp and T. Hall (Eds.): XP 2016, LNBIP 251, pp. 209–216, 2016.
DOI: 10.1007/978-3-319-33515-5_18

2 Background

The introduction of agile techniques at Kainos started with development. This began in the late 1990s with the introduction of DSDM, but has subsequently been overtaken by the use of Scrum. As noted in surveys carried out in 2010 and 2012 [2], the use of an agile approach in the company was mostly dictated by the requirements of each client. At that time, this did not include the public sector part of the business. Now, however, following a strong government commitment to agile practice in public projects [3], roughly 70 % of the work at Kainos is currently agile-based.

The use of agile techniques in the Service Support Department is a relatively recent innovation, starting in 2013. Like software development, this has largely been client-led. Because of its significant involvement in the public sector, maintenance practices in the company are ITIL-based [4], with ISO20000 IT Service Management accreditation [5] awarded in 2009. As a result, all aspects of the maintenance process are defined in detail, and audited for conformance annually. The process definition includes the role and content of Service Level Agreements (SLAs) and the provision of specific services, such as a Service Desk and the management of incidents and third-party suppliers. The transition process from development to maintenance is also specified and this will be considered further in the next section. Overall, the resulting process has proved very effective, for both Kainos and its clients.

The Service Department at Kainos supports over 80 clients. Each client has an assigned service manager and an engineering team, the composition of which varies according to need. There is also a more senior group of service delivery managers who handle the commercial side of the work, including competition for contracts, contract agreement, and the pricing of new work as it emerges.

Conceptually, the engineers form a single pool of staff, where often each engineer will work with several clients simultaneously. Because of this flexible structure, and a focus on responding quickly to client needs, agile techniques were first introduced through Kanban, supplemented with selected Scrum practices. The approach was based on the three key elements of Kanban identified in [6]:

- *Visualize the workflow*: using a Kanban board (whiteboard/wall), mark out columns showing the left to right stages in handling a client request/incident; split the work into pieces, write each item on a card and put it on the board.
- *Limit work in progress* (WIP): assign explicit limits on how many items may be in progress in each workflow column.
- *Measure the lead/cycle time* (average time to complete one item): optimize the process to make the lead time as small and predictable as possible.

Each Kanban board was set up for the clients associated with a specific client manager. All boards started with the same base process but the associated engineers were encouraged to adjust them as they saw fit, in line with Kanban principles. As with any innovation, this worked best where a 'champion' emerged to lead the initiative. Where possible, daily stand-ups were used to review progress with client work and, initially, reflect on the effectiveness of the Kanban approach.

As well as refining the structure of each Kanban board there was also a need to align its content with an existing Kainos Incident Management system (KIM), where clients report issues or make requests for change. KIM held all of the information associated with each work item. The Kanban cards simply recorded KIM references and brief summaries of the tasks involved. Aligning these parallel descriptions required discipline and, for most engineers, felt unsatisfactory. Another difficulty was that some engineers occasionally worked offsite, which meant they couldn't see the board or keep it up-to-date with their own activity. To help address both problems an electronic Kanban system, KanbanFlow [7] was introduced in early 2014 and the physical boards replaced by electronic screens. To retain most of the benefits of the original boards, each screen was dedicated to representing the board it replaced. Since then, the only change has been to switch from KanbanFlow to Trello [8], because of its adoption as the general agile support platform within Kainos.

3 The Transition Challenge

Kainos has experience of all three types of software transition [9]:

- *Self-to-self*, where the transition occurs entirely within the developing organization, continuing with the same process, and largely using the same personnel.
- *Intra-organizational*, where the system is passed from a development team to a separate maintenance team within the same organization.
- *Inter-organizational*, where the system is transferred to an entirely separate organization.

One significant example of self-to-self transition is Evolve [10], its electronic medical records system, which currently has 29 Healthcare Trust clients across 70 hospitals in the UK. As a major product, Evolve has a pool of dedicated staff responsible for its promotion, deployment and support. This includes: (i) a client-facing analysis team who work with each new Trust to identify its specific requirements; (ii) a back-end technical team who handle the implementation and deployment of each instance of Evolve, together with the ongoing enhancement of the base product; and (iii) a support team with the maintenance role of responding to client incidents and their requests for change. All of this work is managed using Scrum.

Roughly 75 % of the projects at Kainos are intra-organizational, involving the transfer of responsibility for systems developed by a Kainos team to its Service Support Department. In some cases, client contracts allow for one or more years of maintenance support on top of initial development. More commonly, however, the company has to win a competitive tendering process to obtain such work.

The remaining 25 % of projects at Kainos are inter-organizational, either in receiving systems developed in other organizations or in passing on systems that it has created. Such arrangements often reflect the preferences of individual clients. For example, some organizations, such as the UK Government, generally develop in-house and then contract out support responsibility for the resulting systems. Similarly, there are organizations that commission the initial development of systems with the intention of taking responsibility for them after deployment.

When competing for projects, Kainos transition arrangements are made explicit, as part of the contract. These are defined around its ITIL-based support service. In particular, this involves the creation of a Support Handover document for each transition. The document is instantiated from a general template that identifies all of the information that has to be provided by the client. This ranges from basic contact details, through descriptions of the software and associated tools, to a summary of known issues. Checklists are used to ensure that no relevant information is overlooked.

The many activities associated with transition in Kainos fall into three areas:

- *Software transition*, covering the transfer of all software-related artefacts from the development team to the maintenance team, including documentation, test suites, and product backlog, in addition to the software itself.
- *Process transition*, covering the introduction of the way in which the client and maintenance organization will interact.
- *Knowledge transition*, covering the acquisition of knowledge by the maintenance team to the level necessary to take over full responsibility for future changes.

Each of these areas is discussed separately in the sub-sections that follow.

Software Transition. With modern configuration management practices, Kainos find that software transition can usually be completed without difficulty. As well as gaining access to software-related assets, there is a need to examine wider environment arrangements. This involves reviewing:

- *Assets and licenses*, rationalizing if possible.
- *Current infrastructure*, to ensure appropriate environments are in place to resolve software issues and facilitate change; typically, this means ensuring that there are development, test and training environments in place, and that these are consistent with the live environment.
- *Existing environments*, to identify potential security issues, and make recommendations for their resolution, as necessary.
- *3rd party agreements*, if any.

Software transition is largely independent of agile practice, though with agile projects less documentation is expected and a more comprehensive test suite is likely to be in place.

Process Transition. Process transition in Kainos involves the alignment of the working practices of the client with those of the company. This allows for adjustments on both sides to achieve a process that is efficient, effective and satisfactory to all, within the context of the contracted Service Level Agreement. The resulting process covers day-to-day interaction in managing incidents, and higher-level interaction associated with the planning, review and release of new content. This is also the time to introduce support technology, such as the use of an electronic help desk and/or incident management tools.

Process transition is generally straightforward regardless of the practices on either side of the transition. Generally, the maintenance organization adapts to client requirements, though small adjustments on the client side may be necessary. For example, clients accustomed to reporting issues at the end of a sprint cycle, will need to report them immediately in the maintenance phase.

Knowledge Transition. The most difficult aspect of the development-maintenance transition is the acquisition of knowledge by the maintenance team. Training courses can help but there is really no substitute for hands-on experience, preferably with suitable members of the development team available to provide guidance. In Kainos, maintenance teams have found it useful to document their acquired knowledge in an Operations Manual, which is essentially a 'how to' guide for the system they are acquiring.

It is important for clients to be aware of the difficulty of knowledge transfer and allow for it in their planning and costing of maintenance support. The options available are discussed in the next sub-section.

Transition Strategy. The software, process and knowledge transition activities, discussed in the sub-sections above, identify *what* needs to be done during transition, but equally important are the decisions on *where*, *how* and *by whom* these are to be performed. Although, in principle, transition responsibilities could be shared between a development and maintenance team, the work is typically led by the maintenance team, as it is affected most by the success or otherwise of the process.

One major factor influencing the efficiency and effectiveness of transition is the degree of overlap between development and maintenance. With self-to-self and intra-organizational transitions, both occurring within Kainos, there is flexibility in when and how transition is handled. For inter-organizational transitions, however, the process has to be treated formally. There are three situations to consider. The first is where there is no significant overlap between development and maintenance, implying an immediate transfer of system responsibly from one team to another. In such cases, knowledge transition is more difficult, because typically there is little to no communication between the two teams involved, except through documentation. This is more of a problem for agile development projects where less documentation is produced.

Where there is an overlap in transition between development and maintenance, there are two options available:

- *Maintainer-site transition*, where one or more of the development team works on-site with the maintenance team to facilitate transition activities, mostly in a coaching role.
- *Developer-site transition*, where one or more senior members of the maintenance team work on-site with the development team to complete all necessary transition activities; in doing so, the maintenance team members would be involved in production tasks, as an aid to knowledge transition.

Maintainer-site transition has the advantage of occurring at a less pressured time, after deployment, but is typically less satisfactory overall. In particular, development team members have a weaker role, as they are not driving the transition; also, they are unlikely to be senior members of the team and so may lack a full understanding of all aspects of the system and its support.

Developer-site transition can be a pressured situation if performed around a 'go live' date, which is often the case. A cyclical agile development structure is very helpful here, however, in that it allows the maintenance staff to join a project at the beginning of a sprint, and so be directly involved in its planning and subsequent review. Therefore, while developer-site transition is preferable to having no transition overlap at all, embedding maintenance staff in the development team appears to be the better option. This is the approach described in the next section in a project for the UK Government Cabinet Office.

Transition Example. The UK Government Cabinet Office project is an example of an agile-oriented inter-organizational transition from development to maintenance. It is significant for Kainos in being its first and, so far, only example where a client wished to extend the sprint structure used in development, into maintenance. It is also the first project where the client facilitated transition by supporting service support staff working on-site with the development team. From an agile perspective, the system is additionally significant for the Government Digital Service (GDS) [11] who developed the system, in being their first example of a "*major transactional service delivered all the way to live as an agile project*" [12].

The system, IER (Individual Electoral Registration), provides a single hub through which those eligible to vote in England, Scotland and Wales can register online. This covers 46 million people, across 387 local authorities. The service went live on 10 June 2014. The maintenance contract was awarded to Kainos in the same month, with the transition to maintenance occurring across July and August 2014. Thirty days of Kainos staff time were agreed to support the transition process. Two senior Kainos support engineers (normally based in Belfast) travelled separately to the developer site (in London) for part of each week; one engineer focused on web operations and the other on the remainder of the application (the first named author of this paper). The transition occurred after the 'go live' date, so developers were less pressured, although it did mean that fewer of them were available for consultation.

A full schedule of activity was developed and approved ahead of the on-site transition, indicating the work to be completed each day by each Kainos engineer. As part of their transition schedule, the Kainos engineers worked alongside their counterparts in GDS, assisting with the sprint backlog and working through incidents that occurred.

4 Lessons Learned

The main lessons learned from the Cabinet Office transition project were:

- The timing and general structure of the transition felt close to optimal. Tackling the transition a month after the system went live meant that the development team were available to provide initial support in the crucial first few weeks of release, and then had time to support transition. There were 20 + lower priority items in the backlog at the go-live point, meaning that there were tasks available to facilitate knowledge transition and keep developers busy when there were no incidents to handle.

- Using developer-site transition proved very effective. With this approach, Service Support in Kainos was able to take on a substantial system, cover all incidents reported (there were very few) and move its development forward — all without any interruption in service. One significant achievement was taking responsibility for the system being rolled out to Scotland, which was delayed until after the independence referendum on 18 September 2014 [13].
- Scheduling transition activities around an agile process is very straightforward. The cyclical nature of the work, and its detailed breakdown in a backlog, meant that it was relatively easy to identify tasks that could be shadowed, and others that could be tackled by the Kainos engineers to build up their experience.
- The GDS development team was very supportive of the transition process, making it fully effective. Greater efficiency may be possible, however, through a tighter collaboration. Specifically, this would involve inserting the transition tasks directly into the sprint backlog of the development team. In that way, transition activities would be covered in sprint planning meetings, daily standups, sprint reviews and sprint retrospectives, with a possibility of reducing the elapsed time of the transition and total effort expended. Further experimentation is needed to evaluate this possibility.
- The Cabinet Office requirement to run support with the same sprint structure as development was largely straightforward. The scale of the work involved meant that a support team could be dedicated to the contract, and work in Scrum cycles. The only difficulty encountered was a need to obtain approval for an exception to ISO 20000 certification to allow for changes to be specified as user stories rather than the usual, more detailed definitions.

Acknowledgements. We are very grateful to the Cabinet Office and GDS for their facilitation of the transition project described in the paper. With their understanding and accommodation, the transition process proved very successful. Thanks also to Kainos for supporting the creation of the paper, especially Tom Gray, the CTO, for his interest and enthusiasm throughout. Finally, of course, we are grateful to our 'shepherd', for his guidance on the structure and content of the paper.

References

1. Kainos. www.kainos.com
2. Bustard, D., Wilkie, G., Greer, D.: Towards optimal software engineering: learning from agile practice. Innovations Syst. Softw. Eng. **9**(3), 191–200 (2013)
3. UK Cabinet Office: Government IT Strategy (2011)
4. Cannon, D.: UK Cabinet Office: Key Element Guide ITIL Service Strategy: Aligned to the 2011 Editions. Stationery Office Books (2012)
5. Cots, S., Casadesús, M.: Exploring the service management standard ISO 20000. Total Qual. Manag. Bus. Excellence **26**(5–6), 515–533 (2015)
6. Kniberg, H., Skarin, M.: Kanban and Scrum-making the most of both. Lulu. com (2010)
7. KanbanFlow. https://kanbanflow.com/
8. Trello. https://trello.com/
9. Khan, A. S.: A Framework for Software System Handover, Doctoral Thesis. Software and Computer Systems, School of Information and Communication Technology (ICT), KTH Royal Institute of Technology, Sweden (2013)
10. Kainos: Evolve Electronic Medical Records Platform. https://www.kainosevolve.com/
11. Government Digital Service. https://www.gov.uk/government/organisations/government-digital-service
12. Government Digital Service Blog: Individual Electoral Registration - changing the way we register to vote (2014). https://gds.blog.gov.uk/2014/06/10/individual-electoral-registration-changing-the-way-we-register-to-vote-2/
13. Wikipedia: Scottish Independence Referendum (2014). https://en.wikipedia.org/wiki/Scottish_independence_referendum,_2014

University of Vienna's U:SPACE Turning Around a Failed Large Project by Becoming Agile

Bernhard Pieber[1(✉)], Kerstin Ohler[2], and Matthias Ehegötz[3]

[1] Agile coach, University of Vienna, Vienna, Austria
bernhard@pieber.com

[2] Vienna University Computer Center (Zentraler Informatikdienst - ZID), University of Vienna, Vienna, Austria
Kerstin.Ohler@univie.ac.at

[3] Teaching Affairs and Student Services (Studienservice & Lehrwesen), University of Vienna, Vienna, Austria
Matthias.Ehegoetz@univie.ac.at

Abstract. In 2012 the University of Vienna started a project, named Student Service Portal (SSP), to create a new portal for the universtiy´s students, university teachers, and administrative staff. The university signed a fixed price project with an external main contractor. Although a lot of effort was put into writing detailed requirements documents, it remained unclear what the exact scope was. Project management was lacking, technical problems arose, and finally the university and the supplier got caught up in each other's blame instead of working together. After two years without tangible results the rectorship of the university stopped the project and ordered a restart – this time with an agile approach. The main contractor was replaced. The IT and the business department took over full responsibility for the product together.

Keywords: Agile · Agile transformation · Agile organizational development · Change project · Scrum · University organization

1 Introduction

In 2012 the University of Vienna started the SSP project, a software development project to implement a new service portal to be used by the university's 93.000 students and 9.000 staff members. In 2014 it became apparent that the project was going nowhere. An important project milestone came nearer. However, the results were practically unusable. Morale was low, trust between business and IT was low, fighting with the main contractor started. The rectorship – the university's board – and the project's managers decided they needed nothing short of a complete restart. This time around they decided to use an agile software development process. It was to be the first large project within the complex organization of the university to which agile methods would be applied for real. Could it work this time? To say the sceptics were the majority would be an understatement. But what else should they do?

H. Sharp and T. Hall (Eds.): XP 2016, LNBIP 251, pp. 217–225, 2016.
DOI: 10.1007/978-3-319-33515-5_19

So they started change2agile, an organizational change project to prepare the IT department and its project partners to switch to an agile development organization. The business departments they worked together with and other stakeholders were invited to participate. The organizational change project itself was run as a Scrum project, with change teams, sprints, reviews, retrospectives etc. After half a year of intense preparation the IT department started four cross-functional Scrum teams, two of which were assigned to the restarted SSP project. To bring in real world experience they hired an external operational project manager and an external agile coach.

More than one year later, the project is on a great track. The relationship between business and IT has reached new levels of trust. The rectorship and managers are very pleased with the project turn around. Enthusiasm, optimism, and fun, missing for so long, are back. Of course, not everything went smoothly. A lot of planned functionality is still missing. Some things still need to be improved. However, we are convinced that together we will succeed. In this experience report we would like to share with you what we learned.

2 Road to Perdition

In this chapter we will describe the different phases of the first attempt at the SSP project from the beginning until the decision to restart in new a setup in April 2014.

Phase 1 – "Ignorance is bliss"
In 2012 the Federal Ministry of Science and Research approved the project. In 2013 the project started with an external company as general contractor. They sent a development team including an operational project manager. The collaboration between business and IT had been difficult. From IT's point of view, business had inflated expectations on the features that were to be delivered while the contractor did not see what they had gotten into. At the same time, IT and business hoped to solve a lot of put off problems in the project. The moment the contractor realized that they tried to reduce project scope.

Phase 2 – "Fear is the path to the dark side …"[1]
Even though the detailed scope was still being negotiated and the contractor's analysts were still writing detailed specifications, the developers had to start. As a consequence the project was off to a very uncoordinated start. The process was like this: the analysts talked with business about the requirements, then went to the UI designers and developers, and after that brought their feedback back to business. The requirement feedback loops were endless. At the end the contractor set deadlines for the approval of specifications by business, even though they were not really finished. Project management tried to impose an ever more detailed process of deadlines and deliverables. While this was meant to clarify everyone's responsibility it had the opposite effect – it lead to each party blaming the other. Everyone was driven by fear.

[1] George Lucas, Star Wars, Episode I: The Phantom Menace, 1999.

Phase 3 – Acceptance Tests or "You shall not pass"[2]

The team members' good mood and motivation disappeared over these disputes. 9 months into project this development cumulated when the target date for the first release was not met because the acceptance test was not successful. It became clear that this mode of working did not yield any useful results. The release date was postponed twice. Yet the resulting software still could not be accepted by business.

Phase 4 – "Nobody has any intention of building a wall"[3]

At this point project goals did not matter anymore. The team members blamed each other for the failure to meet the release dates. As a consequence project management imposed more process and rules, documented in multi-page flow diagrams. By now no one even remotely believed the project could be turned around by a joint effort.

Phase 5 – The War of Roses

At that point in time, the whole project team stopped working on the product. Letters were sent back and forth between the rectorship and the contractor, trying to find a way out. There was none. From now on discussions moved to the legal level. 16 months into the project the partners agreed to cancel the contract. Overall, more than 1500 pages of specification and thousands of lines of codes were written. We spent hours in emergency meetings, the contractor changed their project managers 3 times. But none of the modules passed the acceptance tests. When the contract was terminated, none of our goals was achieved.

Phase 6 – Returning to meaningful life

Finally the last stage of grief began. Morale hit rock bottom. Both departments involved in the project met to lick their wounds. Lessons learned were identified and various ways were discussed how the project could be turned around. Many could not believe this was even possible. The following things were clear: IT and business had to find a way to work together more closely and take full responsibility for the project. No one ever wanted to depend on a single external contractor anymore. And finally: the restart should be agile.

3 The Restart: change2agile

Two years earlier the IT department had invited some other business units to experiment with agile methods in a smaller project. The experiences with the SSP project reinforced those ideas, both in the project departments and the rectorship. So the IT department decided to switch all software development to Scrum. Before the SSP project could be restarted, the project team members had to prepare for the new agile process.

---

2 J.R.R. Tolkien, The Fellowship of the Ring, 1954.

3 GDR head of state Walter Ulbricht in a press conference in East Berlin on June 15, 1961, when asked whether GDR intended to build a wall separating East and West Germany (which they actually did).

What did we do when?

After two restart workshops, one in the IT department, and another one together with the business units, an organizational development project was started in June 2014 – named change2agile (c2a). People of all relevant departments united and set up three cross-department teams to define the new agile working process. To gain practical experience in it we decided to run the change project as a Scrum project. As the IT department is also servicing other business units and they would be affected, we invited them to join the change process.

What type of change stories did we have?

As c2a was a change project the user stories were a little bit different to a normal user story. Here are some examples of our change stories:

- How should the teams be constituted, so that everyone is happy?
- How do we organize the release process?
- Define roles and responsibilities.
- What should be in a feature team's user story?

The change stories had acceptance criteria, e.g. "there exists documentation in the Wiki", "all relevant stakeholders have agreed". In addition to the Wiki documentation a newsletter was sent to a wider group of stakeholders after each sprint.

How did we organize?

Each of the three Scrum teams included people from IT (software development, streaming department, operations and support) and business departments. Some of the line managers were part of the teams. However, they had no more rights than the other team members. There were two product owners, one from IT and one from the SSP business unit. Three members of IT volunteered to be Scrum Masters. Every team member was allowed to spend 20 % of her/his work time for the change project. The rest of the time people worked on their normal duties in their departments.

Sprints were two weeks long in the beginning, later extended to three weeks. All the teams agreed on using JIRA for tracking c2a's backlog. There was a weekly Scrum of Scrum. Planning meetings and reviews were held with all three teams together, retrospectives were done in each team separately. The teams organized themselves, some met twice a week, some less regularly, depending on their change stories. The teams used planning poker to estimate story points in order to decide what stories could be done in the upcoming sprint.

What worked well?

The cross-department setup proved to be essential. Communication improved substantially. The time boxes helped focusing on the tasks to define how the projects should be run. It was a good vehicle for the IT and business units to get to know each other and to learn to collaborate. It increased self-confidence in our ability to really execute the switch to agile. It helped to reduce the fear of such a big organizational change. It allowed team members to experience the success they had lacked for so long. It helped avoid surprises. It helped to convince some of the sceptics. We had wanted to take our fate in our own hands and were finally allowed to do it.

Who/what helped?
Line management helped by not interfering, encouraging self-organization and self-responsibility. All groups could participate in all decisions, e.g. the business team members on questions regarding software development. This was unheard of and helped building trust. It showed that transparency is a good thing.

What did not work so well?
Although all departments were invited some of them did not participate enough in the change process in hindsight. Some of the decisions stayed only theoretical and were never put into action, even although some of them would have been useful and were needed, e.g. the Definition of Done was not often followed. The Definition of Ready is still not used. Why? It was not possible to take care of every single aspect when the team started. It turned out to be difficult to put theory into practice immediately. It took some practice and retrospectives to finally get there.

A small group of team members were fundamentally opposed to the agile process. They were sure that moving away from detailed analysis would lead to bad quality and chaos. This resulted in long and exhausting struggles and discussions. Which cost quite some energy. Two of them eventually decided to leave the university.

What did we achieve?
We successfully developed a clear common picture of how the agile process should be lived and practiced. This included a set of definitions and rules. Everything was documented in a wiki. The change2agile team members spread this know-how in their respective units. Also, the change2agile team members decided to recruit external help for the SSP project: an operative project manager and an agile coach. In September 2014 they started working.

On October 27th 2014 four Scrum cross-functional development teams officially started. They were built from members of the IT department's groups project management, analysis & test, and software development. As a result every team consists of software developers, one to two analysts, one tester and one Scrum Master. The team members still report to their respective line managers. In the first step the group operations & support was kept separate. This was a major milestone in the agile transformation. From then on the SSP project had become a truly agile project. However, it was clear that this actually was just the beginning, the first step in a longer journey.

4 U:SPACE – The Agile Way to SSP

With the most important questions on how to restart, we could begin the next step of the project leading to the release of the new portal, now named U:SPACE.

How are we organized?
Currently the IT department is running five Scrum development teams, two of which are assigned to the SSP project. In addition there are two external teams, one from a software development company and one from the Faculty of Computer Science. In total there are four SSP Scrum Teams. They work in sprints of three weeks starting with planning on Wednesday. The university uses a university management software package

based on standard software with extensive customization. This system is the data backend for the new portal. Three freelancers, which are specialists for this system, are part of the IT Scrum teams. They are not based in Vienna but work from Germany. They fly in every three weeks for the refinement meetings. They participate in the other meetings using Skype.

What is special?

The SSP business unit decided to have 10+ product owners (PO) for four teams. The product owners are responsible for different topics and their respective stories. They meet once a week, in the PO board, and try as good as they can to reach an agreement about the user story priorities. In case of an unresolvable conflict the SSP business unit lead decides. This means that a team has more than one PO in a sprint. At the same time, one PO has stories for more than one team. This allows us to concentrate all teams on one bigger epic if needed. This means that POs and teams need to coordinate well to ensure all software parts fit together.

To help coordinate between the POs themselves, the role backlog owner was introduced. One of the product owners fills this role. He is responsible for the JIRA backlog; he moderates the PO boards, but does not have more rights in prioritizing than the other product owners.

How do we report?

To bridge the gap to the non-agile departments a unique reporting process was initiated iteratively. The rectorship gets one report with the results from all four teams after every sprint, every three weeks. Project management assisted by the Scrum Masters and Product Owners writes it. It includes a calculation of the achieved business value.

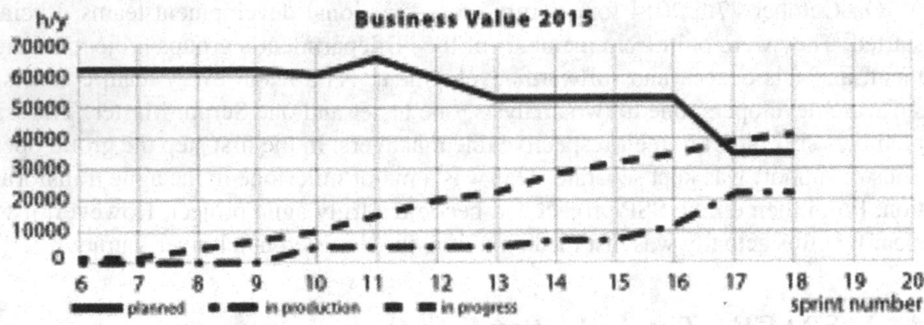

Feedback is very positive. One vice rector expressed that now for the first time she has the feeling to really know the status of project, which gives her peace of mind.

What did we deliver?

In 2015 we put the first version of the portal online. A major new module for modelling the curricula was put into production. New versions of existing applications for students were introduced into the new portal, such as new records of examinations, study overview, course directory. The process for admission to degree programs is now supported online the first time. Students have to visit the admission office less often, which was one major goal of the SSP project. For university teachers a new application for grading exams was introduced. Feedback from them was generally positive.

In December 2015 the rectorship decided to go with a recent high court ruling allowing universities to charge fees for entrance exams in the course of registration. The rector asked the teams if they could create the new function in U:SPACE. It had to be finished by March 1st, 2016. The teams took the challenge. Although it was hard work and time was running out in the end, the teams made it. The most critical success factor was the intense and very good collaboration within and between the teams. All this cumulated in a perfect review presentation. Agility at its best!

What happened to change2agile?

After the successful start of the Scrum teams many of the responsibilities of change2agile shifted to Scrum teams. However, the project members decided not to stop the project in order to address organizational issues concerning all teams. Some of the less important change stories had also not been finished. To account for the new responsibilities, some adaptations were made to the project.

As the number of team members was reduced the project now consists of just one core team. The amount of time reserved for the change project was reduced significantly. The change2agile team is run as a governance team. The team members meet once a month. For each change story a volunteer assembles a smaller ad hoc team of experts to work on the change story. Because the people working on the change stories vary so much, Scrum turned out not to be ideal. Therefore the team members decided to switch to Kanban, which allows us to work on stories over a longer duration than a sprint's length.

Team Building and Human Factors

As in any collaborative endeavor human factors play a major role. After the restart it took some time to build up trust again. Conflicts about various topics are unavoidable and pose valuable challenges for improving team collaboration. The agile coach is there to help the teams with these and other communication issues, by sharing his observations, giving feedback, clarifying dynamics in the teams' communication, and suggesting helpful models of communication psychology, such as Friedemann Schulz von Thun's[4] four-side model of communication, value and development square, or Kerth's retrospective prime directives.

All team members and the management agree on the importance of the following values: open communication, business and IT working together on a daily basis, team autonomy and self-organization. The culture of retrospectives was established and improves transparency and honesty on all levels. In June 2015 all project team members met for a two-day team-building workshop. It was run as an Open Space and moderated by the external agile coach. It helped the participants to get to know each other better and discuss topics for which there had not been enough time in the day-to-day project work. Many of those topics led to change2agile backlog items. As feedback was positive management approved a repetition in 2016. Other regular team-building measures

[4] Friedemann Schulz von Thun, Miteinander reden 1-4, 2010.

organized by the Scrum Masters include sprint drinks, team days, release parties, visits to Vienna's Christmas fair, and a solemn Christmas party.

A Survey on the Agile Transformation

Between July and October 2014 a survey was conducted among 17 members of four business units regarding their experience and satisfaction with the agile transformation on the one hand and the agile process on the other. The results show a median satisfaction of 7 out of 10 for the agile transformation and a median satisfaction of 8 out of 10 for the agile process at the time of the survey.

Overall, we consider this a great result, with still some room for improvement. In one business unit the results were less positive, especially the satisfaction with the agile transformation. Not surprisingly, this was one of the business units, which did not participate much in change2agile. An important result of the survey was that some areas of improvement were identified. In the meantime many of them have already been dealt with, either by the respective Scrum teams or by the change2agile team. The head of the IT department together with his management team decided to repeat this type of survey at least once a year.

Lessons Learned

We learned that working together between departments is the basis for successfully achieving our goals. This is possible if everyone is respected as an individual with her/his skills and shortcomings, which we found to be a prerequisite for trusting each other. Trust is essential within the project teams, and also to departments not fully involved in the agile process. One key factor is encouraging social contacts beyond the daily business. We learned that for taking on full responsibility for the project instead of solely relying on our external partner, we also need the management's confidence. Regular delivery of software, regular, transparent reporting, and solving problems within the teams as much as possible are key factors.

In order to achieve our change to agile working it is absolutely essential that our management is fully behind the agile values. They themselves engage in Management 3.0 theory and practice to better support the teams' self-organization. We still have some problems with the fact that in the past there was a strict separation of roles (analysts, developers, and testers), which makes it difficult to work cross-functionally.

Last but not least, we learned that to successfully introduce agile software development we also needed to develop our organizational structures and process in a fundamental way. Using agile practices for doing that was essential to develop the right mind set. To everyone's surprise, working in an agile way proofed to be entirely possible in such a huge, old, politically overloaded organization as an university.

Acknowledgements. We would like to thank all involved teams for their enthusiasm, trust and respect. We thank our management Mrs. Oberhuemer, Msc MAS, ADir. Riedel-Taschner, DI (FH) Busch and Mag. Steinacher, and the vice rectors Univ.-Prof. Dr. Hitzenberger, ao. Univ.-Prof. Mag. Dr. Schnabl and Mag. Dr. Schwaha for their support and trust. Last, but certainly not least, we thank our shepherd Johanna Rothman for her feedback on this paper, her optimism and her kindness.

The Journey Continues: Discovering My Role as an Architect in an Agile Environment

Avraham Poupko(✉)

Cisco, SPVSS, Shlomo Halevi 5, Jerusalem, Israel
apoupko@cisco.com

Abstract. This paper continues telling the story begun in "It has been a long journey, and it is not over yet" (published in *Agile Process in Software Engineering and Extreme Programming XP2015*, Helsinki – 2015). This experience report tells the tale of the quest to define the role of the architect and of architecture in an agile environment. The primary observation here is that people skills are a key factor in that role.

Keywords: Experience · Journey · Extreme programming · XP · Architecture

1 Introduction

"When you come to a fork in the road…Take it."
Yogi Berra

In my last experience report I described my long journey along the agile road. I ended the report saying that the journey is far from over, and that it should be exciting to see how things evolve. I was right. It is very exciting, with surprises, twists and turns along the way. This second chapter of the story goes on to tell of an Architect trying to find his place within the agile environment.

2 Background

Since 1994 I have been working for NDS (acquired in 2012 by Cisco). I write code and design systems. I take great pride in a job well done. Having fun is a major objective. My current role is defined as Senior Systems Architect. I am expected to be deeply familiar with the core products, to understand the customers' needs, and to lead the task of building something that meets or exceeds expectations, while remaining in line with the company's technical and business objectives.

I work directly with customers, developers and development leads. In addition to being an architect, I manage a large team of architects, and as such I am expected to provide them with leadership and technical guidance.

The company I work for (Cisco) is committed to agile, and continues to adopt many of its practices and values. The Agile Transformation includes a deep look at the current roles in the organization and an attempt to understand how they will adapt to an agile world. As one that has been with the organization from early on, I am deeply involved in that

H. Sharp and T. Hall (Eds.): XP 2016, LNBIP 251, pp. 226–234, 2016.
DOI: 10.1007/978-3-319-33515-5_20

transformation. So it is natural that people often ask me, "What *exactly* does an architect do in an agile environment?" (Often, when asking the question, they will emphasize the word *exactly* and accompany that emphasis with tone and gesture that express more skepticism than genuine curiosity). And the honest answer is that I do not know *exactly* what an architect does or should do, but I can tell them what *I* do, and by way of generalization, deduce what an architect does.

3 The Scary Problem

Often people in the agile community will say something like, "The architecture is emergent." They go on to say that we do not really need architects any more, as agile does not believe in upfront planning. This really has me quite challenged or even worried. I am an architect, I do architecture, and as such, I like to feel that I bring real value to the organization I work for. If the architecture is emergent and we don't need an architect, then what does the architect do? How can the role of the architect be justified?

Put a bit more formally the question can be formulated thus: Agile means responding to change. The Agile Manifesto item that most strongly represents the agile spirit is *we value responding to change over following a plan*. Looking up the word "agile" in a dictionary, I came across the definition, "able to move quickly and easily". On the other hand, architecture is about long term planning; the architect has a long term vision of the domain and of the software system, and engages in technical planning. One of the definitions of architecture is "a unifying or coherent form or structure". At first glance, long term planning and responding to change seem to be at odds with each other. Hence the question. Why do we need an architect in an agile environment?

Historically, one of the drivers behind the agile movement was frustration with the architects. Architects design a system based on requirements. Developers implement a system as described by the specification. However, for many reasons requirements might not really carry the true intent of what the customer wants. Furthermore, the requirements even when clear and well understood, are in constant flux, and as a result architects are often in the business of predicting the future. Not only do we define what requirements the system needs to fulfill, but we also define what the future requirements are likely to be. In that environment, an architect makes decisions based on predictions, many of which are wrong to some extent or another. As Yogi Berra quipped, "It's tough to make predictions, especially about the future." If the predictions are wrong, then an implementation based on the design stemming from those inaccurate (or just plain wrong) predictions will not meet the customer expectations.

Frustrated with these wrong predictions, the agile community adopted the practice whereby all decision-making is deferred to a time of greater certainty. Now we can restate the question. If architecture is emergent, and it is difficult to say anything meaningful about the future, what is the role of the architect? It was this question that forced me to better define what exactly is architecture, and more importantly, what an architect does. I raised this question with many of my colleagues. All of them agreed that agile projects need architecture and architects. They differed on what exactly those architects and architectures are needed for, and quite a few of them were not able to clearly articulate that need. But through the aggregation of all those answers, I was able to come up with some meaningful insights.

4 The Weekly Meeting

About two years ago, I started a weekly meeting with other architects and technical leaders. Since many of us live and work in different countries, these meetings were often phone calls. We would hang around for an hour or so, and discuss the contributions we have made as architects, any interesting issues we faced that week, and what about our implementation of agile needs to be fixed. This turned out to be a great platform for discussion and idea sharing. I discovered that some architects are often great at retrospection and introspection, and others are quite good at understanding people and how they interact with each other. Agile is about people more than it is about technology. So these insights on how people work turned out to be extremely valuable.

One key insight that we kept returning to is that whether or not it is defined in the role of the architect, the agile architect deals with people, and a large part of the architect's role is a people role. For example, we were discussing the responsibility of the architect to communicate design decisions. We asked the question, to what extent should the architect feel obligated to *convince* the team of the wisdom of his decisions? We all agreed that not only must the architect explain the rationale behind his technical decision; he must convince the team of that rationale. Why? Because a team that understands and agrees with what they are doing, have a better chance of doing the right thing. If they identify with the work they are doing, they will do high quality work.

5 No Design Phase

I think that part of the question regarding the role of an architect emerges when agile is compared to waterfall. In a waterfall environment, there is an explicit stage called the *design* phase. This phase is **led by the architect**. He designs and documents the solutions. The design is prescriptive. The assumption is that if the developers follow the design, then the software will be OK. This design phase is the most demanding and solemn of the entire software phase. If you get the design phase wrong, you will end up paying a high price for years to come.

On the other hand, in an agile environment, there often is no design phase. In consequence, the reasoning often goes: "If in an agile environment, there is no design phase, so there is no designer hence no architect." So we must clarify. No design phase does not mean "no design". No design phase means that there is not an explicit phase during which design happens exclusively. Rather, **design happens all the time**. Likewise, when we say that the architecture is *emergent,* that should not mean that we do not need architects because architecture just happens. That is not true. It means something much more subtle. When we say that the architecture is emergent, we are saying that as the system evolves, a certain structure emerges. Someone needs to keep an eye on that emerging structure. When it is emerging according to plan, the architect will strengthen it, and when it is starts diverging, the architect will act accordingly. Maybe adjusting the plan, or maybe pushing the development in a particular direction – or both. Personally, this was the most dramatic change for me as an architect when transitioning to an agile environment. The fact that I am designing all the time, and not just during the design phase, has a significant impact.

So in my current role, I am always designing. The domain is changing, the requirements are changing, and our understanding of the world is changing. Agile realizes and accommodates these changes. As a result, I am always designing.

5.1 Reservation

I'll be honest. Not because I have to, but because I choose to. Making a decision at the "most responsible moment" is a great slogan. In reality it is somewhere between very hard and impossible. We often do not know what the most responsible moment is until that moment is long gone. That has often happened to me. I defer a decision to a later moment, because I feel that it would be irresponsible to decide now. At that later moment, I realize that I missed the opportune moment. This happens much more often than I care for. Every time it happens, I realize (once again) that my responsibility as an architect is not only to make and communicate technical decisions, but to make them at the right time.

It is safe to say that as an architect I am always designing. I am always trying to find the right time to make design decisions, and I am often fixing mistakes when I missed the right time for a particular decision[1].

6 Retrospection

Looking inward, I notice more and more that most of what I do as an architect is to interact with people. As an architect, even when I write technical documents, I am dealing with people. When a developer writes code or script his primary audience is the compiler or interpreter. If he writes something that is clear and unambiguous, but is not clear to the compiler he has not delivered. His secondary audience are human beings. The developer writes clear code with useful names for classes and functions, he writes comments that are concise and do not contain too many lies.

On the other hand, when the architect designs something, or creates an artifact of any sort (diagram interface and so forth), his primary audience is the human being reading that artifact. The architect is constantly learning and explaining. On further inspection, architecture itself is a very human thing. Structure or lack of structure are how humans perceive the system. This is captured beautifully by Christopher Alexander in the introduction to *The Nature of Order*. Order and symmetry are perceived by humans and used by humans. Even when humans cannot find formal

[1] For an insightful discussion of last possible moment as opposed to most possible moment see http://wirfs-brock.com/blog/2011/01/18/agile-architecture-myths-2-architecture-decisions-should-be-made-at-the-last-responsible-moment/.

words to express what it is they are feeling, they share a sense of *orderliness* that can be communicated through aesthetic design.

"The structure I identify as the foundation of all order is also *personal.* As we learn to understand it, we shall see that our own feeling, the feeling of what it is to be a person, rooted, happy, alive in oneself, straightforward and ordinary, is itself inextricably connected with order. This order is not remote from our humanity. It is the stuff which goes to the very heart of human experience".

Wow! Does that mean that when I, as an architect, deal with order, I am dealing with the stuff that "goes to the very heart of human experience"? That is way more than I bargained for when taking this job.

7 Domain Knowledge

Even when the architecture is emergent, the domain certainly is not. The domain is the real world. It is the business need that the software is there to solve. The business needs and the rates of change of those business needs are not emergent. What might be emergent is the understanding of the domain, and the software structures that support that understanding.

Domain understanding is critical for the success of the software. Good architecture will not emerge from software being developed, unless the developer of the software has a good understanding of the problem she is solving.

Someone needs to understand the domain, and be capable of organizing that understanding and explaining it, and then, by observing how that understanding is reflected in software, confirm that indeed the understanding was correct. And in cases where the understanding was not correct, that someone needs to fix things.

That someone is the architect.

8 Dependencies

One of the most complicated things that the architect deals with is dependencies. It is easy to state, "A is dependent on B", as though dependency was a binary value that either exists or does not exist. In reality, it is the nature of the dependency that matters. The architect understands the dependencies between the domain elements (human and otherwise) as well as the dependency between the solution elements (human and otherwise). She is able to offer guidance based on her understanding of those dependencies.

An example can illustrate this point. In one particular project, we recorded dependencies in Rally. Each user story had a list of other user stories it was dependent on. Those user stories had to be implemented first before the current user story could be implemented. One time, after we put all the dependencies in place, we realized that we have a cycle or gridlock where A (Optimize Bandwidth Usage) was dependent on B (Configure Channel), and B (Configure Channel) was dependent on A (Optimize Bandwidth Usage). That caused a few moments of panic until I pointed out that the dependencies have different meanings. When A was dependent on B, we meant to say that we cannot implement A until we have a proper understanding of B, because B is the primary client of A, and thus if we do not understand B we cannot implement A. On the other hand, when B was dependent on A, we did not mean to say that B is of zero value without A, all we meant to say was that B cannot provide its full business value without A.

The nature of these dependencies were clear to me as an architect, and were quite clear to many on the team that understood the domain and the project. However, the graph of the features in Rally seemed to indicate a circular dependency. Once I pointed out the nature of the dependencies, the way forward was obvious, and we decoupled A's implementation from A's interface in a way that allowed development of B to progress.

9 Metaphors

Rebecca Wirfs-Brock elaborates on the various types of architects ("Why we Need Architects and Architecture on Agile Projects" – Most recently presented at ILTam Conference 2015). I would like to propose some additional metaphors that describe the architect. These are not distinct. Rather in an agile world each architect has all of them. Personally, I have acted in all these roles, often in many of them simultaneously.

9.1 The Tribal Elder

In this role, the architect acts as the guardian of the collective memory. He has seen the domain evolve and the architecture evolve. He understands why decisions were made. He understands the deeper meaning of the various dependencies. He is also very experienced beyond the scope of the particular problem. He remembers mistakes that were made, and how they can be avoided. He remembers useful lessons. He has seen how many predictions that were made with certainty do not materialize, and he has seen many surprises. He has a wealth of stories that he is happy to share to make his point. He might not be as "hands on" or as quick on his feet as some of the younger ones, but he more than compensates for that with maturity, understanding of human nature and experience.

One of the challenges with retrospectives and with lessons learned, is how do we preserve these insights over time? How do we maintain a record of these lessons? In a lean or agile environment, this tribal elder is constantly making sure that lessons that were painfully learned are not forgotten.

The challenges for a tribal elder are many. Too often he expects that people will accept his word on authority alone, rather than on the merit of his idea. On occasion we might find that the tribal elder has lost touch with the times, as lessons learned a long time ago might not be relevant any more, and the tribe elder will try to keep us in line with dogmas that are no longer relevant. So this architect needs to be humble and to have a very good sense as to when his experience is of value, and when it is outdated.

In my group, we are constantly caught up in the tension between a generic product and a customized product tailored to meet the customer. This tension has existed for over twenty years, and we periodically cycle from one extreme to another. Now, when someone suggests a shift from a generic product to a customized product or vice versa, the tribal elder (me) will tell stories of what worked and what failed in the past. The tribe elder will warn of pitfalls, while taking care not to dampen any enthusiasm.

9.2 The Architect as the Human Document

A document is a source of information and of agreement. If you need information consult the document. If you are in an argument, the document might be able to arbitrate. The architect can fulfil some of that need but even better.

Sometimes code is referred to as the "Living Document" – meaning that the code is always up-to-date in communicating what the system does. (This is as opposed to a "dead document" that at best was correct at some point in the past.) However, code will only tell you what the system *does* and *how* it does it. It will never tell you *why* the system does what it does, or what the system *should* be doing.

The architect is able to actually explain all the relevant knowledge that is not captured in code. Relevance is a matter of context. Because the architect is contextually aware, he can give the information that is relevant in a particular context.

There are several dangers that the architect as a human document must be aware of.

First and foremost, the architect must not think that he can forgo clear, concise and accurate documents, just because he is smart and articulate. Good documents have the advantage of being unambiguous, context free, and they never change their minds. Interfaces must be documented. This is especially true for teams that work over long periods of time or across great geographical distances.

In the role of the human document, the architect must take care not to become a bottleneck. If everyone is waiting in line to get the time and attention of the architect, then the work gets held up. It is the responsibility of the architect to ensure that does not happen.

9.3 The Architect as the Potter

Looking at a potter working, you will notice that the interaction between the potter and the clay is very light and very accurate. The illusion is so strong that the clay might actually think that it is molding itself into a vase or bowl. The clay does not fully understand the role of the potter, and might see him as redundant. But that is not true. Without the potter's continued presence and intervention, the clay will find itself all over the walls of the workshop. On the other hand, the potter needs to be gentle. If the potter is too aggressive, the clay will resist, and the result will be a shapeless mass. The "potter architect" does the same. He **allows** the architecture to emerge on its own, and only makes featherlight touches here and there when he sees that things need a little fixing. If he is really good, the people will say that the architecture is emergent. He might be so effective the team will start asking what they need him for.

10 Qualities

As I mentioned in the opening of this paper, it is becoming apparent to me that the role of the architect in an agile environment has a great deal to do with people skills. In my own personal journey I am discovering that quite often I need to call on those skills in order to be an effective architect.

I would like to outline some traits that I find particularly useful. While these are good qualities in any person, they are critical for the architect. I am not including the standard qualities such as a quick understanding and good memory. I am focusing on social skills.

Teacher at Heart – The architect must be able to explain complex material at the depth that is appropriate to the audience. He must be able to tell if the audience understands what he is saying, and if not, he must explain it again. He will use all tools that a teacher uses. Metaphor, drama, humor, multisensory, example, tonality and so forth.

Empathy – The architect must be able to see things from someone else's perspective. That will allow the architect to understand the domain and to be able to explain the domain as well as the solution to people that have experiences other than his own. The empathetic architect understands that his perspective is not the only perspective, and that the underlying assumptions of the audience, are very different from his own.

Sense of Humor – The architect must take himself seriously, but not too seriously. A sense of humor will allow the architect to see new and surprising angles on things. A sense of humor will allow the architect to break patterns in interesting ways and find a solution to an elusive problem.

Humility – The architect holds power, authority, and a great deal of respect. His word is often the final word on technical matters. He often gets to set the technical direction of a product or a project. However he is not immune to mistakes, and his mistakes can often have far reaching consequences. Agile is about recognizing and admitting mistakes. An architect that sticks to a decision just because it was his decision will fail. The architect must be prepared to admit that he made an error in judgment, or was not diligent enough in his research.

11 Summary

Agile is about responding to change. Architecture is about structure, uniformity and stability. The architect has a high awareness of how to balance the two. As the system undergoes change, the architect will understand and communicate what parts of the system need to stay the same and what parts should change.

The architect is the bridge between the people and the technology. He not only understands what the software does and knows how to get there. He is deeply aware of the human aspect, and uses his human understanding to lead the project forward.

Acknowledgements. The ideas in this article have been evolving over a long time. I thank all my friends and colleagues that patiently listened to my musings and provided feedback and adjustment. Thanks to my colleagues from Cisco, David Russ and Warren Pratten for many hours of fruitful discussion. I look forward to more such discussions in the future.

Special thanks to Rebecca Wirfs-Brock who encouraged me to write this paper and who provided a great deal of valuable insight and feedback.

Lessons Learned from a Failed Attempt at Distributed Agile

Mark Rajpal(✉)

ARC Business Solutions, Calgary, AB, Canada
mrajpal@arcbus.com

Abstract. What do you do when you have endured an Agile experience where things didn't go so well? You can abandon Agile altogether or you can take those lessons learned and apply them to future Agile projects. This paper discusses the journey travelled from that painful experience to becoming a more confident and experienced Agile practitioner. We will also look at some of the challenges that I still encounter today.

Keywords: Organization · Project · Team · Agile · Scrum · Extreme programming

1 Introduction

The 12 principles of Agile [1] indicate what is needed to make Agile effective. However, it does not specify what elements can render Agile ineffective. Agile (like anything) can only be successful in the right situation. There are components that pair well with Agile, but there are also factors that may not be well suited for Agile.

Some organizations have experienced failed attempts at Agile and claim that Agile does not work. In many cases this is a fallacy. Sometimes Agile uncovers pre-existing issues that have been around for years that were simply neglected. In other cases, the organization is structured in such a way that it is not conducive to the Agile mindset.

In this paper, we examine a failed Agile project that uncovered many practices that were not in fact Agile. These elements range from non-technical to technical. In each case we discuss the journey from the failed project to today where we apply common practices as a result of lessons learned.

The rest of the paper is organized in five separate sections. In Sect. 2, the failed project is explained in detail. Section 3 indicates the lessons learned that were applied. Section 4 discusses the remaining challenges. Finally, Sect. 5 summarizes the key points in conclusions.

2 The Failed Project

In 2008, an ambitious initiative was undertaken to implement a scheduling system for a large organization in the energy sector. The Scrum methodology was selected in an attempt to deliver high quality software in a short amount of time using month long

H. Sharp and T. Hall (Eds.): XP 2016, LNBIP 251, pp. 235–243, 2016.
DOI: 10.1007/978-3-319-33515-5_21

sprints. Consequently, teams were allocated at various locations including Alberta Canada, North Carolina USA, and various parts of Europe. Matters were complicated by the multi-vendor approach where one vendor provided the Canadian teams and the other vendor provided the USA/European teams.

The project was scheduled for just one year. At completion, the project took over 3 years and was over 5 times its initial budget. As a result, the project was considered a failure and the Agile approach was to blame. I was not convinced of this and I decided to explore the truth behind what really went wrong.

This paper will focus on some of the challenges and lessons learned from the failed project. These lessons learned aided me on ensuing projects. That is not to say these subsequent projects were free from challenges. Instead, the failed project provided a starting point, and the successive projects provided a means of moving forward while continually learning and improving.

The lessons learned can be categorized into two main categories– communication and requirements.

2.1 Team Communication Problems on the Failed Project

2.1.1 Intra-Team

I was part of a Scrum team (1 of 2 Scrum teams for Vendor A) consisting of 5 team members where everyone (except the ScrumMaster) was collocated. Team members started their day by updating the time remaining on each of their tasks before the standup meeting. The standup meeting was usually in excess of the standard 15 min as team members typically asked questions instead of answering the 3 questions. Sometimes these meetings went on for over an hour as problem solving was incorporated that unnecessarily occupied everybody's time.

At sprint end, a retrospective was held. The team discussed what did not work well. But the problems continued to exist as no corrective action was taken. Furthermore, the retrospective was cancelled once the project schedule started to slip.

2.1.2 Inter-Team

In all, there were a total of 4 Scrum teams. Vendor A was responsible for 2 Scrum teams located in Edmonton and Vendor B was responsible for 1 Scrum Team that was distributed across North Carolina and Europe. Additionally, the client provided an operations team that was also located in Edmonton but not dedicated to the project.

Communication between Vendor A and Vendor B teams was problematic from the beginning. The teams were uncomfortable talking to one another so they avoided it until they absolutely had to. Phone calls were rarely used. Instant messaging tools were not used. Instead, email was overused so there was no sense of any kind of real-time information. The problem was further complicated having the Vendor B resources in completely different time zones and geographies. It became an "us vs. them" mentality especially after failed integration attempts at the end of each sprint.

A similar relationship existed between the client operations team and the Vendor A teams. There was no sense of team unity between these collocated teams. Both sides did the bare minimum in terms of supporting one another. Complications arose mostly due to the fact that the operations team was not dedicated to the project. As a result, they had various demands that they could accomplish themselves but did not have the time to do because they were inundated with other tasks and projects.

With so many teams and participants, pressure was introduced to refrain from talking which led to less effective communication [2].

2.1.3 ScrumMaster

As mentioned, the ScrumMaster for both Vendor A teams was not collocated with the team and had an additional role of project manager. Even though the ScrumMaster attended the standup via conference call, it was evident that he was not an active part of the process. The ScrumMaster would often ask for the progress of certain tasks that had already been completed or in some cases ignore tasks that were incomplete. Although the ScrumMaster visited the team approximately once a month, during this time he was immersed with meetings amongst senior management.

2.1.4 Product Owner

The Product Owner was only collocated (in Calgary) alongside a single team member from Vendor A. This allowed that team to gain an edge in terms of face time but the team also suffered in terms of effective communication with a distributed team member. The Product Owner had a difficult job mostly because each team competed for her time. As a result, much time was wasted as teams waited for their turn.

In the early stages, the Product Owner travelled to the various teams. While on-site, the particular team she was visiting was productive. Unfortunately, the other teams were at a standstill. As the project schedule slipped and the overall budget escalated, travel was limited.

In one sprint, each team travelled to Calgary for sprint planning. Even though everyone had face time with the Product Owner, the same problem persisted in that the Product Owner was constantly bombarded.

2.1.5 Executives

The relationship between the client and Vendor A's management was turbulent from the beginning. Their interpretation of Agile seemed to be the core of the problem. The relationship declined even further when milestones were not achieved.

Sprint reviews were held with the client's senior management asking questions about why things were done in a certain way. Then in one review, the application crashed. The management team was convinced this was a waste of their time, and sprint reviews were cancelled.

2.2 Requirements Issues on the Failed Project

2.2.1 Confusion

The project was engulfed with many different forms of requirements. This led to much confusion as to what was acceptable and what was not.

Before the project initiation, the client incurred a sizable cost to conduct requirements gathering that resulted in a vast amount of documentation. Consequently, their expectation was that no further requirements were necessary. Upon project commencement, it was obvious that the requirements were outdated and was of no use. This angered Vendor A's management because their fixed price bid was based on the Big Design Up Front (BDUF) requirements and they were concerned about the impact to their profitability. BDUF is where the architecture phase is accompanied with a vast amount of documentation [10].

2.2.2 Process

Before developers could begin coding, they were required to write a design specification. This deliverable was not contractually bound and was only stipulated upon project commencement and yet all vendors agreed to adhere to this. In some cases, developers spent an entire sprint writing a specification and delivering nothing. What I found quite peculiar is that many people agreed that this was a good use of time even though sprint deliverables were not being met.

2.2.3 Change

Change requests were frowned upon because they implied a change to the requirements. As mentioned, there was an assumption that the large cost of BDUF negated the need for any changes. As change requests arose, executives required that the vendors provide thorough documentation. Consequently, teams stopped working on their sprint goals as they context switched to accommodate the executives. In most cases, the change request was rejected and the vendors had to absorb the cost.

3 Lessons Learned Applied

3.1 Good Communication is Important

Be Serious About the Standup: On subsequent projects I experienced many different interpretations of the daily standup. For some teams, the meeting turned into a 1 h water cooler discussion that included the weather and the sporting events from the previous night. Other teams used the time to problem solve. In some cases, my team members decided that the meeting was optional and decided to attend when it suited them or when they felt like it. On a more recent project, I stressed the importance of the standup meeting by explaining "why" it was important. Team members began to realize that it was in their best interest to understand what other team members were doing. At first, they struggled with the 15 min rule. However, I received a really good tip at an Agile conference. The session speaker suggested that at the start of the meeting, the ScrumMaster should set a 15 min timer on their smart phone. When 15 min expires, simply end the meeting. After 3 or 4 times, teams will get the hint and start adhering to the timebox. In fact, one of my teams introduced a post standup discussion. Immediately after the meeting, any team member was allowed to discuss anything they chose as long as it benefited everyone. This included anything from upcoming vacation schedules to the progress of testing.

Aim for Totally Integrated: We live in a world were distributed teams are becoming the norm. According to Sutherland [5], there are three types of Scrum implementations when teams are distributed. Isolated scrums, where teams work completely independent of one another and have very little communication. In fact, some teams abandon Scrum and fall back to waterfall. Distributed scrum of scrums, where teams are mainly isolated but are integrated by a scrum of scrums that meet regularly. Totally integrated scrums, where teams are cross-functional [6] and the project is integrated as a whole. Overall, I would describe the failed project as the isolated scrums model. Not only did the teams work independently, they had very little knowledge of what the other teams were doing. Despite my best efforts, the totally integrated model was never reached on any project. However, having those aspirations allowed for the progression from isolated scrums to distributed scrums of scrums on more than one occasion.

Collocate the ScrumMaster: On ensuing projects the distributed nature of the ScrumMaster greatly affected the team. There was little to no confidence in the ScrumMaster figurehead who was rarely seen and had very little involvement. Also, it seemed that on most projects it was assumed that the project manager should take on the role of ScrumMaster. Much more success was achieved when one of the team members (that was collocated) took on the role of ScrumMaster. On one project in particular, we decided to rotate the role amongst ourselves which made the experience much more enjoyable. Even though this approach worked much better, I'm not sure this would have been successful with a non-collocated team member facilitating the role of ScrumMaster.

On another project we split the role of the ScrumMaster. Essentially, we had a team ScrumMaster who was collocated with the team. Additionally, we had a client facing ScrumMaster who was mainly tasked with communicating with the Product Owner. Initially I thought the "co-ScrumMaster" approach would not work because Agile evangelists do not seem to support it. However, this allowed the junior Agilists to feel more comfortable taking on the team facing ScrumMaster role.

I am not aware of success stories where the ScrumMaster was distributed from the team. That does not mean it cannot exist. In fact, it is highly probable that there are such cases but the lack of supporting information could indicate there are rare cases or that more research needs to be explored in this area.

Involve the Users Early: After one year from the start of the project, the client brought in an additional resource that functioned as a subject matter expert. The idea was to alleviate the barrage of questions on the Product Owner. However, the subject matter expert was not empowered to make decisions. Often she would have to go back to the Product Owner for clarification or confirmation. This approach introduced an unnecessary layer of communication. Furthermore, neither the Product Owner nor the subject matter expert was an active user and Agile projects require active participation from the users [7]. The users did not have an active role in the project.

On later projects, the end users were more than happy to provide feedback. As we listened to their concerns, they felt their trepidations were being addressed. Including users early on in the process tends to give them a finer grain of control over the project [8].

Get Buy-in From the Top: It seemed that the executives (or possibly the organization) were not quite ready to make the switch the Agile. Or maybe they just assumed it would be seamless. Agile migrations are not free from issues and there will be obstacles to overcome. "If you don't involve your executives in the move to Agile, there is a good chance that they will stop the move as soon as they learn of any issues with the migration." [9]. Having dismissed the sprint review, the executives were even less engaged at a time where they needed to be more involved.

On successive projects, we posted displays (aka information radiators) for everybody (including executives) to see. Posting an impediments list prompted executives to inquire about the impediment and eventually aid in removing it. For example, one of my teams listed "Administrator Access" as an impediment. Essentially, the team did not have the ability to install tools on their development machines without going through a formal approval process. It turned out that one of the executives heard this from other people and also experienced this pain point. Consequently, the executive authorized all team members to have Administrator access. However, this example worked well because the executive walked past the information radiator many times a day. In many cases, executives are not located anywhere near Agile teams.

Retrospectives Are Necessary: Even though the retrospectives encouraged good discussion, they were completely ineffective especially once they were cancelled. Following the project, I researched various techniques. Almost everyone I reached out to pointed me to the book, "Agile Retrospectives: Making Good Teams Great". There were many helpful suggestions for the novice and also the more experienced. On most projects I introduce the "Timeline" activity [3] for the Sprint 1 retrospective. It seems to be a good way to get the team (as well as a rookie facilitator) accustomed to retrospectives. The book provides many other activities for the other retrospectives so the team is not repeating the same thing again and again.

Incorporate the Necessary Tools: On the failed project there were many areas that could have been incorporated to bridge the communication gap. For instance, equipping all computers with webcams would have allowed distributed resources to have a face-to-face conversation. Also, teams could have adjusted their working hours to have some overlap with the other teams. Even a one-hour overlap would have made a significant difference. Furthermore, it seemed that the travel budget was not adequate. When travel was requested it was quickly denied due to cost. It is difficult to say whether or not these things would have made a noticeable difference. However, it is likely that these modifications would have gotten the teams closer to a totally integrated scrums model.

On other projects, I have used add-on tools that facilitated more collaboration. For example, Jira is a popular issue tracking system I used on some Agile projects. There are many supporting tools for Jira but one that stands out is Hipchat. Hipchat facilitates instant messaging, screen sharing, and video. It can also produce notifications once the state of a Jira item has been modified. On smaller projects, my teams benefited from Kanban boards by using tools like Trello and AgileZen. While these tools can make our lives easier it should be noted, "technology can maintain relationships but it won't build them" [4].

3.2 Managing Requirements is a Necessity

Time and Materials (T&M) Over Fixed Price: Fixed price can lead to false expectations and mistrust [8]. On this fixed price project, the client felt they could change the requirements whenever they wanted, and the end product would be delivered as expected, at the same cost, and on time. Ensuing projects that were T&M based allowed the client to make modifications but it also allowed the teams to incorporate quality, present alternatives, and build trust by delivering often. In fact, it was noted that while extreme programming (XP) practices are possible for fixed price, it is not proven because accurate estimates of scope are necessary [6].

Change is Inevitable: Requirements will change regardless of how much analysis is spent before the development work commences, so change requests are inevitable. However, many large organizations cause change requests to be as tedious as possible. In this case it simply detracts from getting the work done. Later projects involving smaller organizations viewed change requests as a waste of time. Other projects addressed changed requests by accepting the fact that change will happen. Sometimes that meant the user stories were pushed to another sprint. In other cases, the team put in extra time to accommodate the change to meet their sprint goals.

Requirements Must Be Understandable and Decomposed: For the most part, the new requirements were very complex and the teams were pressured to complete them in a single sprint, which rarely happened. Since the team did not have the necessary availability of the Product Owner, there were many times where they had to guess which seldom ended well. Subsequent projects incorporated user stories as their primary means of acquiring requirements. This worked much better for everyone. The requirements became much clearer when the business analysts were able to write user stories as crosscutting layers. For example, instead of taking on a pure database user story, we developed a screen (will some functionality) that crossed the user interface, business logic, and database layers. Developers favored this approach because it allowed them to complete the user stories within the sprint.

4 Remaining Challenges

This report has explored the challenges associated with communication and requirements using Agile approaches. The results provide information that can be useful in overcoming these challenges. However, there are some challenges that require further investigation.

Lack of Support: Many Agile implementations (especially from a grassroots movement) struggle to gain support from the organization. In fact, there are those that are never going to accept Agile and they may even demean you for trying to promote it.

Empowerment: It is often the case that people are given a title of empowerment without the power to go with it. In Agile, there are cases where ScrumMasters are not empowered to remove roadblocks or Product Owners are not empowered to make decisions without the approval of their superior.

User Involvement: Sometimes users do not want to take part in the Agile process as they feel it adds to their workload. As a result, the task of writing user stories may fall upon the requirements engineer. In other instances, management may decide that the end users do not need to be involved until the modifications are deployed to production.

Scrum Ceremonies: Some (if not all) of the ceremonies can become redundant. Teams often get bored of repeating the ceremonies in the same manner. This may cause the effectiveness to come into question.

5 Conclusion

The paper presents challenges that prevent Agile teams from performing at a high level. Ultimately, organizations need to decide whether or not Agile is a good fit. If it is a good fit then they need to be prepared to make changes (in management style, working environment, team's skills, and close relationships with users [8]) and support it across all relevant levels. When individuals or teams are placed in a situation to fail, they often do just that. Agile is no different.

Of the 12 principles, the one that most resonates with me is "working software is the principal measure of progress" [1]. There have been many times when people have denounced my Agile efforts. What they cannot argue with, is success.

References

1. Beck, K., et al.: Twelve Principles of Agile Software (2001). http://agilemanifesto.org/
2. Hogan, B.: Lessons learned from an extremely distributed project. In: Proceedings of AGILE 2006, pp. 321–326. doi:10.1109/AGILE.2006.37

3. Derby, E., Larsen, D.: Agile Retrospectives: Making Good Teams Great. The Pragmatic Programmers. LLC, USA (2006)
4. Heffernan, M.: Willful Blindness. Anchor Canada, USA (2012)
5. Sutherland, J., Viktorov, A., Blount, J., Puntikov, N.: Distributed scrum: Agile project management with outsourced development teams. In: Proceedings of the 40th Annual Hawaii International Conference on System Sciences, HICSS 2007, p. 274a. doi:10.1109/HICSS.2007.180
6. Hossain, E.: Coordinating mechanisms for Agile global software development. In: IEEE International Conference on Global Software Engineering, 2008, ICGSE 2008, pp. 257–263, 17–20 August 2008. doi:10.1109/ICGSE.2008.24
7. Wells, D.: Extreme programming: a gentle introduction (2009). http://www.extremeprogramming.org/
8. Chen, J.Q., Dien P., Wang B., Vogel, D.R.: Light-weight development method: a case study. In: ICSSSM 2007 International Conference on Service Systems and Service Management, 9–11 June 2007, pp. 1–6. doi:10.1109/ICSSSM.2007.4280199
9. Smith, G., Sidky, A.: Becoming Agile in an Imperfect World. Manning Publications Co., Greenwich (2009)
10. Hadar, I., Sherman, S.: Agile vs. plan-driven perceptions of software architecture. In: 2012 5th International Workshop on Cooperative and Human Aspects of Software Engineering (CHASE), 2 June 2012, pp. 50–55. doi:10.1109/CHASE.2012.6223022

Tailoring Agile in the Large: Experience and Reflections from a Large-Scale Agile Software Development Project

Knut H. Rolland[1,3(✉)], Vidar Mikkelsen[2], and Alexander Næss[1]

[1] Westerdals Oslo School of Arts, Communication and Technology, Oslo, Norway
rolknu@westerdals.no, nesale14@student.westerdals.no

[2] Sopra Steria, Oslo, Norway
vim@soprasteria.com

[3] SINTEF, Trondheim, Norway

Abstract. It is not surprising that agile methods are tailored or customized in various contexts and projects. However, there is little advice for practitioners for how to go about tailoring agile methods in large-scale projects. Henceforth, the aim of this experience report is to highlight some of the challenges with large-scale agile software development and especially how to deal with these challenges involves continuous tailoring of the agile method in use. In so doing, we report from a large-scale agile software development effort involving more than 120 participants in a Governmental organization and running for 3,5 years. The project consisted of three deliverables, partly developed in parallel after a delivery model based on Scrum. After a much troubled start related to scaling challenges and architecture complexity during the first deliverable, the project was turnaround and the second and third deliverables were portrayed fairly successful by both supplier and customer. From a practitioner's perspective, we found that novel practices emerged through out the project that improved the way of working – especially across teams and stakeholders. Based on this, we describe some guidelines for tailoring agile in the large.

Keywords: Large-scale agile software development · Method tailoring · Software development practices

1 Introduction

In this experience report we draw from a recent large-scale agile software development project in a Norwegian Governmental organization. The project involved over 120 participants and was delivered through three distinct deliverables over 3,5 years. The project was highly prestigious and critical, as the Governmental organization had failed in two previous projects in replacing their core IT-systems. The specific context and complexity of the project with numerous external stakeholders, integration with existing portfolio of IT-systems, public contracting legislation, and replacing core legacy IT-systems made tailoring of a Scrum-based delivery model necessary. Existing literature on agile methods has for long underscored the need for tailoring to fit specific contexts and different types of projects [1–3]. However, the empirical literature on tailoring is not substantial, and there is little concrete advice for

H. Sharp and T. Hall (Eds.): XP 2016, LNBIP 251, pp. 244–251, 2016.
DOI: 10.1007/978-3-319-33515-5_22

practitioners for how to go about doing tailoring and what to tailor in practice. Arguably, especially when agile methods and practices are scaled to larger projects in terms of involving multiple teams, heterogeneous users needs, complex software architectures, and numerous integration efforts with existing IT-systems, there is a pressing need to tailor and blend different agile methods [4]. Henceforth, *the aim of this report is to contribute to a richer understanding of tailoring agile methods in the context of large-scale projects – and based on this, to carve out some guidelines that would be useful for others.* We believe our experience and reflections from this project would be of interests to both project managers and developers as experience and guidelines for tailoring agile methods are hard to come by.

The remainder of this experience report is structured in the following way. The next section explains the case context. Then, we describe and analyse some of the experiences through out the project. Next, based on our experiences and some literature we try to give advice for tailoring agile in the large.

2 The Case: The Brownfield Project

Context. A case study of a major software development project was conducted from September 2014 to December 2015. The project, referred to as the Brownfield project, was a large-scale agile development effort involving over 120 participants over 3 years from 2011 to late 2014. The project was organized as four development – or 'Scrum' teams and one team loosely related to the project developing a business intelligence solution. Experience from this project is especially interesting in many respects. Firstly, the supplier, the Consulting company had just recently before starting on the Brownfield project been part of a prestigious large-scale agile software development project that was especially known nationally for being a success – and often used as a template for other large-scale agile projects in Norway. Secondly, the customer had tried two times before earlier in the 2000s to implement the Brownfield project and failed considerably in both cases.

This report is written based on 20 in depth-interviews of project participants, 2 workshops, project documents as well as numerous meetings with different participants. Additionally, one of the authors was the project manager for the Consulting company on the project during the third deliverable.

Three authors have written this report: one practitioner, one student, and one academic. One of us was the project manager for the project during the last of three deliverables. He has more than 10 years of experience as a project manager on large software development projects and agile projects in particular. The other author is currently a researcher working on a scientific case study of the project. Previously, he has also been a practitioner for many years participating in large-scale agile software development projects. The third author is a student of information systems management and innovation, who also has a background in industry. Obviously, our differences in experiences and background made the writing process especially interesting, as we were able to challenge each other's biases.

The scrum-based delivery model. The project followed a Scrum-based model that interestingly had been used by a recent large-scale project where the Consulting company was involved. This previous project was perceived as highly successful, and is generally regarded as 'best practice' for doing large scale agile in the Norwegian IT industry.

The Scrum-based delivery model is characterized by splitting up a large project in different deliverables as shown in Fig. 1 below. For each deliverable then, a semi-agile process is followed by first defining user stories, then architectural design, overall UX design, and refinement of user stories – but with a minimum of effort not to plan things in too much detail.

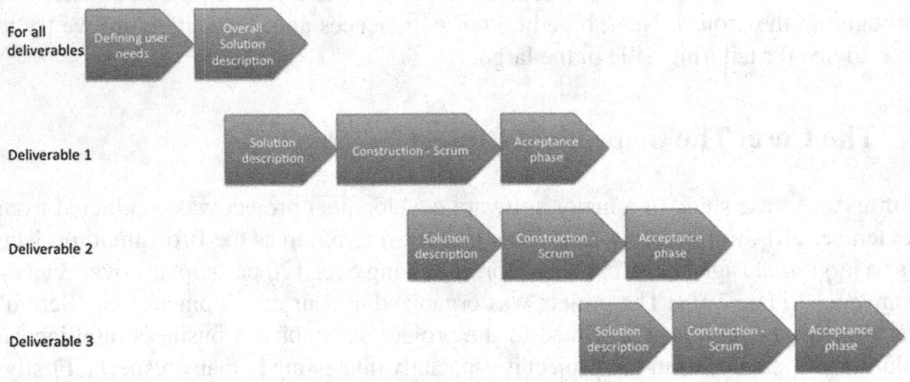

Fig. 1. Scrum-based delivery model of the project.

Project description and goals. The Brownfield project was established in order to replace The Client's outdated legacy IT systems with a new integrated system for case management. The new system was to be based on a Service Oriented Architecture, with support for integration with a large number of external and internal systems. In addition, the new system would include a web-based self-service solution aimed at the general public, as well as a rule-based application processing engine reducing the need for manual processing.

The project thus set out with four main goals:

- To replace fragmented case management systems with one integrated system.
- To replace manual processing with automated, rule-based processing.
- To establish a self-service web interface for the general public.
- To decommission legacy systems.

These goals were further elaborated in the form of a "dual goal matrix", specifying main business goals and main IT goals for each deliverable. The business goals were divided by functional areas, reflecting the existing organizational and system structure. The IT goals were more focused on architectural requirements, cutting across the functional areas in order to establish what was seen as a desirable "future state" of architecture in the organization. The background for the two subsets of goals was somewhat divided: The business requirements were related to limitations of the existing system portfolio in supporting new government regulations, interfacing with external parties, and efficiency in case management and processing. The technical requirements were driven by the strong internal technical organization's vision of a future-proof, platform independent architecture which would allow the organization to "pick and choose" technical components in a vendor independent manner. These technical requirements were communicated in the form of architectural standards and policies. In addition, the Customer had already purchased a number of technical components as part of existing vendor purchasing agreements for related database systems. The Consulting company was asked to consider the use of these components in developing the new architectural platform. At the outset of the project, it quickly became clear that the Customer was overwhelmed by the amount of work required in order to determine and specify requirements. The technical and architectural requirements seemed especially unclear, and resulted in a lot of time being spent by both parties in order to better understand what was actually required to be developed by the Consulting company. As a result, the first deliverable was delayed, and ultimately merged with the second planned deliverable in an effort to save time by skipping one of the planned production migrations.

3 Agile Method Tailoring in the Project

After a much troubled start related to scaling challenges and architecture complexity during the first deliverable, the project was turnaround and the second and third deliverables were portrayed fairly successful by both supplier and customer – including their end users. Noteworthy, we came across the following new practices as the project had been 'turned around':

(1) 'Task forces' were established across teams to deal with common challenges such as performance issues;
(2) 'Champion roles' were implemented working across teams on specific technology issues for example databases or java scripting;
(3) 'Specifying up front' in terms of close collaboration between customer and supplier in preparing user stories, uncovering dependencies and prototyping prior to sprints;
(4) 'Re-distributing development tasks' within the current sprint in order to utilize competence across teams and scale the project.
(5) 'Mini demos' were improvised in the middle of sprints to get users' feedback as soon as possible, and to do smaller adjustments to features and/or interaction design;

We will briefly describe these practices in more detail in the following sub-sections below.

Task forces. In traditional agile development, participants in projects are supposed to work within teams. In this project, however, an informal role of temporarily 'task forces' was formed. Task forces were formed on developers' own initiative for tackling specific pressing problems relevant across the four development teams. These were typically problems related to non-functional requirements. For example, security issues, performance problems and ways of integrating with external systems and standardized components.

Task forces were initially not initiated by management, but grew out of a need recognized by some developers at one of the development teams. The developers recognized that they had common problems across teams and started informally to sit together with fellow developers belonging to a different team. This practice was later sanctioned and even facilitated by team leaders and project management for better solving problems across teams.

Our analysis is that task forces not only solved common problems, but also greatly helped coordinating work across teams and helped building a more common understanding across teams both regarding software architecture and business domain. In this respect, task forces became a necessary addition to scrum-of-scrums in that they had a much more detailed focus on solving specific problems.

Champion roles. While the task forces explained above were of a more temporary nature, the champion roles were more permanent. Champion roles also started bottom-up from a perceived need in the teams to coordinate and standardize certain ways of doing things in the project. For example, it was established champion roles for java scripting and databases ensuring a common way of working with and implementing these technologies across teams.

Champion roles rotated among competent individuals, and over time this also became more sanctioned and facilitated by management.

Similar to task forces, but more stable – champion roles implied better inter-team coordination and standardization of working. Additionally, it also increased learning among teams and members from different teams.

Specifying up front. In collaboration with the customer, the project started to have a more formal process before a new sprint was initiated and sprint planning started. This process where referred to as the 'ready-to-sprint' processes, and engaged all the relevant actors for coordinating and planning of the work to be conducted in the upcoming sprint in more detail. Depending on the specific challenges and type of work to be conducted the process ensured that all involved actors had contributed and were coordinated. This process could include further specification of user stores, flow diagrams, description of technical as well as functional dependencies, and more overall architectural issues.

A crucial skill in agile development is to conduct the Product owner role and the ability to create Epics and user stories upfront the sprints. The project organization addressed these issues by including two persons from the customer in each scrum team with the role "functional responsible". The role was part of the customers Product owner team, and participated both in specification work and to cope with functional clarifications throughout the sprints.

Already from the first sprints conducted, it proved major challenges to establish effective ways of handling the product backlog, agile collaboration that supported both common understanding of specifications, ensure consistent architecture implementation across teams and handling clarifications of upcoming issues. Corrective actions were issued by training the Product owner in necessary skills and adding trained functional architects to the scrum teams. The actions, which were taken, did help to some extent, but it was necessary to make some fundamental adaptations to ensure a more robust process.

Our analysis is that this made the initiation of the sprints more effective and ensured that key participants were coordinated irrespective of team and role in the project. Although this practice inevitably implies more planning up-front seemingly in conflict with the agile principles and practices, we will argue that this practice is more aligned to the characteristics of large-scale agile where there is an increased need for more standardization and coordination across teams and roles.

Re-distribution of work tasks. Partly as a consequence of the previous practice, the project got increased flexibility to re-distribute work tasks across teams within a sprint. This practice was a part of striking a balance between the need for competence and efficiency at the one hand, and the evenly distribution of work among teams on the other. The practice was especially useful in the last sprints of a deliverable when user stories belonging to different domains did not imply equal distribution of work effort between teams.

Again, this practice may seem odd, and even unproductive, from the perspective of 'textbook agile'. However, this gave the project as a whole better utilization of the teams and also helped spread competence across teams. On the other hand, we also see that this practice should be used with care and only for smaller tasks when necessary typically late in the project.

Mini demos. The project had some especially competent project members who had long experience from other large-scale agile projects. Some of the practices they adopted from a previous project were the practice of 'mini demos'. The crucial point in doing mini demos in the middle of sprints was to demo features as soon as they were developed irrespective of when. Typically, this was practiced as a way of negotiating and getting feedback on details regarding functionality and interaction design. In that way, developers and designers could easily do the last finishing touches right away, without going through a more formal demo and going back to those details in the following sprint.

Thus, these mini demos both made the ongoing communication and collaboration with the customer smooth and at the same time reduced the administrative cost for both parties.

4 Implications for Tailoring Agile in the Large

In this section we propose some practical guidelines for tailoring agile in the large. We do not want to be too bold and generalize too much, as guidelines as these could easily be misinterpreted and used in contexts that are not comparable to our project. However, we argue that there is something more general worth mentioning based on our experience. The suggested guidelines are:

(1) **Experiment with new practices.** For tailoring agile in the large, projects should experiment with practices that highlight functional and technical interdependencies in the software being developed. This would help improve coordinating and communicating across teams and roles.
(2) **Facilitate novel practices to emerge.** It should be underscored that project managers should be wary of trying to enforce predefined tailored practices. However, although agile methods and principles tend to emphasize bottom-up initiatives, successful tailoring can be both bottom-up or top-down initiated.
(3) **"Record, and move on".** Do not wait for sorting out contractual details. Try to establish trust to that pragmatic decisions can be made and temporary solutions can be sought.
(4) **Improve inter-team coordination.** Establish both long term 'communities of practice' and short term 'task forces' across teams.
(5) **Scale the project in an evolutionary manner.** Plan for a ramp-up phase allowing customers to get accustomed to the working process. Conduct training activities to ensure customers are aware of what is required of them.
(6) **Adjust content in sprints.** Allow time for customers to absorb and process new information, and coordinate requirement elicitation with stakeholders in their organization. This can be done by inserting technical sprints where programmers focus on technical tasks, in order to allow customers a "programmer's holiday" [5].

5 Concluding Remarks

In this experience report we have emphasized the ways in which a large-scale agile software development effort has been tailored during the process. Here, tailoring was not done up-front, but rather emergent during the development over 3,5 years. Especially in this report we have highlighted and described five different practices and roles: (1) 'Task forces', (2) 'Champion roles', (3) 'Specifying up front', (4) 'Re-distributing development tasks', and (5) 'Mini demos'.

We argue that these novel practices are good examples of agile method tailoring reflecting the complexity and large-scale characteristics of the project. We do not argue that these actual practices denote any 'ultimate way' of tailoring agile projects, but more on an analytic level – that in succeeding with large-scale projects continuous tailoring throughout the process is necessary.

In reflecting upon the establishment of these practices we discuss how some are *bottom-up initiatives* (1, 2 & 4) largely initiated, planned and coordinated among team members themselves with no or little management involvement. Whereas some practices can be described as a *blend of bottom-up and top-down* (3 & 5) where management are much more involved.

Furthermore, we recognize that all of the practices turn out more *emergent*. They were not deliberately planned and adjusted ahead of starting the project – but emerged over time based on the involved actors' experiences. Collectively, then, the project seems to preserve a sense of agility in terms of 'learning from change'. Additionally, interestingly, some of these practices are seemingly also in conflict with the agile principles – notably (3) focusing on planning.

Acknowledgments. This article was written with support from the project Agile 2.0, which is supported by the Research council of Norway through grant 236759/O30, and by the companies Kantega, Kongsberg Defence & Aerospace, Sopra Steria and Sticos.

References

1. Williams, L., Cockburn, A.: Agile software development: it's about feedback and change. IEEE Comput. **36**, 39–43 (2003)
2. Dingsøyr, T., Moe, N.B.: Towards principles of large-scale Agile development. In: Dingsøyr, T., Moe, N.B., Tonelli, R., Counsell, S., Gencel, C., Petersen, K. (eds.) XP 2014. LNBIP, vol. 199, pp. 1–8. Springer, Heidelberg (2014)
3. Haugset, B., Hanssen, G.K.: Automated acceptance testing: a literature review and an industrial case study. Presented at the Agile 2008, Proceedings, Toronto (2008)
4. Jones, C.: Software quality in 2012: a survey of state of the art. Presentation by Namcook Analytics LLC. www.namcook.com
5. Martin, A., Biddle, R., Noble, J.: XP customer practices: a grounded theory. In: Proceedings - 2009 Agile Conference, AGILE 2009, pp. 33–40

Hire an Apprentice: Evolutionary Learning at the 7digital Technical Academy

Paul Shannon(✉) and Miles Pool(✉)

7digital, Technology Team, 69 Wilson Street, London, UK
{Paul.shannon,Miles.pool}@7digital.com

Abstract. Hiring senior software engineers with experience in Agile and Lean has always been difficult. Training university graduates or engineers from other backgrounds takes time and can cause disruption to software teams. 7digital addressed both of these problems by starting a Technical Academy; a 6 month programme of classroom sessions, pairing, deliberate practice, personal project work and guided learning. Backed by key metrics and qualitative data, the paper explores the positive impact that the technical academy has had on the technology team and wider organisation at 7digital. It investigates the changes in technique, curriculum and structure that the team made over the three iterations of the academy. It goes on to detail the challenges that the team faced around justifying the time away from usual activities, measuring the impact, attempting to predict the long term benefit and make the result of extra diversity in the team more apparent.

Keywords: Lean · Agile · Diversity · Learning · Coaching · Apprenticeships · Mentoring · DevOps · Inspect-adapt · Continuous improvement

1 Introduction

7digital are the power behind innovative music experiences. Their diverse, highly regarded team of software and systems engineers build the music streaming and download platform that powers services for global brands. The industry in which they operate is fast paced and ever-changing, and the team needs to grow to react to those changes. Growing the team with the right type of people has often proven difficult but was addressed in 2012 by the inception of the 7digital Technical Academy. The academy programme has completed its third iteration and has evolved through continuous improvement with regular inspection and adaption. In the first iteration, a key retrospective resulted in a move to pull based learning; asking apprentices to solve real business problems and request sessions on the skills they needed to accomplish their objectives. The second iteration saw peer to peer learning and a self organising community develop amongst apprentices. The third iteration brought a wider set of people to the academy and was used to expand understanding of Lean and Agile principles across the organisation.

H. Sharp and T. Hall (Eds.): XP 2016, LNBIP 251, pp. 252–260, 2016.
DOI: 10.1007/978-3-319-33515-5_23

The authors have been heavily involved in the Technical Academy with Paul Shannon, now VP Technology, being the founder of the programme, and Miles Pool, the coordinator of the third iteration and a second iteration graduate.

2 Background

When searching for software development roles on the most popular recruitment websites the ratio of jobs requiring greater than two years' experience to those requiring fewer is eight to one. Additionally, finding senior software developers, with greater than 5 years' experience is notoriously difficult – so how do we provide the opportunity, to those with less experience, to work in a welcoming and learning oriented culture so that they can become senior members of our community?

These problems are not unique to any company working in the tech sector but became more prevalent at 7digital when they focused on quality driven software development practices, as the requisite skills made experienced people even harder to find.

7digital was established in 2004 as a small start-up in London's "Silicon Roundabout". After establishing itself in the first 5 years there was a marked switch to quality driven practices with the appointment of key people experienced in Agile and XP. The two development teams at the time totalled around twenty people, over half of the total organisation. As the technology platform expanded, so did the teams and the need to fulfil roles, and by 2011 the total head count for the Technology Team was forty with further plans for expansion.

2.1 Apprenticeships in Software Development

In early 2012, senior members of the team looked to solve the common problem of a lack of experienced hands available to join the team. They researched efforts in the Software Craftsmanship community to utilise the master/apprenticeship format of more traditional trades. 8th Light [1] ran a programme that defined levels of craftsmanship in the team, with newer members joining as apprentices and being mentored by master craftsmen on a one-to-one basis.

Other efforts of this one-to-one tuition style were attempted by Codemanship, and an interesting initiative at Accenture assigned groups of people to particular learning projects as they joined. One of the team leads at 7digital had experience in a classroom based training scheme during the agile transformation at Codeweavers Ltd [2] involving short, focussed sessions away from the usual team room for new team members to try intensive learning on a particular topic.

While many of these schemes had benefits, they didn't directly fit with the team's desire to expand and invest in the future.

"Education is the kindling of a flame, not the filling of a vessel." – ***Socrates***

2.2 Diversity

A major opportunity the team saw with expanding through internally trained developers, was that they could attract a more diverse cohort.

Gender diversity in the tech industry is a perennial yet slowly improving issue. The 7digital team hoped to improve the diversity of their team by offering a lower barrier to entry than their usual recruitment process. Research suggests [3] that female applicants are less likely to apply for positions that require assertions about experience or achievement - they would only apply if they meet 100 % of requirements whereas men would apply when meeting only 60 % - so a programme which provided training and which emphasised a lack of requirement for experience was believed to be beneficial.

Software development candidates are often products of education in a narrow field of study – Computer Science. The team felt that more diverse backgrounds would provide a wider selection of opinions, so a scheme that would be attractive to people in any field was most desirable.

3 Timeline

Before the academy was created, a first attempt at addressing our recruitment needs with a lower barrier to entry began with an apprenticeship model similar to that at 8th Light. New team members, with some experience in programming, were assigned a mentor and were expected to pair and learn from that person during their daily development tasks. This proved disruptive to teams as they effectively lost a senior developer who spent most of their time teaching, especially in the initial three months.

The following year, in 2012, we decided that a new approach should be taken and the Technical Academy was created. Following a gap of two years the second iteration began and then an opportunity one year later led to the running of the third. The programme is based in the London headquarters of 7digital with co-located teams.

3.1 The Inception of the Technical Academy

Research into other organisations' attempts at apprenticeship programmes led us to believe that we needed some structure, a curriculum and a clearly defined career path for the Technical Academy. While the efforts at Codeweavers Ltd. proved useful, the lack of direction meant it was not a key part of the team's learning there. Efforts elsewhere resembled the initial efforts at 7digital so a committee was formed to discuss and decide upon how to proceed.

An early agreement was reached that apprentices should be hired as full time developers, with a permanent role and that the offer of a position was not dependent on completion of the academy. This would give the apprentices confidence and security that they had a job at 7digital and were just at the start of a potentially long and prosperous career. To ensure a level of protection for both the apprentices and the organisation they were given an extended six month probation period.

3.2 Hire an Apprentice: The First Iteration

For the initial iteration we hired two new developers by advertising the role and contacting universities externally, and recruited one internal candidate through transfer from the operations team. Interviewing candidates with little or no experience in programming posed a challenge as the usual recruitment process involved working through a simple code kata. We decided that as the candidate was joining to both learn, and to write software, that this was still the best form of early assessment. Candidates paired with a senior developer on a simple test-driven development coding exercise. An observer would take notes, paying particular attention to how the candidate reacted to new concepts, such as test automation and refactoring, and how soon they could contribute to the conversation.

Once apprentices had been selected the committee planned a curriculum. This included skills related to Agile software development and Lean practices, with sessions on subjects such as Test Driven Development, Theory of Constraints, Databases, DevOps, Continuous Delivery and Design Patterns.

To help clarify what the apprenticeship entails, we produced a "path to becoming a 7digital developer" - this was a timeline encompassing an intensive "bootcamp", tapering to less frequent sessions on basic techniques before moving into a term of specialisation and project work; it ended with graduation in week twenty-six. Graduation was a company-wide event involving presentations, drinks and gifts.

3.2.1 Adoption of Pull Based Learning

It was identified early that apprentices were being asked to pair on tasks involving concepts they had not yet been taught. A problem here became evident when a team member was struggling to explain to an apprentice the concept of Dependency Injection - a complex but widely used solution to software modularity. This was raised with the Academy coordinator who organised a dedicated classroom session on the topic. Following this the apprentice rejoined his previous pair, with an understanding of the concept and was then able to contribute to the continuing work.

At a similar time we met with Professor Dave West, who had been running a unique degree programme at New Mexico Highlands University, USA [4]. This course had students, with no software development skills, working on commercial projects and requesting the skills they wanted to learn in order to accomplish their task. They used regular feedback, retrospectives and planning meetings to ensure they were developing the right skills to develop software.

The success seen on Prof. West's course, and in conjunction with our example above, led us to adopt pull-based learning; coordinators would talk to apprentices, tutors and team leads to organise group sessions on the topics that were currently of most relevance.

3.3 Evolution in the Academy: The Second Iteration

Following a two year hiatus, we decided to reinstate the Technical Academy under a new coordinator. The driving force behind this decision was from members of the team, including prospective internal candidates, perceiving the successes of the first iteration.

Internal apprentices were thus self-selecting - one transfer to the Technology Team, and for the first time, one apprentice looking to up-skill in their existing, non-development role. Two external candidates were recruited as we had done in the first iteration.

The broad structure of this iteration was much like the first, however each of the four apprentices was now assigned a tutor who was on hand to assist with any technical issues. During the "bootcamp" first term these tutors felt superfluous.

In the weeks before the second iteration, the coordinator collated project ideas from teams in the wider business.

> *"The proposal should have clear interest to the business, but its implementation will be a proof of concept."*

At eight weeks the apprentices chose a project to implement over the following four months. Each project had a product owner who would help define requirements, and ensure continuous delivery practices were observed. With projects framed as real business products, apprentices were also encouraged to adopt practices such as test-driven development and Kanban, with Technical Academy stand-ups attended by stakeholders. While helping the apprentice, the tutor would check for clean code and good automated testing.

In the latter terms the pull for technical sessions allowed the structured learning framework to fall away in favour of "just-in-time" planning. The cohort situated in disparate development teams, built up a strong community with equally disparate technical skills; an environment highly conducive to peer-to-peer learning.

Following a term two retrospective, apprentices took to pairing on their projects; this was of particular benefit to the apprentice not based in a development team. It also allowed apprentices to work confidently on a new and unfamiliar codebase.

3.4 Reflective Practice: The Third Iteration

Just six months after the second 7digital Technical Academy the opportunity arose to take on another two apprentices. The academy was reinstated, this time coordinated by a Technical Academy alumnus. The academy started up with a total of six apprentices, after a short recruitment process and a number of existing speculative applications. Two new hires were made along with one internal transfer, with three apprentices from Operations and QA Teams looking to up-skill.

Termly retrospectives produced a number of valuable actions. To foster an open environment for discussion, a weekly reading group was set up in which apprentices would discuss several, occasionally conflicting articles. Further, it was felt that some crucial topics were introduced, and swiftly left behind. The solution was to theme the week's practical, classroom and reading group sessions, and then to gauge the apprentices confidence level in that week's topic.

3.4.1 Selecting Tutors

Often the developer working directly with an apprentice is not the most suitable person to teach a given subject. It is thus more beneficial to select an appropriate tutor from a wider group, on a subject-by-subject basis.

In the Technical Academy it is important that many and varied members of the organisation have direct contact with the apprentices. In contrast with the master-apprentice pattern, being exposed to diverse views within the team aids the apprentices in drawing their own perspectives on the values the team hopes to instill. It is felt that this is important in a team with a strong culture of shared responsibility. The academy is also a learning experience for the tutors themselves, many of whom are previous apprentices, and the more people involved, the greater this benefit.

4 Discussion

Making the academy visible was a key goal from early on; both in terms of its operation and its efficacy. We managed the first part by advertising sessions more often and getting people outside the team involved in project work. The graduation ceremonies and project demonstrations also increased visibility. Within the teams though we wanted to show that the academy had a positive effect on throughput and cycle time. This was difficult as many other factors could influence these measures (continuous improvement, absence, team changes, changing business needs) but the general trend for teams with apprentices was that, after week six, apprentices were making a positive contribution. This was attributed to the additional person available for pairing and - following their intensive classroom sessions - apprentices were now adding valuc during these pairing sessions.

Having someone with a new perspective, focusing on the detail and asking novel questions was itself advantageous, - one example being a simple observation resulting in a complete change in operation when an apprentice questioned whether we were encoding audio files in a mathematically suboptimal way.

Qualitatively, the benefits of placing apprentices into development teams as soon as they arrived helping the apprentices to feel as though they were already an important and valued member of the Technology Team - this was crucial in fostering a supportive community. It also allowed the apprentice to easily join existing pairs and gain exposure to the team's domain; something which cannot easily be taught during academy sessions.

The feedback cycle of pairing, and subsequently discovering missing knowledge helped drive the tuition, through pull based learning. This "just-in-time" planning of sessions ensured tuition only on subjects that had a direct impact on the daily work of the apprentices, minimising the gap between learning and practicing those skills. Apprentices thus honed new skills through use, adding business value quickly. This resulted in a natural progression from isolated student to fully engaged team-member over the course of the six months.

Retrospectives in the Technical Academy gradually became more frequent as the value they delivered to the learning process became apparent, and with regular continuous improvement these idcas were instilled in the apprentices' daily practice.

With larger cohorts, the community in the academy was slower to develop; a larger group meant apprentices would speak less readily in early open-forum sessions. Furthermore, with a larger cohort less one-to-one tuition was available. While one-to-one tuition has its advantages, group tuition was more efficient when introducing the fundamentals of a new concept. Pull-based group tuition also exposes apprentices to topics they may not yet have faced. On the whole, a balance of group tuition and pairing with other developers is more effective than either technique alone. Eventually a larger cohort became advantageous as the drive for technical sessions rapidly increased as the apprentices made progress with their technically-diverse work. With so many ongoing projects, the challenge then came in keeping up with the pull for such a diverse set of topics. Grouping these topics in a loose, longer-term curriculum was a method introduced to prioritise the sessions.

Tutors and coordinators also benefited from the academy, through areas of personal development and daily variety in their work. The sense of purpose and achievement garnered from contributing to the next generation of software developers, and ensuring they were taught quality driven practices, made it worthwhile for those donating their time. Tutors and team members that were helping apprentices were also challenged on their knowledge, as they were suddenly required to teach what they'd previously taken as rote. When Technical Academy graduate, Sophie, was asked to pair with a new apprentice she said:

> *"You have to really think about what you're doing and it makes you realise how much you do actually know. I still question myself though, but that helps me to learn too."*

4.1 The Tech Academy in the Wider Organisation

A key change in the third iteration was to have projects backed by the 7digital product team. This improved alignment with adding business value and the projects gained more prominence in the wider business.

There were some initial disagreements from other teams about the impact of the academy as it does require team members to spend time away from their usual daily work. We investigated ways we could measure and adapt, and elected to look at the things already measured (throughput and cycle time) while getting regular feedback via retrospectives, one-to-one meetings and reports to senior team members. One of our teams that took on an apprentice in the third iteration had a cycle time of around 2 days

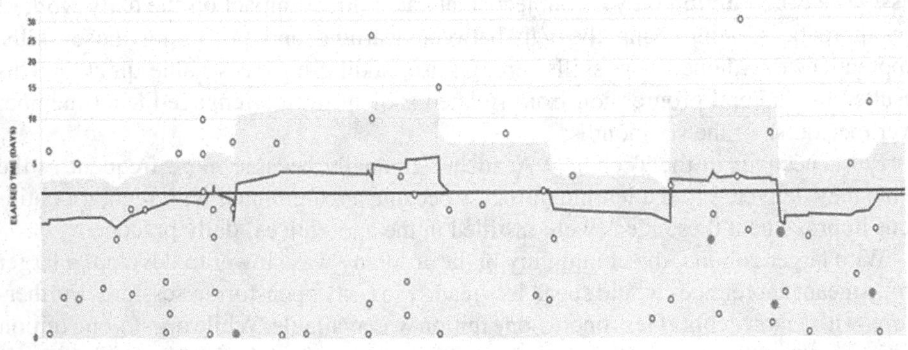

Fig. 1. Cycle time for content discovery team during their apprentice's tenure

before she joined. For the following 6 weeks the cycle time rose to 4.3 days peaking at 5 days before reducing again back to 1.7 days (see Fig. 1).

When Miles joined the Content Development Team he initially had a detrimental effect on their throughput, reducing it to 1–2 minimum marketable features delivered per week for about 8 weeks. The middle period of his tenure in that team saw a stable throughput which then increased towards the end of his apprenticeship. We also added more people to the team in his sixth month which saw the momentum in the team further accelerate with a peak of 13 features delivered in one week.

The pattern based on our metrics appears to make a team slow down for the initial 6–8 weeks, then return to the team's previous pace for the middle part of the apprenticeship. Within the last month or two of an apprentice's tenure a team sees the throughput increase and cycle time decrease as the apprentice contributes more. While other factors could be affecting this, the general feeling of teams is that apprentices add value early on but notably from 4 months onwards.

4.2 Future Directions

An interesting consideration is the comparison between former Technical Academy developers and those hired from other companies. Shared team values seem to be more prominent in the academy graduates as they've been trained specifically by the existing team, and not had to forget the ways of their previous teams. However, this meant that fewer tried-and-tested ideas come from apprentices versus seasoned developers so the trade-off meant that a balance between new ideas, team cohesion and well known practices exists.

We considered alternative approaches prior to setting up the first Technical Academy (Sect. 3) but have since adopted new practices that should aid in training inexperienced developers. Mob programming is a good example of a practice we now use more often that is well positioned to easily spread knowledge. We'll investigate its use as a learning tool in future academy iterations.

With the experience of three successful Technical Academies behind us, and a Technology Team comprised of nine strong graduates and numerous experienced tutors, 7digital is in a stronger position than ever to run a fourth iteration. One might question if we should ever stop, or why we would wait between iterations, or why we might limit the number of apprentices in each cohort, and the answer is quite simple; we do not want to overload the team with apprentices. Having more apprentices will still require effort from teams during the time spent pairing, and diluting the number of senior developers in the team would burden them with additional responsibility. We have discussed the possibility of sharing sessions with other local organisations though, so that we can get more value from each session by teaching their apprentices too.

5 Conclusion

There is a strong feeling at 7digital that the Technical Academy programme has been a success. All of the externally hired apprentices are still with the team, and despite their experience being lower than that of their peers, they contribute at an equivalent level. The team's gender balance is higher than it was with a notably more relaxed and open atmosphere that promotes a variety of ideas. The mixture of people's background also contributes to this. Engagement in team development throughout the team has improved, with discussion on career progression, increased knowledge sharing and collaboration between teams.

As more senior developers have grown in their careers they have appreciated being given the chance to pass on their knowledge through the academy. This interesting side effect has increased retention of more experienced team members. Having their knowledge questioned too has surprisingly resulted in a motivation to ensure we are following good practices and promoted learning at all experience levels.

Hiring has been easier; the best example with the replacement of a senior developer with two apprentices in half the time it took to find the previous senior hire. We've also hired more women into a variety of roles than previous years.

The existence of this paper is a key example of the benefit the Technical Academy has had on the team and organisation. It is motivating for the team to know that they are well regarded by peers in the community and that they have done something unique to solve a common industry problem. It gives team members a sense of purpose other than satisfying the needs of the organisation so 7digital will definitely be running the programme again in the future.

Acknowledgements. Thanks to Allan Kelly, Neil Kidd, Matt Butt, Rob Bowley and everyone at 7digital.

References

1. 8th Light Inc., Apprenticeship (2016). https://8thlight.com/apprenticeship
2. Rutherford, K., Shannon, P., Judson, C., Kidd, N.: From Chaos to Kanban, via Scrum. In: Sillitti, A., Martin, A., Wang, X., Whitworth, E. (eds.) XP 2010. LNBIP, vol. 48, pp. 344–352. Springer, Heidelberg (2010)
3. Lark, N.F.: Act Now To Shrink The Confidence Gap (2014). http://www.forbes.com/sites/womensmedia/2014/04/28/act-now-to-shrink-the-confidence-gap
4. West, D.: Experience Report: Agile Development Apprenticeship at NMHU (2016). http://www.infoq.com/articles/NMHU-scrum-university-apprentice

How XP Can Improve the Experiences of Female Software Developers

Clare Sudbery(✉)

IT Department, LateRooms.Com,
The Peninsula, Victoria Place, Manchester M4 4FB, UK
AWomanInTechnology@gmail.com

Abstract. This paper describes my experience as a female software developer with 17 years' industry experience. Originally I worked with a more traditional waterfall approach to software design and development, but in recent years I have worked with XP. I have experienced many difficulties associated with being in a minority, but a lot of those problems have been alleviated since I started working with XP. My belief is that XP creates a more conducive environment for women and other minorities within the industry. I believe that XP can – and should – pave the way to making the tech industry a more welcoming and attractive place for women.

Keywords: Women in technology · Women in tech · Women in XP · Women and agile · XP · Agile · Women · Gender · Skills shortage · Balance · Feminism · Stereotypes · Assumptions · Challenging assumptions · Recruitment · Role models · Gender roles · Gender equality

1 Introduction

In every workplace for 17 years, I have found myself in a significant minority as a woman. This is not unusual. In 2014, the average percentage of women working in 11 of the world's largest tech companies was around 30 %. But the average percentage of women occupying tech roles within those companies was around 16 % [1]. According to the Harvard Business Review in 2008, 41 % of women working in technology ended up leaving the profession - compared to 17 % of men [2].

The experience of being in a minority[1] has caused me various problems throughout my career. The most obvious one - which is shared by many women in my situation - is a feeling of insecurity. To put it simply, my chosen profession is one in which it is unusual for women to persevere or succeed. I have had to work hard to maintain belief in my own abilities. I have more than once had to resist or reverse attempts to "promote" me into non-technical roles, which I have found less satisfying and have had less aptitude for.

[1] I will use the term "minority" to refer to women throughout this paper. Clearly women are not a minority within society, but they are within technology.

H. Sharp and T. Hall (Eds.): XP 2016, LNBIP 251, pp. 261–269, 2016.
DOI: 10.1007/978-3-319-33515-5_24

At one point I left the profession altogether, but luckily I realised my mistake and returned four years later. It was at this point that I discovered XP, and I believe this resulted a significant reduction in the difficulties I face as a woman.

XP is a forward-looking movement which emphasises flexibility, change and progress - so this is the ideal group of people to be addressing the low proportion of women entering IT. As agilists, we value individuals and interactions over processes and tools. The diversity of our teams, and specifically the encouragement of the participation of all members of our populations, is a crucial part of this.

The rest of this paper will be split into the following three sections: My Journey as a Female Software Engineer; Discussing Lessons Learnt: Attracting More Women Through XP and finally Conclusions.

2 My Journey as a Female Software Engineer

In this section I will describe the experiences I have had within my career, the difficulties that I have faced as a woman, and how my journey has become easier and more enjoyable since I started working with XP. I will cover the following topics: Non-XP Workplaces, Imposter Syndrome and its Effects, and finally The Welcoming Environment of XP.

2.1 Non-XP Workplaces

I have 17 years' experience in the profession, but due to a four-year career break in the middle, it is twenty-one years since I started my first software engineering job. At that point I had just graduated from an MSc in Computation, which was a "conversion" course - designed to transform people from diverse academic backgrounds into computer graduates. My previous degree was a BSc in Mathematics and Philosophy. It was 1995, and Agile and XP were barely heard of.

During the course of the MSc, we were told that the main careers available to us would fall broadly into two categories: Analysis, and Development. The course was a popular course, and split quite evenly between men and women. It was noticeable that the women tended to be drawn towards analysis, with the men being attracted to coding. But personally I was more excited by code than anything else. The object-oriented C++ we were taught was very attractive to my logical, analytical, puzzle-loving brain.

It didn't surprise me to find that I was the only female developer in my first job. I was used to being in a minority – as a mathematics undergraduate, myself and my fellow female students represented approximately 10 % of the total population. I was also used to an accompanying feeling of inferiority: In this case it seemed to me that my male colleagues knew everything there was to know about computing, whereas I had walked straight into the job after a year's study.

I suppose it was at this point that a thought took root in my brain, which I have never quite lost: *These men know so much more than me. I'm only a girl, I'll never catch up.* This is a common experience for women in our industry, and in fact for anyone operating in an environment as a member of a group which suffers from an adverse stereotype.

That is to say, assumptions are often made about women in technology which suggest they will not have the skills they need to succeed. The general term for the way people respond to this is Stereotype Threat, and it is discussed at more length in section three of this paper.

It's worth stating at this point that I have never seriously believed that men have a superior intellect to women. But the inner voice which tells me I'm inferior is one that sneaks in without my permission. It curls up without me noticing, and can stay there for quite a while before I spot it and shoo it away (I now know that this voice has a name: It is called unconscious bias, and I will describe this more in section three).

Between them, my first three jobs in software engineering lasted twelve years (four years, then one, then seven). There was one feature that all these experiences had in common: I found it hard to ask questions. When I was struggling with a piece of work, my approach tended to go like this:

1. Try to work it out on my own. I was proud, and hated the thought that people might think I was ignorant – particularly if they thought I was ignorant because I was a woman.
2. Stall. If I was stuck and too proud or scared to ask for help, I would simply cease work. Daily stand-ups were unheard of, we worked alone, and we were given large tasks which could last several weeks, so it was possible to do very little work for some time before anyone noticed.
3. Ask for help. There were three problems with this approach:
   a. It meant admitting that I didn't know what I was doing.
   b. It meant interrupting someone. Everyone always seemed to be very busy.
   c. When people explained things, this involved me looking over their shoulder while they whizzed through complex concepts at break-neck pace. I would sometimes end up none the wiser.

2.2 Imposter Syndrome and its Effects

For those first ten years, I suffered significantly from self-doubt. I rose to the position of senior developer very quickly, and always got good feedback. I loved writing code and took it seriously. By all objective standards, I was in fact good at my job. But I still believed that most of my colleagues knew more than me.

I frequently suffered from imposter syndrome, i.e. the idea that I was not good enough for the role, and would be "found out". This is not unique to women – men can suffer from it too – and not all women have it. But it tends to be common amongst women in IT, and it's not difficult to see why: If you're part of a minority, you feel like you don't fit in. Like you're an imposter.

After those first twelve years as a software engineer, I was made redundant. At that point I had been with the same company for seven years, but my interest in the job had waned significantly. There were several factors at play:

1. I had several times asked to work on the more interesting and complex software, but had repeatedly been denied this opportunity.

2. I had started working a four-day week. My best guess as to why I might have been denied the opportunity to work on the more interesting software, based on conversations with other colleagues, was that because I worked reduced hours, I wasn't taken seriously. People working on the really exciting stuff were expected to work evenings and weekends, and of course five days during the week.
3. I wasn't giving the job my full attention. It was a vicious circle: I wasn't given interesting work to do, so I focused more on hobbies and family, which meant that I was taken less seriously, which resulted in me paying less attention to my job.

So, when I was offered voluntary redundancy, the decision to leave was not hard. In my exit interview, it was suggested I might try being a social worker! This did not appeal to me.

2.3 The Welcoming Environment of XP

By the time I was made redundant, I was very bored of my job. My skills had stagnated so much, that as well as having very little enthusiasm for finding another software role, I doubted my ability to find anything new. As a result of these factors, I left the career altogether.

After four years out of the industry, I realised that I was more suited to software development than anything else. I decided to return. I was honest about my out-of-date skills, and got myself a job with a company that specialised in taking on graduates and training them up. It was a revelation. Because of the emphasis on training, employees were not only encouraged, they were exhorted to ask as many questions as possible. There was no problem with people being too busy to help. Everyone in the company was expected to both ask and answer as many questions as possible.

The teams I worked with had daily stand-ups, where each team member would report on what they were doing and flag up any problems. The company's design methodology was largely waterfall, but the cultures of communication and collaboration were filtering through from XP working practices in other parts of the industry. This included regular and in-depth code reviews, and an introduction to the concept of clean code.

All of this helped to counter the problems I had experienced before, in the following ways:

1. If I got stuck, I knew that someone would be eager to help me.
2. Daily stand-ups meant that there was nowhere for me to hide. If I had problems, I had to admit them. This was liberating.
3. My code was regularly reviewed in depth – so that I was always getting feedback.
4. The emphasis on clean code meant that I and my peers were focused on making our code accessible to each other.

I was now back in the career and enjoying myself enormously. The idea that it was OK to ask questions was exhilarating. It also helped that I had those twelve years of experience behind me, so I no longer felt like everybody else was more experienced than me.

I deliberately made coding my hobby, and got involved in events run by organisations like XP Manchester [3]. This meant that I was learning about such practices as TDD and pair programming. This excited me, and I was able to move to a more XP-focused company. My progress at this point accelerated rapidly. It wasn't long before I gained the confidence to become a contractor, at which point I moved between several companies on various contracts, and experienced several different implementations of XP.

My confidence increased, but when I felt the old insecurities creeping back in, I decided to approach specific colleagues and ask them to act as sponsors or mentors on my behalf. I also gained the security to discuss the value of positive feedback with my line manager. I have learnt over time that, because of the various insecurities I face as a minority within this profession, I benefit enormously from explicit encouragement. I believe that there is level of openness and communication implicit within XP that has given me the strength to ask for this kind of support.

3 Discussing Lessons Learnt: Attracting More Women Through XP

This section describes the lessons I have learnt as a woman working with XP, and how they might be used in order to encourage more women into XP teams, and enhance the experiences of the women already there. This will include the following sub-sections: The Importance of Diversity Within XP, Stereotype Threat and Unconscious Bias, and finally The Positive Impact of XP.

3.1 The Importance of Diversity Within XP

It may or may not be true that the number of women in XP is a bit higher than elsewhere in the industry, but even if it is, they are still in the significant minority. It's important that we don't simply sit back, cross our arms and say "Oh, we use XP. We don't have a problem with women in IT. We've solved that one already." There is still room for improvement, and XP practitioners have an even greater responsibility than elsewhere in the industry to increase the numbers of women in tech. This is true for several reasons:

XP emphasises the importance of seeing things from the end user's perspective. This is helped when we have things in common with our end users. Obviously those end users are as diverse as our populations are. The more diversity we have within our teams, the better chance we have of appreciating our end users' experiences.

Also, XP is a forward-looking movement which emphasises flexibility, change and progress. As agilists, we value individuals and interactions over processes and tools, therefore if there is any group of people (for instance, women) whose ability to contribute towards their teams is compromised in any way, then this should be a matter of importance within the XP community.

3.2 Stereotype Threat and Unconscious Bias

Stereotype threat describes the experience of any group who suffer from negative stereotypes. In the case of women in technology (and also men in the caring professions, as just one other example), these negative stereotypes manifest as a general assumption that they will not have the skills they need to succeed. Such damaging ideas put people under threat, because they constantly feel they have to disprove them.

There is a large body of research which supports the statements I will make in this section. Several examples are referred to in the excellent book *Delusions of Gender* by Cordelia Fine [4], and I will quote some of them here. For instance, research shows that women's ability to perform is hampered by their anxiety about negative stereotypes. Instead of being able to concentrate on difficult tasks, a significant proportion of their mental concentration is taken up by trying to quell their fears about their potential lack of ability [5].

My own experience bears this out. I have described in this paper how, after a few years in the profession, I found myself in a job where my requests to do more interesting work were denied. There was always a part of me which believed I was less capable than my male peers, and that it was therefore quite reasonable for those requests to be denied. I decided that I would be better off looking for success in other areas of my life – my family and my hobbies – and that I would accept that my job was simply something whose purpose was to pay the bills, rather than something I could expect to excel at or enjoy.

Another problem is that the more successful a woman becomes in a male-dominated profession, the more she will be affected by stereotype threat. This is for several reasons: The more she moves up the ladder, the more of a minority she will find herself in. This will make her more anxious about other people's assumptions, but will also encourage her to believe – by sheer force of statistics – that those assumptions are true. "One study found that the more men there are taking a mathematics test in the same room as a solo woman, the lower women's performance becomes" [6].

The problem is not that girls are inherently less good at technology, or even that they're less interested; it is that people expect less of them. For instance, some men and women were given a difficult mathematics test. Before they started, they were told that it was designed to better understand what makes some people better at mathematics than others. A control group were told the same thing, but were also told that thousands of students had been tested and no gender difference had ever been found. In all groups, the average score for men was 19 %. In the first group, women also averaged 19 %. But in the second group, women averaged 30 %. Even though gender was not explicitly mentioned to the first group, it did not need to be. They could make that connection for themselves, and their performance was affected. But once that stereotype threat was removed, the potential of the women appeared to be unlocked [7].

As well as stereotype threat, another important phenomenon is "unconscious bias". This is effectively the technical term for what I have referred to in this paper as an "inner voice". It refers to the automatic connections that most of us make, for instance between women and the arts, and between men and technology.

One effect of unconscious bias can be that even when women are working within technology, both they and their colleagues do not see them as being in the correct role. This can be particularly true of women doing purely technical roles, such as software engineers. During my own career I have twice faced significant pressure to move out of a software role and into an organisational or management role. Luckily I was quite clear that I wouldn't enjoy those roles. In both cases I did temporarily make the change, but quickly recognised that I was moving in the wrong direction, and fortunately I had the confidence to move myself quickly back into a technical role.

The good news is that both unconscious bias and stereotype threat can be mitigated against by education. When people become aware that the problem exists, and how wide-ranging its effects are, they can start to do something about it. There are various organisations which offer "unconscious bias" training: this allows people from across a company to become aware of how unconscious bias and stereotype threat affect both the recruitment process and the ability of individuals to progress within the workplace. We are hoping to introduce this at LateRooms later this year.

3.3 The Positive Impact of XP

The inner voice which whispers, "But you're a girl," has never entirely gone away. But the following working practices have allowed me to take positive actions to improve my own experience and counter all the problems caused by being in a minority:

1. Daily stand-ups: I have frequently flagged up problems, and the resulting help and reassurance have helped to alleviate any insecurities.
2. Team retrospectives: When my team at LateRooms recently experimented with mob programming, we found that we were sometimes getting carried away with strong opinions, which led to some colleagues feeling excessively judged and criticised. We agreed to be kinder to each other as a result. This highlights how effective the culture of the retrospective can be in helping team members who might potentially be discriminated against.
3. Pair programming: My skills have improved more quickly since I have been able to pair program. I assume I will always have something to learn. I assume the same is true of my colleagues. Although I may occasionally worry that my male colleagues are more proficient than I am, this is proved wrong on a daily basis when we sit side by side and I see that they learn from me as much as I learn from them.
4. Iterative development: The focus on iterative development and a good working relationship between developers and stakeholders allows me to contribute towards a diverse and comprehensive understanding of the context in which my team finds ourselves.
5. Communication: The general supportive spirit has given me the confidence to explicitly ask for the support and encouragement I need to overcome any lack of confidence caused by being in a minority.

All of these practices should already be present in XP teams, but it is worth being aware what a positive impact they can have on minority groups, and therefore consciously practising them with that in mind.

4 Conclusions

After many years in the industry, I have encountered several problems to do with being a woman. The main problems have centred on my own lack of confidence in my ability to perform effectively in a technical role, and the tendency for colleagues to encourage me away from technical roles. The available literature - and my discussions with other women - would suggest that these are common problems for women in this industry.

However, since I have been working with XP, I have experienced several benefits and improvements. I believe these are due partly to the emphasis on communication and collaboration, particularly in the form of pair programming, daily stand-ups and retrospectives; and partly to the focus on iterative development and a good working relationship between developers and stakeholders. These aspects have given me the opportunity to evaluate my own skills more objectively, share knowledge and both give and receive the support I need. They have also allowed myself and my colleagues to evaluate and act upon any negative experiences within the team.

Clearly the experience of women is important to all workplaces in our industry, whether they use XP or not. But because of the emphasis placed by XP on people over process, and because XP understands the very important relationship between developers, business owners and stakeholders, then XP teams should not only care more about this, but are particularly well-placed to do something about it.

Acknowledgements. This paper was made significantly easier and more pleasant by the involvement of my shepherd, Jutta Eckstein. Her input has always been supportive, insightful and constructive. Thank you also to Esther Derby, Wendy Closson, Arlo Belshee, Philip Brock, and Lisa Crispin for responding to my emails. I would like to thank my employers, LateRooms.com, for their encouragement - in particular my team leader Arwel Griffith and our Director of Delivery, Alastair Brown. And finally many thanks to my partner Ally Fogg, for his input and support.

References

1. United States Census (2014). http://www.cnet.com/uk/news/women-in-tech-the-numbers-dont-add-up/, http://www.census.gov/quickfacts/table/PST045215/00, http://www.census.gov/quickfacts/table/SEX255213/00 (2015)

2. Hewlett, S.A., Luce, C.B., Servon, L.J., Sherbin, L., Shiller, P., Sosnovich, E., Sumberg, K.: The Athena Factor: Reversing the Brain Drain in Science, Engineering, and Technology. Harvard Business Review, Boston (2008)
3. XP Manchester. https://xpmanchester.wordpress.com/
4. Fine, C.: Delusions of Gender. W.W. Norton & Company, Inc., New York (2010). (p. 63)
5. Johns, M., Inzlicht, M., Schmader, T.: Stereotype threat and executive resource depletion: examining the influence of emotion regulation. J. Exp. Psychol. Gen. **137**(4), 691–705 (2008)
6. Inzlicht, M., Ben-Zeev, T.: A threatening intellectual environment: why females are susceptible to experiencing problem-solving deficits in the presence of males. Psychol. Sci. **11**(5), 365–371 (2000)
7. Good, C., Aronson, J., Harder, J.A.: Problems in the pipeline: stereotype threat and women's achievement in high-level math courses. J. Appl. Dev. Psychol. **29**(1), 17–28 (2008)

Pair-Programming from a Beginner's Perspective

Irina Tsyganok(✉)

YOOX NET-A-PORTER Group, NAP Commerce,
1, The Village Offices, Ariel Way, London, UK
irina.tsyganok@net-a-porter.com

Abstract. This experience report offers a beginner's perspective on pair-programming with experienced developers. It discusses issues faced by juniors and seniors when working together and highlights the importance of emotional maturity in pairs with disparate skill sets. This paper considers personal characteristics of junior and senior developers in identifying their needs from the pairing session and shares tactics used to improve pair-programming experience on individual and team-wide levels.

Keywords: Pair-programming · Knowledge-sharing · Collaboration · Culture · XP

1 Introduction

I joined YOOX NET-A-PORTER (YNAP) Group as a Technology Graduate in September 2014. During the 12 months of the company's graduate training programme I worked in the roles of a developer in testing, UX researcher, front-end developer and back-end developer, in multiple teams. As a junior, I was paired up with experienced developers to work on each story. It was the company-wide assumption that senior developers were the best candidates to introduce new team members to the technology stack.

Interestingly, most (if any) of my pairs had not practiced pair-programming in their daily work and working with me was, for many, the first exposure to pairing across skill levels. Having no framework to follow, we were largely guided by our instincts in conducting pairing sessions. It is through that experience I realised that social skills and emotional intelligence were powerful influencing factors in the success of pairing relationships.

My inspiration to explore Extreme Programming (XP) came from working with Nat Pryce, combined with support and insights from my manager. Nat introduced me to XProLo - a meet up on XP, which he attended along with other like-minded software engineers. Having become a regular member of the group myself, I have learned different ways of applying XP behaviours in the workplace and gained reassurance in my belief that pair-programming experience if approached appropriately, could benefit our team in many ways.

H. Sharp and T. Hall (Eds.): XP 2016, LNBIP 251, pp. 270–277, 2016.
DOI: 10.1007/978-3-319-33515-5_25

2 Getting Started with Pair-Programming

YNAP provided a consistently supportive learning environment across all teams I worked with. My input was always welcome and mistakes were treated as learning opportunities. I had the opportunity to join any team on any project at any time, which gave me complete control over my professional development. This autonomy allowed me to accelerate progress in areas, which I found most interesting and relevant.

But despite the thriving external environment, pair-programming with senior developers was much less of a success. It was not rare for me to feel frustrated, overwhelmed, disengaged and even insecure when pairing. Granted, a lot of these symptoms are a natural human reaction to facing a steep learning curve. However, six months into my role I repeatedly faced similar problems.

3 Getting Frustrated with Pair-Programming

"If I were given one hour to solve the planet, I would spend fifty five minutes defining the problem and only five minutes finding the solution" – Anonymous, often attributed to Albert Einstein

When considering our issues with pair-programming, I found it useful to categorise the challenges we faced into three groups: physical, session management and social.

Physical challenges are concerned with physical comfort. They can take the form of unsuitable equipment or inadequate personal space and can result in poor posture and discomfort. Session-management challenges are interruptions to the session caused by developers without consideration of the schedule of their pairing partner.

For junior/senior pairs, the biggest challenge is frequent unavailability of senior developers. Social challenges are less tangible and are therefore, the hardest to deal with. They are dependent on the personality traits and emotional intelligence of both partners. Physical and session management challenges can be more easily resolved if the social challenges are eliminated first.

3.1 The Vicious Cycle of Non-learning

I discovered that most of my senior pairs were reluctant to allow me to experiment with solutions. At the slightest sign of uncertainty, they were very eager to take over the keyboard and demonstrate the solution by coding it themselves. Although instinctive and seemingly efficient, this tactic undermines the purpose of knowledge-sharing in pairing across skill. It is also easily developed into a pattern, which if becomes systematic, leads to the vicious cycle of non-learning, as illustrated in Fig. 1.

The pattern illustrated in Fig. 1 sets traps of short-term convenience at each step. It is more convenient for an experienced developer to type in the code than to watch their junior pair struggle through an imperfect solution. Similarly, watching someone writing code for prolonged periods of time almost always leads to disengagement. Breaking this pattern requires taking a step outside one's comfort zone, and can be difficult to achieve.

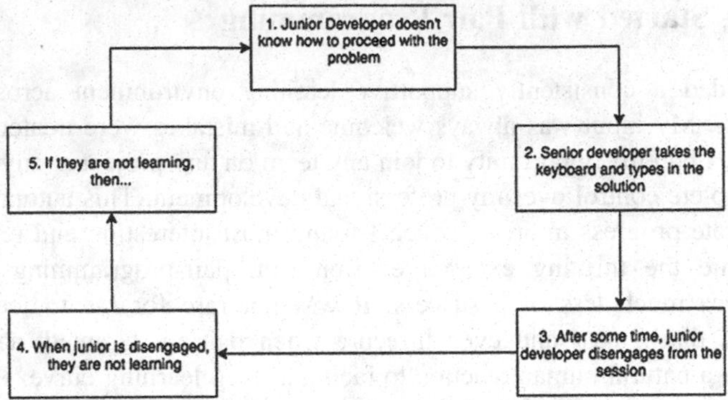

Fig. 1. The vicious cycle of non-learning

4 Observations

To investigate the relationship between social characteristics and levels of technical expertise in software developers, I drew up high level personas for the novice and the expert in the context of a programming session.

The diagram in Fig. 2 shows that behaviours of these personas oppose one another. For my analysis I chose the two extremes of professional spectre - the very junior and the very senior, as they most accurately reflect my experience at YNAP. However, despite obvious differences, junior and senior developers have one goal in common - they both want to learn in the course of the pairing session.

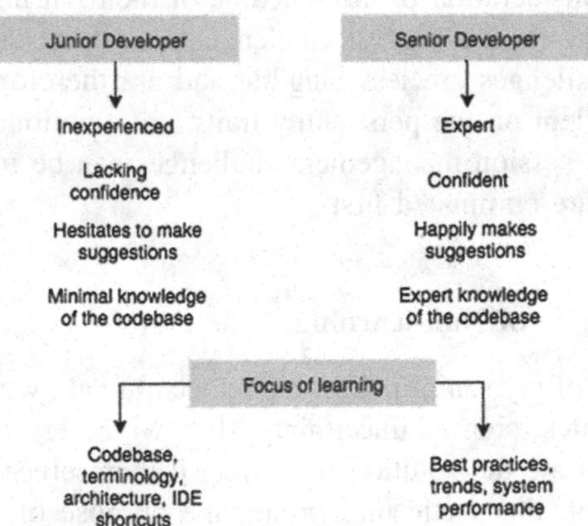

Fig. 2. Junior and senior developer personas

4.1 The Needs of Each Persona

Considering the disparate learning focus of the expert and the novice, I identified the expectations of each one from the pairing session. To analyse the needs of the novice, all I had to do was reflect on my own experience. And this is what I identified to be the most important:

- opportunity to experiment with solutions
- permission to make mistakes
- constructive feedback
- engagement in the session
- a flowing dialogue
- friendly disposition from my pair

In order to find out what the seniors need from the pairing session, I turned to my technical team at YNAP. I gave a presentation 'Pair-programming From a Beginner's Perspective', in which I shared my observations, concerns and proposed solutions with my team. When I asked my senior colleagues about their needs, we were all surprised to discover that the needs of experienced developers are identical to the needs of the junior.

I repeated the talk and the question at XProLo meetup in front of a very experienced audience, and the results were the same.

Through these discussions I learned that senior developers can also be prone to insecurity and that just like the juniors, they need opportunities to experiment with solutions and desire a flowing dialogue from their pair.

5 What We Learned

> "A teacher-student relationship feels very different from two people working together as equals, even if one has significantly more experience." - extremeprogramming.org

Industry perception of pairing across skill often assumes a *teacher/student* relationship. Such teacher-student role division promotes a familiar classroom teaching style, whereby the teacher talks and demonstrates and the student listens.

My experience has shown that pair-programming is most effective when both developers are equally involved and proactive throughout the session. Therefore, I propose to view pairing across skill in the light of the *leader/adopter* pattern. The latter suggests equal participation of both developers in the session, with the experienced developer acting as the leader and the junior, as the adopter. The skill set of the leader should include both technical excellence and emotional intelligence - one or the other alone is insufficient. The skill set of the adopter is incomplete, hence the role.

During my time at YNAP I have had to heavily rely on my social skills to facilitate my own learning. This led me to a conclusion that technical expertise of an individual does not imply emotional maturity; consequently not all senior developers are good leaders. A simple metaphor of a parent teaching their child to ride a bike might help. The parent tasked with teaching is expected to not only be a confident cyclist themselves, but to be also adequately patient and articulated to lead their child through learning experience. From the adopter's perspective, quality of pairing experience is heavily influenced by the emotional expertise of the leader. Continuing the cycling metaphor, the most effective teaching method involves a parent and a child working together as equals. In contrast, a parent demonstrating the technique by cycling around their child in silence, is obviously ineffective. Yet, when it comes to pair-programing, senior developers often choose the leading strategy of cycling around their junior pair.

5.1 Can Anyone Be a Leader?

Just like teaching a child to ride a bike, pairing with the junior demands patience, a teaching plan (that can change), time and willingness of the leader to get deeply involved. The latter is the deciding factor, yet in my experience it has not always been considered.

The cycling analogy demonstrates the importance of acknowledgement and consent. A child who wants to ride a bike has no choice but to master cycling first. The parent, on the other hand, has a choice of either teaching their child themselves or asking someone else to do it.

In making this decision, the parent has to analyse whether the amount of time they can spare for teaching, their own physical fitness and emotional skills needed to guide their child throughout learning experience are sufficient at a given point in time. If a parent identifies that for whatever reason they are unable to meet one or more of the suitability criteria, it is probably better to ask a friend or another family member to lead the teaching. To the child on the other hand, quality of teaching is more important than the person providing teaching.

The suitability and unsuitability of the senior are not permanent. Circumstances may change over time to enable the parent to teach their now eagerly racing child new stunts on their bike.

Coming back to pair-programming, in addition to acknowledging the fact that their pair is inexperienced, a senior developer has to asses whether they are willing and able to take on the role of a leader at a given moment in time.

5.2 The Social Aspect of Pair-Programming

I have learned that for two developers to work enjoyably and productively together, they need to get on well socially. This applies to all pairs regardless of technical expertise, but the experience may feel less natural in a junior/senior pair.

I observed that the act of pair-programming despite being emotionally intense, can be socially isolating. Work environment places focus on technical expertise and professional status and filters social interactions through a prism of organisational culture.

However, when two developers engage in an informal activity, such as having lunch or a drink after work together, their professional status matters much less and so does the organisational culture. Instead, the focus of their interaction shifts to personal and emotional. Those developers are no longer ‘a junior’ and ‘a senior’, they are just two people having a conversation. I have found that positive effects of informal communication transcend environments. That is, once the two developers get back to work, they find that their communication flows better, which in turn, empowers the pair to overcome challenges imposed by the experience gap, status and other constraints of the work environment.

5.3 Pair-Programming – Child's Play?

In the final year of my degree, I organised a Code Club at my local primary school, where I taught a class of seventeen children programming for one year, using a project-based curriculum and encouraging a free-form learning environment. My only two objectives throughout the year were that the children learn to code and have fun. Whether they wanted to work solo, in pairs or in a mob, was entirely up to them.

Throughout that year, I observed most organic transitions of my students' learning through various techniques.

All children started the year in the classroom learning style. They had a computer and a project sheet each and worked solo, raising their hand as they needed my help. As projects became increasingly complex, many children chose to pair up with their friends - in a grown-up XP world we call this 'pair-programming by association'. In their pairs, the children conversed freely, exchanging jokes and clearly enjoying each others' company.

However, as the difficulty of learning the material continued to increase, some children gravitated towards pairing with their more able classmates who were not necessarily their buddies outside of the classroom. Their conversations became more focused on the task, but the dialogue kept flowing at all times. In each pair there was a leader and an adopter, and both remained engaged throughout.

Finally and very importantly, two of my students chose to work solo throughout the whole year. They did not object to helping their peers when prompted, but they clearly performed better and seemed more content having their own space.

All children made amazing progress and many of them have taken their learning further. Reflecting on our experience, it is clear to me that the children loved the social aspect of our club just as much as they loved problem-solving. Another observation I made that year is that not everyone is happy in the role of leader despite displaying excellent technical aptitude. And that is a personal choice everyone should be entitled to. Unless these individuals want to step out of their comfort zone and take a leadership role, forcing them into pairing with a less experienced partner will never lead to a good experience.

The children gracefully demonstrated the significance of emotional intelligence in pair-programming. In comparison, as adults, we seem to have a harder time to effectively apply the practice in the workplace

6 Fixing Pair-Programming

"In theory, theory and practice are the same. In practice, they are not." - Anonymous.

During my time at YNAP I learned that communication is the foundation of successful pairing. Therefore, I focused on improving social interactions with my pairs and team-wide by including jokes, casual conversations and team socials into our day.

Specifically to pairing across skill, I gave a talk to my team, in which I offered a beginner's perspective on pairing with experienced developers. The talk drew attention to the challenges, which senior developers did not know existed and initiated interesting discussions in the team. Our improved communication enabled us to make sound team-wide decisions, which included:

- Swapping pairs to promote pairing fluidity
- Agreeing on the WIP limit and adhering to it
- Setting up our desks and pairing stations to provide comfortable working environment
- Giving each other sufficient time apart and synchronising our breaks
- Working on a story from start to finish, in the same pair
- Finding time for small talk in pairs and socialising more as a team

6.1 How We Can Improve

Pair-programming culture in our team has significantly improved as a result of the increased awareness and positive changes we made. However, we are still working on the assumption that all our senior developers are equally good at pairing with juniors. Going forward, I would like to adopt a more personalised approach in forming junior/senior pairs, particularly, when new graduates join our team. I would also like for us to pair with other stakeholders, such as designers, testers, product owners and data analysts more often.

7 Conclusions and Way Forward

Over the last six months, pair-programming in our team transitioned from being a subconscious training tool to becoming a considered cultural choice for everyone. Working in pairs brought us closer as a team, sometimes as opposing parties of long debates and sometimes as good friends truly collaborating and learning from each other. Even at this early stage of adopting the practice, pair-programming has formed a core part of our work ethos.

Our cultivation of a thriving pairing culture has not been smooth and it is far from over. After many frustrating sessions, it was the acknowledgement of the importance of good communication and emotional maturity in pairs that allowed us to make key positive changes in the way we work together. I am confident that a little more perseverance will take our team to new strengths in applying pair-programming effectively across skill and beyond.

This extract from an email, which Ward Cunningham sent to pdxruby mailing list in 2012 sums up this experience report beautifully: "…Our willingness to work together could be the juice that will push computers forward. We will all have to master pair-programming (not just mentoring) to make this work. It will be awesome".

Acknowledgements. I would like to thank Nat Pryce for the inspiration, support and honest feedback. I appreciate the opportunity to work on the report and attend XP2016, presented to me by Claire Lamb and James Wyllie. Thank you to all my senior pairs for providing the material for this paper. Finally, a special thanks to Avraham Poupko for having faith in this project, and for his undeniable support and valuable insights at every stage of its life.

Empirical Studies Papers

Empirical Research Plan: Effects of Sketching on Program Comprehension

Sebastian Baltes[1] and Stefan Wagner[2(✉)]

[1] University of Trier, Trier, Germany
research@sbaltes.com
[2] University of Stuttgart, Stuttgart, Germany
stefan.wagner@informatik.uni-stuttgart.de
http://orcid.org/0000-0002-5256-8429

Abstract. Sketching is an important means of communication in software engineering practice. Yet, there is little research investigating the use of sketches. We want to contribute a better understanding of sketching, in particular its use during program comprehension. We propose a controlled experiment to investigate the effectiveness and efficiency of program comprehension with the support of sketches as well as what sketches are used in what way.

Keywords: Experiment · Sketching · Program comprehension

1 Introduction

Software is inherently abstract and has no natural representation except source code. Thus, especially for program comprehension, visualizations are important [1]. Sketches are an example for informal visualizations that are often created when understanding or explaining source code [2]. In the past, however, these informal artefacts did not get the amount of attention by the software engineering research community that their relevance in software development practice could imply. With our proposed study, we want to analyse if and how sketching improves program comprehension when explaining source code. Furthermore, we want to gain a better understanding of what sketches are used in what way to explain the source code. In the description of our experiment, we follow the guidelines of Jedlitschka, Ciolkowski and Pfahl [3].

2 Related Work

One of the main purposes of sketching in software development is communication [2,4]. To this end, developers often employ ad hoc notations that rarely adhere to standards like the *Unified Modeling Language* (UML) [2,5]. The ambiguity in sketches is a source of creativity [6] and they support problem solving and understanding [7]. In other areas like engineering, controlled experiments

H. Sharp and T. Hall (Eds.): XP 2016, LNBIP 251, pp. 281–285, 2016.
DOI: 10.1007/978-3-319-33515-5_26

have shown that the possibility to sketch has a positive effect on the quality of the solutions [8]. In our study, we want to analyse if sketches improve program comprehension in a setting where one developer explains a piece of source code to a colleague. To be able to compare the effect of sketching on program comprehension, we measure task correctness and response time [9].

3 Experiment Planing

The overall goal of our research is to better understand the use and usefulness of sketches in software engineering. In this experiment, we especially focus on sketching as a means of program comprehension in the communication between two developers. The goal of our experiment is:

Analyze sketching while explaining source code
for the purpose of evaluating its impact on program comprehension
with respect to its effectiveness and efficiency
from the viewpoint of the developer
in the context of the conference XP 2016.

From this, we derive three research questions. The first two are more descriptive and exploratory to better understand which sketches developers use and how they use them while explaining source code to another developer. The third covers then the causal relationship of using sketches onto the effectiveness and efficiency of comprehending the source code.

RQ 1: Which sketches do developers use to explain code?
RQ 2: How do developers explain code with and without sketches?
RQ 3: How does the effectiveness and efficiency of the understanding of the code differ when it was explained with or without a sketch?

3.1 Experimental Units and Materials

The participants of the experiments will be pairs of developers. They will explain source code to each other. They have to be professional software developers.

We will use four different small open-source software systems in commonly known programming languages such as Java or C#. As the developers do not know the source code beforehand but have to explain them, we limit the systems to 500 LOC at most.

3.2 Tasks

The basic task for each pair of developers is to understand the source code of a small software system and then explain certain aspects to each other. The source code will be made available on an iPad. In case they should sketch, this will be done on paper. The aspects to explain will be low-level and code-centric. Afterwards, the developer the aspect was explained to, will answer questions evaluating how well they understood the explanations.

3.3 Hypotheses, Parameters and Variables

The central independent variable of the experiment is the use of sketching. The dependent variables we are going to measure are the time needed until the explained aspect is understood and the correctness of the understanding. For the explorative part, we also document which types of sketches (e.g. different UML diagrams) they used and how they themselves judged the difference in explanations.

The two null hypotheses we are going to investigate are:

H_{01}: *There is no difference in the effectiveness of comprehension with or without sketches.*

H_{02}: *There is no difference in the efficiency of comprehension with or without sketches.*

Furthermore, we will document further context variables such as the experience of the developers with the programming languages and whether they have previously worked together.

3.4 Experiment Design

We will employ a blocked and balanced design. Hence, from each developer pair, the first developer will first read and explain a software system with sketching and then read another software system and explain it without sketching. The second developer will do the same but first without sketching and then with sketching.

We will openly invite the XP 2016 participants to join the experiment in pairs. Therefore, the sample is a convenience sample.

3.5 Procedure

We need a separate location for the experiment so that the participants can concentrate on understanding and explaining. We could hold it as one event during the conference or continuously over the whole conference depending on the fit to the conference schedule. We will put up lists in which the developers can volunteer to participate.

The first step when a pair starts the experiment is that they receive an iPad each with their two software systems to explain together with the question concerning the aspect they later have to explain to the other developer. Then (step 2) both get time to read the first system. In step 3, participant 1 explains the first system to participant 2 without a sketch. The time for this is measured on the iPad. Step 4 is a short questionnaire for participant 2 to check the correctness of their understanding. In step 5, participant 2 explains their software system aspect to participant 1 with the help of sketches on provided paper (including time measurement on the iPad). In step 6, participant 1 answers the short questionnaire concerning correctness.

Next, in step 7, both participants read the next question and source code. Then, the same procedure is repeated but participant 1 gets to use sketches while participant 2 does not. We will ask about the general experience and context factors in a final questionnaire.

3.6 Analysis Procedure

We will analyse the quantitative data to test the two hypotheses using an ANOVA analysis (RQ 3). Furthermore, we will qualitatively analyse the sketches and the answers to the open questions in the final questionnaire (RQ 1 and 2).

4 Summary and Future Work

In summary, we want to conduct a controlled experiment to better understand how developers use sketches in explaining source code as well as the effects on effectiveness and efficiency of the comprehension. The results of the experiment allow us to reduce the discrepancy between research concentrating on more formally defined modelling languages and the relevance of sketching in practice. Furthermore, we want to use the gained insights to work on a sketching language and tool support to aid practitioners in sketching in an efficient and effective way.

References

1. Storey, M.D.: Theories, tools and research methods in program comprehension: past, present and future. Softw. Qual. J. **14**(3), 187–208 (2006)
2. Baltes, S., Diehl, S.: Sketches and diagrams in practice. In: Proceedings of the International Symposium on Foundations of Software Engineering (FSE 2014), pp. 530–541 (2014)
3. Jedlitschka, A., Pfahl, D.: Reporting guidelines for controlled experiments in software engineering. In: International Symposium on Empirical Software Engineering (2005)
4. Cherubini, M., Venolia, G., DeLine, R., Ko, A.J.: Let's go to the whiteboard: how and why software developers use drawings. In: Proceedings of the SIGCHI Conference on Human Factors in Computing Systems (CHI 2007), pp. 557–566 (2007)
5. Petre, M.: UML in practice. In: Proceedings of the International Conference on Software Engineering (ICSE 2013), pp. 722–731 (2013)

6. Goldschmidt, G.: The backtalk of self-generated sketches. Des. Issues **19**(1), 72–88 (2003)
7. Suwa, M., Tversky, B.: External representations contribute to the dynamic construction of ideas. In: Hegarty, M., Meyer, B., Narayanan, N.H. (eds.) Diagrams 2002. LNCS (LNAI), vol. 2317, pp. 341–343. Springer, Heidelberg (2002)
8. Schütze, M., Sachse, P., Römer, A.: Support value of sketching in the design process. Res. Eng. Design **2**(14), 89–97 (2003)
9. Dunsmore, A., Roper, M.: A comparative evaluation of program comprehension measures. Technical report EFoCS 35–2000, Department of Computer Science, University of Strathclyde (2000)

The 4+1 Principles of Software Safety Assurance and Their Implications for Scrum

Osama Doss(✉) and Tim Kelly

High Integrity Systems Engineering Research Group, Department of Computer Science, University of York, York YO10 5DD, UK
{osad500,tim.kelly}@york.ac.uk

Abstract. As part of our research concerning the integration of assurance case development with Scrum, we are planning to conduct semi-structured interviews with participants to gain feedback on a proposed approach. We will be interviewing individuals who have been involved with safety-critical systems development and Agile methods. Participants will be presented with an overview of the challenges associated with applying the 4+1 software safety assurance principles to Scrum. Initial recommendations concerning how the principles can be accommodated within a Scrum development will also be presented. Participants will be led through a series of questions to gain feedback on the feasibility of the approach, and for an assessment as to whether the 4+1 principles can be addressed without compromising agility. The motivation behind this research is to gain a deeper insight into the difficulties experienced when integrating assurance case in to Scrum process.

Keywords: Scrum · Safety · Assurance · Certification · Assurance case · Software safety

1 Research Aim

This study is part of the research under the High Integrity System Engineering Group, Computer Science Department, of the University of York. This paper introduces the 4+1 Principles of Software Safety Assurance [1] and their implications for Scrum [2], specifically, the impact on the processes, roles and artefacts associated with Scrum development.

Historically, there has been a reluctance to adopt agile methods within safety-critical systems development. However, feedback from our initial research in this area suggests that there are benefits to be gained from the application of agile methods to safety critical systems [3, 8]. Following this feedback we have done further work to assess how the 4+1 principles of software safety assurance can be integrated with Scrum, and have developed an initial proposal for how Scrum could be modified to better address the principles. The aim of the proposed study at XP2016 is gain practitioner feedback on these proposals. The feedback we receive will ultimately be used to help refine the proposal before further empirical evaluation.

H. Sharp and T. Hall (Eds.): XP 2016, LNBIP 251, pp. 286–290, 2016.
DOI: 10.1007/978-3-319-33515-5_27

2 Research Questions and Their Motivations

Our research, as a whole, is focused on answering the following questions:

- RQ1 What are the current concerns and opportunities voiced by safety-critical systems professionals regarding the use of agile development methods for safety-critical systems development?
- RQ2 Can the integration of incremental assurance case development and evaluation within the existing "Scrum" methodology alleviate the concerns identified in answer to RQ1?
- RQ3 What changes can Scrum Process has to undertake in order to be compliant with the safety standard?

This study, specifically furthers our investigation into RQ2 and 3. We now how have initial proposals for changes and a description of assurance case development integrated with Scrum. However, what we lack is a substantial and varied practitioner base to help assess the credibility, feasibility, and efficacy of our proposals.

3 Importance of Research

Despite progress in the use of agile development methods in safety critical systems development (e.g. [4]), there are still those with doubts about the potential for successful integration. There are also reported experiences [5] that highlight the complementary nature of the iterative and incremental approach underlying many agile methods, and recognised best practice in risk management in safety critical systems development. Rather than start with a theoretical evaluation of the compatibility of the principles of agile development with software safety assurance, we decided to draw out these experiences, opinions (and possibly preconceptions) by means of a practitioner's semi-structured interview. In particular, our first round of semi-structured interviews drew out specific responses relating to (possible) incremental and iterative nature of safety requirements development, hazard analysis and safety (assurance) case developments. The responses we received showed both the potential for benefits from agile development of safety-critical software, together with residual concerns about the ability to provide software safety assurance in a manner compatible with current software safety assurance standards. Rather than focusing on a single safety assurance standard (as some have done, e.g. [4]) we have used the framework of the 4+1 software safety assurance principles to tackle the common and broad issues of software safety assurance that exist across multiple industry domains and safety standards. These principles have been developed to highlight the commonality of purpose of multiple existing safety standards, and are being adopted by industry (e.g. in Defence Standard 00-55) as a framework against which software safety assurance can be judged.

The importance of this research is that it represents one step along the path of pushing beyond simplistic and over-generalised preconceptions of the compatibility of agile and safety-critical systems development, and potentially unlocking the benefits of agility within the safety domain.

4 Data Collection Methods to Be Used, Including

- ***Who the participants should be***

It is not easy task to find practitioners with both experience in the field of Agile and Safety. However, XP2016 will involve various categories of experts (software engineers, industry and academia etc.) as well there being a significant opportunity to link this study with the XP2016 workshop Agile Development of Safety-critical Software (ASCS).

We would like to interview individuals who have been involved with Safety Critical-Systems, Agile methods, or both, during XP2016 in order to use their experience and insight to gain feedback on our proposed approach.

- ***What methods will be used and why these have been selected.***

The study will be conducted as a qualitative survey using "semi-structured interviews" for data collection [6]. Shull et al. [7] illustrate the advantage and disadvantage of conducting semi-structured interview. The interview will include some simple (e.g. Likert scale-based) question, as well as more open-ended questions that allow for greater depth of response.

The responses received from XP2016 will also be compared with 1-to-1 semi-structured interviews conducted with some of the respondents from our initial survey [3]; the purpose of this interview study is to investigate the success of the proposed integration of 4+1 principles and assurance safety case development with Scrum.

Interviews will be conducted face-to-face at the XP2016 location. Further interviews (with further participants) may be conducted over phone. Interviews will be recorded and transcribed to facilitate subsequent analysis.

- ***What will happen during data collection activity?***

Participants would take part in an approximately 40 min interview to explore perceptions around the 4+1 Principles of Software Safety Assurance and their implications for Scrum.

The interview will start by introducing the research aims and the topics to be discussed. Then the 4+1 principles will be explained, together with an outline of the proposal for integrating these principles within a Scrum development. Questions will then be asked relating to the proposal – picking out specific features one-by-one (e.g. our recommendations for team composition). The questions will tackle both aspects of (a) whether the proposed approach challenges agility and (b) whether the proposed approach challenges safety assurance.

Documents that will be prepared for the interview:

1. Interview guide - main pointers to guide the interview
2. Information sheet - to be provided to the interviewee to provide the context of the interview
3. Consent form - for interviewee to sign.

5 Data Analysis Methods to Be Subsequently Used

Transcripts will be analysed using thematic analysis. One researcher will read all of the interview transcripts, and will code the transcripts using first-cycle coding (Open Coding or Initial Coding), supported by the NVivo 11 software package. Main categories (or topics) will be identified through clustering of codes in project review meetings. Codes and categories will be constantly compared with the data and revised or refined as appropriate.

The results of the thematic analysis will then be written up in a form suitable for sharing with participants and subsequent publication.

6 How the Results Will Be Used

Initially, we will present the key findings within the High Integrity System Engineering Group at York. The findings will also potentially form part of the final thesis of the ongoing PhD research on Assurance Case Integration with An Agile Development Method. Our findings will be submitted, in the future, for publication in peer-reviewed journals.

Ultimately, the findings will be used to refine our proposed approach before proceeding to empirical case studies.

References

1. Kelly, T.: Software certification: where is confidence won and lost? addressing systems safety challenges. In: Anderson, T., Dale, C. (eds.) Safety Critical Systems Club (2014)
2. Rubin, K.S.: Essential Scrum: A Practical Guide to the Most Popular Agile Process, 1st edn. Addison-Wesley Professional, Upper Saddle River (2012)
3. Doss, O., Kelly, T.: Challenges and opportunities in agile development in safety critical systems – a survey. In: Agile methods applied to development and certification of safety-critical software Workshop, XP 2015, Helsinki, Finland (2015)
4. Stålhane, T., Myklebust, T., Hanssen, G.K.: The application of safe scrum to IEC 61508 certifiable software. ESREL (2012)

5. Bedoll, R.: A Tail of Two Projects: How ‘Agile’ Methods Succeeded after ‘Traditional’ Methods Had Failed in a Critical System-Development Project, Extreme Programming and Agile Methods-XP/Agile Universe 2003, pp. 25–34. Springer, Heidelberg (2003)
6. Flink, A.: The Survey Handbook, 2nd edn. Sage Publications, Thousand Oaks (2003)
7. Shull, F., Singer, J., Sjberg, D.I.K.: Guide to Advanced Empirical Software Engineering, 1st edn. Springer, London (2010)
8. Doss, O., Kelly, T.: Assurance case integration with an agile development method. XP 2015, LNBIP, vol. 212, pp. 347–349 (2015)

Development Tools Usage Inside Out

Marko Gasparic(✉), Andrea Janes, and Francesco Ricci

Free University of Bozen-Bolzano, Dominikanerplatz 3, 39100 Bolzano, Italy
marko.gasparic@stud-inf.unibz.it, {andrea.janes,francesco.ricci}@unibz.it

Abstract. The software engineering community is continuously producing tools to tackle software construction problems. This paper presents a research study to identify which tools, artifacts, and commands developers use during task solving and how one can design software that can suggest and convince the developer to use specific software construction techniques. We want to understand under which conditions developers accept suggestions for a more efficient and effective usage of the available instruments, and if observed usage patterns correlate with observable improvements in the process or product. The expected results include detailed logs of how developers construct software during XP 2016, their preferences for software construction recommendations, and which effects accepted suggestions have on task execution and outcome.

Keywords: Tool usage · IDE command recommendation

1 Aim of Research and Research Questions

The aim of the proposed study is to observe in depth how developers solve their tasks, how developers accept different types of suggestions to support their work, and what are the effects of different behaviors.

Concretely, the research questions we want to answer with this empirical study are:

- RQ1: Which tools and artifacts developers use during task solving?
- RQ2: If a better way to solve a task exists, how can we design software that can persuade the developer to change his or her behavior?
- RQ3: Which effects on task execution and task outcome (i.e., the code) do different tools and command suggestions have?

To solve their daily tasks, software developers are using tools, such as integrated development environments (IDEs), web-browsers, communication tools, etc. The choicc of tools and their usage have a strong impact on the productivity of developers. Understanding how developers work is therefore important to understand how to support their work.

We already performed a preliminary study, by analyzing interaction patterns within the IDE of eight developers, comparing the patterns in different contexts. In a conference setting, such as the XP 2016 coding sessions, we now

H. Sharp and T. Hall (Eds.): XP 2016, LNBIP 251, pp. 291–295, 2016.
DOI: 10.1007/978-3-319-33515-5_28

have the opportunity to build on our experience and observe a bigger sample of skilled, focused developers, solving a predefined programming task. This is an experimental setting which is rare to find. Collecting such data from experienced programmers, all executing a similar task is difficult: companies are rarely willing to invest time to perform such experiments as they do not obtain a direct benefit from it.

We assume that in a conference setting developers will be less exposed to interruptions, which will make the results easier to interpret. This allows us to better understand how experienced developers are spending their time interacting with tools and how they are using the functionality provided by the IDE, solely for the purposes of programming.

To answer RQ1, we want to answer the following sub-questions:

- RQ1.1: Which tools (e.g., text editing, communication, source code management) are developers using to solve a particular task?
- RQ1.2: Which artifacts (e.g., websites, documents, source code files, text files) are they reading, writing, and modifying?
- RQ1.3: Which IDE commands are they invoking?

RQ2 addresses the question if and how we can write software that identifies and suggests to the developer more effective ways to solve a specific task. In this context, we want to focus on the tools developers are using, in particular the IDE. Many developers are not using even some basic features provided by their IDE, even if certain features are recognized as highly useful by the community [1].

To alleviate this problem, first researchers developed and validated IDE command recommendation algorithms [2]. These algorithms were either evaluated offline or by interviewing the study participants. We are not aware of any designed and tested user interface for IDE command recommendations. Consequently, we do not know how persuasive and effective such systems would be in practice and whether the developers would accept recommendations, even if the recommendations would be 100 % accurate.

The most precious resource that development tools require from the developer is the attention. Due to the low usage of tools that the scientific community developed in the last years, it is questionable if the developers are willing to accept them in practice at all [3]. We would like to investigate whether it even makes sense to start building new tools that would change the development process or will the developers rather stick to the current practices. To answer RQ2, we will answer the following sub-questions:

- RQ2.1: How do developers perceive the current integration of the various tools they use?
- RQ2.2: How will developers react to different types of user interfaces for persuasive and effective IDE command recommendations?
- RQ2.3: How efficient are the proposed user interfaces and how can they be improved?

Finally, RQ3 asks which effects on task execution and task outcome tool usage and command suggestions have. We will observe work patterns and interactions with tools and artifacts, as well as the effect on the source code itself.

In parallel, we want to observe the acceptance of command recommendations generated specifically for the task at hand and delivered at the beginning of the coding session; also, we want to observe the effects of the recommendations. Thus, we want to perform an experiment according to the "one factor with two treatments" design type [4], where the treatment group will have access to the IDE command recommendation mockups.

Since the duration of the experiment is short, we plan to investigate RQ3 qualitatively through the following sub-questions:

- RQ3.1: How does the usage of different tools, commands, and artifacts affect the produced source code?
- RQ3.2: How do command recommendations change the interaction with the IDE?

2 Importance of Research

The software engineering community is continuously producing tools that help developers to tackle what Fred Brooks calls "essence and accidents" [5]. Currently, a particularly dynamic field is the field of recommendation systems for software engineering [6]. By obtaining the answer to RQ2, we would like to better understand under which conditions software developers accept the promotion of more efficient and effective usage of tools, by improving their accessibility (RQ2.1) and discovery (RQ2.2). This will pave the way to construct a recommender that can deliver useful recommendations in a real-life setting.

RQ3 is targeting the meaningfulness of the proposed tools and commands. We aim to better understand whether the suggestions to use additional tools, features, web-pages, etc. lead to observable improvements, i.e., cause a change in the data collected in RQ1. Knowing the effect of the usage of certain tools nurtures the motivation to develop new tools and facilitates the introduction of existing tools in practice. Some examples are: the diffusion of innovation within an organization, the training of newcomers, or the support for teaching.

3 Data Collection Methods

The majority of the data will be collected automatically by the following tools:

- A tool that logs the currently focused window, together with its process name and caption. The window caption often contains the path to the currently opened artifact, which can be used to infer the type of the artifact. The obtained log contributes to answer RQ1.1 and in part RQ1.2.

- Eclipse UDC[1] to collect command executions, user interface elements activations, and start and stop events of bundles. In addition, a modified version of Eclipse Mylyn[2] will be used to record the currently focused artifact within the IDE, together with the active perspective, including editors, and views. These Eclipse plugins contribute to answer RQ1.2 and RQ1.3.
- A tool to collect all the logged data to a central location.

We will provide the environment in the cloud and allow participant's to install the necessary tools on their own machines at the beginning of the session. If developers agree, we will use eye tracking devices to understand on what developers are looking during their work.

To investigate the motivations behind the manifested decisions following the display of an IDE command suggestion (RQ2), we will perform qualitative interviews (based on [7]) and an online survey, which will take less than 20 min.

4 Data Analysis and Data Usage

The collected data will be anonymized and studied using descriptive and inferential statistics, data mining techniques, and manual inspection. To study the results of the interviews, we will use quantitative and qualitative research methods. To study the impact of the recommendation on the code, we will use the data provided by code smell detection tools, e.g., FindBugs[3], but mainly manually study which effects the invocation of the suggested commands has on the code. The obtained data will be used to provide feedback to the participants, improve the understanding of development tools usage, and in the development of recommendation systems in software engineering.

References

1. Murphy-Hill, E.: Continuous social screencasting to facilitate software tool discovery. In: International Conference on Software Engineering (2012)

[1] http://www.eclipse.org/org/usagedata.
[2] http://www.eclipse.org/mylyn.
[3] http://findbugs.sourceforge.net.

2. Murphy-Hill, E., Jiresal, R., Murphy, G.C.: Improving software developers' fluency by recommending development environment commands. In: ACM SIGSOFT International Symposium on the Foundations of Software Engineering (2012)
3. Gasparic, M., Janes, A.: What recommendation systems for software engineering recommend: a systematic literature review. J. Syst. Softw. **113**, 101–113 (2016)
4. Wohlin, C., Runeson, P., Höst, M., Ohlsson, M.C., Regnell, B., Wesslén, A.: Experimentation in Software Engineering: An Introduction. Kluwer Academic Publishers, Norwell (2000)
5. Brooks, F.P.: No silver bullet essence and accidents of software engineering. Computer **20**, 10–19 (1987)
6. Robillard, M.P., Maalej, W., Walker, R.J., Zimmermann, T.: Recommendation Systems in Software Engineering. Springer, Heidelberg (2014)
7. Venkatesh, V., Morris, M.G., Davis, G.B., Davis, F.D.: User acceptance of information technology: toward a unified view. MIS Q. **27**, 425–478 (2003)

Pitfalls of Kanban in Brownfield and Greenfield Software Development Projects

Muhammad Ovais Ahmad(✉), Jouni Markkula, and Markku Oivo

M-Group, University of Oulu, Oulu, Finland
{muhammad.ahmad,jouni.markkula,markku.oivo}@oulu.fi

Abstract. In the last two decades, Agile and Lean approaches have gained wide acceptance in the software industry. In this realm, Kanban emerged in 2004 with a strong practitioner-driven support movement and today, Kanban is increasingly adopted to complement Scrum and other Agile methods. Kanban tends to focus on fast production, rapid and continual user feedback and interaction.

1 Background

In the last two decades, Agile and Lean approaches have gained wide acceptance in the software industry. In this realm, Kanban emerged in 2004 with a strong practitioner-driven support movement [1–3], and today, Kanban is increasingly adopted to complement Scrum and other Agile methods. Kanban tends to focus on fast production, rapid and continual user feedback and interaction.

Used for controlling the logistical chain from a production point of view, Kanban was developed and applied in the Japanese manufacturing industry in the 1950s [6]. Kanban's success in the manufacturing industry has convinced software engineers to adopt this approach, with practitioner-driven support furthering this trend. In 2004, David Anderson introduced Kanban to a small IT team at Microsoft, aiming to help the team members visualise their work and put limits on their work in progress (WIP). Kanban has five underlying principles [4], the so-called Kanban properties [5]: *visualise the workflow, limit work in progress, measure and manage flow, make process policies explicit and use models to recognise improvement and opportunities.*

The motivation behind visualisation and limiting WIP was to identify the constraints of the process and to focus on a single item at a time. Additionally, instead of pushing work on to software developers, Kanban promotes a pull approach: when a team member finishes an existing task, he or she automatically pulls the next item to begin work. In brief, Kanban aims to provide visibility to the software development process, communicate priorities and highlight bottlenecks [6]. This process results in a constant flow of releasing work items to customers, as the developers focus only on a few items at a given time [7]. The proliferation of Kanban in software engineering boomed after the publication of key books. These seminal books included David Anderson's *Kanban* [5], which introduces the concept of Kanban in systems and software development, and Corey Lada's *Scrumban* [8], which discusses the fusion of Scrum and Kanban. The key motivation for Kanban use involves a focus on flow and the omission of the obligatory iteration cycles in Scrum.

H. Sharp and T. Hall (Eds.): XP 2016, LNBIP 251, pp. 296–299, 2016.
DOI: 10.1007/978-3-319-33515-5_29

2 Empirical Study Plan

Kanban has received considerable attention from software industry. The existing limited literature explored dynamics of Kanban which is tend to be more concentrating on its obtained benefits and less on Kanban pitfall [6, 7, 9, 10] in Brownfield project. Whereas, there is no evidence of Kanban use is reported for Greenfield project. The reason can be that in software industry Kanban is still in the early adoption phase. A Greenfield project could be one developing a system for a totally new environment, without legacy systems. Brownfield development could be one developing and deploying new software feature or systems in the existing legacy software applications or systems. This study explores the hidden pitfalls of Kanban in software development projects. The aim is to discover the reasons behind the Kanban pitfalls and failure. Additionally, to shed light on a phenomenon by discussing similar experiences among industry experts and find out what topics are most challenging for software companies. The study finds answers relevant to following research questions:

RQ1. What are the hidden pitfalls of Kanban in software development projects?

In our research group we have strong collaboration between the authors institute and Finnish leading software industry. In order for our research to have relevance, we need to work on problems that have been identified by practitioners. We work with organisations in the following way: we identify a relevant topic or challenge, conduct case studies to explore the topic or challenge within its organisational context, and conduct a literature review to identify suggested solutions. We discuss our findings with the organisation, engage in a dialogue with them about mitigation strategies and undertake research into changes made. We then publish our findings as academic papers for the research community [6, 9, 12].

2.1 Data Collection and Analysis Methods

We will deploy a 'Kanban pitfall wall' at XP Conference 2016. The participants can be a mixture of Agile and Lean practitioners, business representatives and academics researchers. The Kanban pitfall wall can be positioned with Kanban poster in a visible place in the conference venue with a stack of pens and small cards. The small cards will be used for writing individual pitfall as shown in Fig. 1. Participants can fill out the cards anonymously and attached it to the wall next to the poster for others participants to read. Similar data collection approach is used in earlier studies [13].

Participants can write one pitfall per card, and could fill in as many cards as they wished. The pitfall wall will be a trigger point for discussions between participants of the conference and the interviewees. The discussion central point will be the nature and context of the identified hidden pitfalls.

After compiling the Kanban pitfalls, separate one to one interviews will be scheduled with the interested volunteers and "key informants" to discuss it in more detail. The key informant technique is used to identify experts and assures rich and high quality data acquisition from them [14]. Interviews could be conducted face to face or remotely via appropriate communication channel such as Skype.

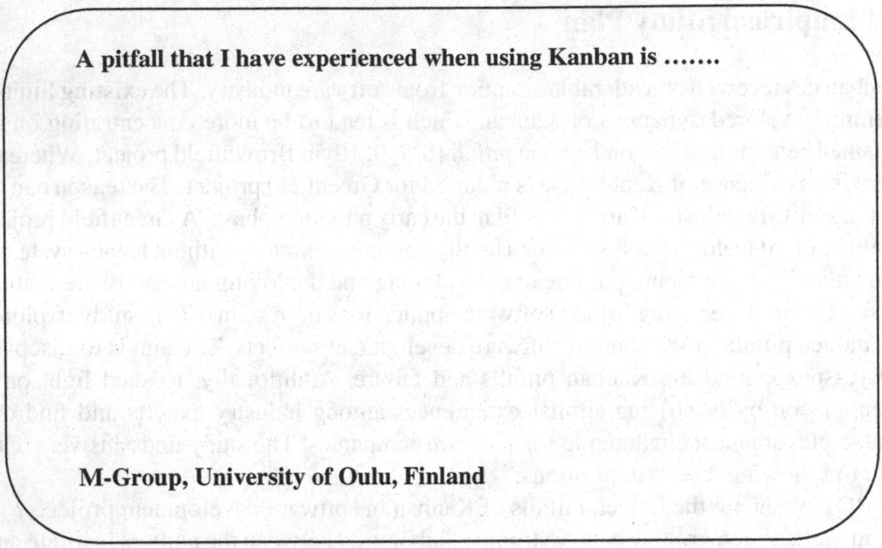

A pitfall that I have experienced when using Kanban is …….

M-Group, University of Oulu, Finland

Fig. 1. A Kanban pitfall card

We will use a thematic analysis approach for data analysis. It describes and organises the data set in rich detail and interprets different aspects related to the research topic [11].

References

1. Hiranabe, K.: Kanban applied to software development: from agile to lean, InfoQ. 11 Nov 2015. http://www.infoq.com/articles/hiranabe-lean-agile-kanban
2. Shalloway, A., Guy, B., James Trott, R.: Lean-agile Software Development: Achieving Enterprise Agility. Pearson Education (2009)
3. Ahmad, M.O., Kuvaja, P., Oivo, M., Markkula, J.: Transition of software maintenance teams from Scrum to Kanban. In: 49th Hawaii International Conference on System Sciences (2016)
4. Boeg, J.: Priming Kanban: A 10 step guide to optimizing flow in your software delivery system, 2nd edn. Trifork (2012)
5. Anderson, D.: Kanban – Successful Evolutionary Change for Your Technology Business. Blue Hole Press, Sequim (2010)

6. Ahmad, M.O. Markkula, J., Oivo, M., Kuvaja,P.: Usage of Kanban in software companies: an empirical study on motivation, benefits and challenges. In: Proceedings of the 9th International Conference on Software Engineering Advances (2014)
7. Boeg, J.: Priming Kanban: A 10 step guide to optimizing flow in your software delivery system, 2nd edn. Trifork (2012)
8. Ladas, C.: Scrumban – Essays on Kanban Systems for Lean Software Development. Modus Cooperandi Press, Seattle (2009)
9. Ahmad, M.O., Markkula, J., Oivo, M.: Kanban in software development: a systematic literature review. In: Proceedings of the IEEE 39th Euromicro SEAA (2013)
10. Ikonen, M.: Lean thinking in software development: Impacts of kanban on projects. Doctoral dissertation (article-based). https://helda.helsinki.fi/handle/10138/28453
11. Braun, V., Clarke, V.: Using thematic analysis in psychology. Qual. Res. Psychol. **3**, 77–101 (2006)
12. Rodríguez, P., Markkula, J., Oivo, M., Turula, K.: Survey on agile and lean usage in Finnish software industry. In: ESEM. pp. 139–148. ACM Press, New York (2012)
13. Gregory, P., Barroca, L., Taylor, K., Salah, D., Sharp, H.: Agile challenges in practice: a thematic analysis. In: Lassenius, C., Dingsøyr, T., Paasivaara, M. (eds.) XP 2015. LNBIP, vol. 212, pp. 64–80. Springer, Heidelberg (2015)
14. Kumar, N., Stern, L.W., Anderson, J.C.: Conducting interorganizational research using key informants. Acad. Manag. J. **36**, 1633–1651 (1993)

Towards a Lean Approach to Reduce Code Smells Injection: An Empirical Study

Davide Taibi(✉), Andrea Janes, and Valentina Lenarduzzi

Free University of Bozen-Bolzano, Piazza Domenicani, 3, 39100 Bozen-Bolzano, Italy
{davide.taibi,andrea.janes,valentina.lenarduzzi}@unibz.it

Abstract. Software Quality Assurance is a complex and time-expensive task. In this study we want to observe how agile developers react to just-in-time metrics about the code smells they introduce, and how the metrics influence the quality of the output.

1 Introduction and Aim of the Research

Software Quality Assurance (SQA) is still a complex task that requires effort and expertise. The reasons for this are manifold, e.g., that quality-related information is difficult to collect [2, 4] or that investment into quality is often still put aside in favor of other activities, e.g., adding new functionalities [4]. Thanks to current SQA tools available on the market, developers are able to increase their awareness on SQA. However, those tools often require substantial effort to understand the provided results.

In particular code smells, a set of structural characteristics of software that may indicate a code or design problem that can make software hard to evolve and maintain, can be easily identified with SQA tools. Developers are often not aware of the code smells they introduce in their source code; with the result of producing products with a maintainability that constantly decreases over time, due to the growth of code smells. For this reason, the identification of code smells is gaining acceptance in industry [1] but the application to agile processes is still not clear since the effort required to apply SQA tools and techniques is usually considered too high and not compliant with agile processes.

The goal of this study is to understand if SQA tools, and in particular SonarQube[1], one of the most common SQA tools, can be effectively applied in agile processes increasing the developers' productivity and the number of generated bugs.

Therefore, we formulate our research questions as follows:

- RQ1: Is the continuous application of a SQA tool (SonarQube) applicable to agile development processes?
- RQ2: Does the continuous application of a SQA tool (SonarQube) help to improve the developers' awareness of code smells in agile processes?

[1] SonarQube: http://www.sonarqube.org.

H. Sharp and T. Hall (Eds.): XP 2016, LNBIP 251, pp. 300–304, 2016.
DOI: 10.1007/978-3-319-33515-5_30

The execution of this study at XP2016 gives us the opportunity to understand if SQA tools can be effectively applied in agile processes, considering industry practitioners that would not participate in an industrial context because of effort reasons.

This paper is structured as follows: after the introductory section containing the aim of our research, we briefly discuss the background and related work in Sect. 2. Section 3 describes the design of the proposed case study.

2 Background and Related Work

Software Engineering, as every other engineering discipline, develops ways to analyze the produced artifacts with the intention to learn how to improve the various engineering methods and to produce outputs of an increasing quality. Approaches like the Experience Factory [7] recommend to have a dedicated team that studies how to improve quality and which packages the collected data into reusable knowledge so that the development teams can reuse it later. In many agile environments, this is not feasible. Developing approaches tailored for Agile and Lean environments requires understanding the specific information needs and the period in which the needed information is valuable. Particularly in Lean, a **just-in-time** approach to feedback is required: the right information at the right moment.

Moreover, the complexity of the QA domain makes results hard to interpret within small companies, since they cannot afford a dedicated team or to pay external consultancy for QA. From this point of view, a tool like SonarQube helps companies to analyze the source code with respect to different quality aspects presenting the results in form of a web page. Unfortunately, SonarQube encourages a "one size fits all" QA model in which users can analyze their source code with a set of predefined measures. This is an additional impediment for teams to use SonarQube to apply a customized QA model within their context, as it requires time and expertise. To apply QA within agile, **a tailored set of metrics has to be used** [9, 10].

3 The Case Study

The objective of our case study is to understand if the continuous application of SonarQube, tailored to an agile development process (as suggested in [9]), helps to reduce the number of injected code smells without influence the developers' productivity and if it helps developers to learn how to avoid code smells in the future.

According to our expectation, we formulate the goal of the study as follows:

analyze the continuous application SonarQube
for the purpose of evaluating and comparing
with respect to applicability and the code smells awareness
from the point of view of the developers
in the context of agile software development.

3.1 Data Collection Methods

The case study targets developers with at least three years of development experience. We aim at collecting data from developers alongside existing programming exercises in existing workshops, during the XP2016 conference.

The data will be collected in two steps: (1) during the development process (2) at the end of the development process.

Before the beginning of a coding session, we will provide the access to our tailored SonarQube platform. Our researchers will configure the platform for the projects to be developed, to avoid adding any extra task to the participants. Moreover, for those who accept to track their development activities, we will also install a tool we developed [8] that simply logs the current application on focus. Using this tool, we track the time spent by the developer per application and the time spent reading our reports. We will ask to manually track the time needed to check the report to those who prefer to not install our tool.

During the development, we will ask participants to commit the source code related to the development of a specific user story, reporting the user-story-id number. After the commit, the platform will present a short report with the list of code smells introduced in the current commit and the list of all previously introduced code smells. For usability reasons, we will also provide a printed version of the report to the developers who prefer to not switch to SonarQube to see the reports. Developers will be free to decide if the code smells should be removed or not.

To understand what participants think about our approach, we will distribute a questionnaire at the end of the development process. To answer this question, we will collect the time overhead needed to read and understand the results provided by the tools and the opinions of the participants by means of the Technology Acceptance Model [5], collecting the metrics listed below.

All statements will be evaluated based on a 5-point ordinal Likert scale with the following options: 1 (strongly disagree), 2 (disagree), 3 (neither agree nor disagree), 4 (agree), 5 (strongly agree).

Perceived usefulness: measures the degree to which the participant considers the approach useful.

- "I learned which kind of code smells I usually introduce in the source code."
- "The report pointed out code smells I was not aware of."
- "The identified code smells do not make sense."
- "The effort required to analyze the report is too high compared to the provided benefits."

Perceived understandability: measures the effort needed by the subject to understand the approach built or whether the participants will need to exert little effort to understand the relationship with the system concepts.

- "It was easy for me to understand how the approach works."

Perceived easiness: measures the degree to which the subject believes that he or she was able to make project decisions easier than without the approach.

- "It was easy for me to decide to remove the code smell or not, based on the information provided by the tool."
- "It was easy for me to identify the code smell."
- "After using the tool I was able to remember previous code smells and how to not introduce them anymore."

Self-efficacy by applying the technique.

- "The approach helped me to increase my productivity reducing refactoring time."

3.2 Data Analysis

For our fist research question (RQ1), we will analyze separately the results for the participants who will install our window tracking tool to calculate the time spent on each window with those who will report the time by manually. Then after statistical tests to check data normality, we will analyze the code smells trend in each commit, to understand the percentage of time spent on the report and on developing.

Q2 will be analyzed first performing a descriptive analysis of the collected data and then with a One-Sample Wilcoxon Signed-Rank test for comparing the obtained medians to the hypothesized median ($\boldsymbol{\alpha} = 3$). Moreover, to make sure that the statements on the given scale will measure the same underlying assumption, we will perform a reliability test by calculating the Cronbach's α reliability measure.

References

1. Fontana, F.A., Braione, P., Zanoni, M.: Automatic detection of bad smells in code: an experimental assessment. J. Object Technol. **11**(2), 5:1–38 (2012)
2. Hampp, T.: A cost-benefit model for software quality assurance activities. In: Proceedings of the 8th International Conference on Predictive Models in Software Engineering (PROMISE 2012), pp. 99–108. ACM, New York (2012)
3. Kamp, P.: Quality software costs money–heartbleed was free. Commun. ACM **57**(8), 49–51 (2014)
4. Diaz-Ley, M., Garcia, F., Piattini, M.: Implementing a software measurement program in small and medium enterprises: a suitable framework. IET Softw. **2**(5), 417–436 (2008)
5. Caldera, G., Rombach, H.D., Basili, V.: Goal question metric approach. In: Encyclopedia of Software Engineering, pp. 528–532. Wiley, New York (1994)

6. Venkatesh, V., Davis, F.: A theoretical extension of the technology acceptance model: four longitudinal field studies. Manage. Sci. **46**(2), 186–204 (2000)
7. Basili, V.R., Caldiera, G., Rombach, D.H.: The experience factory. In: Encyclopedia of Software Engineering–2, Volume Set, pp. 469–476. Wiley (1994)
8. Janes, A.: Squirrel: an architecture for the systematic collection of software development data in microenterprises to support lean software development. In: International Conference on Software and System Process (ICSSP 2015), New York, USA, pp. 171–172 (2015)
9. Davis, C.W.H.: Agile Metrics in Action: Measuring and Enhancing the Performance of Agile Teams, 1st edn. Manning Publications Co., Greenwich (2015)
10. Lavazza, L., Morasca, S., Taibi, D., Tosi, D.: Predicting OSS trustworthiness on the basis of elementary code assessment. In: 2010 ACM-IEEE International Symposium on Empirical Software Engineering and Measurement (ESEM 2010) (2010)

Doctoral Symposium Papers

Towards a More User-Centred Agile Development

Silvia Bordin(✉)

Department of Information Engineering and Computer Science,
University of Trento, via Sommarive 9, 38123 Trento, Italy
silvia.bordin@unitn.it

Abstract. The integration of user-centred design and Agile development is becoming increasingly common in companies and appears promising. However, it may also present some critical points, or communication breakdowns, which manifest in working practices. A solution is likely to be found in a supportive organisational context: in this sense, communication breakdowns can become focal points to drive action and decision for establishing an organisational environment acknowledging the value of user involvement and actively endorsing it also with the customer.

Expected graduation year: 2017.
Supervisor: prof. Antonella De Angeli, Department of Information Engineering and Computer Science, University of Trento, Italy.
Email: antonella.deangeli@disi.unitn.it

1 Motivation

This research proposal aims at addressing the growing interest in the integration of Agile methodologies with user-centred design (UCD), with the goal of achieving a more holistic software engineering approach [14]. In fact, available literature gathers a rich collection of experience reports highlighting several points in common between the two, but also several calls for a more systematic convergence of them.

On the one hand, in fact, Agile methodologies do not explicitly address usability or user experience (UX) aspects in their understanding of the development process, although valuing customer satisfaction [17]. Yet, a carefully designed UX can provide an advantage over competing products [9], giving "positive effects on both system success and user satisfaction" [10]. On the other hand, UCD does not explicitly address how implementation should be performed, despite needing to ensure that no "design drift" [14] occurs. Agile methodologies, popularised by their intrinsic embracing of change and constant involvement of the customer in the process [7], appear as a suitable match to this.

H. Sharp and T. Hall (Eds.): XP 2016, LNBIP 251, pp. 307–311, 2016.
DOI: 10.1007/978-3-319-33515-5_31

2 Related Work

User-centred design (UCD) is an umbrella term used to denote a set of techniques, methods, procedures that places the user at the centre of an iterative design process [13]. Since the benefits of involving users in systems design are widely acknowledged [1,10], several attempts at integrating UCD with Agile have emerged in recent years [9,14], leveraging on the large common ground that the two approaches seem to share. However, literature also highlights some divergences between them, or communication breakdowns [3], i.e. examples of disruptions due to the sudden ineffectiveness of existing working practices:

- in UCD, user involvement can range from informative, to consultative, to participative [8]; in Agile, the emphasis is put on the customer instead, who acts as a representative of users, but whose meaningfulness in this sense is often questioned (e.g. [17]);
- the role of documentation may be interpreted differently: Agile methodologies encourage mostly face-to-face communication [2], while UCD also relies on artefacts to record design rationales [15];
- there are different opinions about whether UCD and Agile should proceed in parallel (e.g. [18]) or should be merged into the same process (e.g. [11]), and to the amount of design to be performed before implementation [11].

3 Methodology

The research process has combined theoretical grounding and action research, performed in two main field studies. The first field study concerned a social innovation R&D project where UCD and Agile were both adopted and where the author served as interaction designer. This context provided several insights about critical aspects, or communication breakdowns [3], that may hamper the integration of the two approaches [4]; a subsequent literature review confirmed that such breakdowns had already emerged previously, but had not been systematised yet. The second field study, performed in a software and interaction design company, allowed to further reinforce and extend the framework defined by identified breakdowns, turning these into focal points for driving decision in companies, facilitating communication between designers and developers, and supporting the management in the construction of a favourable context for a fruitful integration of UCD and Agile [5].

During both studies, data were collected from a number of sources, in particular through interview studies, ethnographically-inspired personal observations [12], and investigation of artefacts used to support working practices. These qualitative data were then thematically analysed [16] and resulting findings were supplemented with a more top-down stream of research, i.e. a literature review.

4 Results

The two case studies described above have led to the identification and validation of a framework constituted by the following four communication breakdowns [4,5].

User involvement. Its perception may vary both between designers and developers, and between the company and the customer: in any case, involved parties should explicitly share the same understanding of its extent.

Documentation. In co-located teams, besides tracing history and design rationales, documentation can help balance the power relationship with the customer, shielding the company from unsustainable changes in requirements.

Synchronisation. If the team is not co-located, or has to incorporate a large amount of feedback, balancing the paces of design and development can be tricky, as it is not always possible or sufficient to rely on face-to-face communication.

Task ownership. While it is advisable that the whole team shares a common language, the responsibility over design tasks should be clear and endorsed by the management, in order to fully support the added value that UCD can provide to the product.

5 Future Agenda

A third field study is under way in an IT company with no UX expert, but needing to design and develop a software interface in a few months. Weekly workshops are being run drawing inspiration from design thinking [6]; the development team is exposed to tools deriving from both UCD and Agile (e.g. personas, use-case diagrams, backlogs) in order to sharpen their understanding of the intended user and subsequently of the functionalities to offer, while keeping in mind the issues represented by identified communication breakdowns. The goal is to assist the working process of the team to assess whether and how their understanding of the user evolves and whether the introduction of mentioned tools may have an observable impact on the quality of the resulting interface.

6 Publication Plan

Envisioned venues for future publications span between the human-computer interaction and the software engineering communities; given the industry-oriented nature of present work, particular interest is paid to conferences bringing together researchers and practitioners. Targeted venues include HCSE 2016 (International Working Conference on Human-Centred Software Engineering), XP 2017, CSCW 2017 (Conference on Computer-Supported Cooperative Work and Social Computing) and its European homologous ECSCW 2017. Thesis defense is foreseen for summer 2017.

References

1. Ardito, C., Buono, P., Caivano, D., Costabile, M.F., Lanzilotti, R.: Investigating and promoting UX practice in industry: an experimental study. Int. J. Hum Comput Stud. **72**(6), 542–551 (2014)
2. Beck, K., et al.: Manifesto for Agile Software Development. http://www.Agilemanifesto.org
3. Bjørn, P., Ngwenyama, O.: Virtual team collaboration: building shared meaning, resolving breakdowns and creating translucence. Inf. Syst. J. **19**(3), 227–253 (2009)
4. Bordin, S., de Angeli, A.: Communication breakdowns in the integration of user-centred design and Agile development. In: Cockton, G., Larusdottir, M.K., Gregory, P., Cajander, A. (eds.) Integrating User Centred Design in Agile Development. Springer, London (2016, to appear)
5. Bordin, S., de Angeli, A.: Focal points for a more user-centred Agile development. In: Proceedings of XP (2016, to appear)
6. Brown, T.: Design thinking. Harvard bus. rev. **86**(6), 84 (2008)
7. Cajander, Å., Larusdottir, M., Gulliksen, J.: Existing but not explicit - the user perspective in scrum projects in practice. In: Kotzé, P., Marsden, G., Lindgaard, G., Wesson, J., Winckler, M. (eds.) INTERACT 2013, Part III. LNCS, vol. 8119, pp. 762–779. Springer, Heidelberg (2013)
8. Damodaran, L.: User involvement in the systems design process-a practical guide for users. Behav. inf. Technol. **15**(6), 363–377 (1996)
9. Jurca, G., Hellmann, T.D., Maurer, F.: Integrating Agile, user-centered design: a systematic mapping and review of evaluation and validation studies of Agile-UX. In: Agile Conference (AGILE), pp. 24–32 (2014)
10. Kujala, S.: User involvement: a review of the benefits and challenges. Behav. inf. technol. **22**(1), 1–16 (2003)
11. Memmel, T., Gundelsweiler, F., Reiterer, H.: Agile human-centered softwareengineering. In: Proceedings of the 21st British HCI Group Annual Conference on Peopleand Computers: HCI... but not as we know it-Volume 1, British Computer Society, pp. 167–175 (2007)
12. Neustaedter, C., Sengers, P.: Autobiographical design in HCI research: designing and learning through use-it-yourself. In: Proceedings of the Designing Interactive Systems Conference, pp. 514–523. ACM, June 2012
13. Rogers, Y., Sharp, H., Preece, J.: Interaction Design: Beyond Human-Computer Interaction. John Wiley & Sons, New York (2011)
14. Salah, D., Paige, R.F., Cairns, P.: A systematic literature review for agile development processes and user centred design integration. In: Proceedings of the 18th International Conference on Evaluation and Assessment in Software Engineering, p. 5. ACM (2014)
15. Sharp, H., Robinson, H.: Integrating user-centred design and software engineering: a role for extreme programming? (2004)
16. Smith, C.P.: Motivation and Personality: Handbook of Thematic Content Analysis. Cambridge University Press, New York (1992)

17. Sohaib, O., Khan, K.:Integrating usability engineering and agile software development: a literature review. In: International Conference on Computer Design and Applications (ICCDA), vol. 2, pp. V2-32–V2-38. IEEE (2010)
18. Sy, D.: Adapting usability investigations for Agile user-centered design. J. Usability Stud. **2**(3), 112–132 (2007)

Responding to Change: Agile-in-the-large, Approaches and Their Consequences

Kelsey van Haaster(✉)

Charles Sturt University, Bathurst, NSW, Australia
kvanhaaster@csu.edu.au
http://www.csu.edu.au/

Abstract. Empirical studies covering Agility at the organisational scale are few in number. Organisations seeking clarity about the efficacy of any approach to business Agility must turn to the commercial literature for information and guidance. As a whole, research into Agile Software Development suffers from a lack of rigour and theoretical grounding, a problem also evident in Information Systems research in general. These issues have led to recent calls for a clear research agenda for scaling Agility and for the quality of contributions to be addressed. Diffusions research has a long history in a wide range of domains and provides a clear theoretical framework for this qualitative PhD study.

Keywords: Scaled agility · Transformation · Diffusions research

1 Statement of the Research Problem

Over the last few years, Australian organisations have become increasingly interested in the concept of business Agility, which appears to offer a way forward in an increasingly disrupted and digital world [1]. However, those embarking on this path have found that the process of becoming an Agile organisation is not straightforward. Large scale organisational transformation is complex, expensive and inherently risky with few successful examples. Organisational governance teams find that accessing high quality, independent advice is a significant challenge. This contrasts with the extensive body of academic literature and practical experience through which we understand Agility from the software team perspective.

In order to progress understanding and support further research into Agility and organisational transformations, this PhD study will seek to answer the following overarching question:

Expected graduation year - December 2017.

Primary Supervisor: Associate Professor Oliver Burmeister, Charles Sturt University, Faculty of Business, School of Computing and Mathematics, Bathurst Campus, NSW, Australia; E-mail: oburmeister@csu.edu.au; Phone: 61 2 6338 6233.

Associate Supervisor: Dr Padma Nathan, Charles Sturt University, Faculty of Business, School of Computing and Mathematics, Wagga Wagga Campus, NSW, Australia, E-mail: pnathan@csu.edu.au; Phone: 61 2 6933 2532.

H. Sharp and T. Hall (Eds.): XP 2016, LNBIP 251, pp. 312–315, 2016.
DOI: 10.1007/978-3-319-33515-5_32

How should a given organisation evaluate the applicability of existing and emergent approaches to implementing or scaling Agile, based on their goals for such an implementation and the environment in which the organisation is operating?

2 Motivation, Contribution and Originality of the Proposed Study

Recently a lack of theoretical underpinnings for Agile research has been highlighted by researchers as a cause for concern [2,3]. Criticisms include; a lack of empirical support for claims about the efficacy of Agile methods; no unified framework to guide the various streams of research; and a lack of methodological and theoretical rigour [4]. Addressing these concerns results in the selection of Diffusion of Innovations (DOI) [5] as a suitable theoretical framework to guide the research.

DOI theory [5] has a strong theoretical basis and has been widely used to explain the diffusion process across a broad range of domains and disciplines [6]. Within these traditions, studies have investigated different aspects of the diffusion process, including the consequences of innovations, this final aspect contributing less than 1 % of diffusion studies and will be key vehicle through which the results will be framed [5].

As an applied discipline, Information Systems research should result in findings that have both a theoretical and a practical application [7]. This latter requirement will be addressed by the development of a taxonomy allowing organisations to position themselves according to their organisational characteristics. The theoretical contribution of the study will arise from the application of (DOI) [5] to an emergent area, business Agility. This will serve the dual purpose of testing the applicability of the theory to the domain and at the same time offers a repeatable, verifiable model through which to support further research, development of the existing theory, or the generation of new theory [8].

3 Brief Literature Review

Since 2001 much of the early focus and research into Agility has been tightly focused on the practices and processes of Agile software development teams. A number of researchers have synthesised and thematically categorised this extensive body of work [2,9–11]. These meta-analyses suggest that the existing body of work is focussed on a subset of practice based topics.

Whilst software Agility focusses on the practices contributing to software and product development, business Agility is a broader concept. In this regard Agile practices are often combined with the ideas behind Lean thinking [12] which share a close philosophical alignment. A number of high profile digital organisations have successfully demonstrated Agility as a whole of business approach [13]. One of the best know of these is Spotify though its own particular model of scaled Agility, generally known as the Spotify Model [14]. Organisations that have attempted to transform to an Agile business model have found the landscape replete with complex challenges [15]. A relatively small number of case studies documenting the experiences of such organisations demonstrate this [16,17]. A more recent development of interest to the business community are a number of frameworks which claim to address some of these issues and provide a transformation pathway to business Agility [18–21].

4 Description of Proposed Research Methodology

A two-part adaptive case study design is proposed; part one will focus on the development of a narrative description of the organisational characteristics and innovation diffusion process for each case. Multiple sources of evidence will be used to generate thick descriptions of each case. Part two of the study will examine of the consequences of the diffusion approach chosen by an organisation. For each case, this will be guided by the factors identified in part one of the study and will focus on: positive and negative outcomes, the role of change agents and the extent to which an organisations social structure and socioeconomic gaps have been impacted.

5 Results Achieved so Far (if Any)

Ethics approval for the study has been granted and initial data collection is currently underway.

6 Plans for Publication of the Proposed Study or Set of Studies

The study will be published as a PhD thesis.

7 Future Agenda

As both a researcher and a practitioner in this field it is hoped that further publication of the outcomes of this study will lead to the development of considered approaches towards organisational transformation. The study may also provide a sound basis for ongoing research into specific aspects of business Agility.

References

1. Papatheocharous, E., Andreou, A.S.: Evidence of agile adoption in software organizations: an empirical survey. In: McCaffery, F., O'Connor, R.V., Messnarz, R. (eds.) EuroSPI 2013. CCIS, vol. 364, pp. 237–246. Springer, Heidelberg (2013)
2. Dingsøyr, T., Nerur, S., Balijepally, V., Moe, N.B.: A decade of agile methodologies: towards explaining agile software development. J. Syst. Softw. **85**(6), 1213–1221 (2012)
3. Stavru, S.: A critical examination of recent industrial surveys on agile method usage. J. Syst. Softw. **94**, 87–97 (2014)
4. Torgeir, D., Nils, B.M., Dingsoyr, T., Moe, N.B., Dingsøyr, T., Moe, N.B.: Research challenges in large-scale agile software development. ACM SIGSOFT Softw. Eng. Notes **38**(5), 38–39 (2013)
5. Rogers, E.M.: Diffusion of Innovations, 5th edn. The Free Press, New York (2003)
6. Börjesson, A., Martinsson, F., Timmerås, M.: Agile improvement practices in software organizations. Eur. J. Inf. Syst. **15**(2), 169–182 (2006)
7. Hart, D.N., Gregor, S.D.: Information Systems Foundations: Theory Building in Information Systems. Australian National University Press, Canberra (2012)
8. Eisenhardt, K.M.: Building theories from case study research. Acad. Manage. Rev. **14**(4), 532–550 (1989)
9. Hasnain, E.: An overview of published agile studies: a systematic literature review. In: Proceedings of the 2010 National Software Engineering Conference, Rawalpindi, Pakistan, pp. 3:1–3:6. ACM (2010)
10. Chuang, S.W., Luor, T., Lu, H.P.: Assessment of institutions, scholars, and contributions on agile software development (2001–2012). J. Syst. Softw. **93**, 84–101 (2014)
11. Hummel, M.: State-of-the-art: a systematic literature review on agile information systems development. In: 2014 47th Hawaii International Conference on System Sciences, pp. 4712–4721 (2014)
12. Lean Systems Society (2012). http://leansystemssociety.org/credo/
13. Power, K.: The agile office: experience report from cisco's unified communications business unit. In: Agile Conference (AGILE), pp. 201–208 (2011)
14. Vlietland, J., van Vliet, H.: Towards a governance framework for chains of Scrum teams. Inf. Softw. Technol. **57**, 52–65 (2015)
15. Houston, D.X.: Agility beyond software development. In: Proceedings of the 2014 International Conference on Software and System Process - ICSSP 2014, pp. 65–69. ACM, Nanjing (2014)
16. Van Waardenburg, G., Van Vliet, H.: When agile meets the enterprise. Inf. Softw. Technol. **55**(12), 2154–2171 (2013)
17. Petersen, K., Wohlin, C.: The effect of moving from a plan-driven to an incremental software development approach with agile practices: An industrial case study. Empirical Softw. Eng. **15**(6), 654–693 (2010)
18. Ambler, S.: Enterprise Unified Process (EUP), Strategies for Enterprise Agile (2014)
19. Ambler, S., Lines, M.: The Disciplined Agile Framework (2014)
20. Larmen, C., Vodde, B.: Practices for Scaling Lean & Agile Development: Large, Multisite, and Offshore Product Development with Large-Scale Scrum, 1st edn. Addison-Wesley Professional, Boston (2010)
21. SAFe Lean-Agile Principles Scaled Agile Framework

Hybrid Effort Estimation of Changes in Agile Software Development

Binish Tanveer(✉)

Fraunhofer Institute for Experimental Software Engineering,
Fraunhofer Platz-1, 67663 Kaiserslautern, Germany
binish.tanveer@iese.fraunhofer.de

Abstract. Unlike traditional software development approaches, Agile embraces change. The resulting dynamism of requirements makes it challenging to estimate effort accurately. Current practice relies on expert-judgment that can be biased, labor intensive and inaccurate. Therefore, a systematic yet lightweight effort estimation methodology is needed to support expert judgment and improve its effectiveness. Such an approach will utilize the quantification of the impact of a requirement on software artifacts potentially affected by it. It will further introduce an explicit consideration of effort drivers that contribute to effort overhead. The aim is to synthesize research from three often orthogonal areas of research: (1) change impact analysis, (2) effort estimation (model and expert driven) and (3) software visualization. Hence, resulting in a hybrid methodology with tool support that incorporates expert knowledge, change impact analysis and enables an explicit consideration of cost drivers by experts to improve the effectiveness of effort estimation process.

Keywords: Effort estimation · Hybrid · Expert judgment · Agile

1 Research Problem

Effort estimation in Agile relies on expert judgment, which is labor intensive, can be biased and inaccurate. Moreover it does not consider the data e.g. quantification of the impact of a change on the existing artifacts, as well as an explicit consideration of effort drivers contributing to effort overhead that affects the accuracy of estimates.

2 Motivation

In software development, the requirements typically cannot be completely specified upfront and are developed as the project progresses. Therefore, the effort estimates need to be adjusted for every sprint in order to deliver project increment in time-boxed release. In such an environment, systematic effort estimation

Supervisor: Prof. Dr. Dr. h. c. H. Dieter Rombach, Email: dieter.rombach@iese.fraunhofer.de

H. Sharp and T. Hall (Eds.): XP 2016, LNBIP 251, pp. 316–320, 2016.
DOI: 10.1007/978-3-319-33515-5_33

is challenging. While estimating the size of the change, its impact on other artifacts and context specific effort drivers need to be considered.

Currently, effort estimation in this context relies heavily on human judgment. A cross-functional team of experts estimate by consensus how much effort a certain change will entail. This approach is not only labor intensive but also has limited prediction accuracy due to the use of limited information (subjective judgment) and human judgment bias (individual and group effects).

Moreover, it does not objectively consider the potential impact of a change on existing software artifacts which makes effort estimates obtained, less reliable. In Agile development, the strict distinctions between various phases of software development are blurred. With cross functional teams and a shared responsibility for the product instead of individual artifacts, software development also includes e.g. testing and user-documentation beyond just writing the source code. Thus, an effort estimate has to consider the impact of a change on various software artifacts e.g. regression testing at unit and functional level is now often considered part of development teams responsibility as part of a sprint.

Therefore, an improvement potential exists with respect to systematic effort estimation in this environment and marks the contribution to the body of knowledge.

This thesis proposes combining expert knowledge with quantitative data i.e. quantification of the volume/size of change, and its impact on other artifacts. Moreover, the explicit consideration of the most relevant effort drivers that contributes to the effort overhead. This data and expert knowledge will constitute towards an effort model that will support the experts in making more accurate estimates. Furthermore, the organizational estimation knowledge including effort model will be stored for future reuse. This will help in mitigating the risk of estimation performance drop due to staff turnover as well as reducing the effort of expert involvement each time estimates are required.

3 Related Work

Three main related areas are briefly discussed below:

3.1 Effort Estimation Methods

In traditional software development, numerous effort estimation methods have been proposed in research. These may be classified as [1]: **Data-driven** (model-based, memory-based and composite) methods, (e.g. COCOMO I, Case-based reasoning and COCOMO II). **Expert-based methods** like Wideband Delphi, Planning Game, Analytic Hierarchy Process. **Hybrid methods** like Expert-COCOMO, Bayesian Belief Nets, and CoBRA® [2].

Each of these methods claims to have addressed a problem in effort estimation, however very few of them actually demonstrated the claims in industrial setting. Also very few individual studies are found that address the effort estimation specifically in the Agile context. Expert-based methods are found to be the most used estimation method in Agile context but their estimation accuracy is hampered by inconsistencies and wishful thinking al. [3]. However, due to the lack of evidence that model-based methods like COCOMO produce more accurate estimates than expert judgment, the use of the former approach is widespread [5]. None of the existing estimation methods (in traditional or Agile development) so far have considered the quantification of the impact that a change has on existing software artifacts. Further, explicit consideration of the most relevant effort drivers is also not addressed in Expert-based methods. In Data-driven methods, to collect and analyze these effort drivers a huge amount of data and cost are required. The Hybrid methods, these effort drivers though are considered, but need to be adapted to Agile context.

3.2 Techniques for Change Impact Analysis

A secondary study on change impact analysis [6] has identified 23 techniques which are broadly based on dependency and traceability analysis. In the context of this thesis, these techniques will be analyzed for their support in estimating the impact of a change.

3.3 Tools for Visualizing Change Impact

To support experts in judging the impact of change, visualizations will be used. For example, to show which software components will be effected by an added functionality heat-maps can be created. Several of the techniques identified by Bixinli et al. [6] have tool support which will be considered in this research.

4 Research Methodology

The aim of this thesis is to develop a data driven, light-weight hybrid effort methodology supported with a prototype tool adapted to the Agile context.

In this regard, we need to understand and answer the following questions:

1. For what purpose do practitioners perform effort estimation (project bidding, resource allocation, sprint planning, release planning etc.)?
2. For the various uses identified for effort estimation, what are the *required* and *current* levels of estimate accuracy?
3. How is effort estimation currently performed (which methods, data and tools are currently used)?
4. What support do practitioners need in their effort estimation tasks?
5. Which existing approaches for effort estimation are appropriate for an Agile context?
6. How can existing approaches be adapted for the Agile context (e.g. identifying a minimal set of effort drivers, identifying appropriate change impact analysis methods, necessary tool support)?

A literature review will be used to formulate and design further studies to explore questions 1–4. A web-based survey will be used to generate a broader understanding for the questions 1–3. While an exploratory case-study will be done to explore in-depth the concerns in questions 1–4. A secondary study will be conducted to answer question 5. Question 6 will be answered by utilizing the findings from answering the other questions and existing secondary studies on the related topics. Answering question will help to achieve the overall aim of the thesis.

This thesis work is being conducted in close collaboration with an industrial partner and the resulting solution will be evaluated in their company.

5 Results Achieved so Far

- An exploratory case study was conducted in a large software company to investigate and understand their effort estimation process. The study revealed the purpose of doing estimation, estimation techniques used and effort drivers that affect effort estimation accuracy. It further emphasized the need of tool support for experts when making estimates.
- Results of existing secondary studies on effort estimation in Agile development have been aggregated and will be used to design a web-based survey.

6 Publication Plan

The plan is to publish the results obtained from the exploratory case study conducted in a large software company. Moreover, the overall methodology including all the aspects i.e. change impact analysis, effort drivers and the underlying effort model. Finally the evaluation of the resulting methodology and supporting tool in an industrial setting are also planned to be published.

7 Future Agenda

Firstly designing and execution of an industrial survey to investigate the effort estimation practice. Secondly, existing secondary studies on effort estimation in traditional development have been identified. They will be analyzed with respect to their strengths and limitations, adaptability and extendibility to Agile context. Thirdly, the identification of variables to be used in estimation model for generating estimates with error and identification of requirements regarding quantification of impact of change. Fourthly, secondary studies on change impact analysis have been identified. These tools and techniques identified in these will be investigated for the purpose of change impact quantification. Lastly, the identification of requirements for tool support and the evaluation of both the resulting methodology and tool in an industrial setting.

References

1. Trendowicz, A., Jeffery, R.: Foundations and Best Practice Guidelines for Success. Springer, Heidelberg (2014)
2. Briand, L.C., Emam, K.E., Bomarius, F.: Cobra: a hybrid method for software cost estimation, benchmarking, and risk assessment. In: Proceedings of the 20th International Conference on Software Engineering, IEEE Computer Society, pp. 390–399 (1998)
3. Jørgensen, M., Boehm, B.W., Rifkin, S.: Software development effort estimation: Formal models or expert judgment? IEEE Software **26**(2), 14–19 (2009)
4. Boehm, B., Clark, B., Horowitz, E., Westland, C., Madachy, R., Selby, R.: Cost models for future software life cycle processes: COCOMO 2.0. Ann. Softw. Eng. **1**(1), 57–94 (1995)
5. Molkken, K., Jrgensen, M.: A review of software surveys on software effort estimation. In: ISESE 2003, Proceedings of the 2003 International Symposium on Empirical Software Engineering, pp. 223–230. IEEE (2003)
6. Li, B., Sun, X., Leung, H., Zhang, S.: A survey of code-based change impact analysis techniques. Softw. Test. Verif. Reliab. **23**(8), 613–646 (2013)

Planned Research: Scaling Agile Practices in Software Development

Kathrine Vestues[(✉)]

Department of Computer and Information Science,
Norwegian University of Science and Technology, 7465 Trondheim, Norway
kathrine.vestues@idi.ntnu.no

Abstract. Agile methods are increasingly being applied to large scale and distributed software development. While there is much evidence to support the efficiency of agile practices in small co-located team, less is known about the applicability of these practices to large scale projects. This paper gives an outline of planned research on the scaling of retrospectives. By using retrospectives as an empirical lens I will try to gain insight into the limitations and benefits of agile practices in large scale and distributed development.

Keywords: Agile · Large scale agile · Distributed agile · Retrospectives

1 Introduction

Agile methods were originally seen as best suited for small co-located teams with easy access to users and business experts, developing non-life-critical systems [1]. However, the good results achieved in small, co-located teams has led organizations to apply agile practices and principles to large scale and distributed software projects. Several papers and surveys show that both practitioners and researchers recognize a need for further knowledge about scaling of agile practices – a need that is further emphasized by the apparent gap in research revealed by a preliminary literature review.

This paper gives an outline of planned research on the scaling of retrospectives. By using retrospectives as an empirical lens, I hope to contribute to a better understanding of how agile practices scale in distributed and large projects.

The next section contains a short overview of some of the literature in the field, tying it to the research proposed in this paper. I will then go on to present the research problem, research methods and future agenda.

2 Background

Early research on agile methods focused mainly on implementation and adaption of agile practices in small, co-located teams [2]. As the use of agile methods became more popular, and the number and quality of studies increased [3], the research scope gradually expanded to include use of agile in new contexts. Two such contexts are agile in distributed teams, and agile in large scale projects.

H. Sharp and T. Hall (Eds.): XP 2016, LNBIP 251, pp. 321–325, 2016.
DOI: 10.1007/978-3-319-33515-5_34

2.1 Distributed Agile Development

In most multi-team project settings distribution will be an inevitable side effect. While team members often are co-located, the different teams tend to be distributed across multiple buildings or even countries. When looking at large scale agile, it will therefore be relevant to look at how practices scale across distances, as well as across teams.

Several papers have been written about distributed agile. Among the topics treated are pair programming in globally distributed projects [4], whether distributed development can be agile [5], and inter team coordination in large scale Scrum [6, 7]. Little seems to have been written about scaling of retrospectives across distributed teams.

2.2 Large Scale Development

At the XP2010 conference, Freudenberg and Sharp [8] compiled a list of "top ten burning questions" based on feedback from practitioners. Agile and large projects were on top of the list. Dingsøyr and Moe [9] summarize the large scale agile research challenges that were discussed at the International Conference on Agile Software Development (XP2013). Among the 8 topics listed, two of them concern scaling of practices: "Which agile practices scale and which do not? Why and when do agile practices scale?" and "How can agile practices be adopted efficiently in large projects?". Following the taxonomy given by Dingsøyr et al. [10], project size is determined by the number of team. A project is considered large if it has 2–9 teams.

The literature review revealed several papers on large scale agile [7, 11, 12], but none discussing the scalability of retrospectives.

2.3 Retrospective Practices

The secret to more successful project management is learning from the past [13]. Dybå et al. also emphasis the importance of reflection and learning in the IEEE special issue on reflective practices [14]. Retrospectives are one way of achieving such reflection and learning.

The term "retrospective" was first used by Kerth [15], but was soon adopted by the agile community. Being a key practice within agile methods, the retrospective has been given much attention by both practitioners and researchers. Several books offer practical advice on planning and running retrospectives [16, 17]. There has also been done research on specific retrospective techniques [18] and how retrospectives contribute to the software improvement processes in agile development [19]. Little research has been dedicated to retrospectives in large scale and distributed projects.

The interest of practitioners and researchers in scaling of agile practices, and the lack of research on retrospectives in large scale projects makes the research questions presented in the next chapter highly relevant.

3 Research Problem

The (main) goal of the research is to contribute to a better understanding of how agile practices can give value in large scale software development.

To reach an answer, I will look into the following underlying research questions in detail:

Research question 1: How can retrospectives be adapted to suite large scale and distributed projects?

Research question 2: How does the retrospective practice contribute to process improvement and sharing of knowledge across teams?

4 Research Methodology

The research will be done using interpretive case studies, divided into 3 phases:

Qualitative survey: To indicate relevance of the above research questions, I will start by performing interviews with 5–6 key informants. These informants will be chosen among project managers and Scrum masters in large scale, distributed projects in public and/or private sector in Norway.

Exploratory interpretative case studies: Initially, 2 cases will be chosen; one normal and one critical case. Data will be gathered through observation and interviews of projects members from different organizational levels.

Descriptive interpretative case studies: Not yet specified.

5 Dissertation and Publication

- Two workshop article synthesising the findings from literature review
- Two conference article on the preliminary findings from the case studies
- One journal article at the end of the study reporting on the full case studies

6 Future Agenda

Future work will be to select a theoretical foundation, conduct field studies and analyse and communicate the results.

References

1. Williams, L., Cockburn, A.: Guest Editors' introduction: agile software development: It's about feedback and change. Computer **6**, 39–43 (2003)
2. Dybå, T., Dingsøyr, T.: Empirical studies of agile software development: a systematic review. Inf. Softw. Technol. **50**(9), 833–859 (2008)
3. Dingsøyr, T., Nerur, S., Balijepally, V., Moe, N.B.: A decade of agile methodologies: Towards explaining agile software development. J. Syst. Softw. **85**(6), 1213–1221 (2012)
4. Flor, N.V.: Globally distributed software development and pair programming. Commun. ACM **49**(10), 57–58 (2006)
5. Ramesh, B., Cao, L., Mohan, K., Xu, P.: Can distributed software development be agile? Commun. ACM **49**(10), 41–46 (2006)
6. Lee, S., Yong, H.-S.: Distributed agile: project management in a global environment. Empirical Softw. Eng. **15**(2), 204–217 (2010)
7. Paasivaara, M, Lassenius, C, Heikkila, V.T.: Inter-team coordination in large-scale globally distributed scrum: Do scrum-of-scrums really work? In: 2012 ACM-IEEE International Symposium on Empirical Software Engineering and Measurement (ESEM), pp. 235–238. IEEE (2012)
8. Freudenberg, S., Sharp, H.: The top 10 burning research questions from practitioners. IEEE Softw. **27**(5), 8–9 (2010)
9. Dingsøyr, T., Moe, N.B.: Research challenges in large-scale agile software development. ACM SIGSOFT Softw. Eng. Notes **38**(5), 38–39 (2013)
10. Dingsøyr, T., Fægri, T.E., Itkonen, J.: What is large in large-scale? *A Taxonomy of Scale for Agile Software Development*. In: Jedlitschka, A., Kuvaja, P., Kuhrmann, M., Männistö, T., Münch, J., Raatikainen, M. (eds.) PROFES 2014. LNCS, vol. 8892, pp. 273–276. Springer, Heidelberg (2014)
11. Dingsøyr, T., Moe, N.B.: Towards principles of large-scale agile development. In: Dingsøyr, T., Moe, N.B., Tonelli, R., Counsell, S., Gencel, C., Petersen, K. (eds.) XP 2014. LNBIP, vol. 199, pp. 1–8. Springer, Heidelberg (2014)
12. Moe, N.B., Šmite, D., Šāblis, A., Börjesson, A.-L., Andréasson, P.: Networking in a large-scale distributed agile project. In: Proceedings of the 8th ACM/IEEE International Symposium on Empirical Software Engineering and Measurement, 2014, p. 12. ACM (2014)
13. Nelson, R.R.: Project retrospectives: evaluating project success, failure, and everything in between. MIS Q. Executive **4**(3), 361–372 (2005)
14. Dyba, T., Maiden, N., Glass, R.: The reflective software engineer: reflective practice. IEEE Softw. **31**(4), 32–36 (2014)
15. Kerth, N.L.: Project Retrospectives: A Handbook for Team Reviews. Dorset House Publishing, New York (2001)
16. Derby, E., Larsen, D., Schwaber, K.: Agile Retrospectives: Making Good Teams Great. Pragmatic Bookshelf, Raleigh (2006)
17. Kua, P.: The retrospective handbook (2013). E–book https://leanpub.com/the-retrospective-handbook

18. Lehtinen, T.O.: Development and evaluation of a lightweight root cause analysis method in software project retrospectives. Aalto University (2014)
19. Salo, O.: Enabling Software Process Improvement in Agile Software Development Teams and Organisations. VTT Publications, Espoo (2006)

Architecting Activities Evolution and Emergence in Agile Software Development: An Empirical Investigation

Initial Research Proposal

Muhammad Waseem(✉) and Naveed Ikram

Riphah International University, Islamabad 44000, Pakistan
m.waseem@iiu.edu.pk, naveed.ikram@riphah.edu.pk

Abstract. This proposal is design to address the proposed research work on agile software development and architecture co-existence. The objective of this research is to answer how architecting activities emerge and evolve with agile software development in industry. The architecting activities are architectural analysis (AA), architectural synthesis (AS), architectural evaluation (AE), architectural implementation (AI), architectural maintenance and evolution (AME), architectural recovery (AR), architectural description (ADp), architectural understanding (AU), architectural impact analysis (AIA), architectural reuse (ARu) and architectural refactoring (ARf). This research objective could achieve by using multiple research methods. We are planning to use comprehensively report the pure 'state- of- practice' for architecting activities in ASD from industry and practitioners point of views. Therefore, we decided to use the case studies, survey and semi structure interview as research methods. The result of this research work can provide the baseline information for architecture evolution frameworks for agile software development, challenges and solutions in ASD for SA activities, expected evolvable dimensions of the software system, methods that may help for minimizing the architectural and agile co-existence issues and architectural technical debt in agile software development.

Keywords: Software architecture · Agile development · Architecting approach

1 Introduction

Agile methods widely accepted by the software organization in reaction of heavyweight software development processes. Agile software development(ASD) respond to the changes, people collaboration and working software instead of emphasizing on bureaucratic and upfront planning [1]. Many classical software development activities can align with agile software development such as requirements, architecting, coding, testing and deployment. However, researcher have doubt that practitioners do not pay the sufficient attention to architectural activities in agile software development [2, 3]. Software architecture and agile related research reports two extreme views [4]: First, upfront design and SA evaluation are highly time and effort consuming activities therefore you don't need to go with architecture centric activities, refactoring would help to resolve most of

H. Sharp and T. Hall (Eds.): XP 2016, LNBIP 251, pp. 326–332, 2016.
DOI: 10.1007/978-3-319-33515-5_35

structural problems [2, 5]. Second, the proponent of SA is sure that the sound architectural practices (SA analysis, design, description or documentation) cannot be followed completely in agile software development, which may effects on the project quality. Naturally, *a question arises then what happen with architecture in agile software development?*

In recent years, a good number of studies have investigated the architectural related challenges and solutions in agile software development [5–9]. These studies focus on different perspective of software architecture for example a study of Boehm identify the organizational and technical challenges that involved in integrating the traditional and agile software development process [8, 10]. Acuna et al. reports agile methods do not pay sufficient attention to the architecture centric activities as compares to traditional process so that's we could not found the significant guidance on SA activities in agile context [11]. MA Baber identifies the architecture related challenges and issues which agile teams could face. It has been observe that, architects should have the sound skills and knowledge about implementation domain [12]. Boehm argues for hybrid approach for agile architecting and development. According to him, combine the necessary characteristics from agile and plan driven development for projects implementation.

The aim of this research is to empirically investigate: how software architecture and agile used in combination and how architecture emerge and evolve in agile software development.

2 Problem Statement and Motivation

Software evolution may analyze through different ways; for example releases histories, source code analysis and architecture analysis. This proposes research plan focus on architecting activities evolution and emergence in agile software development. First, software architecture provides the base to software system [13]. Second, the architecture of software system presents the high level structure and behaviors of the system which are expected to evolve with passage of time [14] and provide bases for evolution [15]. Thirdly, it is supposed to be agile and software architecture is proponent to each other. For example, if teams spend too much time on software architecture it may possible working software may delay. If teams pay little time to SA then the team may face high risk of system failure (how much upfront). Fourth, SA and agile combination received the significant consideration in recent years for research but there are very less number of studies that consider the architecting activities emerge and evolve [16]. Therefore, we decided to come up with following problem statement.

Problem statement: "How does architecting activities emerge and evolve in agile software development?"

Software architecture consists of numbers of activities that explain the process and stages of software architecture. We have select following activities from systematic mapping study [16] and formulated in a questions for our proposed research.

RQ 1: *How does an architectural significant requirement are identified and maintain in agile software development?*
RQ 2: *How does architectural solutions are be provided for ASRs in agile software development?*
RQ 3: *How does scenario base architectural evaluation (AE) is conducted in agile software development?*
RQ 4: *How much detailed design is enough in agile software development?*
RQ5: *How does architecture emerge and evolve in agile software development?*
RQ6: *How does architecture maintain in agile software development?*
RQ7: *What are the possible benefits of architectural recovery (AR) in agile software development in term of quality time and cost?*
RQ8: *What are most useful architectural views are being used in agile software development and why?*
RQ9: *How does Architectural Understanding (AU) is used to comprehend the architectural elements (e.g. architectural decisions) and their relationships in an architecture design for agile software development?*
RQ10: *Does Architectural Impact Analysis (AIA) really have worth in agile software development?*
RQ11: *How does existing architectural reusable components such as architecture frameworks, decisions, and patterns are used in agile software development*
RQ12: *How does Architectural Refactoring (ARf) is happen in agile software development?*

3 Description of Proposed Research Methodologies

Architecture is very much depended on architect and teams so we need to investigate the people and there interactions over the process (architecting in agile). We are covering major architecting activities in agile software development that may identify by using different research method. So we have decided to use qualitative and quantitative research (where required) method for evaluating our research questions. We will design the case studies, survey and semi structure interview for exploring the practitioners experience about architecture evolution in agile software development. We may also use the experiments for particular architecting activities such as in architecture evaluation.

3.1 Survey

Considering the objectives of our research and available resources, we could go with survey research method to understand the architectural and agile practices from architecting activities perspective. A survey research method is considered suitable for gathering self-reported quantitative and qualitative data from a large number of respondents [17]. Our survey design will be a cross-sectional. Survey research can use one or a combination of several data gathering techniques such as interviews, self-administered questionnaires and others [18]. Our possible method will be questionnaire as a data collection instrument because we want to obtain the information from a relatively large number of practitioners, many of whom we would not be able to contact personally. Our proposed survey may consist on following activities.

- Instrument construction and evaluation
- Instrument deployment
- Target population identification
- Instrument deployment
- Sampling techniques selection and invitation mechanism
- Data validation and data analysis

3.2 Case Studies

Our proposed research questions may answer through 'Multiple Embedded Case studies' from industry and practitioner. Following are the generic outline that may follow for achieving our research goal(s).

- Devising unit of analysis
- Deciding case selection criteria
- Data collection technique and process
- Sctting up population
- External validity
- Reporting study limitation
- Scheduling and
- Reporting

We are interested to apply both Primary and secondary data collection techniques on collected data. Our data may consist of on field notes, audio recordings of meetings and discussions, photographs and copies of artifacts. We will apply the triangulation approach to incorporate multiple vantage points. We can achieve this diversity by using different data sources and types, and by engaging multiple observers. Additionally, we are interested to discuss our findings with the respective teams for initial verification.

3.3 Semi Structure Interviews

Architecture is very much depended on architect and teams so we need to investigate the people and there interactions over the process (architecting in agile). Semi structure interview is good technique when depth is required for particular phenomena. Interview question will be design before taking the interview from participant(s). It would not be not necessarily to ask questions in same order as they are listed. So we would ask the questions according to situation. Further, semi structure interview allow 'improvisation and exploration' in study subject. During the interview session, we will record the participant response in audio/video format and we will take the notes where things need to write. Our focus would be, how individuals/team qualitatively and quantitatively experience about architecting activities.

Our potential participant would be experienced architect, senior developer, team leads and those who have significant development experiences in agile way.

4 Data Analysis Method

Data analysis methods are different for qualitative and quantitative data. Our collected data may consist of large amount of qualitative data, so we are decided to analyze this data through constant comparison method that originally presented by Glaser and Strauss [19], it has been practically explained by the some other [20]. We will use the guide lines that has been presented in [20] for constant comparison method. Steps involved for our data analysis are

- Preformed coding field notes periodically
- Grouping into patterns according to code
- Writing of field notes

For quantitative data, analysis may include descriptive statistic (mean values, standard deviations, histograms, scatter plots etc.), correlation analysis, development of predictive models, and hypothesis testing [21].

5 Future Agenda

This research study could provide information on the issues of agile architecture co-existence including how architectural analysis and description change over the time? Further, this study would also be exploring architectural models evolution on different level, particularly on system level. This could be beneficial for analyzing traceability between changing requirements, features and architectural model to improve the evolution process. Furthermore, this study would also be analyzed the architectural and design pattern evolution, this would expectedly heighten the awareness about different kind of design and architectural practices and there possible threats in agile software development. To the future researchers, The result of this research can provide the baseline information for architecting activities frameworks for agile software development, expected evolvable dimensions of the software system, methods that may help for minimizing the architectural and agile co-existence issues and architectural technical debt in agile software development.

References

1. Kent Beck, M.B., van Bennekum, A., Cockburn, A., Cunningham, W., Fowler, M., Grenning, J., Highsmith, J., Hunt, A., Jeffries, R., Kern, J., Marick, B., Martin, R.C., Mellor, S., Schwaber, K., Sutherland, J., Thomas, D.: Manifesto for Agile Software Development, Feburvery 2001. http://agilemanifesto.org/
2. Abrahamsson, P., et al.: Mobile-D: an agile approach for mobile application development. In: Companion to the 19th Annual ACM SIGPLAN Conference on Object-oriented Programming Systems, Languages, and Applications. ACM (2004)
3. Boehm, B.: Get ready for agile methods, with care. Computer **35**(1), 64–69 (2002)
4. Babar, M.: Making software architecture and agile approaches work together: foundations and approaches (2014)
5. Nord, R.L., Tomayko, J.E.: Software architecture-centric methods and agile development. IEEE Softw. **23**(2), 47–53 (2006)
6. Abrahamsson, P., et al.: Mobile-D for Mobile Software: How to Use Agile Approaches for the Efficient Development of Mobile Applications. VTT Technical Research Centre of Finland, Finland (2005)
7. Bass, L., Clements, P., Kazman, R.: Software Architecture in Practice, 528 p. Addison-Wesley Longman Publishing Co., Inc., Boston (2003)
8. Lycett, M., et al.: Migrating agile methods to standardized development practice (2003)
9. Parsons, R.: Architecture and agile methodologies-how to get along. In: Working IEEE/IFIP Conference on Software Architecture. IEEE Computer Society, Vancouver (2008)
10. Boehm, B., Turner, R.: Management challenges to implementing agile processes in traditional development organizations. IEEE Softw. **22**(5), 30–39 (2005)
11. Acuña, S.T., et al.: A systematic mapping study on the open source software development process. In: 16th International Conference on Evaluation & Assessment in Software Engineering (EASE 2012). IET (2012)
12. Babar, M.A.: An exploratory study of architectural practices and challenges in using agile software development approaches. In: Joint Working IEEE/IFIP Conference on Software Architecture, 2009 & European Conference on Software Architecture, WICSA/ECSA 2009. IEEE (2009)
13. Clements, P., Kazman, R., Klein, M.: Evaluating software architectures (2003). 清华大学出版社
14. Garlan, D.: Software architecture: a roadmap. In: Proceedings of the Conference on the Future of Software Engineering. ACM (2000)
15. Medvidovic, N., Taylor, R.N., Rosenblum, D.S.: An architecture-based approach to software evolution. In: Proceedings of the International Workshop on the Principles of Software Evolution (1998)
16. Yang, C., Liang, P., Avgeriou, P.: A systematic mapping study on the combination of software architecture and agile development. J. Syst. Softw. **111**, 157–184 (2016)
17. Kitchenham, B.A., et al.: Preliminary guidelines for empirical research in software engineering. IEEE Trans. Softw. Eng. **28**(8), 721–734 (2002)
18. Lethbridge, T.C., Sim, S.E., Singer, J.: Studying software engineers: Data collection techniques for software field studies. Empirical Softw. Eng. **10**(3), 311–341 (2005)
19. Glaser, B.G., Strauss, A.L.: The Discovery of Grounded Theory: Strategies for Qualitative Research. Transaction Publishers, Piscataway (2009)

20. Miles, M.B., Huberman, A.M.: Qualitative Data Analysis: An Expanded Sourcebook. Sage, Thousand Oaks (1994)
21. Runeson, P., Höst, M.: Guidelines for conducting and reporting case study research in software engineering. Empirical Softw. Eng. **14**(2), 131–164 (2009)

Author Index

Printed in the United States
By Bookmasters

Printed in the United States
By Bookmasters